Local Economic Development
in Europe and the Americas

This book is to be returned on
or before the date stamped below

UNIVERSITY OF PLYMOUTH

PLYMOUTH LIBRARY

Tel: (0752) 232323
This book is subject to recall if required by another reader
Books may be renewed by phone
CHARGES WILL BE MADE FOR OVERDUE BOOKS

Local Economic Development in Europe and the Americas

EDITED BY
CHRISTOPHE DEMAZIÈRE
AND PATRICIA A. WILSON

MANSELL

First published 1995 by
Mansell Publishing Limited, *A Cassell imprint*
Wellington House, 125 Strand, London WC2R 0BB, England
215 Park Avenue South, New York, New York 10003, USA

First published 1996

British Library Cataloguing in Publication Data
Local Economic Development in Europe and the Americas
I. Demaziere, Christophe II. Wilson,
Patricia A.
338.9

ISBN 0–7201–2269–4

Library of Congress Cataloging-in-Publication Data
Local economic development in Europe and the Americas / edited by
Christophe Demazière and Patricia A. Wilson.
    p. cm.
    Papers originally presented at a conference held in Lille, France,
March 16–18, 1994.
    Includes bibliographical references and index.
    ISBN 0–7201–2269–4
    1. Economic development—Congresses. 2. Community development—
—Congresses. 3. Regional planning—Congresses. 4. Urban renewal—
—Congresses. I. Demazière, Christophe. II. Wilson, Patricia Ann
HD73.L63 1996
338.9—dc20   95–18499
                                                                  CIP

Printed and bound in Great Britain by
Biddles Ltd, Guildford and King's Lynn

Contents

Part VI: Outlook

List of Contributors

KEVIN ARCHER Department of Geography, University of South Florida, Tampa

IAIN BEGG Department of Applied Economics, University of Cambridge, Cambridge

WILHELM BENFER Regionale Planungsgemeinschaft Uckermark-Barnim, Eberswalde

MICHAEL CHAPMAN School of Planning and Housing, Edinburgh College of Art, Heriot-Watt University, Edinburgh

JYAPHIA CHRISTOS-RODGERS University of New Orleans, New Orleans

ANDREW CHURCH Department of Geography, Birkbeck College, University of London

FRÉDÉRIC COROLLEUR IREPD, University of Grenoble, Grenoble

FABIENNE CORVERS MERIT, University of Limburg, Maastricht

BEN DANKBAAR MERIT, University of Limburg, Maastricht

CHRISTOPHE DEMAZIÈRE CLERSE, University of Lille 1 and IFRESI-CNRS, Lille

ROBERT HASSINK MERIT, University of Limburg, Maastricht

FRANK MOULAERT CLERSE, University of Lille 1 and IFRESI-CNRS, Lille

BERNARD PECQUEUR IREPD, University of Grenoble, Grenoble

PETER REID Department of Geography, Birkbeck College, University of London

ARANTXA RODRIGUEZ Department of Applied Economics, University of the Basque Country, Bilbao

LISA J. SERVON Department of City and Regional Planning, University of California at Berkeley, Berkeley

DIANE-GABRIELLE TREMBLAY Télé-Université du Québec, Montréal

PASCALE VAN DOREN RIDER, Université Catholique de Louvain, Louvain-la-Neuve

ANNA WHYATT South Bank University, London

PATRICIA A. WILSON Community and Regional Planning, University of Texas at Austin, Austin

ALMA H. YOUNG University of New Orleans, New Orleans

Preface

This book grew out of the conference 'Cities, Enterprises and Society at the Eve of the XXIst Century' organized by IFRESI[1] with PIR-Villes, the multidisciplinary research programme on cities of the French National Council for Scientific Research (CNRS) in Lille, France, 16–18 March 1994. We are indebted to a number of people and organizations who helped to make the conference possible. DATAR/PIR-Villes provided funds for the scientific preparation of the conference, while the European Science Foundation, the Conseil Régional Nord Pas-de-Calais and the Urban Development Agency of Lille among others, had a crucial part in the realization of the project. We also have a special debt to the conceiver and scientific co-ordinator of the conference, Frank Moulaert, for his inestimable knowledge, his comprehension and his constant support.

The conference attracted 400 people and more than 200 papers were presented. Four key issues were addressed:

1   economic globalization and urban dynamics;
2   restructuring strategies of firms within the urban economy;
3   local labour markets and social polarization;
4   local economic development strategies and policies.

This book grew out of the latter question which, by and large, attracted most of the contributions. The contributions that were selected were subsequently updated and revised. Other chapters are invited papers. The translation and finalization of the papers benefited from the financial support of PIR-Villes and the Conseil Régional Nord Pas-de-Calais.

The concept of the book was developed during the late spring of 1994 when, thanks to the support of PIR-Villes, Patricia A. Wilson could be invited to spend three months at IFRESI. The editors are very grateful to the contributors for their co-operation and efforts. We also wish to thank to the staff of IFRESI and its director, Patrice Grevet, for their help. After organizing and running the conference efficiently, Cécile Soudan made our editorial tasks much easier; she also translated several chapters. Fariza Marécaille typed and corrected the manuscript, while Kourosh Saljoghi was resourceful in deciphering encoded floppies and helping the editors to keep in touch accross the Atlantic. We are most grateful to them all. Christophe Demazière also wishes to acknowledge his debt to his colleagues and companions of the local economic development unit at IFRESI, Frank Moulaert, Jean-Cédric Delvainquière, and Pavlos Delladetsima. Most of his knowledge about local economic development comes from their joint work during the last three years, so that, even if they did not take part in the editing process, this book is theirs as much as his (but the usual disclaimers apply!).

Finally, we would like to thank our editor at Mansell, Veronica Higgs, for her interest, advice and commitment to the project.

C.D. and P.W.
Lille and Austin

Note

1. IFRESI (Federative Institute for Research on Industrial Economies and Societies) was created in Lille in 1986, by CNRS (French National Centre for Scientific Research), and five universities in the Nord Pas-de-Calais. On the basis of a pluridisciplinary programme, it federates research carried out in social and human sciences.

   For a list of the other publications, please write to Frank Moulaert, scientific co-ordinator of the conference, IFRESI, 2 rue des Canonniers, F-59800, Lille, France.

Introduction

CHRISTOPHE DEMAZIÈRE

The world crisis that started two decades ago remains as an intriguing phenomenon, due to its intensity and length. In the 1970s advanced societies experienced inflation, rising unemployment, and instability of exchange rates. The macroeconomic policy instruments, set up after World War II to regulate the economy at the national or international level, seemed to have reached some inherent limits. Since then, the overwhelming changes in the organization of production, the fragmentation of demand, and the continued expansion of international trade have increased the ineffectiveness of nation-states' regulatory structures and institutions. Transnational corporations have never been so powerful, while regions and localities, and within such setting a vast array of agents and individuals, are looking for and acting to create an alternative economic growth. An outcome of the two-decade-long economic crisis, local economic development (LED) is a vast field of experiments.

The first aim of this book is to present systematically to the wider audience the enormous variety of LED initiatives, their aims, mechanisms, and outcomes. This is certainly an age of intense adoption, but at the same time of increasing standardization of LED strategies. Nevertheless, local economic development is certainly not a one-direction movement. Anyone who has attended conferences or seminars on local development has experienced this variety and, mixed with the wish of the participants to exchange their concrete experiences, the great difficulty of knowledge transfer.

The second aim of the book is to review the local economic development literature, which has changed extensively over the last fifteen years. Since the pioneering writings by scholars such as John Friedmann (1979), Walter Stöhr (1981), Arnaldo Bagnasco (1977) and others, the numerous LED initiatives taking place all over the world have been documented and classified. In this process, places like Route 128, Prato, Baltimore's waterfront, or Mondragon, have become incredibly famous. A number of 'models' of local economic development have appeared, notably the Marshallian Industrial District model. And a number of debates have taken place, relating to both theoretical and empirical/policy matters. These debates and the related questions which have been raised can be summarized in the following groups.

1 Geographical debates: what is the logic behind the rise of new industrial spaces and the fall of former loci of accumulation? Are there regular spatial forms of economic restructuring from one country to another? Are 'local/regional economies' resurgent?

2 Economic debates: what do local strategies mean in an age of economic 'globalization'? What are the concrete outputs of local development strategies? Is there any economic/social cost to economic redevelopment? At a macro level, is LED a zero-sum game?

3 Policy/political debates: is LED only a local matter? Should there be a national policy for LED? What are the respective contributions of public authorities, firms, and citizens to the development of strategies? What is the democratic content of LED strategies?

To deal with the complexity of these questions a number of contributions review and examine critically the dominant trends in LED, especially endogenous development (Chapters 1 and 15), strategic planning (Chapters 4 and 5) and the physical redevelopment of cities (Chapters 4, 12 and 13). Some of these chapters explore the possibilities of applying these models to 'losing' localities. In a complementary way, other chapters explore recent, innovative trends in LED, like microcredit (Chapter 14), the growing implication of the third sector (Chapters 10 and 11), and the internationalization of LED strategies (Chapters 7 to 9).

The third aim of this book is to develop a comparative approach to LED initiatives, especially between countries and between continents. The variety of approaches and their comparative study are researched by means of a 'global scan' of LED experiences. The presentation covers nine European countries, and the Americas, including Latin America (Chapter 10), are also analysed. In addition to the conclusive piece, two contributions (Chapters 3 and 11) are devoted to a comparison between the American and the European experience. Nevertheless, Parts I, II, and III are mainly concerned with European cases, while Parts IV and V are devoted to the Americas.

Part I: Global economic restructuring and the rise of local economic development policies in Europe

In the first chapter, Frank Moulaert and Christophe Demazière, on the one hand, place local economic development in context and on the other construct a theoretical agenda shared by most contributors. They examine thoroughly the spatial impacts of global economic restructuring in France, Great Britain, Germany, Spain, Portugal, Greece, and Italy, and demonstrate how the different levels of public intervention have been reorganized. The variety in timing, scope, and nature of local responses leads the authors to examine critically the local economic development literature. They argue that in spite of its influence on LED strategies, the Marshallian Industrial District model only applies to a very small part of current trends; justice should be done to the involvement of large firms in local dynamics. The institutional framework which should foster development initiatives by regional and local authorities is also of critical importance. In the conclusion, Moulaert and Demazière examine the many deprived areas in Europe and the possible strategies that could be devised for redevelopment. They suggest that these strategies should be based on a non-technical reading of the local potential, and need not reproduce the models which are drawn from 'success stories'.

The two following chapters pursue the theoretical agenda set out in the introduction and also detail the framework of local economic development policy in the two largest countries of the European Union. In Chapter 2, Wilhelm Benfer highlights the specificity of local economic policies in Germany (FRG), especially with respect to the American literature on local development. He argues that theories of LED are important because they shape the orientations of the concrete programmes adopted by local authorities. A theoretical framework allows Benfer to compare trends in LED between countries, pointing to the distinct character of LED policies in Germany. The chapter concludes with a summary of similarities and differences concerning LED policies in Germany and the United States.

In France, the local development 'movement' roughly started with the Decentralization Act of 1982, which allowed local public institutions to increase their intervention in the local economy. Frédéric Corolleur and Bernard Pecqueur show in Chapter 3 that in France the goals and means of LED strategies have almost evolved in the same direction over the last fifteen years. In the early 1980s local authorities used their new powers to act as 'fire-fighters' for local firms, which frequently involved financial support. This approach has proved to be inefficient and public authorities have recently been more concerned with providing a favourable business environment. The numerous public/private partnerships have contributed to the construction of territorial specificities. This new policy orientation seems to be relevant in the context of an increasing economic globalization (i.e. of a lesser spatial fixity of enterprises). But it may lead to a growing competition between local authorities, and between localities and regions.

Part II: Planning the redevelopment of industrial cities

The first three chapters of this section document the different national contexts of LED, as well as relating the mushrooming of LED strategies to the tendencies of economic restructuring in the last two decades. This second part adds crucial details to this broad picture. Each chapter contains an in-depth case study of large cities in their attempt to gain a new prosperity. Interestingly, these chapters illustrate contrasting strategies and conceptions of LED.

In Chapter 4, Arantxa Rodriguez documents the case of Bilbao, one of the main industrial centres of Spain and also one of the most severely affected by economic recession, environmental degradation and social exclusion. De-industrialization has paved the road for a service-based strategy of metropolitan recovery. But tertiarization is, arguably, dependent on extensive physical restructuring. To lead this process, several policy schemes have been designed by the local and regional authorities. Rodriguez critically discusses the effects of this property-led regeneration. She also examines the limits of urban policy innovations, notably the lack of integration between the different policy tools.

Chapter 5, by Pascale Van Doren, examines the LED strategy of Charleroi, the fourth largest city in Belgium. As a typical early industrial city, Charleroi has experienced several sectoral crises since the late 1950s. Nowadays the steelmaking industry is still the biggest local employer and it seems obvious that Charleroi's development trends need a dramatic reorientation. In that respect, the local authorities have adopted a pro-active attitude: Charleroi was one of the first cities in Belgium to formulate a strategic plan. Van Doren discusses the situation and prospects of Charleroi by resorting to the notion of innovative milieux, a concept developed by Aydalot (1986) and the Groupe de Recherche Européen sur les Milieux Innovateurs (GREMI). According to Aydalot, local environments are undoubtedly the relevant scale to analyse the current economic restructuring and its spatial dimensions. The milieu creates local entrepreneurship and accounts, to a certain extent, for the performance of local firms. This view is a far cry from traditional growth pole theories, for which the environment is, rather, an output of production. The characteristics of early industrial regions (vertically integrated plants with stable, if few, relationships with subcontractors; a hierarchical division of labour; a 'paternalistic' management of human resources) need to be reversed. In Charleroi the redevelopment strategy is concerned both with creating local resources and benefiting from the completion of the Single European Market. Van Doren shows that there is no articulation between those two aims and advocates a strategy that would take the larger environment around Charleroi into account and, especially, the fast-growing urban region of Brussels.

In contrast to Bilbao or Charleroi, London is certainly not a traditional industrial city. Nevertheless, as Iain Begg and Anna Whyatt point out in Chapter 6, its economic development prospects are quite worrying. Although it produces 15 per cent of the GDP, the metropolitan area of London has some of the most deprived communities and highest rates of unemployment in the United Kingdom. De-industrialization has been extreme, while the significant growth of advanced services has not (not yet?) produced any significant 'trickle-down effect'; on the contrary, it has been producing social polarization. Begg and Whyatt discuss three scenarios for London's future, of which the continued decline seems to be the most likely. In any case, they argue, London's future cannot be left entirely to the private sector, let alone developers. But herein lies London's second weakness: the territorial fragmentation of the economy is echoed by the institutional fragmentation and the absence of any executive body at the metropolitan level (probably unique in the advanced world). In this context, the contradictory interests of the individual London boroughs are exacerbated, making LED initiatives a mere caricature. Begg and Whyatt point out the need for a sound development strategy. A strategy that above all should seek to provide the social as well as the physical infrastructures that might appeal to new industrial investors.

Part III: The internationalization of local economic development strategies

Local development has sometimes been depicted as being localist, naive, and, consequently, of little significance. At the present time these views seem to be weaker. Local development strategies increasingly acquire an international dimension. In Europe, this tendency is clearly related to the rising influence of EU policies. On the one hand, the structural funds act as spatially targeted instruments. On the other hand, the European institutions have contributed to the development of infrastructures, to the narrowing of the skills mismatch, and to the fight against poverty and social exclusion. In Chapter 7 Michael Chapman presents a detailed overview of these EU policy actions. He also reviews the new programmes that are of direct relevance to economic initiatives at a local level (like urban, etc.).

In this part, the notion of an 'internationalization' of LED has two meanings. First, there is the constitution of international networks of institutions involved in LED strategies. Whereas the European Commission is not likely to respond to special demands made by individual localities, the international coalitions of localities have not only been extremely successful in attracting European funds, but have recently proved to be extremely influential in the development of the EU spatial policy (Fothergill, 1994). The second meaning is more precisely spatially focused: it concerns LED strategies which target cross-border co-operation. This latter aspect is documented in the two chapters that follow Michael Chapman's analyses.

Chapter 8, by Peter Reid and Andrew Church, examines international strategies from the point of view of local institutions. Often accompanied by the retreat of the national state, economic globalization is the very driving force. But what economic globalization means may be interpreted differently by local authorities. As a result, cross-border policy initiatives vary greatly; this is very clear in the cases of co-operation between Kent and Nord Pas-de-Calais, and between the South Coast of England, Picardy and Normandy. Reid and Church also examine the future development of international LED strategies and their possible advantages and disadvantages.

Because they are located at the periphery of economic and administrative centres of the nation-states, border regions are generally regarded as structurally weak regions. In this context the opening of the Single European Market brings new opportunities as well as new threats to private and public agents. This is why the European Union now encourages cross-border co-operation, especially in the form of the 'Euregions', i.e. institutionalized contacts between governments on either side of the border. In Chapter 9, Fabienne Corvers, Ben Dankbaar, and Robert Hassink analyse cross-border co-operation between local institutions in the context of the Maas-Rhine Euregion, situated along the Dutch-Belgian-German border. They argue that the Euregion formula has not proved, so far, to be the best way to overcome the economic borders, because the collaboration between administrations has been privileged. The policy should rather be to help economic agents to increase their cross-border exchange. On the basis of an extensive empirical research, Corvers, Dankbaar and Hassink show that many sources of technological innovation are left untapped and they recommend the adoption of a 'Euregional' innovation policy.

Part IV: Community-based economic development in the Americas

In Chapter 10, Patricia Wilson draws a parallel between the diminishing role of the nation-state in both North America and Latin America and the rise of community-based strategies. In the United States, from the Johnson to the Clinton administration, the successive local development policies all pushed the public sector to call on the private sector. This can be seen as a zero-sum game, because it led to intense competition between local governments to attract outside private investors. In Latin America, the governments impulsed privatization and an institutional decentralization which failed to give any significant economic power to the local authorities. Both in the United States and Latin America, the retreat of the central state without the emancipation of local authorities left the floor to the involvement of the civil society in local economic development. This took the form of the community development corporation movement in North America and of community-oriented non-governmental organizations in South America. Patricia Wilson argues that, in contrast to the 1960s, community-based economic development is no longer either naive or localist, but has become a sophisticated, internationally connected force, without losing, it seems, the sense of community.

In Chapter 11, Diane-Gabrielle Tremblay first compares the scope, extent and meaning of LED in Europe, with community-based economic development in the USA. She then illustrates the importance of community-based economic development in the context of French-speaking Canada. She presents the different types of community-based economic development organizations active in Quebec and Montreal and explores two leading issues: how they are able to work with local government, and how their strategies relate to the global context of increasing free trade in North America.

Part V: Progressive local economic development strategies and their effects on social exclusion

Several chapters of the book critically discuss the capacity of local strategies to regenerate local economies. This part pushes the discussion even further by examining 'progressive' LED strategies and their effects on social exclusion. Progressive conceptions of LED put the stress on the possible benefits of local growth for the least privileged social groups. In brief, they aim at combining the promotion of economic development and the alleviation of urban poverty. The question is to what extent are these goals compatible.

In Chapter 12, Kevin Archer illustrates the continuation and ruptures from urban entrepreneurialism to progressive LED strategies. In its extreme form, urban entrepreneurialism consists of 'selling a city' as an image to outside investors. The Walt Disney Company provides a most inventive example: in a few decades, it has turned Orlando, a small town in Florida, into a major international city. Orlando's larger industrial neighbour, Tampa, experienced a slow growth throughout the 1970s and 1980s, probably due to the proximity and thrift of Disney World. Cast in the shadow of Mickey, Tampa's local 'growth élite' first tried to gentrify its waterfront. Later, a more progressive mayor tried to include working-class and minority groups in the development strategy. Archer shows that this intended progressive policy has several limits. In particular, what he calls the 'rhetoric of inclusion' hides a policy process that still excludes the least privileged segments of the population. For Archer, democratic politics of local economic development may not be easily achieved (a view also expressed in Chapters 1, 5, and 7).

Alma Young and Jyaphia Christos-Rodgers have a more invigorating tone. Their contribution (Chapter 13) is a richly detailed case study of community organizing strategies in a deprived neighbourhood of New Orleans. The grassroots organizations have challenged the dominant discourse on economic restructuring and its consequences for New Orleans, and developed other discourses, on institutionalized racism, community power, well-being, land use, etc. These discourses have helped to build a sense of community building and dialogue, rather than confrontation and protest. The local community has developed a holistic development strategy and has received backing from several national non-governmental organizations.

This part of the book ends with an account of one of the most innovative tendencies in LED: microcredit. Microcredit is an economic development tool that provides training and small loans to low- and moderate-income people who want to start their own businesses. In Chapter 14, Lisa Servon addresses three main questions: (i) how do microenterprises programmes work?; (ii) who do they serve?; and (iii) how do they fit the historical context of economic development and urban poverty policies? She presents findings from a research project which is organized around case studies of three microenterprise pro-grammes in the United States. She analyses the evolution of microcredit since the early 1980s and illustrates how the lessons learned can be applied to other local economic development policies and strategies.

Part VI: Outlook

In the concluding chapter, Patricia Wilson draws on the contributions to the book in order to reflect on future directions in local economic development. The LED literature, she argues, shows that the tension between global and local can be managed creatively. It also illustrates the innovative roles of local partners of economic development such as local authorities and firms, and the arrival of new actors, e.g. non-profit organizations, both community based and on a larger, even international, scale. Other emerging issues are the rise of the informal sector in developed countries and networking – among localities, firms, practitioners, etc. Finally, the LED literature illustrates the decline of grand theory, and the use of more partial, post-modern, methodologies. This opens the possibility for the analyst to redefine his/her role and, especially, to be of more service to front-line actors in local economic development.

References

Aydalot, P. (ed.) (1986) *Milieux innovateurs en Europe*. Paris, GREMI.

Bagnasco, A. (1977) *Tre Italie. La problematica territoriale dello sviluppo italiano.* Bologna, Il Mulino.

Fothergill, S. (1994) 'The impact of regional alliances. The case of the EU coalfields', *European Urban and Regional Studies*, 1: 177–80.

Friedmann, J. (1979) 'Basic needs, agropolitan development, and planning from below', *World Development*, 7: 607–13.

Stöhr, W. (1981) 'Development from below: the bottom-up and periphery-inward development paradigm', in Stöhr, W. and Taylor, D., *Development from Above or Below?* Chichester, John Wiley and Sons.

Part I

Global economic restructuring and the rise of local economic development policies in Europe

1

Local economic development in post-Fordist Europe: survey and strategy reflections[1]

FRANK MOULAERT AND
CHRISTOPHE DEMAZIÈRE

Introduction

For over a decade now, the Western world has witnessed a 'local economic development movement': local initiatives have become a preferred instrument for economic development in regions and communities. The functional decentralization of business activities, the exclusion of many areas from the geography of the new production systems, the failure of top-down national and regional economic restructuring policy to solve the problems of localities, the rise of regional and local autonomy movements, have encouraged the local perspective in tackling problems of local development and underdevelopment.

The diversity of local economic development strategies and models, combined with the relative absence of systematic classification work hitherto, have logically led to terminological ambiguity. Somewhat in correspondence with the lack of unifying analytical efforts, different types of literature and partial systems for classifying regions, areas and development strategies have emerged. The purpose of this chapter is to create some order in the abundance of scientific literature on local economic development in Western Europe. Therefore, not descriptive exhaustiveness but a targeted analysis of development approaches is stressed.

The first part of this chapter provides an overview of the economic and political contexts in which local economic initiatives have appeared. The second part assesses national experiences of the impact of economic restructuring at the local level in six countries of the European Union: Great Britain, Germany, France, Spain, Portugal, and Greece. In the third part, experiences with industrial districts are examined for different countries, especially Italy. The industrial district is often considered the prima donna of local development models and strategies. For this reason, it should be examined in a critical way. Part of this examination concerns the question as to which types of localities with restructuring problems can draw lessons from experiences with local production systems of the industrial district type. In fact, research shows how areas with a low profile in industrial tradition, a long rural history and a significant disconnection with leading growth trajectories, find little value in the industrial district model.

The fourth section of this chapter addresses the changing role of private firms in local economic development. Without denying their key role in many local development strategies, small firms must be demystified, and justice should be done to large enterprises which today play a vital role in some of the regional and local development networks in Western Europe. However, private initiative seems to be more successful in regions and localities with a certain level of division of labour between the public and the private sector. Elements of a comparative analysis are provided and it is argued that regionalized state systems, with well-established local agents, seem to be the most effective in more or less balanced development strategies.

The chapter concludes with a provocative question: what lessons for peripheral regions and localities can be drawn from the West European development experiences as they have been screened in the literature? A plea is made for a more careful understanding of such areas, their development needs and the appropriate redevelopment strategies.

Local economic development: concepts, agents, challenges

The meaning of the term 'local development movement' is far from unequivocal. In its generality, it refers to the diversity of initiatives taken by different social agents, all meant to promote local economic development. However, the objectives of these initiatives can be quite different, the instruments by which they are pursued witness to differentiated levels of creativity and the amalgam of local socio-economic structures for whose revival, survival or further prosperity they are meant, is hardly susceptible to coherent classification.

Different social agents

Far from being exhaustive, we may distinguish the following categories of agents:

(a) local entrepreneurs demonstrating a strong identification with their community;
(b) socio-economic institutions: chambers of commerce, local sections of unions;
(c) social and political movements rooted in the local communities;

(d) political decision-making agents at different levels in the spatial hierarchy (local, regional and national administrations, supranational authorities such as the European Commission);
(e) mixed agents, such as local development agencies with private and public partners.

The actions undertaken by these different agents can be combined (e.g. in the form of networks or partnerships) or occur independently. Normally, they will be determined by the institutional nature and competence of the agent in question, be it that this nature can be modified by the dynamics of co-operation. For example, in many cities or groupings of municipalities, combined actions of local capital, labour and government administrations, as well as political authorities at a higher spatial level have led to the establishment of local development agencies. These agencies have taken different types of initiatives: services to investors (advice, training, preparation of investment projects), lobby for financial support, organize public infrastructure, etc. In the setting of such actions, local governments have to a certain degree adopted an entrepreneurial role. At the same time, in many localities, local business people have become more community concerned, unions have partially identified with the profit logic of capital, and regional, national or European public authorities have entered into partnerships with their local counterparts.

Of course, this tendency to unite differently coloured hands in a local development movement should not blind us to the other dimensions of the complexity of co-operation, such as the diversity of objectives, the specificity of local socio-economic structure, as well as the plurality of development instruments.

Different objectives

Depending on the divergence in local socio-economic structure, development agents and available instruments, objectives of local development can be very different among localities. In some regions, local development actions are meant to create employment for the employees who lose their jobs through the restructuring of traditional industries. In other cases, it is a matter of strengthening an already strong regional export base in a leading high-tech area or providing employment opportunities for specific target groups (youths, unemployed elderly) in an urban neighbourhood. Although generic approaches to regional and local development stress the communality of problems and objectives, empirical research shows the strategic importance of local forms. For local forms, the complexity of development problems as well as the antagonisms between development agents, may condemn development

strategies to the cohabitation of different, partly or completely conflicting targets.

Different local socio-economic structures

Local social and economic structures are the basis of significant differences in local development actions. Most success stories have been
written for more or less prosperous areas: the Third Italy and its industrial districts, California's Silicon Valley, Britain's M4 corridor or
France's Sophia Antipolis. Traditional industrial regions in decline have
more problems to generate a local development potential: France's Nord
and Lorraine, Germany's northern industrial regions, the manufacturing
Basque country. And localities in rural or semi-rural, often peripheral
areas such as Portugal's northern depressed areas, Italy's Mezzogiorno or
the Greek Thrace, must face their development problems still differently.

In addition, a comparative reading of local development trajectories is
also burdened by the variety in scale of communities and regions, as well
as their modes and degrees of integration within the regional, national
and international economies. The specific economic, political and socio-
cultural features of the local socio-economic structure are important to
evaluate the endogenous development potential of a locality. However,
such features are determined in a dialectical interaction with the embed-
ding socio-economic structure. The weight and place of a region or a
locality in the global economic, political and socio-economic relationships are crucial in determining its endogenous development potential.

Diverse instruments

Instruments of local development depend on the objectives, but are also
determined by the possibilities and socio-economic features of the social
'milieu' of the region or locality as well as the socio-economic structures
to which they belong. Public or private instruments, budget versus fiscal
policy, productive versus infrastructural investments, economic activities, global or local partnerships: all these choices depend on so many
variables which cannot be the object of a general discussion, but which
emanate from the local development practice and its experience.

Global economic restructuring and its spatial impact on Europe: an appraisal

Since the early 1970s the world economy has endured instability. Europe
itself lived through a number of impacts of macroeconomic or macro-
political shocks, notably with the rise of energy prices, the loss of control
on the wage price spiral, monetary crises surrounding the rise and fall of

EMS; and, recently, the difficult political democratization and economic transition of East and Central European countries. During these two decades, the basis of Europe's prosperity has clearly been put in question. An economic and political restructuring has taken place, in three forms at least. First, the hierarchy of industrial sectors – in terms of employment, contribution to the gross national product or innovative capacity – has changed drastically. Traditional heavy industrial sectors like steelmaking, shipyards, etc., experienced an endless restructuring, and sometimes nearly disappeared from the map of some European regions. More modern so-called Fordist sectors, like the car industry or consumer equipment goods, showed a tendency to shift from mass production of uniform products to small batch production of a variety of products. To achieve this major change, they relied massively on information technology and producer services; the qualitative and quantitative importance of these activities for the future economic growth is more and more acknowledged.

Second, there were major changes in the regulation of the world monetary, financial, and commercial system. At the initiative of the United States, the liberal 'deregulation' provoked in the 1980s a fierce competition between nations. Markets became global, economic exchanges intensified between the First World and the Third World, the relevance of the latter term fading with the rise of newly industrialising countries (NICs) (Lipietz, 1985). This dimension of economic restructuring also bore dramatic consequences for localities and regions in Europe.

Third, European governments, whatever their political philosophy, all made the control of inflation the central goal of their macroeconomic policies. As a result, four important changes were made in macro- and meso-policy orientation and in political institutions in all the member states of the European Union:

1   the adoption of policies sharing a common austerity basis;
2   the growing importance of EU institutions and policy;
3   the increasing number of specific target policies at the national level;
4   the multiplication of positive developmental interventions, especially targeting the local level (Moulaert *et al.*, 1994: Chapter 3).

In short, although (or: because?) austerity policy is in the first place a macro-policy, it affects regional and local communities in an uneven way. And the new top-down development initiatives targeting the local level are usually too general in nature, or miscalculate the specificity of local development mechanisms.

This sea-change economic and political restructuring has significantly affected the geography of prosperity and decline of nations, regions and localities. Indeed, economic restructuring has often had dramatic spatial consequences. Throughout the 1980s, important bodies of literature have extensively documented the rise or fall of local productive systems (e.g. Aydalot, 1986; Scott and Storper, 1986; Henderson and Castells, 1987) and it is not our aim to present a catalogue of this literature, but rather a synthesis. In Western Europe, localities have been affected in specific ways, depending on: (i) their own socio-economic structure and agency; (ii) their belonging to certain regional armatures and social formations; (iii) their embeddedness in the global socio-economic and political context; and (iv) their eligibility for positive regional policies (Moulaert, 1995). Although there are many other types which illustrate the reactivity of localities to the global restructuring dynamics (Moulaert *et al.*, 1994), we restrict the illustrations to just two different types of localities: old industrial regions and high technology poles.

Traditional industrial regions have been abandoned by industrial capital in two ways. First, plants were closed because the conditions of profitability had completely changed, especially with the rise of the price of energy (the case of steelmaking or metalworking industries) and the increasing cost competition from the NICs (Hudson and Sadler, 1989). Old industrial regions were also hit by relocations, not only of light manufacturing plants which had settled in the post-war era, but also of heavy industries which had formerly been the driving sectors of these areas (Cuñat *et al.*, 1986). As a result, the dynamism of the whole local economy was affected. With the rise of long-term unemployment, the inadequacy of training schemes, the deprivation of entire districts and, in general terms, the social exclusion of large segments of the population, local communities had to struggle to survive and to develop a new vision for their localities.

On the other hand, a number of regions with little or no industrial tradition benefited from the formation of spatial clusters of high-tech complexes, labelled by Stöhr (1986) as 'territorial innovation complexes'. These are the famous technopoles (Benko, 1991). The rise of technopoles takes place against the background of a considerable growth of new technologies over the last two decades, in terms of investments, output, employment, exports. The crucial point is that this growth is spatially concentrated in only a few areas. Here, the hand of the state, and more specifically of the military state is quite visible. State procurement and investments in military and aerospace equipment had a determining impact on high technology industrial development, reinforcing spatial inequalities in investment opportunities (for the case of France, see Dyckman and Swyngedouw, 1988; Cooke *et al.*, 1992). Localities receiving high technology investments are in general promising localities, but we would like to underline that the new growth takes the form of (cyclical) boom/bust cycles (Swyngedouw and Archer, 1986) and is unlikely to replace jobs made redundant in other industrial sectors (Castells, 1985). Another model of successful local development is the industrial district, which we will analyse on pages 14–15.

The presentation of these two types of localities is deliberate: over the last two decades, the attention of specialists in urban and regional development has shifted from old industrial regions to 'winning' localities. During the 1970s until the middle of the 1980s, the focus was on traditional industrial regions in developed economies, which were hit hard by restructuring. Gradually, it became clear that the economic, social and political mode of development of the post-war era was to give way to radically new forms of production, consumption, and political expression. At the same time, the attention was driven towards places and regions where new industries were born and/or developing (Scott, 1988: 1–7) or where existing production organization models were successful in driving the new production dynamics: industrial districts, local production systems.

This shift is problematic because most localities in Europe do not have the profile of a technopole or an industrial district, but nonetheless develop local development strategies. This is the case in the rural or semi-rural regions of Greece, Spain and Portugal, but also in France, Denmark and Finland, where global economic restructuring had a negative impact, and where new economic growth is needed. There is then the risk of trying out developing strategies that are not adapted to the potential of economic development of such areas. An overview of local development strategies and their origins in six countries in Western Europe should help to understand the specificity of development endeavours.

The emergence of local economic development strategies in six countries of the European Union

There is a great variety in local development subjects among the different European countries. In Great Britain, Germany and France, most of the literature clearly relates local economic development to global economic dynamics. Greece, to some extent, has also devoted particular research interest to the impact of global economic dynamics on peripheral regions. In Portugal and Spain this has been much less the case, with most of the empirical research being devoted to case studies concerning the involvement of public authorities in local economic development. As we shall see, the case of Italy is also specific by its focus on local productive systems.

Great Britain

In Great Britain the first local development programmes, called community development programmes (CDPs), were designed in the late 1960s to address the concentrations of unemployment, poverty, and social malaise in inner city areas. Originally, those problems were attributed to the characteristics of the inhabitants (lack of skills, psychological propensities and sociological characteristics, presence of immigrants) (Hamnett, 1979). However, the research associated with CDPs generally attributed the decline of inner cities to the (late) adaptation of British industrial sectors to Fordist norms of production, which often took the form of plant closures and of an increased centralization of production in large firms (e.g. BCDPRT, 1977). Throughout the 1970s and 1980s urban policy gradually incorporated the finding that the 'inner city problem' could not be solved only by social action, but rather through an action targeted at the structural economic causes of the decline. However, due to the economic crisis, the employment situation of inner cities has worsened. This was extensively documented by the ESRC research programme on inner cities that dealt with Bristol, London, Clydeside, Newcastle Metropolitan Region, and the West Midlands (Hausner, 1987). Ironically, it could be argued that this research developed a framework that was too economistic and neglected issues which received due attention in the 1960s but are in fact also of high relevance today: the informal economy (Stewart, 1988), housing issues, urban social movements, local culture, and so on. These issues are of great significance to the disintegration of inner cities and for assessing their possibilities for redevelopment.

Another ESRC research programme, the 'Changing Urban and Regional System in the UK' (CURS), is of particular relevance here, because it highlighted the interplay between global dynamics and local pro-activity (Cooke, 1989; Harloe et al., 1990). Localities which successfully and unsuccessfully faced the crisis were selected. The industrial and socio-political history of those localities is reconstructed and related to the global economic and political processes at the regional and national level. Considerable attention is given to revival and survival processes: these are analysed from the perspective of the strategy of capital, the cohesion of local communities and the pro-activity of their political and socio-political agents. A major conclusion of the research is that development strategies are not confined to economic issues but often focus on social care, and that local initiatives frequently occur outside the formal sphere of local government (Cooke, 1989: 297).

Germany

In the context of the world macroeconomic crisis, the most competitive industrial sectors of Germany have sought to defend their existing profile of specialization through modernization and flexibilization of their production system, through a closer involvement of SMEs in the production and innovation processes of large firms, and above all through a functional and structural integration of the service sector (Esser and Hirsch, 1989). Because of the large consensus that technological progress should be diversified and decentralized, Länder and municipalities were able to play an active part in technology policy. Influenced by the myth of high-tech regions in the USA, local governments established technology parks; but so far, these have not made noteworthy contributions to local employment (Hilpert and Ruffieux, 1991).

Friedrichs *et al.* (1986) and several other authors have argued that economic restructuring in West Germany resulted in a double spatial tendency: (i) towards a divide between southern prospering Länder (such as Bavaria, Baden-Württemberg) and declining regions in the north (Hamburg, Bremen); and (ii) towards an increasing social/spatial polarization within large cities. This polarization is addressed by municipalities through employment programmes for long-time, low-income unemployed. The major incentive for the municipalities to perform an active employment policy is that social assistance for this category of unemployed is financed out of municipal resources. The majority of the cost of the employment programmes is carried by the social security system; the municipalities bear only 10 to 15 per cent of the total cost of such programmes. This is not to say that German municipalities have currently much room for manoeuvring in local economic development. Due to drastic drops in tax revenues, many towns had to face a financial crisis in the early 1980s and their scope for autonomous expenditure has steadily diminished since then (Krebs, 1991).

The hypothesis of the 'south–north divide' has been contradicted both by analyses of industrial sectors and their growth patterns, and by overall comparisons between Länder (Esser and Hirsch, 1989: 426–8). For instance, Wettmann (1986) pointed out that the restructuring process of shipyards, steelmaking and coalmining industries in the northern regions was certainly not in its early stage. On the contrary, it had progressed a long way, so that there may be a 'stabilization of the north' and possibly, we would like to add, a redevelopment of the large Hanseatic cities. Hamburg, for instance, has begun to benefit from the German reunification as well as from the economic and political transformations in Eastern Europe (Haüßermann, 1994). The case of Hamburg is also interesting because its public authorities found a way out of the economic decline and financial crisis by a shift to enterpreneurialism. On the initiative of the Mayor, a new economic strategy was devised in 1983 by the Chamber of Commerce and other public and private actors. 'Enterprise Hamburg', as it is called, contributed to the creation of 22,000 jobs and attracted investments of about DM5.4 billion (Dangschat, 1993).

France

In France, the recent rise of local development strategies is explained both by economic restructuring and the decentralization of the state apparatus at the beginning of the 1980s. In this view, the transition to a flexible production system would have fed business and public initiatives based on new industrial solidarities and flexible specialization at the local level (see Pecqueur, 1989). To develop a balanced approach of local development in the case of France it is necessary to put it in its historical, political and social context. We argue that two historical elements still influence local development in France, namely the spread of Taylorist principles for the organization of industrial work processes after World War II, and the fact that the political system used to be very centralized until the early 1980s.

It is well known that France, in spite of having experienced the Industrial Revolution quite early, is a country where agriculture has remained important throughout this century. It was not until the 1930s that the number of workers in manufacturing exceeded the figures in the primary sector (Gadrey, 1992). After World War II, the regional economic policy – defined at a national level (*'l'aménagement du territoire'*) – managed to bring modern industries (e.g. cars, and even electronics) to a number of under-industrialized areas, notably in the western part of the country. However, in doing so, this policy did not really achieve its primary goal (i.e. to reduce regional disparities), but rather contributed to the formation of a Taylorist spatial division of labour (Lipietz, 1984). Coing wrote about the Touraine area, which gained numerous branch-plants during the 1960s, that 'firms did not come there in order to "develop" the area, but rather to benefit from its characteristics of under-industrialized area' (Coing, 1982: 25). In fact, throughout the 1950s and 1960s, a model of bipolar development consolidated itself in France, with the highest skilled tertiary and high-tech manufacturing jobs (whether public or private) being created in Paris, and the south-east of the country. Other areas have largely fallen outside the scope of these dominant regional dynamics. Economic development used to be planned at a central level, with local authorities playing virtually no part (Ganne, 1985; Preteceille, 1989); their meagre powers were even trimmed by the central state (Dulong, 1978). Therefore, it is often considered that local economic development started with the laws of decentralization in 1982. The regions were then officially created, while subregional authorities (the '*départements*') and municipalities were given consistent economic competences.

Obviously, politics and policies were historically important for the emergence of local economic development strategies. Nevertheless, it would be simplistic to read local economic development as only a political issue for the local authorities. First, grassroots movements were at the origin of local development initiatives as early as the 1970s (see Chassagne and de Romefort, 1987). As to the present period, Briole and Lauraire (1989) argue in their case study of five technopoles in the South of France that local authorities are not so interested in playing a symbolic part, but rather in developing their own local economic policies, especially in the field of new technologies. In this case, the redefinition of the local state is clearly linked with the shift from Fordist to flexible forms of accumulation and regulation.

Spain, Portugal, Greece

In Spain, Portugal, and Greece, the socio-economic crisis of traditional industrial cities and regions has been well documented and a growing literature assesses the initiatives that have emerged since the late 1980s (for instance, see Chapter 4). Nevertheless the literature in these three countries deals predominantly with the role of public administrations, local planning issues and the conceptualization of local development models and strategies (Henriques, 1989; Rosa Pires, 1990; Evangelinides-Arachovitou, 1989). These foci are not coincidental. Many regions in southern Europe fall outside both the industrialization discourse used to explain the decline of traditional industrial regions in the highly industrialized countries and the post-Fordist utopianism. Either the focus is on industrializing regions and urban centres, whether or not included in a peripheral Fordist division of labour; or the attention is drawn by semi-rural or rural areas, without modern manufacturing basis, and where development strategies depend on a strong impetus from public authorities. In Europe, Italy is probably an intermediary case, since its regions have contrasting socio-economic profiles. Whereas il *Mezzogiorno* is an increasingly 'dependent' region (Giunta and Martinelli, 1995), a metropolis such as Milan thrives and, with 3 per cent of the Italian population, accounts for 21 per cent of the GNP (Bonneville *et al.*, 1993). Nevertheless, most of the Italian literature is devoted to another region – the Third Italy – and its SMEs-based local production systems and industrial districts. Given the importance of the latter model in Western local development literature, its analytical and strategic status must be carefully examined.

Non-Fordist localities in a post-Fordist era: industrial districts in Europe

The term 'industrial district' goes back to Alfred Marshall (1879). It is commonly defined as a geographical localized production system, based on a strong division of labour between small firms which have their own specialization within the same industrial sector, a similar dominant activity, or in a limited number of sectors (Courlet and Pecqueur, 1991). This industrial district concept puts a strong emphasis on the endogenous development potential of the community of people and the population of firms in one naturally and historically bounded area.

Industrial districts were first 'rediscovered' in Italy in the early 1970s. Since World War II, the east and the centre of the country, subsequently called 'Third Italy', have experienced a process of diffuse industrialization, with a certain continuity with the former agricultural mode of development and the social features and values it contained. This diffuse industrialization movement was quite strong: industrial employment grew in the Third Italy by 25.9 per cent during the 1960s, against only 11.8 per cent in the rest of the country; and in the 1970s it increased by 19.7 per cent against only 4.3 per cent for the whole country. Nowadays the Third Italy accounts for as much as 37.3 per cent of the total employment in manufacturing in Italy (Scott, 1988). As Scott points out, diffused industrialization remained for a long time unnoticed because artisanal firms used to be regarded as archaic, with few possibilities to survive, and nearly none to grow. It is only with the works of Bagnasco (1977) and Becattini (1979) that the existence, and later the importance, of the industrial district were acknowledged. Since then, an impressive number of scholars have studied the case of Tre Italia. (Useful bibliographical references can be found in Amin and Robins (1990) and Pyke and Sengenberger (1992)).

With the work of Piore and Sabel (1984) the industrial district has tended to become a paradigmatic case of the future of economic development. Piore and Sabel highlighted Italian industrial districts as examples of territorial aggregations of small and medium-sized firms, interacting within a single production cycle and able to compete on an international level with large firms. The very notion of industrial districts has subsequently inspired several major analyses of economic restructuring in large industrialized countries, such as the United States (Storper and Scott, 1989), or Great Britain (Hirst and Zeitlin, 1989). Empirical research inspired by the notion of industrial districts has also been done in other European countries, like France (for a survey, see Ganne, 1990),

Denmark (Kristensen, 1992), Norway (Isaksen, 1994), or Spain (Costa, 1994). But the industrial district approach has been exposed to both mild and severe criticisms. Some of these criticisms should be taken seriously, others just stem from a careless reading of the literature. Rather than speaking in terms of refuting the industrial district and diffusion model, let us express some warnings.

First, the industrial district model is one which can only properly be applied to societies with an industrial tradition. Replicating this model in localities belonging to regions with no industrial tradition at all is risky. This is particularly clear in southern Europe. We note that in Portugal and Greece, the literature does not devote special attention to the industrial district phenomenon, or is especially critical, calling it a 'new mythology' (Hadjimichalis and Papamichos, 1990). It is true that many regions in southern Europe just do not have the potential to generate industrial dynamics along the district lines; their local development strategies should be different, adapted to peripheral, rural or semi-rural areas. But the argument can be generalized for other large parts of Europe: the industrial district is in many respects not adapted to possible development strategies for the least privileged localities, with an explicitly rural and sometimes also old industrial economic history (Moulaert and Delvainquière, 1994).

Second, one should watch out for the 'locality trap'. Some interpretations and applications of the industrial district concept overstress the endogenous development potential at the expense of the global economic structure to which the local economies belong. It is too easily forgotten that, even if the local content of the development process is strong, its forward and backward linkages bypass the local geography by far. Fortunately, reflections on networks of different types have reintroduced global realism into local development analysis (Pecqueur, 1989) and have weakened the thesis that modern time production systems show a dominant tendency to cluster in space (Amin and Robins, 1990).

Third, there also exists a 'smallness trap'. Certainly, there is a dominant trend to decrease the level of production units, to decentralize the responsibility for production, productivity and profitability to smaller, more easily manageable units. This, however, does not mean that we are witnessing the end of oligopoly and that SMEs will be conquering the world economic scene. In fact, 'Oligopoly is alive and well' (Martinelli and Schoenberger, 1992). Financial concentration of economic activity keeps growing. Quite often, it is a *conditio sine qua non* to allow different business units to become smaller and functionally reorganized. We must therefore not run into the 'smallness trap' and privilege SMEs as prime business candidates for generating local economic development. In fact, large corporations can present an impressive record regarding their role in local economic development dynamics.

Local development and business strategies

During the last two decades the locational strategies of large enterprises (including TNCs) and SMEs have undergone some structural changes. In the Fordist era the spatial organization of large industrial groups and firms was in the first place the reflection of industrial and financial strategies, the search for a critical size and an increasing market share. The functional division of labour, based on the application of Fordist production norms, was reproduced in a spatial hierarchy, in which numerous smaller cities became involved in a relation of dependency within the spatial division of labour of the large industrial groups. Although Fordist geography was in the first instance a national geography, where global production systems and their regulation had an outspoken national territorial articulation (Moulaert *et al.*, 1988; Lipietz, 1990), the search for higher profitability and cost control led to the extension of the Fordist production system in the NICs and their satellite regions as well as in peripheral regions in World War I (in Europe: Southern Italy, Spain, Portugal) (Lipietz, 1985).

The crisis of the 1970s accelerated the reorientation of large business strategy and structure. Tendencies in this process are: (i) return to the core business; (ii) technical and organizational integration of different business functions and activities; (iii) application of new production technologies and modes of organization of the work process (flexible production systems); (iv) combination of intensive and extensive use of space. The latter means that the practice of global production systems, with multiple sourcing and marketing strategies, is combined with the exploitation of local network development and clustering of certain functions in space. In this way, the national Fordist geography breaks down to the benefit of a spatial strategy based on a global–local interplay strategy (Cooke, 1989). Peripheral locations in the Fordist spatial division of labour can be hit hard; or they can benefit from the presence of an 'upgraded branch plant'. For, under the renewed functional logic, TNCs must focus on the supply chain, subcontract more and look for partners in R&D, engineering, marketing, training, service provision, etc. Localities with branch plants may benefit from this development because of the employment of design, engineering and purchasing professionals. Local firms may pick up some advantages from the spatial constraints of, for example, just-in-time delivery and collaborative manufacturing (Morgan and Sayer, 1988).

To qualify this novel spatial behaviour of firms, we want to discuss two elements which are of utmost importance in the local development literature: the networking strategy of firms in their management of the relationship between the local and the global; and the 'size' of the network actors.   As already pointed out in the previous section, a network approach to local development provides a robust safeguard from the 'locality trap' which is implicitly present in the local development approach. However, the terms 'network' and 'networking' must be kept away from the realm of postmodernist buzzwords, so that they can assume a useful analytical meaning. As an 'ensemble of a precise type of relationships between individual and/or institutional agents', the notion of network has no analytical content. To acquire such a content, it should be related to an organizational structure and its different functions (Grabher, 1993). Following different organizational and functional logics, one is soon prompted to talk about different types of networks and their modes of interconnection. From the enterpreneurial point of view, Pecqueur (1989) makes a distinction between: (i) material flow networks; (ii) institutional relation networks (including the firm and its different institutional partners); (iii) informal networks (professional and family relationships). In addition, distinctions should be made between functional and spatial networks (Moulaert and Djellal, 1993) as well as between local, regional and global networks. Moreover, from a spatial point of view, discriminating between different sorts of infrastructure networks and contact networks (Törnqvist, 1990), is of high relevance to capture the local–global interplay.

From the point of view of enterpreneurial strategies in local development, 'network structures' will be developed in view of the strategic objectives of their members (Boekema, 1990). Johannisson (1990) has developed an interesting approach to strategy and networks in local development. He analyses business activity by combining modes of organization (functional and territorial integration) with efficiency criteria (cost minimizing, opportunity management). Opportunity management in a territorial setting requires the pursuit of economies of overview in the setting of personal networks. In fact, the network provides a natural overview of the local setting and replaces physical by social proximity, i.e. creates a 'personal community' on other arenas (Wellman, 1982). The local community may thus operate as an organizing context 'where synergy and economies of overview are achieved, ... the role of the entrepreneur is to operate as a broker' in the different network linkages. The density of networks and network linkages is an important asset for knowledge-intensive production, for the diffusion of technological, organizational and managerial innovations (Johannisson, 1990). Therefore, this approach could mean an important improvement to the seedbed growth hypothesis, stressing the local industrial structure as the main factor of new firm birth. But, as clearly argued by Grabher (1993) and Amin (1993), regional and local networks have their limits, and embedment in larger social structures always remains a major issue in the organization of development strategies.

In the literature on local development we have seen that there is a strong focus on the role of small and medium-sized enterprises. SMEs play an important part in local development dynamics. Arguments in favour of SMEs as development agents are derived from the special-ization of production and customization of demand, the downsizing of functional units combined with flexible production technology and work processes. Together, these developments allow for economies of scope which can be achieved by financially independent, small and medium-sized production units. Therefore, it is important to stress the role of SMEs in local development, and to recognize the specific socio-economic environments in which they prosper (see for example, Guesnier, 1990). But it is of even higher analytical and policy relevance to examine the combined role of large corporations and SMEs in local development dynamics (Pecqueur, 1989). The role of corporate networks or networks animated by industrial groups of 'upgraded branch plants' offering R&D facilities or access to corporate service systems and assuring technology transfer, has been recognized in many case studies on local development. Indeed, it would be a fallacy to exclude *a priori* large or transnational corporations from local development partnerships. In the same way, it is clear that the public sector can play an important part in local economic development.

The significance and rise of local public development policy in western Europe

The institutional framework for local economic development varies greatly from country to country. The institutional, legal and admin-istrative elements of this discussion have been presented and summarized in other publications.[2] We will focus on the significance and rise of local public development policy within nation-states. The growing role of European institutions in local economic development initiatives is analysed by Michael Chapman in Chapter 7. Nor shall we deal with Germany and France, which are examined in Chapters 2 and 3 of this volume.

In most European countries, and over different time spans, local public authorities have received significant powers in the domain of socio-economic policy. This decentralization (or delegation?) of public power to the regional and local level fits the changes in the functional division of labour among different territorial levels in the state apparatus. These changes follow from the crisis of the Fordist system of production and regulation, and the rise of the more decentralized flexible production and regulation system (Lipietz, 1986; Moulaert *et al.*, 1988). Moreover, in countries like Spain, Portugal and Greece, institutional transformations were catalysed by the return to democracy and the search for regional and local self-determination of constituencies and regional ethnic groups. The search for regional self-determination has, in different degrees, also influenced the decentralization of the political system in France, Italy and Belgium.

Great Britain

Great Britain has no outspoken tradition of economic co-operation between the public authorities and private actors. This situation has even worsened under the recent Conservative governments. The policy of Thatcher and Major has been to cut public expenditure, to deregulate, and to reduce public control over private agents' activities. As a result emerging local development strategies have been contained within market boundaries. Pioneering localities which had a strongly interventionist posture in the early 1980s have become far more 'realistic' about the methods of supporting local initiatives. Besides, the Conservative governments have developed a radical urban policy that is targeted against cities, i.e. against local elected authorities (Le Galès, 1988). In the largest conurbations governance has been considerably weakened with the abolition of metropolitan councils (see Chapter 6 on the case of London). Not only have local governments been accused of 'bureaucratism', 'inertia' and the decline of the inner cities, but they also had a budgetary orthodoxy imposed. Moreover, their powers and local leadership have been challenged by a number of governmental initiatives – like task forces, enterprise zones, city grants, city challenge, etc. – which all display an entrepreneurial approach to local economic development.

The Urban Development Corporation is without any doubt 'the flag-ship, the jewel in the crown, of Conservative government urban policy' (Imrie and Thomas, 1993: 3). Created on the initiative of the government, an Urban Development Corporation (UDC) aims at regenerating a spatially delimited urban area in a limited time span, by developing its own projects and by attracting private investors. To achieve this, it can make use of significant land acquisition and planning control powers. The first UDCs, targeting London Docklands and the Merseyside, appeared in 1981 and eleven more have been created since then. In a number of cases, UDCs have been created against the will of local authorities. The dialogue (not to speak of co-operation) with local authorities has often been difficult. Many critics have addressed the role of UDCs; two criticisms are worth mentioning here: (i) UDCs bypass the local democratic system by establishing corporations dominated by business and property interests; (ii) their property-led regeneration strategy cannot succeed in the long run. The latter argument has validity (see Turok, 1992) but it could be objected that the assessment of a local development strategy can follow different sets of criteria, leading to quite opposite views on the achievements of UDCs (Clarke, 1988). As to the first argument, it is observed that in a number of cases, UDCs and local authorities co-operate according to their mutual interests (Imrie and Thomas, 1993). The activities of UDCs are mediated by their local political, social and economic environment.

The debate about UDCs should not make us forget that urban regeneration through leverage planning is only one possible local development approach among many others (see Brindley *et al.*, 1989). For a number of issues in local economic development, the solutions are naturally devised at a local level, e.g. in the field of training. This is why we argue that in spite of the unfavourable institutional context, local economic development strategies may soon mushroom in Great Britain as is the case all over Europe. Stoker and Young (1993) provide details on how local authorities can regain leadership.

Spain

In Spain, the interest in local public economic initiatives follows to a large extent the institutional changes resulting from the transition to democracy. The strength of the political regionalisms is expressed in the recognition by the Constitution of the spatial organization of the state in autonomous regional entities. This new state structure affirms the regional governments as powerful authorities responsible for regional development. Some autonomous governments and local authorities have become key agents in the mobilization of endogenous potential. Ruiz *et al.* (1986) analyse the different possibilities for economic intervention after the changes in political structure. They conclude that the possibilities for regional policy provided by the Constitution should be fully exploited, in order to tackle the major regional restructuring challenges. Vazquez-Barquero (1993) in turn stresses the significance of the provincial and local level for development initiatives.

Portugal

In Portugal, there is general recognition of the high relevance and influential role of local government in the process of spatial, social and economic change. In fact, after the revolution of April 1974, local government became more democratic and gained a certain degree of financial autonomy. Such autonomy favours a high level of local intervention, particularly with regard to the satisfaction of basic needs. In fact, the construction of infrastructure (roads, water supply, sewerage system) took most of the available resources. But many other forms of intervention were also applied. The central state is abandoning its traditionally powerful position in the economic sphere, through privatizations and budgetary cuts. Here, the influence of the membership of the EU is quite clear: 'in order to obtain financial transfers from the EC, Portugal has been forced to review existing policy and develop new policy areas' (Syrett, 1993: 540).

Conclusion

What is the value of the ideas, strategies, policy practices and develop-ment plans outlined in this chapter for areas in Europe which really need a regional and/or local development strategy, i.e. for peripheral regions or localities? We will try to answer this question in three steps:

- how to define peripheral regions or localities?
- how to determine their development needs?
- to what extent is the battery of strategies which was presented here relevant to meet these needs?

Peripheral regions or localities

Peripheral regions and localities can be defined according to different criteria. However, we should beware of falling into the positivist trap of criteria analysis, of trying to calibrate the state of economic development of a region or a locality in terms of quantitative variables only. In fact, economic development or underdevelopment depends on the socio-economic structure of the territorium which is considered (Moulaert, 1995). Between the state of absolute incapacity and that of absolute capacity of development, there are many intermediate situations to be qualified in terms of features of the socio-economic structure. According to Henriques (1989: 104), the notion of 'local underdevelopment refers to the complex interdependency among ecological, economic, political, socio-cultural and psychological factors underlying the inhibition of local initiative aiming at local development'. Three elements are of high relevance in evaluating a state of underdevelopment: (i) 'regional disin-tegration' and the 'local community'; (ii) 'non-emergence' of local initiative and 'local underdevelopment'; (iii) socio-communitarian disin-tegration of human relationships.

Regional disintegration results from the use or non-use of territories in the process of capitalist and pre-capitalist accumulation. Local commu-nities can be almost excluded from stages in the development of industrial capitalism. This holds for certain regions of Portugal, Greece, and Spain, which remained dominated by primary sector activities (agri-culture, fishing). Other regions have been involved in decentralized rural industrialization, and escaped the dominance of corporate capitalism (Vazquez-Barquero, 1993). Still others did not miss any pre-Fordist or Fordist industrialization processes, but were ultimately transformed into cemeteries of scrapped manufacturing equipment, unattractive for new initiatives. In all these cases, regions and localities have either been excluded or marginalized (because of no or later take-off in a new stage of development) in the geography of economic restructuring, or have been seriously affected by the location or dislocation of different types of activity. In any case, these local or regional economies have been 'disintegrated', i.e. functionally cut off or divided up by the locational dynamics of production systems (Lovering, 1988). The economic development potential of these localities is heavily determined by the state of integration or disintegration of the local community.

Development needs

How then to determine the development needs of communities which have been cut off from the geography of accumulation dynamics? This is certainly a political problem, which we cannot tackle in the context of this chapter. More research will be needed to obtain a better insight in how needs are revealed and channelled into policy targets, and how appropriate policy instruments must be designed. It is our impression, however, that the shift from a top-down to a bottom-up approach in development planning (Friedmann, 1978; Stöhr and Tödtling, 1978; Stöhr, 1981) has not really solved the problem of democratic planning practices. Planning at the local level often remained in the hands of local élites; planning was decentralized from the central to the regional and local levels, but not from the élites to the constituencies or to the groups of citizens with particular needs (subsistence income, housing, retraining, socio-cultural organization).

Strategies

Is the battery of strategies discussed in this chapter useful for the development of disintegrated regions? In general, we have the impression from the literature that there is a tendency to replicate strategies fitted for strongly coherent socio-economic structures (such as communities with a developed set of networks of different kinds; or industrial districts; or second-tier urban centres; or regions with a presence of dynamic branch plants of TNCs) in regions or localities with explicit properties of socio-economic disintegration. There is evidence that such replicating strategies do not work (the so-called Silicon Valley syndrome) because they do not take into account the socio-economic structure of the locality or region.

Knowledge of the local-regional structure cannot be developed from a technico-economic perspective. Unfortunately, development specialists remain too economic and technocratic in their approach. Their reading of socio-cultural dynamics, of human relations networks, with ethnical, religious and kinship dimensions, is often done from a social engineering point of view: the endogenous development potential is defined in classical terms of economic assets, work attitudes, capital labour relations, dynamism of public and private institutions. This reading misses an anthropological dimension, an existential history of humankind in the region or locality at stake. To solve this problem, not only renewed scientific efforts, but also applied grassroots democracy is necessary (Friedmann, 1992; Moulaert and Leontidou, 1995).

Notes

1. The origin of this chapter goes back to 1990, when Frank Moulaert, in collaboration with Ricardo Alaez, Phil Cooke, Claude Courlet, Hartmut Haüßermann and Artur da Rosa Pires wrote a feasibility study for the EU (DGV/Poverty III programme). For the purpose of this book, we took the opportunity not only to update the analysis, but to revise some of the original judgements.

2. Several recent publications provide both national monographies and comparative views: Bennett (1989) on Spain, the Netherlands, France, Germany, Finland and Belgium as well as Central European countries; Pickvance and Preteceille (1991) on Denmark, Great Britain, Germany, France (and Canada and the United States); some research by Pavlos Delladetsima is on the institutional framework of local economic development in eight European countries (UK, Portugal, Spain, France, Belgium, Greece, Italy and Germany), with a focus on the role of the EEC (Moulaert et al., 1994: Chapter 3).

References

Amin, A. (1993), 'The globalization of the economy: an erosion of regional networks?', in Grabher, G. (ed.) *The Embedded Firm. On the Socio-Economics of Industrial Networks*. London, Routledge.

Amin, A., Robins, K. (1990), 'The re-emergence of regional economies? The mythical geography of flexible accumulation', *Society and Space*, 8: 7–34.

Aydalot, P. (ed.) (1986), *Milieux innovateurs en Europe*. Paris, GREMI.

Bagnasco, A. (1977), *Tre Italie: La problematica territoriale dello sviluppo italiano*. Bologna, Il Mulino.

BCDPRT (Birmingham Community Development Project Research Team) (1977), *Workers on the Scrapheap*, Final Report nbr 2: Employment.

Becattini, G. (1979), 'Dal settore industriale al distretto industriale', *Rivista di Economica e Politica Industriale*, 2: 7–21.

Bennett, R. (ed.) (1989), *Territory and Administration in Europe*. London, Pinter.

Benko, G. (1991), *Géographie des technopoles*. Paris, Masson.

Boekema, F. (1990), 'Planning local economic development and industrial relations: theoretical and empirical results', paper presented at the 30th RSA European Congress, Istanbul, 28–31 August.

Bonneville, M., Buisson, M.-A., Rousier, N. (1993), 'L'internationalisation des villes en Europe: un même défi, des processus différents', in Bonneville, M. (ed.), *L'avenir des villes*. Lyon, PPSH Rhônes-Alpes.

Brindley, T., Rydin, Y., Stoker, G. (1989), *Remaking Planning*. London, Unwin Hyman.

Briole, A., Lauraire, R. (1989), *Technopoles, services urbains, télécommunications et stratégie des acteurs locaux*, research report to Plan Urbain, Paris.

Castells, M. (ed.) (1985), *High Technology, Space and Society*, Urban Affairs Annual Reviews, 28, Beverly Hills, CA, Sage.

Chassagne, M.-E., de Romefort, A. (1987), *Initiatives et solidarités pour le développement local: l'affaire de tous*. Paris, Syros.

Clarke, M. (1988), 'The need for a more critical approach to dockland renewal', in Hoyle, B.S., Pinder, D.A., and Husain, M.S. (eds), *Revitalizing the Waterfront*. London and New York, Belhaven Press.

Coing, H. (1982), *La ville, marché de l'emploi*. Grenoble, Presses Universitaires de Grenoble.

Cooke, P. (ed.) (1989), *Localities: The Changing Face of Urban Britain*. London, Unwin Hyman.

Cooke, P., Moulaert, F., Swyngedouw, E., Weinstein, O., Wells, P. (1992), *Towards Global Localisation: The Computing and Communication Industries in Britain and France*. London, UCL Press.

Costa, M.-T. (1994), 'Organisation industrielle et compétitivité dans les systèmes productifs localisés en Espagne', in Courlet, C. and Soulage, B. (eds), *Industries, territoires et politiques publiques*. Paris, L'Harmattan.

Courlet, C., Pecqueur, B. (1991), 'Local industrial systems and externalities: an essay in typology', *Entrepreneurship and Regional Development*, 3: 305–15.

Cuñat, F., Daynac, M., Millien, A. (1986), 'La reconversion des zones industrielles en crise', in Guesnier, B. (ed.), *Développement local et décentralisation*. Paris, ERESA.

Dangschat, J.S. (1993), 'Conceptualising Urban Space in Germany', in Mangeen, S. and Hantrais, L. (eds), *Polarisation and Urban Space*, Cross National Research Papers, Third Series. Loughborough, European Research Centre.

Dulong, R. (1978), *Les régions, l'état et la société locale*. Paris, Presses Universitaires de France.

Dyckman, J., Swyngedouw, E. (1988), 'Public and private technological innovation strategies in a spatial context: the case of France', *Environment and Planning C*, 6: 401–13.

Esser, J., Hirsch, J. (1989), 'The crisis of Fordism and the dimensions of a "postfordist" regional and urban structure', *International Journal of Urban and Regional Research*, 13: 417–37.

Evangelinides-Arachovitou, M. (1989), 'Some theoretical aspects concerning local development policies in Greece', in Konsolas, N. (ed.), *Local Development*. Athens, Regional Development Institute/Hellenic Agency for Local Development and Local Government.

Friedmann, J. (1978), *The Active Community: Towards a Political-Territorial Framework for Rural Development in Asia*. Nagoya, UNCRD.

—— (1992), *Empowerment: The Politics of Alternative Development*. Oxford, Basil Blackwell.

Friedrichs, J., Haüßermann, H., Siebel, W. (eds) (1986), *Süd-Nord-Gefälle in der Bundesrepublik?* Opladen, Westdeutscher Verlag.

Gadrey, J. (1992), *L'économie des services*. Paris, La Découverte.

Ganne, B. (1985), 'Du notable au local. Transformations d'un modèle politique', *Annales de la Recherche Urbaine*, 28: 23–32.

—— (1990), *Industrialisation diffuse et systèmes industriels localisés: essai de bibliographie critique du cas français*, report for the International Institute of Social Studies. Geneva, International Labour Office.

Giunta, A. Martinelli, F. (1995), 'The impact of post-Fordist corporate restructuring in a peripheral region: a case study in the Mezzogiorno of Italy', in Amin, A. and Tomaney, J. (eds), *Conflict and Cohesion in the Single European Market* (forthcoming).

Goodwin, M. (1991), 'Replacing a surplus population: the employment and housing policies of the London Docklands Development Corporation', in Allen, J. and Hamnett, C. (eds), *Housing and Labour Markets – Building the Connections*. London, Unwin Hyman.

Grabher, G. (ed.) (1993), *The Embedded Firm: On the Socio-Economics of Industrial Networks*. London, Routledge.

Guesnier, B. (1990), 'Small and medium-sized enterprises' evolution and local development in France', paper presented at the 30th RSA European Congress, Istanbul, 28–31 August.

Hadjimichalis, C., Papamichos, N. (1990), ' "Local" development in Southern Europe: towards a new mythology', *Antipode*, 22: 181–210.

Hamnett, C. (1979), 'Area-based explanations: a critical appraisal', in Herbert, D.T. and Smith, D.M. (eds), *Social Problems and The City – Geographical Perspectives*. Oxford, Oxford University Press.

Harloe, M., Pickvance, C., Urry, J. (eds) (1990), *Place, Policy and Politics: Do Localities Matter?* London, Unwin Hyman.

Haüßermann, H. (1994), Locality case study: Hamburg, Research programme for the EC (DGV/Poverty III), 'Local Development Strategies in Economically Disintegrated Areas: A Proactive Strategy against Poverty in the European Community', Berlin, Humboldt University.

Hausner, V. (ed.) (1987), *Urban Economic Change: Five City Studies*. Oxford, Oxford University Press.

Henderson, J., Castells, M. (eds) (1987), *Global Restructuring and Territorial Development*. London, Sage.

Henriques, J.M. (1989), 'Facing local underdevelopment: challenges to municipal intervention', paper presented at the RSA workshop on 'Theories and Policies of Local Development', Rhodes, April.

Hilpert, U., Ruffieux, B. (1991), 'Innovation, politics and regional development: technology parks and regional participation in high tech in France and West Germany', in Hilpert, U. (ed.), *Regional Innovation and Decentralization*. London, Routledge.

Hirst, P., Zeitlin, J. (eds) (1989), *Reversing Industrial Decline?* Leamington Spa, Berg.

Hudson, R., Sadler, D. (1989), *The International Steel Industry: Restructuring, State Policy and Localities.* London and New York, Routledge.

Imrie, R., Thomas, H. (1993), 'Urban policy and the urban development corporations', in Imrie, R. and Thomas, H. (eds), *British Urban Policy and the Urban Development Corporations.* London, Paul Chapman.

Isaksen, A. (1994), 'New industrial spaces and industrial districts in Norway: productive concepts in explaining regional development?', *European Urban and Regional Studies*, 1: 31–48.

Johannisson, B. (1990), 'Organizing for local economic development – on firm and context dynamics', paper presented at the 30th European Congress of the Regional Science Association, Istanbul, 28–31 August.

Krebs, G. (1991), 'The framework for local economic initiatives in Germany', in Bennett R. and Krebs, G. (eds), *Local Economic Development: Partnership Initiatives in Britain and Germany.* London, Belhaven Press.

Kristensen, P.H. (1992) 'Industrial districts in West Jutland, Denmark', in Pyke, F. and Sengenberger, W. (eds) *Industrial Districts and Economic Regeneration.* Geneva, International Labour Office.

Le Galès, P. (1988), 'Grande-Bretagne: le gouvernement contre les villes', *Annales de la Recherche Urbaine*, 38: 53–62.

Lipietz, A. (1984), *L'audace ou l'enlisement.* Paris, La Découverte.

—— (1985), *Mirages et miracles.* Paris, La Découverte.

—— (1986), 'New tendencies in the international division of labour: regimes of accumulation and modes of regulation', in A.J. Scott and M. Storper (eds) *Production, Work, Territory.* Boston, Allen and Unwin.

—— (1990), 'Le national et le régional: quelle autonomie face à la crise capitaliste mondiale?', in Benko, G., (ed.), *La dynamique spatiale de l'économie contemporaine.* La Garenne-Colombes, Editions de l'Espace Européen.

Lovering, J. (1988), 'The local economy and local economic strategies', *Policy and Politics*, 16: 145–57.

Marshall, A. (1879), *The Economics of Industry.* London, Macmillan.

Martinelli, F., Schoenberger, E. (1992), 'Les oligopoles se portent bien, merci!', in Benko, G. and Lipietz, A. (eds) (1992), *Les régions qui gagnent.* Paris, Presses Universitaires de France.

Morgan, K., Sayer, A. (1988), *Microcircuits of Capital.* Cambridge, Polity Press.

Moulaert, F. (1995), 'Rediscovering spatial inequality in Europe. Building blocks for an appropriate "regulationist" framework', *Society and Space*, forthcoming.

Moulaert, F, Delvainquière, J.-C. (1994), 'Regional and sub-regional trajectories in Europe: the role of socio-cultural trajectories', in Bekemans, L. (ed.), *Culture: Building Stone for Europe 2002.* Brussels, European Interuniversity Press.

Moulaert, F., Djellal, F. (1993), 'Les firmes de conseil en technologie de l'information: des économies d'agglomération en réseaux', in Plan Urbain (ed.), *Métropoles en Déséquilibre.* Paris, Economica.

Moulaert, F., Leontidou, L. (1995) 'Localités désintégrées et stratégies de lutte contre la pauvreté: une réflexion méthodologique postmoderne', *Espaces et Sociétés*, forthcoming.

Moulaert, F., Leontidou, L. Delladetsima, P.M. (eds) (1994), *Local Development Strategies in Economically Disintegrated Areas: A Proactive Strategy against Poverty in the European Community*, final report to the EEC (DGV, Poverty III). Lille, June.

Moulaert, F., Swyngedouw, E., Wilson, P. (1988), 'Spatial responses to Fordist and post-Fordist accumulation and regulation', *Papers of the Regional Science Association*, 64: 11–23.

Moulaert F., in collaboration with R. Alaez, P. Cooke, C. Courlet, H. Haüßermann and A. da Rosa Pires (1990), 'Integrated area development and efficacy of local action', feasibility study for Animation & Recherche in the context of Poverty III.

Pecqueur, B. (1989), *Le développement local: mode ou modèle?* Paris, Syros.

Pickvance, C.G., Preteceille, E. (eds) (1991), *State Restructuring and Local Power – A Comparative Perspective*. London and New York, Pinter Publishers.

Piore, M.J., Sabel, C.F. (1984), *The Second Industrial Divide*. New York, Basic Books.

Preteceille, E. (1989), 'Paradoxes politiques des restructurations urbaines. Globalisation de l'économie et localisation du politique', *Espaces et Sociétés*, 59: 5–26.

Pyke, F., Sengenberger, W. (eds) (1992), *Industrial Districts and Economic Regeneration*. Geneva, International Labour Office.

Rosa Pires, A. (da) (1990), 'Os PDAR e a Diversidade Regional. Elementos para a Construçao de uma Nova Politica Agricola', paper presented at a seminar on 'Programas de Desenvolvimento Agrario Regional', Braga.

Ruiz, G. *et al.* (1986), 'El futuro de la politica regional en la España de las Autonomias', *Pensamiento Iberoamericano*, 10: 299–333.

Scott, A.J. (1988), *New Industrial Spaces*. London, Pion.

Scott, A.J., Storper, M. (eds) (1986), *Production, Work, Territory*. Boston, Allen and Unwin.

Stewart, M. (1988), 'The finding of Wigan Pier?: a review article on the ESRC Inner Cities Research Programme', *Policy and Politics*, 16: 123–32.

Stöhr, W. (1981), 'Development from below: the bottom-up and periphery-inward development paradigm', in Stöhr, W. and Taylor, D. (eds), *Development from Above or Below?* Chichester, John Wiley and Sons.

—— (1986), 'Territorial innovation complexes', in Aydalot, P. (ed.) *Milieux innovateurs en Europe*. Paris, GREMI.

Stöhr, W., Tödtling, F. (1978), 'Spatial equity – some antitheses to current regional development strategy', *Papers of the Regional Science Association*, 38: 33–53.

Stoker, G., Young, S. (1993), *Cities in the 1990s*. Harlow, Longman.

Storper, M., Scott, A.J. (1989), 'The geographical foundations and social regulation of flexible production complexes', in Wolch, J.R. and Dear, M. (eds), *The Power of Geography: How Territory Shapes Social Life*. Winchester, MA, Allen and Unwin.

Swyngedouw, E., Archer, K. (1986), 'Les leçons de l'expérience américaine', in Zoller, H. and Federwisch, J. (eds), *Technologies nouvelles et rupture régionale*. Paris, Economica.

Syrett, S. (1993), 'Local economic initiatives in Portugal: reality and rhetoric', *International Journal of Urban and Regional Research*, 17: 526–46.

Törnqvist, G. (1990), *Sweden in European Networks*, research programme in progress.

Turok, I. (1992), 'Property-led regeneration: panacea or placebo?', *Environment and Planning A*, 24: 361–79.

Vazquez-Barquero, A. (1993), *Política económica local*. Madrid, Pirámide.

Wellman, B. (1982), 'Studying personal communities', in Marsden, P.V. and Lin, N. (eds), *Social Structure and Network Analysis*. Beverly Hills, CA, Sage.

Wettman, R.W. (1986), 'Das Süd-Nord Gefälle – Realität und Perspektiven', in von Voss, R. and Friedrich, K. (eds), *Das Süd-Nord Gefälle*. Bonn, Verlag Bonn Aktuell.

2

Orientations in local economic development policy in the Federal Republic of Germany

WILHELM BENFER

Introduction

An analysis of the efforts undertaken in German local communities to promote economic growth undoubtedly presents a complex task. As this chapter suggests, this task goes beyond a careful examination of the basic question of who does what and how, and in that it should also consider the orientations with which local economic development policies are pursued. The orientations are shaped by the theoretical underpinnings that surround the various activities adopted to promote the economic well-being of places. This book with its wealth of information on local economic development in a number of countries in Europe and the Americas illustrates how these orientations may vary from country to country or even from community to community. The study of local economic development in several localities should not be undertaken, however, only to yield a collection of individual case studies. By using a theoretically oriented, conceptual framework, individual local strategies to promote economic development can be categorized and the similarities and differences that exist between them can be evaluated.

Before this chapter turns to local economic development in Germany, it therefore outlines some basic models concerning the theoretical underpinnings of local economic development policy. Of particular concern in this context is the relationship between the public and private sectors. The particular way in which this relationship is defined in a certain locality is of great significance for shaping the character of the pursuit of economic development initiatives. Since the literature on German local economic development has, so far, largely neglected a theoretical approach to the subject, the chapter will review works by American authors which provide a rich source of material not only with regard to the economic development efforts of local communities in the United States but also concerning the theoretical basis of those activities.

The second part of the chapter focuses on a general description of the approaches to local economic development policy adopted by local governments in Germany. It presents a brief historical review of these activities and discusses the role of local governments in local economic development, and economic development goals and strategies. Based upon this depiction, the chapter argues that local economic development policy in Germany has its own distinct character that deviates in several important ways from a 'model' approach to the pursuit of strategies to promote local economies. This model approach, it is argued, has widely been identified with the initiatives of local communities in the United States to foster economic growth. Especially in Western Europe, various policy instruments, such as public–private partnerships, that were developed in the United States were rather enthusiastically embraced during the 1980s as new and successful ways to stimulate economic development. In this context, a comparison of some of the main characteristics of local economic development policy in Germany and the United States is a useful tool for revealing the distinctive character of the German case. The chapter, therefore, proceeds with a summary of the major similarities and differences concerning the orientations with which efforts to stimulate local economies are undertaken on the local level in both countries which concludes this part of the chapter.

The chapter closes with a review of several issues that warrant further inquiry. These issues concern not only the practice of local economic development in particular, but also the advancement of conceptual knowledge about economic development in general.[1]

Theoretical approaches to local economic development

The literature on local economic development has grown considerably over the last two decades, establishing the study of local economic development as a field of scientific inquiry in its own right rather than a speciality within other fields, such as urban planning, geography, economics, or political science. Today, this body of literature comprises a diverse range of material including practically and theoretically oriented works.[2] While the studies that concentrate on the pursuit of economic development policy will be dealt with later, it can be observed with regard to the theoretical and more general works that, especially during the 1980s, several books were written, not seldom in the broader field of urban development, that contributed significantly to the conceptual development of the discipline. These works provide and elaborate a limited number of key analytical models as the following brief review will demonstrate.

Peterson's book *City Limits* (1981) may be regarded as the first in a number of conceptual works that emerged during the 1980s. In sum, Peterson's analysis represents a somewhat deterministic perspective on urban development. He argues that the market economic framework mandates cities to use their powers and resources actively and efficiently to enhance the economic well-being of their communities. The compelling nature of this systemic characteristic leads to broad support among communities for economic development policies. According to Peterson, these policies, best pursued by an élite who are not directly accountable to the public, are inherently in the interest of cities and will inevitably benefit the whole spectrum of different groups which make up the urban fabric.

Borrowing from basic Marxian theoretical concepts, a surprisingly similar model of economic determinism is offered by structuralist urban scholars. Molotch's work provides an example of this school of thought. Having already introduced the main element of his conceptual view of urban development during the 1970s (Molotch, 1976), in a collaborative effort with Logan, he elaborated the notion of 'growth machines' in the book *Urban Fortunes: The Political Economy of Place* (Logan and Molotch, 1987).

Although Logan and Molotch accept Peterson's principal argument of the primacy of economic forces in market economies with regard to urban development, they come to very different conclusions about the outcomes of such a model. They contest the notion that economic growth, and the development policies which stimulate it, benefit the community at large and are thus in the interest of a city as a whole. Instead, the authors claim that benefits tend to be collected exclusively by relatively few, the people who make up the growth machines. The authors' perspective is similar to Peterson's, however, in the sense that they also consign the public sector to a supportive, if not subordinate, role in relation to the demands of the market and the institutional forces promoting growth.

An alternative model of urban development can be found in Mollen- kopf's work *The Contested City* (1983) which was published only two years after Peterson's study. Whereas the latter identifies economic factors as the principal determinants of urban development and the policies adopted for its promotion, Mollenkopf's analysis rests on the assumption that it is, first and foremost, in the political realm where policies are born and shaped. Mollenkopf suggests that there exists a fair degree of independence between the public and private sectors. His model does not exclude the possibility that private sector interests dominate the content as well as the pursuit of public policies. This happens through the operation of pro-growth coalitions brought together by political entrepreneurs who gather and risk 'political capital or support in order to reshape politics and create new sources of power by establishing new programs' (Mollenkopf, 1983 : 6). At the same time, Mollenkopf's view of the relationship between the two sectors allows for the possibility that in a given situation economic interests are neglected in favour of other interests that exist in the community. This particular relationship between the two sectors may be best summarized in Mollenkopf's own words: 'Politics runs on votes as well as money' (1983 : 9).

Stone and Sanders provide an elaboration of this coalition model in their study of *The Politics of Urban Development* (1987). Based, in part, on a review of an extensive number of case studies, they suggest that coalitions may not necessarily have to include representatives of local government to achieve their goals. The systemic feature of democratic societies, i.e. that governments are controlled by the public, allows organizations outside the realm of elected officials to muster enough political power to influence development policy-making.

The conceptualizations formulated by Stone and Sanders and by Mollenkopf share the view that urban development, and the policies which promote it, are to a large extent shaped by political forces rather than economic ones. However, Mollenkopf suggests that these political forces do frequently align themselves around business élites and institutions in the form of pro-growth coalitions. Stone and Sanders, by contrast, seem willing to advance a more pluralist picture of urban politics that allows for a greater diversity of orientations among coalitions corresponding to specific problems within the local community.

In addition to the above analytical models there exists a body of literature that deals specifically with the roles of the public and private sectors in local economic development. Local economic development and the policies aimed at its promotion require interaction between the public and private sectors to an extent rarely found in any other area of public policy. Local governments are interested in improving the economies of their jurisdictions while private businesses are concerned with the advantages that particular locations offer, many of which are determined by public sector activities. Even on such a very general level it is clear that local economic development involves considerable contact between the public and private sectors.

Wolman and Ledebur (1984) provide a categorization of possible forms of public–private interaction. Distinguishing between different balances in the relationship of the two sectors, they identify seven models, with the '*laissez-faire*' approach at one end of the spectrum and 'public ownership' at the other. Whereas in the former 'the public sector permits the private sector to pursue its activities with as little government interaction ... as possible' (Wolman and Ledebur, 1984 : 26), the ownership form of interaction occurs when 'the public sector assumes and operates some of what ... are commonly assumed to be private sector activities' (Wolman and Ledebur, 1984: 27). With respect to the practice of local economic development, the authors contend that it generally falls within the middle range of the above outlined spectrum, using a 'promotion approach,' or an 'inducement approach', or a 'cooperative or partnership approach'. The element common to all three of these forms of interaction is the fact that they 'are designed to influence the decisions and behavior of businesses in non-coercive ways' (Wolman and Ledebur, 1984: 28).

In their investigation of local economic development policy in the USA and the UK, Barnekov *et al.* (1989) argue that the way the public sector acts in the pursuit of strategies to promote economic growth can be explained and defined within the conceptual framework of privatism. They suggest that privatism and the particular roles it assigns to the public and private sectors have been traditional features of US urban policy. The term privatism was first conceptualized and applied by Sam Bass Warner in his study of Philadelphia (1968). Based upon his historical analysis of Philadelphia's growth during periods of the eighteenth, nineteenth, and twentieth centuries, he described the essence of privatism and its role as the dominant cultural tradition in the United States that has resulted in a basic dependence of cities on the well-being of their economies as follows:

> The first purpose of the citizen is the private search for wealth; the goal of a city is to be a community of private money makers ... (with the result that) what the private market could do well American cities have done well; what the private market did badly, or neglected, our cities have been unable to overcome (Warner, 1968: x).

Based on this premise, privatism implicitly assumes that the role of the public sector is limited and focused only on the removal of barriers to private investment. The general expectation is that this arrangement is the most effective and efficient way to stimulate local economic growth which is beneficial to all segments of a local community.

Compared to numerous studies examining the role of the public sector in the process of local economic development, only a few analyses can be found that focus on the private sector's role. This may be explained simply by the general assumption that in a market economic system it is the private sector which is, almost by definition, primarily responsible for producing economic growth and prosperity. To secure continuous profitability, the private sector always strives for improved efficiency as a means to successfully overcome economic problems. The public sector, by contrast, plays a much more limited role: state intervention is not appropriate for alleviating economic problems because 'planning ... itself [has been] a cause of economic inefficiency' (Fainstein and Fainstein, 1989: 42).

Within the overall context of the privatist tradition that has dominated US local economic development policy, Barnekov *et al.* explain the expectations underlying the above arguments as being

> an assumption that the private sector is inherently dynamic, productive, and dependable; a belief that private institutions are intrinsically superior to public institutions for the delivery of goods and services; and a confidence that market efficiency is the appropriate criterion of social performance in virtually all spheres of community activity (Barnekov *et al.*, 1989: 1).

At a time when local economic problems have been defined mainly in terms of insufficient localized demands for labour (Hanson, 1983), it follows that 'the private sector has the pivotal role in urban economic innovation and development – including job creation' (Barnekov and Rich, 1989: 215). It is assumed that the private sector, when adequately assisted by the public sector, can fulfil this role and benefit all aspects of urban development and segments of local communities. Judd describes the logic underlying this assumption as follows:

> The argument proceeds as follows: [private sector] investment leads to more jobs and an improved tax base. This, in turn, raises the incomes of city residents and provides more resources to city governments so that they can improve public services. Higher incomes lead to increased spending and consumption by city residents. Better public services are evidenced by good streets, lighting, parks, and public buildings and in better schools, police protection, and public health, all of which improve the quality of neighborhood life. Rising spending and consumption create a favorable business environment, which, of course, encourages investment, and on around the cycle again (Judd, 1988: 376–7).

In the tradition of privatism, the public sector assumes a role subordinate to the private sector and its interests. In the pursuit of their role, local governments are primarily concerned with removing obstacles that hinder private investments, and often let the business community participate to a considerable extent in the economic development policy-making process. This role distribution between the two sectors is based on a belief in the inherent superiority of the private sector over the public sector with regard to the efficient and effective pursuit of activities to promote economic growth, and the suitability of the market mechanism to determine and distribute the costs and benefits of economic development.

After reviewing some general theoretical concepts that have emerged in the economic development literature the chapter now turns to the case of local economic development policy in Germany. The following analysis is founded on a broad-based empirical study of economic development strategies as they are pursued by individual local communities as well as on general works as they are found in the literature.

Local economic development policy in Germany

Within the constraints of this chapter, a presentation of such a broad topic necessarily has to be limited in the number of issues it covers. The following section, therefore, concentrates on three aspects of local economic development policy in Germany: its history, local governments and local economic development, and the goals and strategies pursued to foster local economic growth.

History of local economic development policy in Germany

Local government involvement in economic development is by no means a recent phenomenon but rather it has a long tradition in Germany reaching back to the Middle Ages. At that time, two conditions for the emergence of local economic development policy began to be met: the existence of local communities beyond the family or clan, and the emergence of a local economy which no longer comprised primarily small, family-operated enterprises aimed at securing the subsistence of the family members (Schiefer, 1989). Instead, businesses had become more specialized and were producing goods and services in quantities that were intended to satisfy the demand of larger communities. Looking on themselves as 'states within the state', cities engaged in the promotion of their economies to maintain and further strengthen their importance. The means that were available to them to achieve this goal were far-reaching. A local administration could grant or refuse a range of different rights to businesses which originated outside its boundaries – such as the right to do business, to store merchandise, or to trade within the city – thereby effectively controlling external influences on the local economy.

This rather active phase of local government's involvement in economic development came to a preliminary end in the seventeenth century due to the severely weakened position of cities. Apart from an increasingly strong influence of territorial rulers over local affairs, it was to a large extent the Thirty Years' War from 1618 to 1648 that had a devastating effect on local communities and their economies. During the subsequent period of mercantilism, public sector activities to promote economic development became a function carried out primarily by the governments of principalities and kingdoms.

During the nineteenth century, the ideas of economic liberalism, with Adam Smith as its main protagonist, in concert with those of the French physiocrats, contributed to a fundamental change in the relationship between the state and the economy. The state had assumed a strong regulating, if not policing, role *vis-à-vis* the private sector during the mercantilist period, but now its proper role was defined as being subordinate to the economy. The removal of as many barriers to entrepreneurial activities as possible became the main concern of governments in their efforts to promote economic development.

This situation did not significantly change until the economic depression at the end of the 1920s, which dramatically altered the character of local economic development policy. At that time, the assumption that local economic development was a justified and necessary area of local government policy-making was no longer seriously disputed (Schiefer, 1989). Consequently, as local businesses were hit by severe economic problems resulting from the world economic crisis, city halls did not hesitate directly to support ailing individual companies through various forms of financial assistance. After the National Socialists took over the government of Germany, no time was wasted in passing a German Local Government Charter in 1935 which considerably limited the power of municipalities to continue their extensive financial involvement in matters of local economic development.

Following World War II, German local economic development policy evolved through several phases (Schiefer, 1989). During the immediate post-war period, local economic development policy was characterized by rather a pragmatic approach whereby local communities attempted to mitigate the worst consequences of destruction brought about by the war. Subsequently and lasting roughly until the mid-1960s, the economic expansion spilled over into less urbanized parts of the country, spurring many municipalities in these areas to formulate local economic development strategies. The strategies were aimed at attracting businesses seeking to escape the tight labour markets of the big cities. The following decade saw local economic development activities gradually shift in orientation away from footloose businesses towards the companies that were already located within city boundaries. In addition, more and more local administrations established separate offices or departments exclusively devoted to the promotion of local economic development.

Over the last two decades, local governments in Germany have pursued the task of promoting economic growth amid growing challenges to their economies. The transition from an industrial to a post-industrial socio-economic order has created severe problems for local economies such as the erosion of jobs in manufacturing industries and the relocation of businesses away from traditional centres of economic activity. These recent economic problems required local governments to become much more active in stimulating economic growth than before.

Local government and local economic development in Germany

This involvement of local governments in economic affairs is inseparably tied to the country's long tradition of strong local government. Government in its various historical forms has always been accepted in Germany as an institution of authority with the power to regulate a significant part of individual as well as communal life. This regulative authority extends into the economic sphere as a result of a recognition that, despite the power and potential of free market forces, state intervention is needed to avoid or to ameliorate the socially adverse consequences of these forces. As a result of a generally positive view of state activity, German local governments have been mandated a general responsibility to manage their own affairs and to enhance community well-being. Because of its far-reaching impacts upon large, if not, all segments of a community, local economic development belongs to the range of functions that local governments perform as part of this responsibility.

In this context, it is necessary to emphasize that the tradition of strong local government in Germany has developed in a cultural environment in which cities are perceived both as economic and social entities. From the early phases of the development of urban areas, when economic forces were largely directed at securing the subsistence of families, cities served as communities operating within a particular secular or spiritual order and they were governed by institutions responsible for maintaining this order. Economic considerations in communal life gained significant importance with the industrial revolution which led to changes in a system of settlements that had already existed for several centuries. The impact of the industrial and, more contemporaneously, the post-industrial revolution did not, however, significantly change the prevailing perception of cities as communities whose value for society goes well beyond their economic potential.

The brief review of the history of local efforts to stimulate economic growth illustrated the important role that local governments in Germany have played and continue to play in that process. When examining this role in some detail, it can be observed that the public sector is widely regarded among economic development officials in Germany as performing mixed roles in the response to the economic challenge that local communities are facing, i.e. both supporting and guiding private sector participants and activities.[3] In adopting the former role, local governments provide incentives to private enterprises and create a supportive business climate while, in the latter role, they attempt to ensure that private sector activity is compatible with the city's economic development goals. This perception of the public sector role reflects a belief in the ability of local governments to act in different ways with regard to the extent to which their activities influence private sector investment decisions.

By adopting different roles, German local governments are able to erect barriers that may hinder the full realization of private investment opportunities, on the one hand, and assist businesses in managing and coping with these obstacles, on the other. This capacity and orientation of local governments enable them to pursue their own interests for the benefit of the community as a whole as well as to find ways to ameliorate possible negative consequences of their activities for private enterprise. Notwithstanding the strong role of local governments in economic development, private sector participation is generally perceived to be essential for successful economic development. This may appear to be an obvious or even redundant observation in the context of a market economy where most economic activity is supposed to be undertaken by the private sector. Nonetheless, the recognition of the importance of private sector participation has not led to a proliferation of close institutional arrangements between local governments and the business community. Instead, regular contacts and co-ordination between local governments and the business community take place, in most cases, through the local chambers.

Seen from the perspective of local governments, this kind of private sector participation does not preclude close co-operation between economic development administrations and business organizations on specific projects and programmes. Furthermore, the institutional independence of German local governments in economic development facilitates the formulation and implementation of activities that focus on projects which are not viable without public assistance rather than on projects that offer private investors a financial windfall or other economic returns.

The institutional independence of local governments from the private sector is the result of public choice. Deliberate decisions were made in the past which were intended to put municipal governments in an influential position with regard to the process of urban development. These decisions also created organizations that represented the interests of local business communities. The inability of the marketplace to enhance the public good for all segments of society was acknowledged as well as the need to establish strong institutions whose activities were not aimed at profit maximization but at fostering the well-being of local communities. This recognition of the differing roles and responsibilities of the private and public sectors is reflected in regulations that govern the 'business-like' activities of local governments. Limiting these activities is viewed as necessary to ensure that municipalities fulfil their responsibility for enhancing the well-being of the entire community (Habermehl, 1987).

Local economic development goals and strategies

The promotion of community well-being is a basic goal of local economic development in Germany. Similar to the goal of job creation, community enhancement is widely considered the ultimate objective guiding the economic development efforts of municipal governments. In order to understand fully the significance of the goal of fostering community well-being, it is necessary to point out that this goal is understood in terms that go beyond a predominantly economic definition to include a concern for the social well-being of local communities. Economic development efforts that only aim at providing business assistance would result in a loss of the legitimacy with which local governments pursue their function to promote economic growth. This legitimacy is based upon the constitutionally guaranteed right of local communities to manage their own affairs. The principle of self-determination assumes not only that local governments are better suited than higher levels of government to take responsibility for community development; it also assumes that this responsibility cannot be given to the private sector because of its narrow pursuit of self-interest. Local governments, by contrast, possess the capacity to devise and pursue policies that are directed at enhancing the well-being of all segments of a community.

The significance of the goal of enhancing community well-being for local economic development in Germany is clearly reflected in the views of economic development practitioners in Germany. They attach a very high level of importance to their efforts to contribute to a balanced economic and social development strategy for their communities. Furthermore, there is widespread support for the proposition that the community as a whole should benefit from economic development. This commitment fulfils an important precondition that policies are not to be narrowly focused on merely assisting individual businesses but rather designed with an understanding of the wider distribution of costs and benefits.

The comprehensive understanding of the purpose of local economic development in Germany is evident in the design of economic development efforts. Generally, local governments in Germany base their economic development policies on a number of different strategies and make use of a wide range of policy instruments for their implementation. By pursuing a variety of development strategies, economic development policies can be formulated to address several problems of the local economy simultaneously rather than focus only on a few projects with a limited number of beneficiaries. This strategic orientation of local economic development administrations in Germany means that strategies such as targeting development activities and leveraging private investment play a limited role in municipal efforts to promote economic activity.

German local economic development administrations do not spend a lot of attention to targeting particular geographic areas or industrial and commercial sectors. Instead, due to the existence of a considerable number and variety of development programmes established by state, federal, and European Community governments in addition to local governments' own initiatives, public support is made available for a wide range of projects in various geographical areas. It may be argued that an approach that attempts to address a considerable variety of economic problems simultaneously runs the risk of providing too little assistance to too many recipients and, thus, jeopardizes the effectiveness of individual projects. This is an especially serious concern at times when the financial resources available for the pursuit of economic development are limited. Further studies are needed better to assess the effectiveness of an approach which spreads development efforts and resources over a number of programmes and geographical areas.

Leveraging, or the use of public funds to induce private investment, represents another development strategy that is perceived with considerable scepticism by German economic development officials. Presented in the United States by many as a very successful economic development tool for stimulating business investments, leveraging can also pose problems. A local economic development strategy that relies heavily on leveraging as a policy instrument may easily become fragmented because development efforts are concentrated on a limited number of often unrelated projects. Furthermore, public funds may be spent on projects that might be implemented without government assistance. In these cases, it is the private sector that leverages funds from the public sector rather than the reverse. The lack of support among German economic development officials for leveraging not only concerns its use as an effective economic development tool to solve today's problems but also its future usefulness. However, whether the scepticism towards leveraging is based on experiences with the strategy or whether it is due to reservations about a new strategic approach to economic development policy-making are questions that warrant additional inquiry.

Instead of concentrating public assistance on a few selected projects, German municipalities tend to provide support for a wide range of programmes, which are usually offered to the business community as a whole. Whether the different forms of support are used then depends on the initiative of individual companies or the extent to which economic development administrations seek to find beneficiaries for these various forms of assistance. While local governments have traditionally assumed the former, reactive, position, they have recently begun to adopt a more active approach to economic development. In many German cities, the attention of economic development offices has started to shift to the businesses already located within their boundaries, away from the attraction of 'footloose' capital. In addition, greater value has been placed on new business formation, especially in the area of new technologies. Such new foci have required economic development administrations to seek closer contacts with the business community in order to obtain a better picture of the special needs of individual enterprises.

Taken together, the points described above present a picture of the pursuit of local economic development policy in Germany that offers some distinct features. These features differ in part from what has frequently been associated with a generalized 'model' approach to economic development in market economies. In several ways, however, the German case corresponds with such a generalized approach. To highlight the distinct character of local economic development in Germany this chapter proceeds with a review of the similarities and differences between the pursuit of local economic development in the United States, representing the 'model' approach, and German municipalities.

Similarities and differences between local economic development policy in the USA and Germany

The following list of assumptions and expectations characterizes the pursuit of economic development in American municipalities during the 1970s and 1980s:

– local governments must find ways to stimulate the expansion of private activity because the private sector has the pivotal role in urban economic innovation and development – including job creation;
– the best way to stimulate the expansion of private activity in urban areas is for local governments to form partnerships with their private sectors and to use limited public funds to 'leverage' private investments;
– economic development efforts can and should be 'targeted' to disadvantaged groups and/or distressed communities;
– public resources should be concentrated on projects that would not be viable without public subsidy;
– local governments should concentrate economic development efforts on those sectors likely to be in the forefront of a high-technology, service-oriented, post-industrial future;
– to be effective, local governments must address economic development as a technical rather than a political issue;
– local economic development programs are low-cost options for local governments because they rely substantially on private investment;
– communities can capture the benefits of investment in economic development; and
– everyone in the community will share in the benefits of local economic development, and the costs will not be concentrated in any one segment of the population (Barnekov and Rich, 1989: 215).

The following list of characteristics summarizes German local economic development. The format of the list follows that of the list above to facilitate the comparison of the key features of local economic development in the USA and Germany. Municipal efforts to promote economic

activity in Germany are thus characterized by the following assumptions
and expectations:

> – local governments engage in efforts to stimulate the expansion of private
> activity as a result of their responsibility to enhance the well-being of local
> communities;
> – the best way to stimulate the expansion of private activity in urban areas
> is for local governments to devise economic development strategies and to
> coordinate them with the private sector and its representative organiza-
> tions;
> – economic development efforts offer assistance for a wide variety of
> programs and beneficiaries and are not limited to a selected few recipi-
> ents;
> – public resources should be used for a variety of activities and not be
> concentrated either on projects with a high rate of return on the investment
> or on projects that would not be viable without public subsidy;
> – local governments should provide assistance to growth industries and
> those with a high growth potential as one component of their compre-
> hensive economic development strategy;
> – local economic development is a technical as well as a political issue
> where formulation and successful implementation require the co-
> operation of a limited number of public and private sector participants;
> – local economic development programs may be low-cost options for local
> governments because they rely substantially on private investment;
> – communities can capture the benefits of investment in economic develop-
> ment; and
> – everyone in the community will share in the benefits of local economic
> development, and the costs will not be concentrated in any one segment of
> the population (Benfer, 1993: 215).

These two sets of characteristics illustrate the differences as well as
similarities between local economic development in the United States
and Germany.

Economic development has always been an important concern for
American cities since their fate has traditionally depended to a large
extent on the vitality of their economies and the initiatives of local
business communities. In the light of the fundamental dependence of
local communities on private economic interests, much of the American
local economic development literature suggests that the public sector's
role is best characterized as being subservient to the demands and needs
of the private sector (Warner, 1968; Fainstein *et al.*, 1986; Barnekov *et al.*,
1989). In such a 'privatist' environment, the private sector becomes the
prime agent in the process of urban change and development. This
contrasts with a public sector in Germany that pursues a much stronger
role in urban and local economic development. Of great significance in
this context is the general responsibility of municipal governments to
enhance the well-being of local communities as a whole which mandates

the public sector to play an active part in the development of local communities.

This contradiction reflects the influence of culturally shaped views of state intervention in both countries. In their subservient role, local governments in the United States attempt to remove barriers which could have a negative impact on private investment decisions. By contrast, German municipalities are oriented towards assisting enterprises in managing and coping with obstacles through the use of various measures, such as decrees and prohibitive directives, which are firmly placed within the public domain (Naßmacher, 1987).

In a society such as the United States that has traditionally relied on individual initiative, pursued in an environment of great personal liberty, rather than on government regulation and intervention, it is therefore not surprising that local governments seek close ties with the private sector in the pursuit of economic development. As a consequence, American municipalities often enter into institutionalized forms of co-operation with the business community. While the participation of the private sector in German local economic development is also widely regarded as essential for the success of development activities, the participatory forms are significantly different from those prevalent in the USA. The business community in Germany generally participates in the formulation and implementation of economic development policies through its representative organizations, mostly the local chambers. These organizations are regularly consulted by local governments and, as a result, the activities that both sides pursue independently are thereby co-ordinated.

The differences between the two countries with respect to the role and participation of the private sector in economic development have implications also for the pursuit of development efforts. Viewed as a concentrated and thus effective effort to assist a particular industry or, more often, geographic area, targeting has become a cornerstone of local economic development policies in the USA. Although disadvantaged groups and/or distressed communities have frequently been the targets of economic development programmes in the United States, studies of the results of these programmes suggest that success is rather limited (Barnekov and Rich, 1989). Strict guidelines regarding the employment of 'hard-core' unemployed, for instance, were found to reduce the attractiveness of public programmes for the private sector, and the influence of political forces reduced the amount of economic development assistance that was channelled exclusively to distressed communities.

However, local governments have, to a large extent, concentrated their development efforts on downtown areas that deteriorated as a result of widespread suburbanization and overall economic transformation. In those areas, private sector investments, supported by substantial public funds, have often brought about large-scale redevelopment projects. Furthermore, the pressure on local governments to make their development incentives attractive to the private sector has, as critical analyses suggest, led 'public and private participants ... [to be] biased toward minimizing restrictions on private enterprise' (Barnekov and Rich, 1989: 220). As one result, the expectation that public resources should be concentrated on projects that would be viable only with public subsidy often does not reflect the practice of economic development in the United States.

The influential role of municipal governments in German local economic development, by contrast, prevents an orientation from being too focused on the interests of the business community in the design and implementation of economic development programmes. The targeting of economic development assistance towards a few selected recipients, i.e. geographic areas, industrial sectors, or individual businesses, does not play a significant role as a strategy to stimulate economic activity. In addition, it is generally not assumed in Germany that public funds should be concentrated only on projects which would not survive economically without public assistance. Local economic development administrations prefer to devise policies that are, instead, characterized by a considerable scope of activities each addressing different economic problems and needs.

As one element of such comprehensive strategies, many local governments in Germany have begun to pursue initiatives that are oriented towards high-tech industries and other industrial sectors believed to have a high growth potential in a post-industrial economy. Considered important for the promise they hold towards securing local economies in the future, the pursuit of such strategies does not result in the abandonment of the existing industrial base of a community. The promotion and expansion of the innovative capacity of the local economy have also been, for a considerable period of time, an important item on the development agenda of American municipalities. Although such attempts have, at least in the United States, 'yet to demonstrate any consistent pattern of effectiveness as a general strategy of urban regeneration' (Barnekov and Rich, 1989), efforts to promote high-tech industries represent a common phenomenon in both the USA and Germany. With this strategic focus now being given a higher priority than before, local governments in both countries seek to respond to a rapid transition to a new post-industrial order in which the technological and innovative capacity of industries will be vital to their survival and growth.

Another similarity between local economic development in the United States and Germany concerns the issue of citizen participation. The formulation and implementation of policies to stimulate local economies generally take place without extensive participation of local residents. As suggested above, local economic development in the USA is widely considered as a technical issue where the participation of a wider public would only lead to unnecessary inefficiencies. As a result, economic development projects are often negotiated directly between representatives of the local governments and the private sector within the frequently closed environment of public–private partnerships.

Although the political nature of economic development is generally acknowledged by economic development practitioners in Germany, citizen participation is widely rejected. To better understand this unwillingness in both countries to open the economic development policy-making process to a wider range of participants, it needs to be mentioned, however, that the group of participants in economic development in Germany is bigger than in the United States. Participation involves agencies within local administrations as well as organizations from outside local government. Economic development agencies routinely consult with other administrative branches, most often with the land-use planning units, as well as a few organizations that are not part of municipal government, most importantly the local chambers. This level of participation by outside institutions is apparently considered to be an adequate recognition of the political nature of economic development.

Another similarity in the assumptions and expectations with which local economic development is pursued in the United States and Germany is the view that economic development represents a low-cost option for local governments because it relies substantially on private investment. It is commonly assumed that the costs involved in economic development activities are limited to the immediate programme expenditures through which development assistance is provided. Generally, these programme expenditures are designed as incentives that are expected to stimulate economic activity by influencing private sector investment decisions. The incentive nature of economic development policy instruments is most obvious in the provision of various forms of financial assistance to businesses but ultimately it also applies to indirect policy measures, such as local government investments in physical infrastructure, educational and training programmes.

Although the incentive nature of economic development programmes appears as a systemic feature of public sector efforts in market economies to stimulate economic activity, the view that such programmes are a low-cost option for local governments may often be unrealistic. Critical analyses that concentrate on the United States have shown that local economic development programmes contain hidden or unanticipated costs to local governments (Barnekov and Rich, 1989: 86–9). These costs may reach substantial proportions and thus can make economic development programmes an expensive undertaking for local governments requiring a considerable share of total financial resources. However, these shortcomings are either not seen or not considered significant by economic development practitioners in the United States and Germany.

Similarities between the two countries also exist with regard to the belief that local communities can capture the benefits of economic development and that these benefits, as well as the costs of economic development, will not be concentrated in any one segment of the community. While it is not surprising that those who are involved in economic development have a positive view of the effects of their activities, studies of American local economic development suggest that the costs and benefits of economic development programmes are not distributed equitably (for a case study, see Levine, 1986). Costs of economic development projects often have to be borne by groups in the community that are unable to derive significant benefits from these activities.

Although a positive assessment concerning the distribution of costs and benefits of economic development is shared by practitioners in the United States and Germany, however, there are differences in the assumptions that these officials make regarding the responsibilities of government. Studies of American economic development show that – while individual businesses are the immediate beneficiaries – the wider distribution of benefits is left to a succession of trickle-down effects that are assumed to eventually reach the entire community (Judd, 1988). The views of economic development practitioners in Germany confirm that the constitutional mandate of local governments to enhance the well-being of all citizens plays a significant role in directing the orientation of economic development efforts in Germany. Local communities as a whole are intended to be more direct beneficiaries of activities to stimulate economic growth. As one precondition to attain this objective local governments pursue comprehensive economic development policies that seek to address a variety of problems and offer public assistance to a considerable number of different recipients.

The above comparison of some of the main assumptions and expectations underlying the pursuit of local economic development in the United States and Germany has important implications for the inquiry into this field of public policy. These implications are outlined in the closing section of this chapter.

Implications and directions for future research

From an American perspective, perhaps the most obvious conclusion is that a policy orientation which is based on privatism – despite its dominance in the United States – is not the only approach to economic development available to local governments in market economies. The investigation of local economic development policy in Germany shows that, as a result of specific circumstances brought about by public choice, the public sector in a market economy can assume a stronger role in the stimulation of economic activity than is evident in the United States. Such a role allows local governments to take a relatively independent position *vis-à-vis* the private sector and to commit themselves to the goal of community enhancement in a more direct manner than experiences from local communities in the United States would suggest.

Comparative statements of this sort should be phrased in a cautious way. The similar features of American and German local economic development that are discussed above are a reminder that attempts to characterize local government efforts to promote economic development in different market economies cannot be expected to demonstrate radically different orientations. Certain parameters of a market economic framework, such as the basic distribution of functions between government and private capital, do not change radically across country boundaries.

Although the government's recognition of its responsibility to exert some level of control over the otherwise free play of market forces has led to a more active public sector role in Germany's social market economy, the private sector in both countries remains the main economic actor. The federal governments of both the United States and Germany are given the right to determine and regulate certain macro-economic variables such as money supply and taxation levels. Within that basic framework, it is nevertheless largely left to the market and its private sector participants to determine the prices of goods and services. In order to find a radically different approach to the promotion of economic growth by local governments, one would have to leave the politico-economic system of a market economy and consider the pursuit of local economic development in a planned economy where the role of the public sector and its relationship with the private sector are defined in very different terms.

Nevertheless, alternative orientations do exist for local governments in market economies to carry out their economic development function. This proposition, in turn, leads to the question of what factors actually account for the different orientations. Is it, as suggested with regard to both the United States and Germany, the existence of certain country-specific traditions that impact upon and define the character of the public–private relationship? Or is it a matter of public choice where, as Max Weber already suggested, a particular definition of this relationship is only manifest for a single moment in history due to a particular mix of circumstances and decisions by government institutions (as reviewed in Saunders, n.d.)? Obviously, to conclude that local economic development in Germany differs significantly from the approaches adopted in the

American context provides sufficient reason to investigate this matter further. This inquiry could be expected to yield additional qualitative knowledge about the alternative orientations of local government activities to promote economic development.

As has been illustrated before, the character of local government economic development policy depends to a significant extent on the role of the public and private sectors and the relationship they form in the pursuit of this policy. The analyses of individual cities and their efforts to stimulate economic development suggest that this relationship is not defined in the same way in every community (Fainstein *et al.*, 1986; Beauregard, 1989). The balance between the public and private sectors may be tilted to different degrees to either side, depending more upon the particular power structure of a local community than upon the overall politico-economic system in which these communities operate.

In contrast to much of the functionalist and pluralist literature on urban politics and development, the nature of the balance between the public and private sectors is, because of the influence of local circumstances, not fixed. The analysis of selected municipalities produces, instead, a continuous scale between two end points where, at the one end, the private sector is the dominant force in urban development, dictating in various degrees the goals, strategies, and means used to direct the urban development process, and where at the other end, it is primarily political interests and the political process that determine urban development. The local features that help define the relationship between the public and private sectors in a particular community along the continuous scale include, for instance, the reign of a strong mayor and/or city council firmly committed more to redistributive and allocational policies than to developmental policies (to use Peterson's classification), or, alternatively, the dominating influence of a single, large enterprise over an entire local economy supported by a powerful business-led growth coalition determining the economic development agenda.

On a national level of analysis, these stark contrasts between the orientations of public policies of different local communities tend to diminish. The character of local economic development in several market economies and the balance between the public and private sectors may, thus, be located at some intermittent points along the scale from economic to political determinism. This is not to devalue the benefit of studies that attempt to characterize, on a national level of analysis, the orientations with which local governments pursue economic development. General differences do exist between German and American municipalities with regard to their efforts to promote economic growth. But if the question that is to be studied further is whether, in market economies, local governments have in fact a choice between alternative orientations, a community level of analysis appears to hold considerable promise.

It is in this regard that the discussion about the local state – as it has been newly emerging in the late 1970s and 1980s – provides an interesting and potentially valuable, yet very theoretical, perspective. Whereas earlier definitions and conceptualizations of the local state tended to be rather general (e.g. see Johnston, 1982), more recent efforts have attempted to define specifically the local state concept within the context of urban areas and municipalities (e.g. see Gottdiener, 1987; Gurr and King, 1987). This increased level of place specificness in the conceptual development of the 'local state' has contributed to a move away from a purely functionalist definition. Viewed from such a perspective, the local state merely serves the predominant economic interests. This shift towards a more independent nature of the local state is exemplified by Gottdiener's depiction:

> The theory of the local state ... explains public policy as the complex interplay of social interests manifested through forms of the State. Clearly, the premises of this theory suggest that the outcomes of this process must be determined empirically rather than being predicted by some functionalist argument prejudging the nature of the State/society relation under capitalism. Most important it is precisely because of the very nature of the relative independence of the State framework from economic relations or production ... that the State can appear to play a variety of different roles in society. (Gottdiener, 1987: 216)

Although this view recognizes that local governments can indeed establish themselves as independent participants in the process of urban and economic development, it stops short of providing indications of what the roles of both the public and private sectors might be. The analyses that do exist with regard to this latter issue still tend to be non-spatial in their considerations of the relationship between the two sectors (for an overview of recent material see Gottdiener, 1990).

More locally oriented yet theoretical research seems necessary to generate a more specific understanding of the nature of these inherent features of local economic development policy. This theoretical inquiry should be supplemented by additional empirical investigations of how the roles of the public and private sectors in the pursuit of that policy are perceived by representatives of both sectors. Empirical investigations of this kind should define more precisely these roles, taking into account the different phases in the entire policy-making process from formulation to implementation.

There is another important reason for further empirical investigation. Recently, a number of articles have been published in Germany that suggest the advent of a significant change in the way local economic development is being conducted. In many ways, the proposals put forth in this material emphasize the need for changes that would make the efforts by German cities to stimulate their economies resemble much more closely those of their counterparts in the USA or the UK.

The suggestions proposed include the adoption of a business approach by economic development agencies towards managing their tasks (Meissner, 1987; Demokratische Gemeinde, 1988a), the establishment of more independent local development agencies (Demokratische Gemeinde, 1988b), encouragement of cities to work and act as entrepreneurs (Klages and Lichtblau, 1989) and to seek arrangements with the private sector identical to the American public–private partnership model (Lutze and Heuer, 1988). In addition to this literature, a survey of economic development officials has found a clear willingness to seek more intensively co-operation with the private sector (Benfer, 1993).

The search for and examination of factors that explain the differences in policy orientations between various market economies point to another area where additional research is needed. This investigation has already suggested a few of those factors, such as the general acceptance of a strong government and a perception of cities that stresses more their social than their economic qualities and character. Studies aimed at exploring this direction in greater detail may be designed to yield conclusions of a general nature, such as the following:

> The necessity of planning will thus come to depend as much upon politically determined definitions of situations and a historical tradition of state planning, as upon purely objective elements in either the organization of capital or the character of an economic crisis. In other words, necessity can never be defined wholly by an objective situation divorced from ideological mediation. (Fainstein and Fainstein, 1985: 486)

It is hoped that this chapter has demonstrated the need to expand the existing comparative literature to include countries that are characterized by different 'politically determined situations' and 'historical traditions of state planning'. This book with its broad spatial scope including countries in Western Europe and the Americas, clearly, is a reflection of and a response to that need. It, therefore, represents a valuable addition to the yet very limited literature in this field of comparative policy research and analysis.

Notes

1. The author wishes to express his sincere gratitude to Timothy Barnekov of the University of Delaware's College of Urban Affairs and Public Policy. His patience and support greatly facilitated the research on which this chapter is based.

2. The literature dealing with the pursuit of economic development comprises studies that examine the efforts of individual local communities to stimulate their economies (recent examples are, for example, Fosler and Berger, 1982; Organisation for Economic Co-operation and Development, 1987; Pohl, 1988), studies that report the findings of broader, sometimes national, surveys of local government economic development activities (e.g. Heuer, 1985; Robinson, 1987; Grabow *et al.*, 1990), proceedings of conferences where practitioners and/or academics discussed the challenges to local economies as well as successful strategies to revitalize them (e.g. Davis, 1989), and a limited number of cross-national studies of local economic development activities (e.g. Johnson and Cochrane, 1981; Bennett and Krebs, 1991). As perhaps a sign of the growing maturity of the field, the last few years have seen the arrival of textbooks for economic development students (e.g. Blakely, 1989) as well as 'how-to-do' (or even 'how-to-do-best') manuals for local economic development officials and practitioners (e.g. International City Management Association, 1991).

3. This is one result of a recent representative national survey of German local economic development officials. Questionnaires were sent to the economic development offices of all West German cities with a population greater than 50,000. All subsequent details and references to economic development practitioners' beliefs and attitudes are based on the results of this survey. For a complete description and discussion of the survey findings see Benfer (1993).

References

Barnekov, T., Boyle, R., Rich, D. (1989), *Privatism and Urban Policy in Britain and the United States*. Oxford, Oxford University Press.

Barnekov, T., Rich, D. (1989), 'Privatism and the limits of local economic development policy', *Urban Affairs Quarterly*, 25: 212–38.

Beauregard, R. A. (ed.) (1989), *Economic Restructuring and Political Response*, Urban Affairs Annual Reviews, 34. Newbury Park, California, Sage.

Benfer, W. (1993), 'Local governments and local economic development policy in the Federal Republic of Germany', Ph.D. diss., University of Delaware, 1993.

Bennett, R. J., Krebs, G. (1991), *Local Economic Development: Public-Private Partnership Initiation in Britain and Germany*. London, Belhaven Press.

Blakely, E. J. (1989), *Planning Local Economic Development – Theory and Practice*, Vol. 168. Sage Library of Social Research. Newbury Park, Sage.

Davis, B. (ed.) (1989), *Remaking Cities. Proceedings of the 1988 International Conference in Pittsburgh*. Pittsburgh, Pittsburgh Chapter of the American Institute of Architects.

Demokratische Gemeinde (1988a), 'Klaus von Dohnanyi sorgte für den wirtschaftspolitischen Paukenschlag', *Demokratische Gemeinde*, 12: 17–20.

—— (1988b), 'Professionelles Management gibt es nicht zum Nulltarif', *Demokratische Gemeinde*, 12: 26–30.

Fainstein, N., Fainstein, S.S. (1985), 'Is state planning necessary for capital? – the US case', *International Journal of Urban and Regional Research*, 9: 485–507.

Fainstein, S. S. *et al.* (1986), *Restructuring the City – The Political Economy of Urban Redevelopment*, rev. edn. White Plains, Longman.

Fainstein, S. S. and Fainstein, N. (1989), 'The ambivalent state – economic development policy in the U.S. federal system under the Reagan administration', *Urban Affairs Quarterly*, 25: 41– 62.

Fosler, R. S., Berger, R. A. (eds) (1982), *Public–Private Partnerships in American Cities: Seven Case Studies*. Lexington, Lexington Books.

Gottdiener, M. (1987), *The Decline of Urban Politics – Political Theory and the Crisis of the Local State*. Newbury Park, Sage.

—— (1990), 'Crisis theory and state-financed capital: the new conjuncture in the USA', *International Journal of Urban and Regional Research*, 14: 383–403.

Grabow, B., Heuer H., Kühn, G. (1990), *Lokale Innovations – and Technologiepolitik. Ergebnisse einer bundesweiten Erhebung*. Berlin, Deutsches Institut für Urbanistik.

Gurr, T. R., King, D. S. (1987), *The State and the City*. Chicago, University of Chicago Press.

Habermehl, K. (1987), 'Wirtschaftliche Betätigung der Kommunen und Abwehrmöglichkeiten des privaten Konkurrenten', *Verwaltungsrundschau*, 33: 105–10.

Hanson, R., (ed.) (1983), *Rethinking Urban Policy – Urban Development in an Advanced Economy*. Washington, D.C., National Academy Press.

Heuer, H. (1985), *Instrumente kommunaler Gewerbepolitik – Ergebnisse empirischer Erhebungen*, Schriften des Deutschen Instituts für Urbanistik, Bd. 73. Stuttgart, Mainz, Verlag W. Kohlhammer/Deutscher Gemeindeverlag.

International City Management Association (1991), *Achieving Economic Development Success: Tools That Work*. Washington, D.C., International City Management Association.

Johnson, N., Cochrane, A. (1981), *Economic Policy-making by Local Authorities in Britain and West Germany*. London, George Allen & Unwin.

Johnston, R. J. (1982), *Geography and the State – An Essay in Political Geography*. New York, St. Martin's Press.

Judd, D. R. (1988), *The Politics of American Cities – Private Power and Public Policy*, 3rd edn. Glenview, Scott, Foresman and Company.

Klages, K. D., Lichtblau, K. G. (1989), 'Kommunale Wirtschaftsförderung – eine unternehmerische Aufgabe für Städte and Gemeinden', *Städte- and Gemeindebund*, 4: 115–19.

Levine, M. V. (1986), 'Public–private partnerships and uneven development: Baltimore, 1950–1985', paper presented at 1986 Annual Meeting of the American Political Science Association, Washington, D.C., August.

Logan, J. R., Molotch, H. L. (1987), *Urban Fortunes: The Political Economy of Place*. Berkeley, Los Angeles, University of California Press.

Lutze, A., Heuer, B. (1988), 'Stadtentwicklung als unternehmerische Herausforderung and Aufgabe', *Der Städtetag*, 12: 799–801.

Meissner, H. G. (1987), 'Marketing für die kommunale Wirtschaftsförderung', *Städte- and Gemeinderat*, 7: 196–9.

Mollenkopf, J. H. (1983), *The Contested City*. Princeton, Princeton University Press.

Molotch, H. L. (1976), 'The city as a growth machine', *American Journal of Sociology*, 82: 309–32.

Naßmacher, H. (1987), *Wirtschaftspolitik <<von unten>>: Ansätze and Praxis der kommunalen Gewerbebestandspflege and Wirtschaftsförderung*. Basel, Switzerland, Birkhäuser Verlag.

Organisation for Economic Co-operation and Development (1987), *Revitalising Urban Economies*. Paris, Organisation for Economic Co-operation and Development.

Peterson, P. E. (1981), *City Limits*. Chicago, The University of Chicago Press.

Pohl, M. (1988), *Wirtschaftsförderung in Großstädten – Ein Struktur- and Standortvergleich im Bundesgebiet*. Bremen, Rieck.

Robinson, C. J. (1987), 'Economic development policy approaches of city administrations: types and influential local conditions', Ph.D. diss., University of North Carolina.

Saunders, P. (n.d.), *The Relevance of Weberian Sociology for Urban Political Analysis*, Unpublished manuscript, School of Cultural and Community Studies, University of Sussex, U.K.

Schiefer, B. (1989), *Kommunale Wirtschaftsförderungsgesellschaften – Entwicklung, Praxis and rechtliche Problematik. Studien zum öffentlichen Wirtschaftsrecht*, Band 10. Cologne, Berlin, Carl Heymanns Verlag.

Stone, C. N., Sanders, H. T. (eds) (1987), *The Politics of Urban Development*. Lawrence, University Press of Kansas.

Warner, S. B., Jr. (1968), *The Private City – Philadelphia in Three Periods of Its Growth*. Philadelphia, University of Pennsylvania Press.

Wolman, H., Ledebur, L. (1984), 'Concepts of public–private co-operation', in Farr, C.A. (ed.), *Shaping the Local Economy – Current Perspectives on Economic Development*, Washington, D.C, International City Management Association.

3

Local economic policy in France in the 1980s

Constructing specific territorial advantages as a strategic challenge for local authorities

FRÉDÉRIC COROLLEUR AND
BERNARD PECQUEUR

Introduction

The analysis of public sector economic policy is at the centre of two main debates in the field of public sector economics: the first focuses on the circumstances of intervention, the second on its modalities. Analysis has evolved considerably, driven especially by many studies emphasizing the importance of the institutional context in explaining the variable performance of economies, at both national and regional levels. Studies of successful regions in Germany (especially Baden-Württemberg), the USA (parts of New England), Italy (North-eastern regions), Switzerland (the Swiss Jura Arc), and France (Arve Valley, Oyonnax, etc.), or of successful regions based on traditional activities (textiles, shoes, mechanical engineering, etc.) or advanced activities (micro-mechanics, micro-technics, electronics, etc.) have underlined the role played by non-traded relationships and institutional factors: trust, social consensus, local partnerships to support firms, agencies and traditions which foster innovation, training and diffusion of ideas, etc. (Sabel *et al.*, 1989; Grabher, 1993). They have also encouraged new thinking about the role of local public institutions in the dynamics of these regions (International conference, 'Industrial Districts and Local Economic Regeneration', Geneva, 18–19 October 1990).

Thinking about the role of institutions in economic growth can no longer be done independently of changes in modes of production and consumption. The work of the regulation school has underlined the links between principles of production and public sector intervention, as well as how these links evolve over time (André and Delorme, 1983). In assessing public sector economic policy over the recent period, the analyst must therefore take into account the questioning of Fordist principles of production (Taylorist division of labour, standardized products, etc.) and the increasing tendency towards economic integration. Indeed, the interdependence between economic actors is evident at increasingly higher spatial scales, due to the globalization of exchange in goods, services, and financial flows, as well as the globalization of company strategies.

As far as public sector economic policy is concerned, the main consequences of these developments have been to question institutional red tape, criticize the ineffectiveness of national demand stabilization policies, and raise the issue of regulation policies at different scales; either wider than the national (the European Union, the 'Triad', the Pacific rim, etc.) or more restricted (region, localized production systems, etc.).

> As regards either short-term economic policies or mechanisms which may have separated income from actual work, perverse effects start as soon as the benefits of such policies or mechanisms expand while their costs remain localised. (Colletis and Pecqueur, 1993: 497)

The role of local authorities in economic development becomes a particularly important issue. In France, whether and how the local public sector can respond to the challenge of globalization is one of the issues at stake in the debate on government decentralization. This issue forms the context for the present chapter. The first aim is to describe the role of local authorities in the regional dynamics of France during the 1980s. The second aim is to discuss the strategic challenges, generated by current economic changes, which are faced by local authorities. Before this, however, we set out the main difficulties and challenges facing local public sector economic policy in general. Next, we briefly review the development of economic policy by French local authorities during the 1980s,[1] focusing on the appropriateness of these policies to the nature of contemporary change in production systems.

Institutions and local economic development

The nature, frequency and intensity of relationships between actors are influenced not only by shared tacit knowledge but also by stable structures, which include local authorities and their agencies (Société d'Economie Mixte (SEM), Maison de l'Economie, etc.). If institutions in general, and public institutions in particular, can play a role in economic change, it is also true that there remain significant difficulties and that a stabilization change dialectic must continually be confronted.

Institutions and local economic development: the difficulties of collective action

The intervention of local authorities and the development of local economic policies raise several problems of co-ordination. Indeed, local authorities must take into account not only the inter-relationships between their policies but also the various strategies of local firms (small and medium-size enterprises (SMEs) or large firms, private or public firms) as well as the strategies of professional organizations (chambers of commerce, local trade organizations, etc.).

Besides the scarcity of the financial resources, at least two types of difficulties can therefore be identified: (i) those related to the complexity of the institutional framework; (ii) those related to the nature of industrial organization. Some difficulties result, then, from lack of co-ordination between the economic policies of the various public institutions and from lack of correspondence between administrative boundaries (despite their longevity) and actual production systems. Local authorities face problems due to the division of powers among them, duplication of effort, and unnecessarily complex decision-making processes. For instance, the Cholet region in the west of France is recognized to be economically coherent in terms of a shared industrial specialization (shoes, garments) and shared modalities of production organization (high density of SMEs both competing and co-operating). Yet public sector economic policy is fragmented into four departments and two regions (Courlet and Pecqueur, 1989), and does not therefore correspond with the coherent economic region. Inter-governmental co-operation, which might be developed across these borders, is hindered by a 'regional patriotism'.

Local authority economic policy is also made difficult by the multiplicity of types of firms within their jurisdictions and by the varying degrees of attachment of these firms to the region. SMEs are clearly more concerned with their native region than large firms or network-like firms. Their resources are highly localized and their capacity to obtain resources elsewhere is limited. The absence of common interests between a firm and the local authority can be explained in terms of the nature and hierarchical structure of the linkages firms have with others located outside the region. As far as these difficulties are concerned, the analysis of local economic dynamics can be approached in terms of the inter-play between three groups of actors: firms, local authorities, and intermediary institutions (Soulage, 1994). The last category includes all the organizations enabling firms to interact with one another or with public institutions. It is then possible to identify various modes of economic development according to different types of interaction among the three groups of actors:

● The firm is the driving force behind economic change, supported by both local authorities and intermediary institutions. This is the case in the Arve Valley (Haute-Savoie), Oyonnax (Ain) and Thiers (Puy de Dôme).

- However, one of the groups may be inactive. For example, the spectacle industry in Morez and clock manufacture in Haut-Doubs seem to be handicapped by a lack of political linkage and support. In Roanne, by contrast, the other actors are willing but firms are not.
- One or more groups may be opposed. For example, local public institutions in the Lavelanet and Mazamet basins have pursued policies diverging from those of firms, because the political institutions have been governed by social groups opposed to the entrepreneurial system.

Soulage admits that the distinction between firms, intermediary institutions and public institutions is clearly a rough one. It is reductionist since it places different actors within a single category (the category of firms is far from homogeneous, and includes various types: SMEs, large integrated firms, network-like firms, networks of firms, etc.) and it is incomplete in so far as some important actors are missing (the national state, the educational system, etc.). However, Soulage's categories already suggest inequalities among local actors in terms of mobilization of resources for local economic development. Theoretically speaking, even if collaboration were in the common interest of local actors, a problem similar to the prisoner's dilemma arises. Starting from the point that all collective action has a cost, Olson shows that each actor tries to ensure that the costs of co-ordination fall on the others (problem of the free rider), so that the collective good (i.e. the joint action) is generally not achieved (Olson, 1966). Axelrod's work clarifies the logic of collective action by introducing time into the analysis. He shows that repeated interaction enables people to recognize the superiority of co-operative solutions over non-co-operative ones. Investigations in urban economics have drawn on the studies of these authors to explain variations in the success of urban development in the United States (Gittel, 1992).

Beyond the problem of resource mobilization, there is the problem of resource creation. The analytical frameworks developed by Gaffard (1990) and Colletis and Pecqueur (1993) clearly express the need to consider the creation of resources. This is Sabel's perspective when he argues that trust among actors gradually increases as they become aware that there are benefits in social exchange and that mistrust is not inevitable (Sabel, 1990). Trust can therefore be 'created' on the basis of various institutional catalysts: not only ethnic, political or religious belonging, but also more or less formalized collective agreements. This is an important point because reduction of uncertainty is necessary if the division of labour is to be deepened, the specialization of productive organizations and individual actors is to be increased, and growth is to result. On the contrary:

> In a situation of uncertainty, the tendency to specialise does not exist. If
> one does not know if there is the possibility of sanctioning free-riders, and
> cannot be relatively sure about how other members of the group will
> behave, one will not assume the risk of investing in sunk activity which
> could limit one's strategic options. (Bianchi and Miller, 1993: 9)

Thus the role of local authorities may be to facilitate the resolution of
conflicts between the actors involved in local economic development.
The success of industrial districts in the long run emphasizes the importance of such institutional mechanisms (Zeitlin, 1990). More generally,
the role of local authorities is to stimulate the exchange of information
and meetings between the actors so as to facilitate co-ordination and a
deeper division of labour.

Institutions and local economic development: Fordism in question and challenges of globalization

If, by reducing uncertainty, institutions provide the stability required for
the reproduction of society, their impact is ambivalent when it comes to
change. A certain level of institutional stability is necessary for an
innovation to progress along its technological trajectory. However,
stability may become a drawback and slow down the introduction of a
radical innovation that threatens existing behaviours and investment
decisions. No institutional system is able to respond continually to
change: institutions stimulating innovation during one period may block
it during another. We must be all the more careful since the current
period in one of profound change.

The Fordist mode of production is no longer hegemonic. If the current
period remains open as far as alternatives are concerned, it is clear that
firms are now experimenting with more flexible types of production'
organization, to be able to deal with demand which is more volatile and
differentiated. The efficiency of a productive organization, whether large
or small, is less based on the productivity of its individual components
than on the density and nature of the non-routinized interactions
between the different stages of the production process, whether within a
network of SMEs or among the functional divisions of large firms.

The elaboration of a principle of common interest therefore emerges
as an important competitive advantage. Variations in demand, the rapid
development of technology, the need for skilled labour, all these require
a network of stable long-term relations between employers and employees, suppliers and distributors (Campbell *et al.*, 1991). Enterprises no
longer seek only generic quantitative advantages (low labour costs,
abundant and accessible raw materials, etc.) but also, as Porter suggests,
a large local market, a network of high-technology SMEs, a highly skilled

work force, etc. (Porter, 1990). Such advantages are not based on an initial stock of factors of production but on a process of resource creation. The challenge, then, is to create a mode of co-ordination which permits the learning process and the exploration of new productive solutions (Gaffard, 1990).

These changes in principles of production have an impact on economic geography. To address the globalization of competition, firms in effect globalize their strategy by seeking to profit from multiple territorial differentiations. They reorganize their operations, often towards increased integration – for instance, global management of purchasing – and rethink their organization, usually evolving towards decentralization and network forms with subsidiaries or suppliers that are quasi-integrated but legally independent (Veltz, 1994). To Porter's analysis of globalization – which suggests that global firms are engaged in a global competition (territorial differentiation does not influence their strat-egies) can be compared a rival, probably more common, strategy: glocalization (Van Tulder and Ruigrok, 1992). This strategy aims to gain control over the development of a worldwide market and to establish a local subcontracting network and co-operation based on a geographical concentration of competencies.

Here globalization is synonymous with territorial differentiation. The policies of local authorities must not only support co-ordination between the actors involved in local economic development but also make avail-able information on the techno-economic environment (technological and economic scanning) as well as facilitate relations with external actors in order to stimulate innovation. Adaptation to change is most likely to occur only in such an open situation (Bianchi and Miller, 1993). But are the strategies of local authorities evolving in the same direction as changes in models of production? If so, are they evolving sufficiently?

The construction of territorial specificities: a strategic challenge for local authorities

As emphasized by Morel and Zimmerman (1993), the issue of local economic development is rather novel for local public sector actors, and the methods and thinking behind their economic policies have evolved considerably. In France, local public sector actors first became aware of this issue in the mid-1970s when signs of economic crisis became more acute (large-scale closure of factories, growth of unemployment, etc.) along with its regional repercussions (cities and whole regions in crisis), and when at the same time regional institutions were created with the aim of promoting economic and social development. However, the economic policies of local authorities really began to expand with the implementa-tion of the 1982–3 decentralization laws (see also Lajugie *et al.*, 1985).

Douence (1988) and Gerbaux and Muller (1992) show how local economic policy evolved from emergency action focused on the firm itself towards policy more sensitive to the business environment. This development is manifested in the creation of Sociétés d'Economie Mixte (SEMs), the increasing number of industrial parks and technopoles (Certaines, 1988), and the emphasis placed on training and technology. It not only reflects the will of local authorities to go beyond the strict framework of rules governing direct aid, but also and more fundamentally a questioning of the theories and policies underlying that type of intervention.

The evolution of local economic policy in France during the 1980s

Economic policy provided a way for local authorities to react against the economic crisis. It was made easier by the decentralization laws and became widespread during the 1980s. Aid awarded by local authorities to industrial, commercial and craft firms tripled in the period from 1984 to 1990, from FFr2.4 to 6.7 billions (excluding loan guarantees). The main increase occurred between 1984 and 1987. Aid tended to be indirect rather than direct, and within this, focused on particular types of indirect aid (an increase in subsidies, in industrial property, in policy involving SEMs, etc).

Behind this threefold increase in the total sum of economic aid, the greatest increase during the period 1984–90 concerned indirect aid. The growth in aid was concentrated in the first part of the period, with a notably lower pace of growth in the years 1987–90 (17 per cent). If direct aid remained dominant, there was nonetheless a rebalancing of direct and indirect aid. While direct aid to industrial, commercial and craft firms represented two thirds of all aid in 1984, it amounted to a little more than half the total in 1990.

Table 3.1 Evolution of the relative share of direct and indirect aid in total aid (excluding loan guarantees and security bonds) (%)

	1984	1985	1986	1987	1988	1989	1990
Total direct aid	66	63	38	57	56	53	55
Total indirect aid	34	37	62	43	44	47	45
Total excluding loan guarantees and security bonds	100	100	100	100	100	100	100

Source: Ministère de l'Economie des Finances[2]

This trend towards a balance between direct and indirect aid was accompanied by variations in the growth of the various types of aid within each category. Subsidies were the form of direct aid most often used by local authorities (42 per cent in 1990), particularly by regional governments (60 per cent in 1990). Their use increased during the 1980s, unlike allowances (regional employment allowances, regional tax credits for new firms) which significantly declined, especially during the second half of the period. Loans and advances (under more generous conditions than in the market) were the second major type of direct aid (one-fifth of direct aid). Their share was lower in 1990 than in 1984. This relative decrease occurred during the years 1984–6, when the share of loans and advances declined from 38 to 19 per cent of total direct aid and then stabilized between a fourth and a fifth of the total.

As departments and municipalities only granted direct aid to complement aid allocated by regional governments, the gradual withdrawal of direct aid by regional governments led to the withdrawal of the additional aid granted by the other authorities. This happened particularly with the system of allowances. With respect to indirect aid, only a small share is due to guarantee funds and equity participation. However, while the former, mainly operated by the regions, tended to decrease, the latter tended to increase, focusing above all on participation in SEMs.

Most indirect aid is categorized as 'diverse indirect aid' (9/10). This consists of sales of buildings with phased payments, redevelopment of industrial and crafts areas, studies and management consultancy, construction or other work in buildings used for industry, etc. Phased payments and the redevelopment of industrial areas are the most important of these. In both these domains, the main investment is made by municipalities, while regional governments are more concerned with studies and management consultancy.

Table 3.2 Evolution of the share of total aid (excluding loan guarantees and security bonds) going to industrial property

	1984	1985	1986	1987	1988	1989	1990
Building and land purchases (%)	86	90	90	72	80	86	79
Discounts on the sale or rent of land and buildings (%)	14	10	10	28	20	14	21
Total (FFr thousands)	344,159	329,183	537,001	607,616	579,494	943,140	966,493
Share of the total (%)	14	11	10	15	13	18	17

Source: Ministère de l'Economie et des Finances

The share of industrial property in total aid is far from negligible. 'Building and land purchases' and 'discounts on the sale or rent of land and buildings' together amounted to 17 per cent of all aid (excluding loan guarantees) granted in 1990 (FFr966 billions). Together with aid for redevelopment of industrial areas, they account for one third of all aid (about FFr2 billions in 1990). Moreover, the 1980s were marked by a fascination with the phenomenon of the technopole: in 1988 Certaines counted 12 existing technopoles as well as 24 being developed or planned (Certaines, 1988). This fascination can be explained by the expectations they (and more broadly, new technology) generated of a way out of crisis.

Loan guarantees and security bonds are particular types of aid. They are not expenditures in their own right, but mark a financial commitment if the firms receiving them default. This new power, contained within the 1982 Act, gave rise to serious financial difficulties for a few municipalities, which acted as guarantor without sufficient forethought. However, on the whole it was used with caution. The total sum guaranteed increased over the period; from FFr2.4 billions in 1984 to FFr5.8 billions in 1990. But relative to total aid excluding loan guarantees and security bonds it decreased, from 34 per cent in 1984 to only 16 per cent in 1990. While, initially, local authorities granted aid to firms other than SEMs, they later channelled more of their funds through them.

Table 3.3 Evolution of loan guarantees and security bonds granted to SEMs and to firms other than SEMs relative to total aid excluding loan guarantees and security bonds (%)

	1984	1985	1986	1987	1988	1989	1990
Loan guarantees and security bonds granted to							
SEMs	38	25	40	31	65	55	44
firms other than SEMs	62	75	40	69	35	45	56
Total	100	100	100	100	100	100	100
Total aid excluding loan guarantees and security bonds	34	31	24	33	19	11	16

Source: Ministère de l'Economie et des Finances

The orientation towards SEMs was reflected in their increasing powers and domains of activity and by the increased involvement of local authorities in their management:

- in 1993, there were 1,264 SEMs in France, twice as many as in 1983, with capital of FFr63 billions and 50,000 employees (40 per cent higher than in 1983).
- SEMs were initially intended to undertake construction and urban redevelopment activities, but the 7 July 1983 Act expanded their powers to encompass the management of public services. This expansion met the wishes of local authorities. Sixty per cent of SEMs created since 1983 have been management SEMs.

- Finally, local authorities provide a growing share of SEM capital. In 1993 65.3 per cent of SEM capital was held by local authorities. The growth can be explained by the lifting of the legal minimum share in SEM capital that could be held by local authorities. It also reflected a strategy to bypass controls over aid given by local authorities.

The tendency towards a balance between direct and indirect aid can be understood in terms of the reaction of local authorities to a tightly controlled regime of direct aid which was itself allied to a centralized view of economic policy. Indeed, the precision of legal documents, combined with the fact that direct intervention by municipalities and departments depended on the policy of regional governments, limited the freedom of action of local public actors. The regime for indirect aid, however, was much more flexible. It was neither subject to a complementarity principle nor restricted in terms of creation of a minimum number of jobs.

Local authorities therefore developed mechanisms for indirect aid, with its less constraining procedures; indirect aid gradually replaced direct aid or complemented it in pursuit of greater efficiency (Douence, 1988). The development of the SEMs can also be explained by the desire of local authorities to acquire more flexible forms of intervention in place of a strict monitoring regime. These developments reflect not only the desire of local authorities to go beyond the strict framework of rules applied to direct aid, but also and more fundamentally a questioning of policies and ideas behind economic intervention. The ways in which economic policies are conceived and co-ordinated are as important as the resources associated with them (Gerbaux and Muller, 1992). From the same point of view, Greffe suggests that local authorities should not substitute for the private sphere in producing and providing the goods and services that firms require to grow (though their role may be more pronounced where the training of skilled workers is concerned). Their role should consist more of connecting the local partners who have interests in undertaking a project for their own diverse reasons, so that they can act together on it (Greffe, 1988). Similarly, local authority policies appear to be evolving towards the technology dimension. Thus regions like Provence-Alpes-Côte d'Azur, Rhône-Alpes and even Brittany devote 3 to 5 per cent of their overall budgets to research, and the number and activities of the Centres Régionaux sur l'Innovation et le Transfert de Technologie and local economic study units are increasing. Such measures are justified by the need for SMEs to gain access to new technologies, and more generally to receive information about markets. Local authorities have thus clearly focused their efforts on reinforcing their attractiveness, through both the economic policies briefly presented above, and policies to increase the flow of information with themes such as 'regional metropolis', 'international city', 'region at the crossroads of Europe', etc. (see Chapter 4).

These developments raise two main issues. First, the division of powers between municipalities, departments and regional governments is no longer clear. This has led to a growing rivalry between the different hierarchical levels (Gerbaux and Muller, 1992), as illustrated in recent debates on regional planning, with municipalities and departments seeking to underline their prerogatives relative to the regions.[3] Second, attempts made by the authorities to create an environment generally favourable to business and to create a strong international image have paradoxically led to a relative decline in the differentiation between regions (Ganne, 1992). Thus, each municipality has wanted its own technopole, its own technology park, etc., even though in most cases these go no further than the provision of space for production activities or access to communication, not reaching the stage of reviving the region. This homogenization favours the mobility of firms. Indeed, territories become standardized and consequently face the phenomenon of relocation.

In a context of lively competition between local authorities to attract and retain business, the traditional policy of 'accompanying' company strategies no longer suffices. Local authorities would do better to proceed to a third step: to develop territorial specificities.

The creation of territorial specificities as a challenge for French local authorities

We start from an analytical framework developed previously (Colletis and Pecqueur, 1993) from which we draw lessons for local authority economic policy. We utilize a twofold distinction: between resources and assets on the one hand, and between generic and specific qualities on the other hand. The interest of local authorities lies precisely in creating territorial specificities. This strategy is based on economic policy directed towards the business environment but which is designed in terms not of resource transfer but of resource creation. This appears to be the most appropriate strategy for local economic development.

The potential for local economic development can be assessed based on the twofold distinction between resources and assets on the one hand, and generic and specific qualities on the other hand:

- Resources represent a potential for a territory in the sense that they are not yet being used. A further distinction is made between existing resources as yet unexploited for cost reasons and 'virtual' resources, which remain to be discovered or organized (which do not exist as such). Assets are the factors of production which are being used, created on the market.

- Resources or assets are 'generic' when they are available independently of the production process or of social dynamics (e.g. hydroelectric energy, days of sunshine, unskilled labour). They appear as exogenous variables. In contrast, resources or assets are 'specific' as soon as they clearly result from strategies of actors and are devoted to a specific use (e.g. skilled and specialized labour, engineering colleges, technical centres, research laboratories that specialize in a specific sector or competence). A specific resource is the outcome of the dynamic combination of actors' strategies which has been virtual up to that point; it results from the creative relationship among actors tackling a hitherto unknown problem (a group of researchers combining their competencies to solve a new problem).

Table 3.4 The bases of territorial competition

	Resources	Assets
Generic	Non-market	Non-market
	Exogenous 1	Endogenous 4
Specific	Market	Market
	Exogenous 2	Endogenous 3

Source: Adapted from Colletis and Pecqueur (1993)

For firms, the four polar situations in Table 3.4 represent a range of strategic choices which do not necessarily coincide with the strategies of the local authorities where they are located. The firm whose strategy is to utilize generic assets positions itself in the market in terms of cost-based competition. It thus seeks locations offering the lowest production costs. It has no interest in becoming involved in the region where it is located; it can relocate quickly, at low cost.[4] The qualities and organization of the region are of little importance. Other firms seek to develop the region so as to create specific assets, on the basis of which specific resources can be created. To this end, they establish a local network by developing co-operation (traded or non-traded) with other actors (firms, financial institutions, research centres, training centres, etc.). They seek to benefit from relational quasi-rents within a circumscribed territory.[5]

As for local public institutions, it is always in their interest to seek specific territorial assets. In a context of keen spatial competition, the existence of specific assets allows the region to be differentiated and identified. Moreover, these assets restrain the 'volatility' of firms (their propensity to relocate to the lowest cost site). Indeed, a specific asset loses part of its productive value if put to an alternative use. It is therefore costly for a firm to relocate if it cannot find the same assets elsewhere,

immediately and at the same price. This constraint increases over time as
the firm improves the quality of its local relationships (trust makes co-
ordination easier and reduces costs).

Similarly, it is in the interest of local public institutions to play their
role in the specification of resources. Resources can appear in the form of
a reservoir of knowledge which can be mobilized by firms to solve new
problems. For example, the city of Grenoble is considered by outsiders to
contain such a reservoir of knowledge which can easily be activated by
firms: its links between universities, laboratories and firms are widely
acknowledged.

By offering specificities, regions can in part avoid being set in competition with one another in the market. Indeed, only territories able to
supply generic resources at competitive costs (low labour cost, abundant
and cheap raw materials, etc.) are likely to benefit from relocations. For
regions in industrialized countries, development strategy requires withdrawal from the market context and the offer (creation) of specific
advantages that firms cannot find (or only at high cost) elsewhere.

Conclusion

It is therefore in the interest of local authorities to define global projects
for economic development. A project is global in so far as it includes all
the actors capable of producing specificity. Such a project requires a
process of mobilization which articulates economic objectives, social
balance and cultural heritage.

The area of Colombey les Belles in the department of Moselle provides a good example of a development project driven by a territorial
coalition (see *Le Monde*, supplement '*Heures locales*', 6–7 February
1994). Public and public–private organizations are able to play an important role in bringing regions to life and providing dynamism. The Maison
de la Productique in Roanne fulfils a twofold function of technological
transfer and training, thus contributing to reviving local economic
growth. In Oyonnax, the municipality is developing an urban policy
centred on accommodating new strata of technicians and executives
required for economic renewal. It is also active in vocational training by
seeking to turn the technical school into an important centre for training
technicians, or again by launching the initial stages of training for plastics
industry engineers. In the Arve valley, a Centre de Promotion à l'Innovation et à l'Economie is also a development tool for meeting the needs of
local firms. Its aim is to contribute to change in the valley's economic
system by directly or indirectly providing a whole range of services for
firms (see *Usine Nouvelle*, 2458, May 1994).

These projects are different from the standard model of policy, which
does not promote any specific asset and is content with acquiring facilities

and with implementing financial or regulatory measures conceived else-where. To carry out a global development project requires a capability to manage the long term and to manage institutional dynamics (Cuaresma and Pecqueur, 1994). The key is to operate a territorialized institutional system. This can renew local public policy and the way it is conceived. The coming together of institutional interests in a region (firms, citizens, banks, etc.) occurs through a complex game of co-ordination increasingly centred on interface organizations such as the SEMs, technical centres, or even economic development associations.

Further investigation is necessary. We need to know more about the mechanisms of collective action (role of group size, homogeneity, etc.), to observe how it evolves over time (is the coalition progressive or back-ward looking?) and to examine whether it is equitable and fair.[6] There is no necessary linkage between institutions and economic growth. The mere existence of institutions does not induce growth and adaptability:

> The link between institutional thickness and the economic success needs to focus also on questions such as the breadth of interests covered by that which amounts to local collective representation, the degree of co-ordination between institutions, and the capacity of embedded institutions to adapt to changes in economic opportunity. (Amin and Thrift, 1993: 419–20)

The same conclusion is drawn by Grabher when he speaks of the paradox of embeddedness (Grabher, 1993). Only by increasingly ques-tioning collective action will progress be made in resolving this paradox.

Notes

1. We refer here to developments described by many analysts, especially Douence (1988), Greffe (1988), Gerbaux and Muller (1992) or Morel and Zimmerman (1993), and we agree with their main arguments. However, the economic aid considered is only aid granted to industrial, commercial and craft firms. Moreover, while Gerbaux and Muller developed the idea of 'local government' and placed particular emphasis on the financial aspect of decentralization, we specifically focus on the production aspect. We therefore share Morel and Zimmerman's point of view, when they focus on the underlying aspects of policy (rationality, image, self-realizing prophecy, etc.). Our concern is further downstream; our focus is on an analytical framework for observed economic policy and whether the latter is appropriate to the principles of production. Other perspectives can be found in Affichard (1994): (organization theories, game theory, economics of conventions, sociology of organizations, political philosophy, public law).
2. The figures refer only to aid given to industrial, commercial or craft firms.
3. The rivalry between 'departmentalism' and 'regionalism' is not new: see Lajugie *et al.*, 1985.

4. This type of strategy was recently pursued by the firm Hoover, which closed a plant located in Dijon to relocate it in Cambuslang in Scotland. When the relocation choice was made, the firm's wage costs were 37 per cent higher in Dijon. The site in Scotland provided various advantages: lower wage costs and a devalued UK pound.

5. The recent work sharing agreement signed in Grenoble at the Hewlett-Packard component production centre illustrates the firm's strategic choice between utilizing generic assets and constituting specific assets. This firm suffered from competition from low-wage countries in the field of components production. The logic of generic asset utilization would dictate relocation of plants to South-East Asia. However, the other aspect of its activities requires design work and here there are benefits to being located in a dense scientific environment. In this case, two opposing strategies face the same firm. The solution to this dilemma is to play specific assets card while simultaneously seeking to move closer to market conditions as far as components production is concerned (a 40 per cent increase in productivity is permitted by a reorganization of working hours, night and weekend work, compensated by reduced working hours rather than by bonuses).

6. Reference can be made to the special issues of *World Development* (1989) and *Journal of Theoretical Politics* (1994) which deal with the role of institutions in economic development and with issues of size and homogeneity of firms. An unorthodox institutionalist analysis of these same questions can be found in Bianchi and Miller (1993).

References

Affichard, J. (ed.) (1994), *Décentralisation et coordination: les principaux modèles d'analyse*, Proceedings of the conference organized for the Ministry of Equipment, Transports and Tourism, and for the Ministry of Environnement. Paris, Institut International de Paris-La Défense.

Amin, A., Thrift, N. (1993), 'Globalization, institutional thickness and local prospects', *Revue d'Economie Régionale et Urbaine*, 3: 405–27.

André, A., Delorme, R. (1983), *L'Etat et l'Economie*. Paris, Seuil.

Bianchi, P., Miller, L. (1993), 'Collective action, strategic behavior and endogeneous growth', paper to the EAPE conference 'The Economy of the Future: Ecology, Technology, Institutions', Barcelona, 28–30 October.

Campbell, J.L., Hollingsworth, J.R., Lindberg, L.N. (1991), *Governance of the American Economy*. Cambridge, Cambridge University Press.

Certaines, de J. (1988), *La fièvre des technopoles*. Paris, Syros.

Colletis, G., Pecqueur, B. (1993), 'Intégration des espaces et quasi intégration des firmes: vers de nouvelles rencontres productives?', *Revue d'Economie Régionale et Urbaine*, 3, 489–508.

Courlet, C., Pecqueur, B. (1989), 'Un modèle de développement diffus en mutation: l'exemple du Choletais', *Notes et Documents*. Grenoble, IREPD.

Courlet, C., Pecqueur, B., Sanson, G. (1992), 'Diagnostic d'actions et développement local: le cas de la vallée de l'Arve', Final report for the Centre de Rencontres et d'Initiatives pour le Développement Local. Grenoble, IREPD.

Courlet, C., Soulage, B. (eds) (1994), *Industrie, territoires et politiques publiques*. Paris, L'Harmattan.

Cuaresma, M., Pecqueur, B. (1994), 'Le projet global de développement local', *La Lettre du cadre territorial*, dossier d'expert.

Douence, J.C. (1988), *L'action économique locale, décentralisation ou recentralisation?* Paris, Economica.

Gaffard, J.L. (1990), *Economie industrielle et de l'innovation*. Paris, Dalloz.

Ganne, B. (1992), 'Place et évolution des systèmes industriels locaux en France: économie politique d'une transformation', in Benko, G., Lipietz, A. (eds), *Les régions qui gagnent*. Paris, Presses Universitaires de France.

Gerbaux, F., Muller, P. (1992), 'Les interventions économiques des collectivités locales', *Pouvoirs Locaux*, 6, October 1990, reproduced in *Problèmes Economiques*, 2275: 7–13.

Gittel, R.J. (1992), *Renewing Cities*. Princeton, Princeton University Press.

Grabher, G. (ed.) (1993), *The Embedded Firm: On the Socio-Economics of Industrial Networks*. London, Routledge.

Greffe, X. (1988), *Décentraliser pour l'emploi, les initiatives locales de développement*. Paris, Economica.

Journal of Theoretical Politics (1994), special issue on collective action, 6(4).

Lajugie, J., Delfaud, P., Lacour, C. (1985), *Espace régional et aménagement du territoire*, 2nd edn. Paris, Dalloz.

Morel, B., Zimmerman, J.B. (1993), 'Les institutions économiques et le développement économique au plan local', Aix-Marseille, working paper G.R.E.Q.E.

Olson, M. (1966), *The Logic of Collective Action*. Cambridge, MA, Harvard University Press.

Porter, M. (1990), *The Competitive Advantage of Nations*. London, Macmillan.

Sabel, C.F. (1990), 'Studied trust: building new forms of co-operation in a volatile economy', paper to the ILO conference 'Industrial Districts and Local Economic Regeneration', Geneva, 18–19 October.

Sabel, C.F., Herrigel, G.B., Deeg, R., Kazis, A. (1989), 'Regional prosperities compared: Massachusetts and Baden-Württemberg in the 1980s', *Economy and Society*, 18: 374–404.

Soulage, B. (1994), 'La place du politique dans les systèmes productifs localisés', in Courlet, C., Soulage, B. (eds), *Industrie, territoires et politiques publiques*. Paris, L'Harmattan.

Tulder van, R., Ruigrok, W. (1992), 'Globalisation or glocalisation: rival internationalisation strategies. The world car industry as an example', paper to the Conference 'European Firms and Industries Coping with Globalisation', Saint-Malo, CERETIM, 25–26 April.

Veltz, P. (1994), 'Dynamique des systèmes productifs localisés, territoires et villes', paper to the conference 'Cities, Enterprises and Society at the Eve of the XXIst Century', Lille, 16–18 March.

World Development (1989), special issue: 'The role of institutions in economic development', 17: 9.

Zeitlin, J. (1990), 'Industrial districts and local economic regeneration: models, institutions and policies', paper to the ILO conference 'Industrial Districts and Local Economic Regeneration', Geneva, 18–19 October.

Part II

Planning the redevelopment of industrial cities

4

Planning the revitalization of an old industrial city: urban policy innovations in metropolitan Bilbao (Spain)[1]

ARANTXA RODRIGUEZ

Introduction

Over the last two decades, metropolitan areas have been at the centre of widespread economic, social and political reorganization. For some cities, especially those in old industrial regions, the crisis of Fordism and the transition towards a so-called new regime of flexible accumulation (Harvey, 1989a) have brought about systematic divestment in manufacturing activities, plant closures, environmental degradation, massive unemployment and rising poverty and marginality. The dynamic of productive reorganization, however, has not been the only factor shaping the fortunes of cities and regions; the specific character of national, regional and local state responses to the imperatives of structural change has also played a critical part. Indeed, urban revitalization became an important policy arena, during the 1980s, despite the imperious ascendancy of macroeconomic regulation and structural adjustment policies and an almost universal withdrawal of national state institutions from a commitment to spatially oriented policies. In this context, regional and local governments were encouraged to take a more proactive stance and face the challenge of reversing economic decline under conditions of scarce resources, rising demands and, frequently, inadequate or ineffective planning instruments (Granados and Seguí, 1988). This shift posed radically new challenges to local planners and authorities forcing a profound reappraisal and reformulation of spatial planning theories, objectives, strategies and policy tools (Albrechts, 1992).

Against this background, this chapter aims to explain recent trends in urban policy-making in metropolitan Bilbao, one of the main industrial centres of Spain and also one of the most severely affected by economic recession and manufacturing decline. The chapter shows how critical policy innovations in urban planning developed over the last decade in

Bilbao run parallel to dominant approaches in planning in other advanced industrial countries.

Urban planning and revitalization strategies in the 1980s: the search for growth

Almost without exception in the advanced industrial economies, the 1980s were a period of significant change and reformulation in urban planning theory and practice; new policy objectives, strategies, instruments and institutions developed during a decade of steady challenge and fragmentation that has accomplished nothing short of the remaking of urban planning (Brindley *et al.*, 1989). Since the mid-1970s, the crisis of planning brewed as conventional land-use plans and regulations came increasingly under question. Several factors can account for this development. First, as with other forms of spatial policy, the downfall of urban planning owed much to the failure of planning practice to achieve its own self-proclaimed objectives and, especially, to fulfil the high expectations it generated (Ravetz, 1980). Second, rapidly changing economic conditions throughout the 1970s soon rendered the existing regulatory planning system, designed to guide and control growth processes, entirely inadequate to meet the challenges posed by economic recession, industrial restructuring and urban decline. Third, extensive reorganization of state policies, the ascendancy of market liberalism and the ferocious attack launched against all forms of state intervention, contributed significantly to the crisis of planning. Statutory and regulatory interference with the market were charged with the responsibility of bad economic performance of cities and regions, while the ideology of entrepreneurship and *laissez-faire* capitalism accompanied the withdrawal of the state from a commitment to social and spatial redistribution.

As the crisis unfolded, the presumption that planning could master market forces was shattered and with it, largely, the idea that it should. Instead, planning turned unabashedly towards the private sector to lead the regeneration of cities. But, since stagnating urban land markets and low return expectations made unassisted private sector involvement unlikely, planners and local authorities were persuaded to adopt a more dynamic and entrepreneurial approach identifying market opportunities and actively assisting private investors to take advantage of them (Harvey, 1989b; Leitner, 1990). Shifting away from regulatory means and procedures, urban policy gradually assumed more direct forms of support from private capital including the use of leverage funding, direct subsidies, public–private partnerships and the removal of regulatory constraints to make private investments more attractive. The strong redistributive focus and social welfare considerations that had played an important part in much urban policy-making since the mid-1970s were slowly replaced by an increasing concern with the promotion of economic growth and urban competitiveness (Rodriguez and Virizuela, 1987).

Despite mounting criticism, partial dismembering and considerable scepticism, planning remained an important contender in the urban arena (Hall, 1988), but not without substantial reorganization that led to the emergence of new modes of intervention, planning goals, tools and institutions; the abatement of controls, the transfer of planning powers to the private sector and the strengthening of market-led approaches, were dominant features of the emerging planning framework (Brindley *et al.*, 1989). Indeed, the crisis of planning led to critical innovations in urban policy and the creation of a wide array of policy instruments to promote urban growth and revitalization; these included enterprise zones and freeports, local economic development agencies, place marketing, public–private partnerships, urban development corporations, urban regeneration and city grants and other urban funding programmes (Hall, 1988; Ashworth and Voogd, 1990; Gaffikin and Warf, 1993; Atkinson and Moon, 1994). Except for local economic initiatives, these schemes were, generally, devised and financed by central governments and granted the private sector a leading role in urban regeneration using direct public investments and fiscal and financial incentives to stimulate private investment; they revealed the shift in planning priorities and the rise of a more assertive and entrepreneurial style of urban governance (Harvey, 1989b; Albrechts, 1992). Urban funding programmes designed to stimulate private investment in stagnant land markets, property redevelopment and urban regeneration, found their supreme expression in large-scale urban renewal operations, doubtless the most celebrated urban planning procedure of the 1980s. Emblematic, large-scale renewal first became a synonym for effective urban restructuring in the United States after the 'success' stories of the Boston waterfront and Baltimore's Inner Harbor regeneration. Other cities – Pittsburgh, London, Glasgow, Rotterdam, Genoa, Lille, etc. – soon moved to follow their example, rediscovering their own opportunity sites in derelict inner-port and inner-city industrial areas left behind by manufacturing decline, productive decentralization and restructuring.

Large urban renewal operations attempted a profound physical and economic transformation of cities through the reconversion of vast derelict sites into carefully designed mixed-use areas, integrating office space, housing, retail centres, cultural and recreation services and tourist-oriented infrastructures. These schemes were, commonly, tied to radical image reconstruction and city marketing strategies supported by a combination of flagship projects, postmodern architectures, theme parks, art festivals, fairs and other hallmark international events that supplied the initial development impetus and played a propagandist role to attract further investment. Thus, despite an enduring physical and design bias, the adoption of self-promotional marketing techniques as well as the extensive size of the schemes and purposeful combination of land uses, set these projects apart from traditional physical planning and urban renewal operations of the 1950s and 1960s (Ashworth and Voogd, 1990).

Generally portrayed as examples of market-led regeneration, in fact, the massive funds required by these emblematic operations almost always implied the need for strong public support and enormous leverage funding to stimulate the private sector property and land market. Leveraging[2] the private sector involved highly targeted public sector investment in the initial stages, clearing and preparing sites, building basic infrastructure and removing extra-economic barriers, to improve the prospects for private capital gains. Like public–private partnerships and local growth coalitions, two other key innovations of the 1980s, leveraging entailed close collaboration between the public and private sector to enable (re)development at specific locations. These so-called co-operative forms of intervention signalled the ascendancy of a post-Keynesian mode of urban governance where private sector leadership in regeneration is maintained not only through substantial public subsidies but also through the adoption of more entrepreneurial methods on the part of government institutions.

Through the 1980s, urban mega-developments boomed, replacing statutory planning as the primary means of intervention in cities. Against the crisis of the comprehensive plan, the large emblematic project emerged as a viable alternative (Campos, 1985; Mangada, 1991), combining the advantages of flexibility and targeted actions with a tremendous signifying capacity. Essentially fragmented, this form of intervention goes hand in hand with an eclectic 'postmodern' planning style where attention to design, detail, morphology and aesthetics is paramount (Terán, 1985; Harvey, 1989b). The emblematic project captures a segment of the city and turns it into the symbol of the new restructured and revitalized metropolis cast with a powerful image of innovation, creativity and success. Waterfront developments are an archetype of this approach; carefully conceived and designed, they stand out as the ultimate postmodern achievement: the city reconstructed as a stage where a simulacra of difference and heterogeneity mimics the complexity of urban reality. In the words of Hall, 'like theatre it resembles real life, but it is not urban life as it ever actually was: the model is the Main Street, America exhibit which greets entering visitors at the California Disneyland, sanitized for your protection (as the phrase goes) wholesome, undangerous, and seven-eighths real size' (1988: 351).

For cities undergoing severe crisis and restructuring, remaking their urban image through hallmark operations and events is part and parcel of a place marketing strategy designed to enhance their capacity to compete for the attraction of internationally mobile capital and for the acquisition of key command functions and high-level producer services. However, heightening inter-urban competition impinges strongly upon the revitalization potential of this strategy as 'serial reproduction' of cultural centres, international fairs and exhibitions, waterfront developments, etc., erodes the original search for place differentiation and uniqueness rendering competitive advantage an ephemeral achievement (Harvey, 1989b). Now, while economic growth is, doubtless, the primary motive behind large-scale emblematic developments, the production of a more attractive post-industrial urban image also plays a critical part in social representation. These glittering fragments of the city, sites of high-level corporate and finance offices, upper-income housing, luxury consumption and gentrified lifestyles, come to stand for, to represent, the revitalized city as a whole. In doing so, they provide the basis for a new, carefully designed model of collective identification that mirrors the lifestyles and aims of powerful groups, especially, of emerging urban élites; the city becomes, thus, a metaphor for their success. Social and spatial differentiation and exclusion are disguised under a new ready-made image of the bettered city: neat, orderly, innovative and expanding. However, by excluding less successful or less marketable social groups from the new projected identity, it jeopardizes their support and brings in the potential for significant contestation (Goodwin, 1993).

In recent years, the pitfalls of this mode of intervention have become increasingly evident. The proliferation of emblematic mega-developments and place marketing schemes is making it increasingly difficult for latecomer cities to portray themselves as singularly attractive production and consumption centres, keeping up both with earlier innovators as well as succeeding imitators. The downturn of the economy in the late 1980s has also revealed the dangers of speculative investment in urban regeneration epitomized by the disastrous bankruptcy of the Canary Wharf developers in the London Docklands (Merrifield, 1993), and the existence of massive office space surpluses in many urban areas making private investors less prone to engage in these types of developments.

Yet, more than anything else, this strategy has been challenged on the basis of its highly polarizing effects on the urban fabric. Indeed, there is growing evidence that property-led regeneration may have contributed to increasing, rather than decreasing, social and spatial inequalities. A narrow concern with physical factors of regeneration and the central and downtown bias of most of these projects account for this pattern. The concentration of public investments in these locations involves a redistribution of resources away from other less conspicuous uses and areas while the benefits of renewal are far from being evenly distributed among neighbourhoods and social groups. As a result, often, downtown regeneration stands in appalling contrast to an enduring reality of widespread poverty, unemployment and environmental degradation in its surrounding area. The risks of two-speed metropolitanization (Busquets, 1993) with recovering core areas and declining metropolitan peripheries are readily apparent in many so-called successful examples. Thus, Holcomb (1993), for example, notes how Pittsburgh, rated in 1985 'the most liveable city in the United States' by the *Rand MacNally Places Rated Almanac* held, at the same time, the second highest record in unemployment levels for its black population, while in Cleveland 40 per cent of its population still live below the poverty line, despite major downtown redevelopment; in Baltimore, large sections of the city remain under severe economic stress and urban decline is far from reversed despite the attraction of nine million visitors a year to the renewed Inner Harbor (Hula, 1990); likewise, in the London Docklands, multiplier effects and trickle-down benefits from massive redevelopment to the local population are generally recognized to have been minimal (Fainstein, 1991).

However, the highly localized and uneven effects of urban renewal operations are not simply the result of a geographical or political bias; they are also, in a very fundamental sense, the result of a fragmented view of revitalization narrowly focused on flashy physical infrastructure investments and place marketing to activate markets and attract internationally mobile capital to these new sites of production and consumption; a view that portrays cities as growth 'machines' and marketable commodities and where planning has become simply a means 'to oil the machinery' and remove barriers to growth (Hall, 1988). The extent to which this fragmented approach impinges upon the prospects for a more socially and geographically balanced recovery of the whole urban region can be shown by looking at metropolitan Bilbao. In Bilbao, the recent adoption of large-scale emblematic mega-projects as the core of a strategy for urban restructuring and revitalization takes place in the context of substantial debate and innovation in the regulatory framework and practice of urban policy, thus, providing an excellent synthesis of prevailing trends.

Remaking urban and territorial planning in metropolitan Bilbao

Economic and urban restructuring

With close to one million inhabitants, metropolitan Bilbao is one of the main urban industrial centres of Spain and the largest in the Basque country. A traditional port city, this area has been, and still remains, an industrial heartland, highly specialized in heavy manufacturing, notably, steel and shipbuilding, metal products and basic chemicals. Over the last two decades, severe manufacturing decline, a shrinking economic base, falling employment levels, demographic decrease and loss of centrality functions have made it an archetype of a declining industrial area. A rough measure of its poor economic performance is provided by the evolution of employment. Between 1975 and 1991, metropolitan Bilbao lost more than a third (37 per cent) of its total industrial employment, mostly in traditional industries such as shipbuilding, steel manufacturing, chemicals and electric equipment. A net increase (33 per cent) in the tertiary sector, during the same period, helped to balance industrial losses, increasing the share of this sector from 42.0 per cent to 58.2 per cent of total employment; in contrast, the proportion of manufacturing fell from 45.8 per cent to 31.5 per cent. Nonetheless, despite the growth of service activities, total employment in 1991 – even after a short recovery phase between 1986 and 1991 – remained below 1975 levels and unemployment rates, in that year, stayed above 20 per cent for the metropolitan area as a whole. Recent indicators for the region show that this trend has worsened in the early 1990s.

But, changes in total and sector employment, and particularly job losses, have not taken place in a homogeneous manner within the metropolitan area. Economic restructuring has affected different localities of the urban region in different ways and levels of intensity. Barakaldo, for example, the second largest municipality within the area and one of the main industrial locations, is a case in point. During the 1980s, this locality lost 75 per cent of its industrial employment; significantly, more than half of this loss occurred between 1985 and 1993, a period of relative economic recovery in the region and in Spain as a whole. Moreover, in contrast to the aggregate performance for the metropolitan area, tertiary employment fell by 12 per cent. As a result, between 1981 and 1993 Barakaldo lost 56 per cent of its total employment (see Rodriguez *et al.*, 1994). Accounting for intra-metropolitan differences is critical because of the risks of polarization and exclusion mentioned above.

Against this background, institutional responses have often been too little and too late and sectoral approaches have dominated over territorial ones. At the level of the central state, solutions have taken the form of macroeconomic regulation, positive structural adjustment and sector-oriented reconversion policies; regional or other spatially sensitive policies have been very sparse and no national urban policy has been implemented despite the fact that these non-territorial policies have had extremely uneven geographical effects. The Basque government and provincial level institutions have given maximum priority to sector over territorial-based policies. Notably, the lack of an adequate territorial planning framework together with a complex institutional structure, rarely co-ordinated, have caused tremendous dispersal, competition, duplicity and waste in the use of regional resources. Finally, local institutions in metropolitan Bilbao have been extremely reluctant to broaden their field of intervention beyond traditional land use regulations, service provision and compensatory policies and to incorporate socio-economic planning criteria in the drafting of new urban plans. The sudden proliferation of projects, plans, schemes and directives aimed at the revitalization of metropolitan Bilbao, in the 1990s, appears in striking contrast to the passivity of the previous decade. Such overproduction is often presented as evidence of the strong dynamism and concentration of efforts towards the goal of economic revitalization and the eventual placement of Bilbao on the European map of competitive cities. While the abundance of initiatives may, indeed, express a widespread commitment to urban renewal and recovery as well as recognition of the need for new policy tools and instruments, the unrelenting flow of new plans and projects may equally express a lack of sense of direction, unco-ordinated institutional action and lack of decision-making capacity. A discussion of some of the most significant planning instruments related to urban revitalization, the General Urban Plan of Bilbao and the Metropolitan Directive, Ría 2000, and the Strategic Plan for the Revitalization of Metropolitan Bilbao, reveals to what extent this is the case in Bilbao.

Urban planning revisited: from statutory planning to territorial directives

Urban planning in Spain is the competence of municipalities who have exclusive jurisdiction over the production of urban plans, subject to very broad guidelines set by the central government. These normative documents have been, and remain even now, the main policy instrument for urban areas. The fact that, after several failed attempts over the last two decades, to draft a new urban plan, the municipality of Bilbao remained, formally, under the guidance of a metropolitan level plan of 1964, is an indicator of the dismal state of urban planning during this period. The new Plan, approved by the city council in March 1994, was not commissioned by the city council of Bilbao until 1986.

Extremely ambitious, the new General Urban Plan of Bilbao (GUPB) sets out to achieve two basic objectives: to raise the population's income level and to improve the quality of the urban habitat. The first grants the Plan a key role in socio-economic recovery by supplying new sites for the location of expanding economic activities; improving metropolitan and regional accessibility; creating infrastructures and services necessary for the development of new centrality functions; and providing Bilbao with a capital city image through the construction of emblematic spaces (PGOU, 1992). The second macro objective, improving the quality of the urban environment, addresses the physical reconversion of derelict and degraded sites within the city making them available for those purposes. Thus, the Plan identifies a series of 'opportunity areas' left out, or marginally occupied, by activities in recession which can be effectively transformed in accordance with these two objectives. These areas include: two abandoned mining sites, occupying more than ninety hectares, to be reclaimed for housing development; a badly degraded inner-city industrial area to be transformed for mixed residential and tertiary uses; an old freight railway line and station to be reconverted for passenger traffic and residential uses; and thirty hectares of central waterfront land, freed by the recent shutdown of a shipyard and the transfer of inner-port facilities to a newly built outer-port area, to be transformed into a new emblematic downtown area.

Notwithstanding its claims to social and economic regeneration, the GPUB abides resolutely by a long-standing land use planning tradition that treats the city more like the physical support and passive container of various functions and activities, than the dynamic social, economic and political construction it is. A genuine product of the 1980s, the Plan exhibits all the traits of dominant planning practice: the overriding presence of large emblematic projects with a strong marketing and symbolic dimension, intense regard for aesthetics and design, priority of form over function and content, marked downtown bias, massive public support to property-led redevelopment, scarce attention to equity and social justice considerations, no socio-economic content, etc. Indeed, while the GPUB maintains formally the structure of a comprehensive blueprint plan, in practice, it may be more adequately described as an attempt to provide a more or less coherent framework for a number of fragmented and pre-existing proposals that, often, have been conceived and approved without any local participation and with little regard for the planning process.[3]

The production of the GPUB has coincided with a period of intense controversy in Spain over the limits of blueprint and municipal statutory planning (Campos, 1985; Vazquez, 1993) that have led to the elaboration of new regulatory and policy instruments aimed at articulating sectoral, urban and territorial planning (Vegara, 1993). The Basque Autonomous Community has been among the first regional authorities to make use of its regulatory powers to take up the challenge to devise a new integrated territorial planning framework to co-ordinate municipal planning and to guide sectoral policies (Jauregui, 1993). The approval, in May 1990, of the 4/1990 Act for 'Territorial Planning of the Basque Country' provided the legal basis for this framework through the development of three new territorial planning instruments: (a) the *Directrices de Ordenación Territorial* (DOT); (b) the *Planes Territoriales Sectoriales* (PTS); (c) the *Planes Territoriales Parciales* (PTP). The general directives (DOT), approved in the early part of 1994 after a long and complicated negotiation process among the various institutions and political parties, define the broad guidelines for the formulation of all territorial plans, programmes or actions carried out by sub-regional administrations and are charged with ensuring adequate integration of both new and existing territorial planning instruments. The sectoral plans (PTS) and the sub-area plans (PTP) are more specific tools; the PTS are sectoral plans of 'territorial relevance' prepared by different departments of the Basque government and aimed at securing design, in the first case, to achieve a high degree of co-ordination between sectoral and territorial planning; the PTP are functional area plans that designate specific planning guidelines for a series of predetermined functional areas, such as metropolitan Bilbao.

Although, strictly speaking the metropolitan planning directive for Bilbao is still under preparation, its key elements were already included in a preparatory study commissioned jointly by the Department of Urbanism of the Basque government and the Diputación de Bizkaia at the end of 1987 and submitted in 1989. According to this study, the future of Bilbao and the regeneration of its productive structure are considered to be dependent upon the spatial reconversion of the 'urban chassis', a condition that transforms physical renewal into a mediated economic objective (Leira and Quero, 1992). Like Bilbao's General Urban Plan, the report identifies various opportunity sites liberated by plant closures, industrial rationalization and functional reorganization, at the metropolitan level, as the sites of a series of integrated urban operations; the precise content of these operations is to be developed by the PTP.

The metropolitan directive can, therefore, be considered a sort of metropolitan level urban plan that designates particular land uses from a unified perspective, beyond the fragmented initiatives of municipal statutory plans. While a more rigorous evaluation is contingent upon final approval, it is possible to identify critical continuities with traditional functional planning that, in our opinion, undermine its considerable potential and prevent it from becoming a truly effective territorial planning tool. These include the exclusive attention to land use specifications, transport systems and physical infrastructures; the lack of any direct socio-economic dimension; the unresolved administrative hierarchy between sectoral and spatially sensitive policies; its isolation both from municipal plans and other metropolitan revitalization proposals; and the lack of formal implementation mechanisms.

Ría 2000: an urban development corporation

The emerging consensus on the need to concentrate efforts and carry out co-ordinated action towards revitalization in Bilbao received considerable impetus in December 1992, when the central government and the

Basque administrations reached a formal agreement to create Ría 2000, an urban development corporation to promote the regeneration of metropolitan Bilbao. The initiative came originally from the General Directorate of Cities within the Ministry of Public Works, Transport and the Environment (MOPTMA), which, after the monumental urban operations of Seville and Barcelona, was eager to reproduce the same integrated approach in other urban centres. Moreover, the fact that the central state, through various public firms like the national railroad company (RENFE), the national institute of industry (INI) and the Port Authority, held property claims over a large proportion of the potential redevelopment sites, conferred upon it an unlikely leading role.

Formally created as a private firm, Ría 2000 operates in practice as a quasi-public agency, a planning and executive body whose objective is to manage the development of a series of urban renewal operations within the metropolitan area of Bilbao. Although these operations are determined through standard planning procedures, Ría 2000 retains considerable planning powers regarding priorities for intervention, disposal of land and other property and the management of public funds for redevelopment. In the aftermath of the post-1992 hangover, the mandate of Ría 2000 is to achieve maximum efficiency in the use of resources and maximum financial self-sufficiency so as to minimize the need for public investment. Nonetheless, since the high-risk, low-profitability character of the early phases of urban renewal, precludes private sector involvement, Ría 2000 is required to undertake land reclamation and basic infrastructure construction in the hope of obtaining equivalent returns from future sales of land titles to private developers. Indeed, Ría 2000 resembles quite closely a private firm except for the fact that it is public resources (land and money) that take the risk of speculative redevelopment in order to propitiate further private valorization.

During the two years that it has been in operation, Ría 2000 has assessed the proposals for different locations within the metropolitan area, established a priority schedule and initiated three interconnected operations in the municipality of Bilbao. The first, Abandoibarra, is a classic waterfront scheme of close to thirty hectares in the centre of Bilbao; conceived as a new downtown, the project involves the creation of a mixed land use area for advanced services, high income housing, commercial areas and cultural and entertainment infrastructures, in the heart of the city, next to one of the most privileged neighbourhoods of Bilbao. This scheme is the jewel in the crown of the city's urban regeneration, an archetype of the new post-industrial, innovative, competitive and postmodern Bilbao; its symbolic importance is underlined by the presence of flagship projects such as the Guggenheim Museum and a global proposal drafted by the American architect Cesar Pelli. The second initiative, Amézola, involves the reconversion of an underused railway station from current industrial and freight transport uses to urban transport liberating close to ten hectares for residential use and green areas. The third intervention involves the transfer of the left bank metropolitan railroad line that now divides Abandoibarra to the Amé-zola freight line. The total cost of these operations has been estimated at 25.000 million pesetas to be financed by the different public institutions integrated in Ría 2000 and by contributions from the European Com-munity's Structural Funds. However, the benefits obtained from land sales in Abandoibarra and Amézola are expected to cover most of the costs, ensuring a high degree of 'self-financing'.

Although urban development corporations have been widely used during the 1980s, in Spain, they have only recently been adopted. Ría 2000 is one of the first cases, but its significance lies not so much in this dubious pioneer role as in its considerable potential as a co-ordinating and executive agency; its capacity to act as a unified body in urban redevelopment schemes in metropolitan Bilbao has vastly improved the prospects of implementation. However, its status as a private firm poses critical questions regarding the 'privatization' of planning, lack of polit-ical accountability, its limited applicability to sites of high commercial potential and its overwhelming concern with economic feasibility as a guiding principle for intervention. Moreover, its exclusive attention to the physical components of urban renewal make it liable to many of the criticisms addressed to the planning instruments presented above; the question remains whether this form of property-led regeneration can provide a sufficient basis for sustained growth and how it is procured.

Despite a very strong rhetoric of urban growth and revitalization, the three policy instruments discussed so far, the General Urban Plan, the Metropolitan Directive and Ría 2000, abide fully by a tradition of physical, land-use planning that regards socio-economic growth as an indirect outcome. In contrast, a fourth initiative, the Strategic Plan for the Revitalization of Metropolitan Bilbao, is specifically an exercise in socio-economic planning.

The strategic plan for revitalization of metropolitan Bilbao

The rediscovery of territorial strategic planning and its application to large-scale urban renewal has been one of the basic innovations in urban policy during the 1980s. Following the example of widely publicized successes like Pittsburgh, Baltimore or Glasgow, Bilbao too has adopted strategic planning to guide its process of revitalization. This decision was the result of a series of debates initiated, in 1989, by the Basque govern-ment on the prospects for economic revitalization in the metropolitan area. Representatives from various economic sectors and institutions such as the Chamber of Commerce, the provincial government, the Port

Authority, large banking institutions, consultancy firms, economic experts, planners, etc., were brought together, for the first time, to analyse urban decline and growth perspectives in Bilbao region. The outcome of these debates was the commission of a strategic plan for the revitalization of metropolitan Bilbao from Arthur Andersen Consulting.

The production of the strategic plan comprised four phases. The first involved in-depth analysis of the dynamics of the urban economy to determine its strengths and weaknesses, its opportunities and threats.[4] This phase was driven by the search for consensus and commitment from various so-called decisive actors (presumably those with the capacity to carry out the strategies) on a course of action. The Plan identified eight critical subjects or policy areas: investment in human resources, development of advanced tertiary functions, environmental regeneration, urban regeneration, improved intra-metropolitan mobility and external accessibility, development of cultural centrality, co-ordinated public–private management, and social welfare. The second phase undertook detailed examination of the internal and external conditions for each of these sectors and their potential for metropolitan revitalization. The third phase defined specific goals and targets and means and strategies in relation to the eight critical sectors. Finally, after these goals, targets and strategies had been endorsed by all the participants, the last phase involved the production of a series of action plans to be undertaken by the relevant actors.

Having taken so long to come to terms with the reality of urban economic decline, in June 1992 Bilbao could boast of having one of the first strategic plans drafted in Spain. Against the limits of statutory urban planning and the widespread tendency for fragmented emblematic operations, the comprehensive perspective of strategic planning came as a breath of fresh air. Moreover, the attention given to socio-economic factors and processes and its emphasis upon integrative approaches made it appear a superior planning procedure. Likewise, its metropolitan focus was equally welcome after a decade of localism and self-contained municipal planning that made little attempt at co-ordination and neglected the metropolitan dimension. The metropolitan region was established as the adequate functional and planning unit and therefore as the relevant space for the definition of an economic development strategy.

However, despite these fundamental contributions, the Strategic Plan has not succeeded in establishing itself as the uncontested instrument for urban revitalization; without any statutory powers and limited executive capacities it stands as a reminder of everything that should be achieved but without any actual strategy on how to secure it and, after two years since its approval, its implementation still remains uncertain.

It may be something of a paradox to say that some of the basic flaws of the Strategic Plan stem from its commitment to overall 'comprehensiveness'. Too eager not to exclude any substantive project, the Plan has ended up adopting a large number of initiatives frequently without sufficient critical assessment of their need, their compatibility with other proposals, or their feasibility. Moreover, the Plan lacks the legal means to neutralize decisions that conflict with its own proposals and often stands as a passive spectator of resolutions that directly affect the metropolitan area. A clear example is provided by the location of the Guggenheim Museum in Abandoibarra. Despite the fact that the development of cultural centrality and services is one of the specified critical fields of intervention, the Plan played no part whatsoever in the decision to locate the Museum in Bilbao. Other decisions like the expansion of the port and airport facilities, the construction of the high-speed train system or even Bilbao's waterfront redevelopment, lay beyond the influence of the Strategic Plan and decisions have been made without any regard for its position.

A second factor contributing to the limited impact of the Strategic Plan has been the lack of effective mechanisms to ensure that the production of the Plan is integrated with the process of implementation. Unlike corporate strategic plans, territorial strategic planning does not command a hierarchical administrative structure to manage its implementation; on the contrary, once the Plan is drafted, implementation remains a complicated process since it still needs to be determined who does what, when and how. A clear order of priorities has to be set and agreed upon by all members, and an assessment of resources and commitment from the various actors involved is required in order to secure implementation. Indeed, a major deficit of the Strategic Plan for Bilbao is, precisely, that although a great deal of discussion has taken place to reach a consensus on a large number of initiatives, no financial plan has been elaborated, there is not an estimate of the resources necessary to carry them out, and no negotiation has taken place regarding who will invest, how much, and when. The lack of specificity of the projects and the lack of a hierarchy of priorities are no doubt related to this indefinition. Then, one could ask, what is the achievement in bringing more than one hundred organizations to agree that it is necessary to revitalize metropolitan Bilbao and, to that end, carry out the no less than 347 'strategies' contained in the Plan, if no practical commitments regarding actors, resources and schedules from those organizations have been obtained?

Finally, the absence of statutory capacities has favoured the relative isolation of Metrópoli 30[5] from other planning initiatives and institutions. The Strategic Plan remains organically and functionally dissociated from other planning schemes within the metropolitan area, the municipal urban plans, Ría 2000 and the Metropolitan Directive discussed above.

Even if, after all, many of the projects contained in these other instruments are the same, the role of the Strategic Plan is undoubtedly in question. The same can be said for co-ordination with other economic planning agencies such as the SPRI, the regional development agency. Given the importance assigned by the Plan to inter-institutional and public–private co-ordination, this separation remains a puzzle. Thus, despite its strategic component and its ambitious proposals, the Strategic Plan runs the risk of becoming another example of an undeveloped blueprint plan; the lack of statutory powers, the absence of an outright institutional sponsor, the limited command of resources and the want of effective implementation mechanisms, may prove too strong obstacles.

Concluding remarks

During the 1980s processes of economic and urban restructuring have been accompanied by a profound reappraisal of urban planning and the development of new policy instruments, institutions and strategies aimed at urban revitalization. Throughout the advanced industrial societies, the search for economic growth and urban competitiveness has favoured the emergence of an entrepreneurial style of urban governance that assigns the private sector a leading role in urban regeneration while using massive public support to create more favourable conditions for private investment; local growth coalitions, public–private partnerships and quasi-private planning institutions are an integral part of this trend. Urban regeneration has been equated to economic regeneration and property-led regeneration through flagship mega-developments and city marketing strategies. This chapter has attempted to show how these general trends are expressed in recent urban policy-making in metropolitan Bilbao.

The new planning instruments developed over the last decade in Bilbao are the outcome of substantial efforts on the part of the local, regional and central governments to overcome the functional and territorial shortcomings of statutory urban planning and to establish a more effective policy framework for urban intervention. However, these policy innovations are strongly influenced by prevailing trends in spatial planning. Indeed, Bilbao constitutes a primary example of property-led regeneration where physical reconversion of key sites is determined by the need to provide a built environment adapted to the changing requirements of capital restructuring. The presence of emblematic projects serves to advertise the commitment of the city to provide a new, attractive, innovative and entrepreneurial environment for business and, thus, help to attract footloose capital. Yet, while the promotion of economic and urban growth is the ultimate aim of the different initiatives, growth remains, for the most part, an unqualified statement. Economic recovery is treated as an almost automatic outcome of physical renewal and critical decisions about land use designation, large infrastructure developments, the construction of massive office and commercial space, or the creation of emblematic spaces are made on the basis of a very partial view of economic restructuring and growth processes. Yet, while speculative investment may, doubtless, succeed in boosting local growth rates in the short term it is hardly a sufficient basis for medium- to long-term recovery. Similarly, social welfare and redistributive results are expected to follow from 'trickle-down' effects without any necessary mechanisms to ensure them, thus disregarding the latent social and spatial exclusion effects of property-led regeneration. Spatially, the risks of two-speed metropolitanization are not taken into account, despite the downtown and central area bias of these initiatives and the tendency for private sector-led regeneration to concentrate exclusively on the most profitable locations.

More specifically, the fragmented character of these policy instruments and their relative isolation from one another are a critical factor in undermining their regenerative potential. The sharp divide between territorial planning initiatives, on the one hand, and socio-economic planning, on the other, is hardly resolved by these new tools. Territorial initiatives (the GPUB, the Metropolitan Directive and Ría 2000) assimilate urban revitalization to urban renewal and focus exclusively on the reorganization of the built environment. Notwithstanding a strong economic revitalization rhetoric, these proposals remain strictly concerned with land development and infrastructure provision. On the other hand, socio-economic planning (the strategic plan) takes a broader approach that subsumes physical renewal as one more area of intervention along with labour market, social welfare, etc., but lacks the specific intervention mechanisms of urban plans and the statutory power to secure the implementation of priority projects. Therefore, the impressive list of initiatives and projects contained in the different policy instruments does not amount to a coherent metropolitan revitalization strategy but, on the contrary, exposes the highly fragmented and unco-ordinated nature of urban planning in metropolitan Bilbao.

Lack of co-ordination between the different initiatives is only one way in which urban policy fragmentation is expressed. Too often outright competition between different institutional levels can also be an important constraint on the viability of any metropolitan revitalization strategy allowing for contradictory policy outcomes and redundancy in the use of scarce public resources. Except for Ría 2000, metropolitan level co-ordination of the various state levels is uncertain. Moreover, the absence of any organic links of these revitalization proposals to economic development policies of the regional government and the unchallenged administrative hierarchy between sector and territorially based policies are of utmost importance.

On the other hand, while much has been said about the need for private–public partnerships and co-operation, the role of citizens' parti-cipation, both in the planning as well as in the implementation process, has been largely ignored. In fact, critical decisions regarding redevelop-ment of particular sites or the setting up of large infrastructures have, frequently, been made outside the planning process. Apart from the GPUB, the lack of participative mechanisms to voice citizens' concerns is notorious in all instruments. This point is of special significance in the case of large emblematic projects (such as the Guggenheim Museum) that tend to be discussed and approved in isolation, without explicit reference to a global strategy for revitalization.

In sum, the shortcomings of property-led revitalization combined with a very fragmented and unco-ordinated policy framework impinge severely upon the prospects for socio-economic recovery in metropolitan Bilbao. A more socially and economically grounded approach for the entire urban region, better integration of the different initiatives from the local to the central state level, a unified criteria on means and resources and greater consensus on medium- and long-term priorities among social and institutional actors, are urgently required before Bilbao advances effectively on the road to revitalization.

Notes

1. The author is indebted to the European Commission (DG XII) for its support of this research through its programme Human Capital and Mobility.
2. The London Docklands is one of the most often cited examples of leverage planning (Brindley *et al.*, 1989). Taking into account the full range of public expenditures from site preparation and infill to capital allowances and rate-free periods as well as the extensive transport infrastructure programme (a light railway, a Docklands airport, road building and underground extension), it has been estimated than £2.5 billion of public funds went into the Docklands between 1981 and 1991 bringing more than £9 billion private investment, a gearing ratio of aproximately 1:3.6 (Atkinson and Moon, 1994). In Baltimore, $375 million invested by the private sector between 1960 and 1982 in the redevelopment of the Inner Harbour were leveraged by $330 million from the city, state and federal governments (King, 1987). In other large-scale redevel-opment projects leverage funding was provided through the use of Urban Development Action Grants in the United States, Urban Development Grants in Great Britain (Parkinson, 1989).
3. Because of very limited financial autonomy on the part of local authorities, planning initiatives are contingent upon private sector involvement and regional and central administration funding. As a result, local priorities have to be negotiated and likely subordinated to the preferences of private interest or institutions beyond the locality. On this account, local planners often face

a *fait accompli* regarding particular projects. In the case of Bilbao, the existence of a large number of projects supported by provincial or regional authorities and, in some cases, the private sector, has left local planners with little capacity to plan otherwise.

4. Andersen Consulting uses a version of the Harvard SWOT (Strengths-Weaknesses-Opportunities-Threats) model of strategic planning. This model provides a highly systematized and modular methodology than can be applied to any territorial analysis (Vazquez, 1993).

5. The Association for the Revitalization of Metropolitan Bilbao 'Bilbao-Metrópoli 30' was constituted at the end of 1991 by more than 80 public organizations, universities, technology centres, mass media, major metropolitan enterprises and other private organizations. The objective of this Association is to join public and private efforts in the revitalization process of Metropolitan Bilbao. It can be regarded, fundamentally, as a lobbying institution to stimulate and encourage the development of the Plan's initiatives and projects. As of 1994, Metrópoli 30 has more than 100 members that include local and regional institutions, chamber of commerce, the universities, large firms, various non-governmental and private organizations.

References

Albrechts, L. (1992), 'New challenges for urban policy under a flexible regime of accumulation', *Landscape and Urban Planning*, 22.

Ashworth, G. J., Voogd, H. (1990), *Selling the City*. London, Belhaven Press.

Atkinson, R., Moon, G. (1994), *Urban Policy in Britain, the City, the State and the Market*. London, Macmillan.

Brindley, T., Rydin, Y., Stoker, G. (1989), *Remaking Planning*. London, Unwin Hyman.

Busquets Grau, J. (1993), 'Perspectiva desde las ciudades', *CyTET*, 1.

Campos Venuti, G. (1981), *Urbanismo y Austeridad*. Madrid, Siglo XXI.

—— (1985), *Teoría e intervención en la ciudad*. Madrid, Fundación de Investigaciones Marxistas.

Departamento de Economía y Planificación del Gobierno Vasco (1989), 'Bases para la revitalización económica del Bilbao Metropolitano', *Ekonomiaz*, 15.

Fainstein, S. (1991), 'Promoting economic development. Urban planning in the United States and Great Britain', *Journal of the American Planning Association*, 57.

Gaffikin, F., Warf, B. (1993), 'Urban policy and the post-Keynesian state in the United Kingdom and the United States', *International Journal of Urban and Regional Research*, 17.

Goodwin, M. (1993), 'The city as commodity: the contested spaces of urban development', in Kearns, G., Philo C. (eds), *Selling Places: the City as Cultural Capital, Past and Present*. Oxford, Pergamon.

Granados, V., Seguí, V. (1988), 'La crisis de las políticas regionales, un problema teórico', *Revista de Estudios Regionales*, 21.

Hall, Peter (1988), *Cities of Tomorrow*. Oxford, Basil Blackwell.

Harvey, D. (1989a), *The Condition of Postmodernity*. Oxford, Oxford University Press.

—— (1989b), 'From managerialism to entrepreneurialism: the transformation in urban governance in late capitalism', *Geografiska Annaler*, 71B.

Holcomb, B. (1993), 'Revisioning place: de- and re-constructing the image of the industrial city', in Kearns G., Philo, C. (eds), *Selling Places: the City as Cultural Capital, Past and Present*. Oxford, Pergamon.

Hula, R. (1990), 'The two Baltimores', in Judd, D., Parkinson, M. (eds), *Leadership and Urban Regeneration*. Newbury Park, CA, Sage.

Jauregui Fernandez, P.J. (1993), 'Un nuevo modelo territorial para el País Vasco', *CyTET*.

King, D. (1987), 'The state, capital and urban change in Britain', in Smith, M.P., Feagin, J.R. (eds), *The Capitalist City*. Oxford, Basil Blackwell.

Leira, E., Quero, D. (1992), 'Bilbao, territorio y regeneración productiva', *Estudios Territoriales*, 39.

Leitner, H. (1990), 'Cities in pursuit of economic growth. The local state as entrepreneur', *Political Geography Quarterly*, 9.

Mangada, E. (1991), 'Suelo e infraestructura metropolitana: el diseño urbanístico de las grandes ciudades', in Rodriguez, J., Castells, M., Narbona, C., Curbelo, J.L. (eds), *Las grandes ciudades: debates y propuestas*. Madrid, Economistas.

Merrifield, A. (1993), 'The Canary Wharf debacle: from "TINA" there is no alternative – to "THEMBA" – there must be an alternative', *Environment and Planning*, 25: 1247–65.

Parkinson, M. (1989), 'The Thatcher government's urban policy, 1979–1989', *Town Planning Review*, 60: 421–40.

PGOU (Plan General de Ordenación Urbana) (1992), *Avance*. Bilbao, Ayuntamiento de Bilbao.

Ravetz, A. (1980), *Remaking Cities*, London, Croom Helm.

Rodriguez, A., Viriuela, M. (1987), 'El papel de la administración local en la recuperación económica del espacio urbano', II Congreso Mundial Vasco de Geografia, Vitoria-Gasteiz.

—— (1988), 'Apuntes para una política de desarrollo local', in Agencia de Desarrollo Económico y Empleo (ed.), 'La ciudad como instrumento de recuperación económica y empleo', Vitoria-Gasteiz, Ayuntamiento de Vitoria-Gasteiz.

Rodriguez, A. *et al.* (1994), *Estudio del Mercado de Trabajo y de la Estructura Económica de Barakaldo*, Ayuntamiento de Barakaldo, unpublished manuscript.

Terán, F. (1985), 'Sobre la crisis actual de los fundamentos teóricos del planeamiento', in Campos Venuti, G., *Teoría e intervención en la ciudad*. Madrid, Fundación de Investigaciones Marxistas.

Vazquez Barquero, A. (1993), *Política económica local*. Madrid, Pirámide.

Vegara Gomez, A. (1993), 'Cultura urbana y cultura del territorio. Los retos del urbanismos del siglo XXI', *CyTET*, 1.

5

Adopting the innovative environment approach
A programme of regional development for Charleroi

PASCALE VAN DOREN

Introduction

In the light of the new dynamics of territorial organization at a global level, induced by the changing techno-industrial system, new global–local interactions are emerging. This phenomenon gives rise to heterogeneous spatial situations which are difficult to comprehend using the linear development logic of traditional theoretical approaches. Such is the case of declining older industrial regions, a good example being the region around the Belgian city of Charleroi.

 Research carried out by the GREMI[1] group aimed to clarify the redistribution in the 'hierarchy' of territories, through investigating their capacity to integrate the determinants of the new techno-industrial network into the productive fabric. On the basis of the concepts of 'innovative environments' and of 'innovation networks', GREMI attempted to explain the success or failure of certain territories in adjusting to the globalization of the economy by incorporating technological change. In other words, the research drew attention to the difficulties met by territories in adapting to the new techno-industrial system and in establishing a sustainable 'innovative environment'.

Given the current series of activities and initiatives aimed at a yet uncompleted economic restructuring of the region of Charleroi, this particular older industrial region appeared to be a relevant case to be studied within the context of the GREMI research. In consequence, the overall aim of this chapter is to examine whether and how the industrial area of Charleroi is incorporating or generating the determinants of an innovative environment. The analysis is based on the strategic orientations developed within the frameworks of the 'Projet de Ville' and 'Charleroi Futura', the regional development plans.

The chapter is divided into three sections:

- the first section recalls the techno-industrial changes which currently characterize industrial economies and elucidates the challenge to territorial development which they pose (pages 93–97);
- given these new territorial dynamics, the second section spells out the main contributions of the innovative environment theory (pages 97–101);
- finally, on the basis of the theoretical framework outlined in the preceding sections, the third section tries to assess whether the Charleroi region will be able to evolve favourably towards the creation of a viable innovative environment (pages 101–108).

The dominating techno-industrial mutations in industrialized countries

It is almost unnecessary to demonstrate that economic development is based on an ever-increasing incorporation of immaterial factors and new technologies into the production process. Nowadays, this process, which affects all the areas of the economy, i.e. services as well as industry, is characterized by two fundamental and interwoven changes.

The globalization of the economy and the creation of the European Single Market

Since the mid-1980s, the development of economic exchanges has been characterized by a process of globalization going beyond the classical notion of internationalization specific to the economic evolution of the 1960s. Internationalization was a form of economic organization through which firms tried to capture external markets by entering domestic or multidomestic economies; it favoured the internalization of production functions according to the dynamics of the international division of labour (Michalet, 1988; Delapierre, 1990).

Globalization corresponds to a set of conditions in which a growing part of wealth is produced throughout the world within the framework of a system of interwoven networks of enterprises, characterized in particular by:

- the capacity to produce and distribute goods and services from structures organized on a global basis;
- global markets regulated by global norms and standards;
- organizations operating on a global basis with an organizational culture regulated by a system of values codified at the global level;

- systems of alliance in which the rules of the game are based on 'deterritorialized' legal, technological and economical norms;
- a marked trend towards the externalization of inter-firm relations and to transnational co-operation in the fields of R&D, production and distribution.

All these mutations which affect small and medium-sized enterprises (SMEs) as well as the large industrial groups, contribute to the creation of global networks from which a new global industrial structure emerges. The latter no longer directly adheres to the need to gain access to domestic markets and goes beyond classical international specialization. One result is 'new spatial configurations' at odds with classical scenarios of territorial planning (Quévit and Van Doren, 1993a), an issue which will be addressed on pages 97–101.

The rupture of the traditional techno-industrial paradigm

In order to grasp the complex nature of the globalization of economy, it is necessary to stress the emergence of a new techno-industrial paradigm which radically modifies the overall functioning of the most industrialized economies, i.e. the growing predominance of the science–technology relationship in the production of goods and services.

A break with traditional theories of development

The techno-industrial system which governed industrial progress over the last decades was fundamentally dominated by the direct link between the transformation of material resources and their technical adaptation with a view to creating goods. Hence, there was a linear process flowing from the access to raw materials to the penetration of well-controlled markets, within the framework of a relatively stable growth influenced by short-term adjustments and a steady evolution of production techniques.

Such modes of economic activity were widely recognized and they were borne out by the classical theories of regional development, such as: the approach of the neo-classical tradition based on endowments of the factors of production; the Keynesian model based on the cumulative effects of the relationship between demand and local investment; or, more recently, Perroux's approach of polarized development based on the catalytic effect of a leading industry. A brief mention can be made of the main policy instruments proposed by these approaches in order to assess their efficiency and pertinence in the context of the globalization of the economy.

In the neo-classical approach, the policies of local development were mainly concerned with the implementation of instruments aimed at two major goals:

- removing the obstacles to the free circulation of the factors of production;
- removing the institutional or monopolistic elements which prevent the relative prices of the factors from attaining their competitive level (especially in the labour market).

Accordingly, public intervention placed an emphasis on using incentives to compensate at a local level for differential costs of location (e.g. costs of peripherality) or social costs (equal wages throughout the territory despite productivity differentials), as well as on the interventions in favour of main infrastructure (accessibility).

In the neo-Keynesian approach, local development policies were implemented, in particular, by instruments such as:

- aids and subsidies assisting less competitive industrial sectors to ensure an acceptable level of local demand and income;
- direct productive investments through the creation of public enter- prises or through public interventions in the capital of private firms;
- public investments in favour of infrastructure (roads, industrial zones, etc.) to attract potential investors often exogenous to the region.

In the polarized development theory, which can be considered as a step beyond the other two approaches, interventions in the dynamics of local development were directed towards the creation of 'growth poles' dependent on 'leading' industries resulting in spin-off or catalytic effects liable to regenerate the local productive fabric. These interventions focused on policies of local planning favouring urban concentration, and on infrastructures connecting the growth poles at the national and even international level. The older industrial regions are a typical example of polarized growth, in which industrial development is twinned with urban growth.

A number of fundamental observations illustrate clearly that these theories are outdated and can no longer deal with the new constraints faced by the industrialized economies:

1   In the past decades, the traditional industrial regions of the Euro- pean Union implemented widely neo-Keynesian type policies of local development, especially through sectoral restructuring policies (e.g. shipyard, textile, steel and iron industry, etc.) and through policies of polarized territory planning in favour of transport and

communication infrastructure. Despite a significant factor endow-
ment, an industrial base, high population density, and considerable
infrastructure, these regions appear to have relinquished their role as
'motors' of economic growth and, moreover, have been as yet unable
to trigger a new dynamic of local development (e.g. Nord Pas-de-
Calais and Lorraine in France, Wallonia in Belgium, North East
England, Saarland in Germany, etc.).

2   Local development policies initiated by the member-states of the
European Union through the operations of the European Regional
Development Fund (ERDF) were so inspired by these theories that,
over the period 1975–1990, more than 90 per cent of ERDF money
was exclusively dedicated to the development of large infrastructures
in a polarization logic. However, once again, the outcomes of these
policies are not convincing, indeed, as was noted in the last report on
the socio-economic situation of the European regions, interregional
disparities have remained similar to what they were in the early
1970s.

3   Growth poles (technopoles) often remain disconnected from the
local productive tissue when they form part of an offensive approach
of public authorities ('cathedrals in the desert'). Moreover, they may
create difficulties for local small firms through ensuing increases in
the price structure (wages, rents, cost of living, etc.). Finally, technopoles do not necessarily assist local enterprises to increase their
innovative capacity since often relations are restricted to technical
subcontracting.

Emergence of a new techno-industrial paradigm: science–technology–production relationships

A totally different paradigm is at the base of the new techno-industrial
system: the science– technology–production relationship in which
material resources are less and less important compared to immaterial
resources (knowledge, organization, creativity, etc.). Economic activity is
above all influenced by the relationship between science and the market
and is governed by two interactive processes and is constitutive of a
global economy: technological creation whose applications are spread
throughout all the industrial sectors; and the rapid differentiation of
products under the pressure of an increasingly global demand. In contrast, in the previous techno-industrial system, large industrial sectors,
such as the iron and steel or mechanical engineering industries, dominated the productive process and had a driving effect on the economy. In
the current system, the functioning of the global industrial structure is
determined by technological fields such as composite materials, bio-
technology or telecommunications whose developments have an impact

on a series of sectors. Moreover, the rapid rate of change in these technological fields and the uncertainty which it induces generate a greater turbulence in the economic environment and enjoin more flexible modes of organization. The consequences of this new paradigm are numerous, to cite just the most important:

- a greater interaction between industry and the service sector;
- an economy dominated by a plurality of business sectors;
- increasing importance of productive services;
- a continual increase in R&D investments and the creation of R&D technology structures;
- a strategic role for the means and sources of information and communication technologies (quality and rapidity rather than quantity);
- the creation of new occupations based on knowledge.

In general, there is a radical transformation of productive activity in which immaterial factors related to knowledge and organization outclass material factors related to the technical transformation of raw materials and natural resources. This mutation of the techno-industrial system characterized by the mobility of technological factors brings about new effects on the spatial distribution of economic activities generating new forms of territoriality.

Territorial challenges of globalization and the contribution of the 'innovative environment theory'

From bipolarity to multiterritoriality

Under the previous techno-industrial system, mastering spatial planning determinants was relatively simple and unchanging, for economic activity was spatialized according to the bipolar logic of polarized growth. Space was mainly divided into centres (with quantitatively high levels of development accompanied by high concentrations of population, industrial activities and services) and peripheries (with low levels of development, sparsely populated and low levels of industrialization). Within this abstraction, the interaction between the centre and periphery was conceived as a linear process in which spatial planning policies gave priority to the rational organization of a polarized development around strong urban systems. In this framework, peripheries benefited only from an extension of the poles due to the need for additional space or as a function of the diseconomies of agglomeration resulting from an over-concentration of activities.

The technological paradigm makes this approach even more complex, for it leads to a new interaction between the global and local levels, through the impetus given by the mobility of technological factors and innovation-related externalities of organized territorial communities, rather than the immobility of factors of production and decreasing costs. As a result, a multiplicity of spatial situations exists which are difficult to analyse within the parameters of bipolarity. This is illustrated by the decline of old industrial regions or the emergence of areas whose development is founded on comparative advantages related to specific and more diversified 'environmental' conditions, such as research potential, lifestyles, local entrepreneurial traditions, specific know-how, etc.

As a consequence, the bipolar and linear distribution of space is being increasingly replaced by a 'multiterritoriality' resulting from the changing patterns of concentration and deconcentration both in economic and territorial terms (Quévit and Van Doren, 1993a).

Innovative environment and networks of innovation as means of responding to the principle of multiterritoriality

In founding the GREMI approach, in 1984, Aydalot drew explicitly on this observation of the transformation of the hierarchies between territories. Aydalot underlined that the 'u-turn process' ('*processus de retournement*'), as he named it, in which certain central regions commenced a relative decline, while some of the so-called peripheral regions experienced a new dynamism could not be explained by existing theories. Indeed, these theories only explained the hierarchy of spaces and not the modification of this hierarchy. Accordingly, an autonomous dynamic must exist within certain regions which enables them to improve their position. By considering the issue from this viewpoint, Aydalot established certain links with a stream of thought on the analysis of the territorial development process represented, in particular, by the analysts of the Italian industrial districts (Beccatini). This research had drawn attention to the success of certain specific forms of production organization, territorially integrated, and to their capacity to develop relatively autonomously.

On the basis of the industrial district model and the theory of the behaviour of firms, the GREMI studies tried to contribute to the formulation of a theory of spatial development accounting for the capacity of territories to integrate the new paradigm of the techno-industrial system in their productive tissue, using the notions of innovative environment and networks of innovation (Maillat, Quévit, Senn, 1993).[2]

An 'innovative environment' can be defined as the set of economic, political and institutional relationships and multilateral transactions occurring in a given territory which generate externalities specific to innovation and a dynamic process of collective learning resulting in more efficient forms of common management of resources.

Thus, in the GREMI approach, innovation is considered as a process which integrates the elements which determine and favour the dynamics and transformation of the territorial techno-production system (Gordon, 1992). Hence, the innovative environment is characterized by the integration of internal dynamics and external changes. As a result, an environment is innovative when:

- it is capable of acquiring information and additional resources through an openness to the exterior. The quintessential innovative environment is open to diversity and receptive to change;
- when its resources are organized, co-ordinated and inter-connected by economic, cultural and technical structures which make them exploitable by new productive forms.

The innovative environment is a multi-dimensional reality which associates a group of actors in the dynamic evolution of a production system through integrating both the territorial dimension and the techno-industrial paradigm at the basis of the structural changes in the productive capacities.

Thus, the innovative environment concept incorporates:

- a technological dimension referring to a logic of learning, know-how and knowledge related to the technological paradigm; the process of creation of generic technologies and the process of integration of adaptive technologies in specific production systems;
- an organizational dimension with a logic of interaction between interdependent actors: networking of economic and institutional actors at the local level (enterprises, research and training institutions, local public authorities, etc.), modes of organization through partnerships and contracts , etc.;
- a territorial dimension where a certain unity and homogeneity are liable to create locational externalities and generate a comparative advantage specific to the territory.

When collaborative relations are set up between several actors in an innovative environment, when these relations specifically aim at innovation, when they are established on the basis of mutual trust and are not occasional, they become a real mode of organization named innovation network.

The establishment of innovation networks results from the fact that, nowadays, innovation is neither a simple function of the entrepreneur's ability or of the competence of an isolated enterprise or scientific institution nor a simple question of institutional co-ordination. The innovation network concept partakes of the idea that the innovation process is of a multifunctional character which, on the basis of the joint activities of these organizations, involves a complex and non-linear articulation of specific competencies and processes of knowledge acquisition all along the chain of production (Planque, 1993).

Moreover, the research carried out by the RIDER team on the relations between local and global levels in the regional productive tissues led to the identification of three relevant levels of territorial organization with respect to structural adaptations (Quévit and Van Doren, 1993).

1   The local level corresponding to the field of local development directly influenced and characterized by:
    - the existence of local development initiatives of a highly endogenous nature, which seek to maximize the potential of local human, material and financial resources;
    - the existence of interactions between local actors: entrepreneurial partnerships, dialogue between economic and public agents (training, research, etc.), cultural associations, etc.;
    - the existence of a system to organize and manage local development: educational system, public services, local transport facilities, certain business-related services, etc.

2   A supra-local level corresponding to a local development environment, which generates externalities through the agglomeration effect:
    - interconnection between neighbouring cities: the potential of co-operation between medium-sized cities has been highlighted as a means of ensuring an adequate spread of urban functions (business-related services) throughout peripheral areas;
    - connections with research and technological development organizations (centres of transfer of technology, higher education, training, etc.);
    - access to sources of finance and saving in the near proximity, etc.

3   The global level including all the intra- and extra-community exchanges:
    - connections to world wide networks of telecommunication and information (teleports, etc.);
    - access to trans-European networks (links with a major metropolis, global markets, etc.);
    - establishment of interregional forms of co-operation and partnership related to the needs of local firms;
    - the connections to high speed means of transport and communications (motorways, links to TGV (high-speed train) network).

In short, a territory is evolving towards an 'Innovative Environment' type of organizational mode if it integrates the four fundamental and specific dimensions:

- a technological dimension referring to a logic of learning, know-how and knowledge related to the technological paradigm;
- an organizational dimension referring to a logic of interactions among actors;
- a territorial dimension which includes local-global relationships;
- a temporal dimension which takes into account the temporal processes of the restructuring of production system, which assume a flexible mode of transactions over time.

In the last section of the chapter, an attempt will be made to identify each of these dimensions in the case of Charleroi.

The innovative environment approach applied to Charleroi[3]

As was stated in the introduction, and on the basis of the theoretical concepts discussed above, this section will try to assess to what extent the Charleroi region is evolving favourably towards the creation of a viable innovative environment.

The case of Charleroi can be considered as relevant for a number of reasons:

- the zone around Charleroi is an old industrial region challenged by the need to achieve a fundamental restructuring of its production system;
- as it is eligible for Structural Fund support of the European Union under objective 1, Charleroi receives important European funds;
- Charleroi has launched a number of important development programmes which mobilize all the social, economic and political leaders of the area, especially in relation to its recent eligibility under objective 1.

Is this economy 'in transition' going to move towards an innovative environment as previously defined in this chapter ?

Principal diagnostic elements of the territory of Charleroi

Charleroi, an economic area confronted by an industrial past

The industrial belt around Charleroi is located some 60 kilometres south of Brussels. It was based on traditional heavy industry: coal mining, iron and steel industry, glass industry and manufacture of rail equipment.

These sectors were vital for the economy, and largely contributed to the former prosperity of Charleroi. However, they were seriously affected by the backlash of the technological mutations of the European and global economy.

The coal mines bore the brunt of the first shock as early as the 1950s. Subsequently, many mechanical engineering enterprises were to fail on a regular basis. The glass and electrical engineering industries were also faced by a structural crisis. In the 1970s, the difficulties of the iron and steel industry hastened the decline of the older industrial sectors.

However, in the early 1980s, the industrial orientation of the Charleroi basin remained predominant: in 1980, almost 44 per cent of the active population still worked in industry. Over the last decade, the dismantling of these traditional industries has led to the loss of approximately 25,000 jobs in the Charleroi region; in relative terms a reduction of more than 30 per cent.

Nowadays, while significant restructuring has taken place in the area, the imprints of the industrial past still remain vivid:

- the productive system is characterized by the important relative weight of the old industry-related activities which were at the basis of the first industrial revolution (metallurgy industry) and of the second revolution (producer goods and transport industries as well as building and public works industries);[4]
- the industrial activities are mainly concentrated in the upstream low value-added industrial branches.

The weight of this industrial past still affects the economic potential of the Charleroi area and requires the implementation of strong and voluntarist policies and instruments. Indeed, in the European economic space, Charleroi is considered as a declining industrial area whose main symptom is a very high rate of unemployment (compared to a European average of 100, unemployment in Charleroi is equal to 165.4).[5]

In the context of such a structural crisis, Charleroi has benefited from EU actions under objective 2 of the European Regional Development Fund (ERDF) concerning 'declining industrial areas'.

In the current funding period (1995–9), Charleroi will benefit from the EU support under objective 1 of the Structural Funds for 'lagging regions', for it is located in the province of Hainaut which has recently been recognized as eligible.[6]

Faced by a substantial challenge in terms of economic restructuring and the management of considerable means, which options will Charleroi choose in terms of its relative position within Europe? This issue will be dealt with in the section on plos.

A lagging potential of immaterial factors: R&D and human resources

The vulnerability of Charleroi is characterized by various handicaps as far as its potential in research and technological development is concerned. Among the most striking handicaps are:

- a low participation of enterprises in the RTD programmes of the European Community, probably due to the lack of university structures in Charleroi;
- a clear deficit in 'grey matter' especially represented by a relatively low rate of university level students (Charleroi = 70 compared to the index 100 for Belgium);
- a disconnection of local RTD support organizations (nuclear medicine, chemistry) from the main domains of the enterprises (electrotechnics, electronics, telecommunications, material technology);
- a regional approach of services supporting technological innovation (universities, scientific parks, fairs and RTD exhibitions, innovation financing structures, etc.) which remains weak.

In addition, despite all the efforts made to support R&D in the energy and industry sectors in every traditional industrial region undergoing a restructuring of its traditional sectors, the analysis of the outcomes shows that they remained too focused on upstream products in their respective low value-added industries (Quévit *et al.*, 1991).

As far as human resources are concerned, the Charleroi area offers a series of relatively non-encouraging facts:

- a strong proportion of unqualified people of working age;
- a relatively low percentage of young people in full-time education and a low proportion of students starting university studies; therefore, no catching up of the accumulated lag in terms of labour qualification;
- a type of long-run structural unemployment generating a very strong dualization of labour market;
- a relative lack of higher or university training, especially in the domains of RTD, management and marketing.

The level of the openness of Charleroi: a policy of infrastructure investment out of proportion

In terms of business centres in Europe, Charleroi appears ideally located close to the most important flows of commercial exchange.

Indeed, Charleroi is located:

- in a zone delimited by flows of exchanges between the South-East of the UK, the North of Belgium and West of the Netherlands, the

Rhine and the South of Germany, Switzerland and the North of Italy;

- relatively close to the main European ports in terms of global exchanges: Antwerp, Rotterdam and Dunkirk.

From the perspective of maximizing the potential of this strategic location in terms of exchange flows, and with the intention of becoming an efficient and dynamic urban structure within a European context, Charleroi is implementing a policy to increase mobility in all its forms within the dynamic of the global modernization of the various networks of communication. Given this objective of reinforcing its accessibility at the Walloon, European and international levels, Charleroi is mainly investing in transport and telecommunication.

Among the main orientations favoured by the city to reinforce its accessibility can be noted:

1   the desire to promote Charleroi and western Wallonia in Europe through the development of public transportation; in this respect, Charleroi is pursuing five major goals:
- access to high-speed train services for passengers (TGV);
- development of the high-speed goods traffic;
- development of combined transportation;
- completion of the basic subway programme;
- modernization of training workshops and stations.
2   the opening up of the border zone through the completion of the Walloon motorway programme south of Charleroi, i.e. motorway links providing faster connection between Charleroi and the area located between the Sambre and Meuse rivers and the neighbouring French regions (Champagne Ardenne and the Avesnes area);
3   the expansion of the economic function of the regional airport (Brussels South Charleroi Airpole), especially through the building of a large enterprise zone alongside the runways;
4   the development of telecommunications, especially through the creation of a multipolar teleport (access to satellite or to other means of long-distance communication) and the development of an urban cable network (urban tele-management, tele-work, tele-education).

While remaining within the descriptive part of this case study of Charleroi, from the point of view of the establishment of an innovative environment, attention can be drawn to the disparity between the orientations of the infrastructure policy and the effective economic role which a so-called medium-sized city can play in European economic exchanges. The part dedicated to heavy infrastructures to link Charleroi to the outside is more aligned to the needs of a metropolitan development approach rather than that of a medium-sized city even if it has a high potential. Within this framework, it is useful to recall that Charleroi should first ensure the success of its industrial reconversion: a challenge which implies that a particular emphasis should be placed on the role of local development structures related to the techno-industrial system.

A compromised evolution towards an innovative environment: an inappropriate territorial relationship

This section aims at perceiving whether Charleroi – within the framework of its main development programmes[7] – fulfils all the conditions required for the setting up of an innovative environment as defined by the GREMI research. For this purpose, we present the general principles on which these programmes are founded and the main lines of their implementation.

The development programmes of Charleroi were guided by general principles which aimed at establishing plans[8] with the following specificities:

- they should be multiannual (time dimension);
- they should ensure an equilibrium between material and immaterial investments and 'should be innovative in order to favour a different development' (technological dimension);
- they should be coherent with the real socio-economic life of the whole province of Hainaut (territorial dimension);
- they should be integrated, i.e. meet as many economic needs as possible and ensure their positive interaction (organizational dimension).

In order to show more precisely the place of these principles in the GREMI research, we deliberately tried to classify the main orientations of these plans according to the three fundamental dimensions which characterize the dynamics of an innovative environment, i.e. the technological paradigm, the organizational dimension and the territorial dimension. As for the temporal dimension, it is implicitly included in the planning concept. This analysis was carried out over two periods.

A positive response to the technological and organizational paradigms at the basis of the innovative environment

As can be seen in the following table, the orientations selected within the framework of the development plans of the region of Charleroi have largely integrated the concepts originating in the technological paradigm and organizational dimension which characterize the setting up of an innovative environment, as it was defined by the GREMI research.

Table 5.1 Charleroi, technological and organizational paradigms

Technological paradigm	Organizational paradigm
Encouraging strategies of diversification by giving greater place to information and training than to the medium or long-run sectoral trend (market growth prospects, potential technological trajectories, etc.);	Developing enterprises/schools partnerships especially through work and training programmes;
Improving the export capacities through managerial guidance facilities;	Setting up a service pole for firms and international functions especially by improving telecommunications equipment, and through the development of synergy between netwroks of local actors (Chamber of commerce, 'Intercommunales', Club of exporters, etc.);
Increasing the potential of aids to create enterprises aiming at a multiplication of the firm incubator facilities;	Strengthening the connections to the European business poles and decision-making poles through a systematic policy of information and communication-seeking especially based on telecommunications;
Increasing the access to producer services by favouring the structuring of demand for services in the development of enterprises (consultancy, marketing, financial and technical engineering, etc.) through the setting up of information facilities;	Increasing co-operation agreements to consolidate the integration of Charleroi in exchange networks (transborder co-operation agreements, network of the French-speaking community, etc.);

Reinforcing the role of local support in engineering the development of the small and medium-sized enterprises

i.e. an interface role which would also include aids to write down terms of reference, to perform the follow-up and to assess the service provisions;

Encouraging the emergence of local potential in technology-oriented services which would contribute in the assessment of technological potential, access to market opportunities (new products, etc.), and the move towards the downstream of industrial branches;

Improving the means of training and information about the management of innovation;

Intensifying the mechanisms of technology transfers through intersectoral seminars and training courses;

Arousing the need for requalification, training and continuing training through developing awareness in the professional milieus;

Creating an internationalization fund dedicated to help the local SMEs to benefit from financial support for projects related to their internationalization (financial participation in joint ventures, purchase or application for a patent, etc.).

Through the integration into European networks of service providers and partnerships with centres located in the main European metropoles;

Promoting partnerships between enterprises, research centres and universities in the technological fields of the new telecommunication materials;

Encouraging the participation in European groups of enterprises centred on technological targets, especially through European technological programmes;

Promoting partnerships between existing centres and European centres of excellency, possibly through exchanges of researchers.

An incomplete response to the territorial paradigm in an innovative environment

The strategic orientations implemented within the framework of the development programme in the region of Charleroi[9] will not converge as such towards an innovative environment dynamics since they proceed from a discontinuous approach between the local level, confined to the sphere of the directly controllable local development, and the global level confined to the whole set of intra-Community exchanges. In other words, these orientations do not include and benefit from the dynamic realities of the economic and social flows which actually exist in its hinterland, especially with the region of Brussels-capital. Indeed, it is clear that Charleroi is currently experiencing important transformations of its immediate environment, especially as a result of the effects of the diseconomies of agglomeration in Brussels, and of the scientific and technological development of the Brabant-Wallon, another neighbouring region.

However, in the face of the issues at stake at the urban level, this evolution is just embryonic and is yet to be confirmed. Indeed, the globalization of the economy, and especially the development of the intra-community exchanges at the European level and the growing importance of the immaterial and technological factors in the production system, create new urban functions which can only be fulfilled if there is a sufficiently buoyant and large economic and technological hinterland to generate economies of scale and agglomeration. These new urban functions are especially:

- an innovation function: creation of technology, technological transfer, labour qualification, interfirm networks of co-operation, etc.;
- a communication function which enables the local and regional economy to find its place in international competition and to have access to new markets by favouring the speed and quality of communication: airports, high-speed train links, development of information and communication systems;
- a function of international exchange networking with the organization of fairs, the creation of business centres, the development of cultural exchanges, etc.;
- a function of environment and quality of life, especially in the domain of urban regeneration, housing, public transportation and social-cultural facilities.

Despite the numerous and recent efforts to plan and consolidate its urban space, it is clear that the urban system of Charleroi is not suited to these new functions because its dependency on its industrial past remains dominant. The possibility of an innovative environment being created in Charleroi would require it to be open and attractive to a wider economic and social space (supra-local level of proximity). This is the condition for Charleroi to reach a sufficient critical demand and supply size which is vital to it becoming a successful urban system.

This recommendation to widen the area of attraction of Charleroi is based on the mode of development of city networks, increasingly used in Europe, to intensify the international integration of medium-sized cities which are handicapped by their critical size from fulfilling the new urban function already mentioned. However, the success of such networks of medium-sized (and small) cities requires a strong linkage with larger cities (such as Brussels-capital in the case of Charleroi). This implies the priority development of the interdependencies (and not only the dependencies) between the different urban levels. The partition of the European space between different types of urban population systems can have a determining role on the strategies of (multinational or local) firms. If a territory – Charleroi in particular – cannot disown its past, it can without any doubt orientate its future (Rozenblat, 1993).

Thus, the creation of this new socio-economic space in Charleroi should be based on the networking of the economic, technological and urban complementarities of three territorial sub-systems:

1 The contribution of the Brabant-Wallon area (East of Charleroi), endowed with a major university, as a pole of excellence in the field of research and technological development and in the field of tele-communications (teleport).
2 The urban system of Charleroi thanks to the development of a good quality tertiary sector and the expansion of its airport.
3 The complementarities between Charleroi and, to the west, the less developed conurbation of Mons-Borinage and La Louvière in the industrial, infrastructure (multinodal platform) and technological (Mons university pole) domains.

In conclusion, it appears essential to encourage the complementarities between Charleroi and the Brabant-Wallon – two areas which can benefit from the positive effects of the dynamism of Brussels – as the only strategy likely to reinforce the development of the adjoining Mons-Borinage and Centre region. Due to their social and economic situation, both these areas cannot generate by themselves the sufficient critical mass and really competitive externalities of development. On the other hand, if their territories and urban systems were integrated in a networking dynamism, this region could benefit from the buoyant dynamics of development which exist in the two other regions and use their assets to reinforce the urban network required for the future development of the three territorial sub-systems.

Due to its dimension and central position, such an economic space will be able at the same time:

- to find its place in the European urban system;
- to fulfil urban functions of a strategic nature in the face of the globalization of the economy in the single European market;
- to play an active role in the socio-economic life of the western part of Wallonia by benefiting from the economic flows towards France, both Paris and Lille;
- to create an economic and technological space of excellence in the centre of Europe (Quévit, 1993b).

Notes

1. Groupe de Recherche Européen sur les Milieux Innovateurs.
2. The following development is largely inspired by the preamble to '*Réseaux d'Innovation et Milieux Innovateurs: un pari pour le développement régional*' Maillat, Quévit, Senn (1993).
3. *Sources*: Quévit *et al.* (1992).
4. In 1989, these four industrial branches accounted for 75.8 percent of the industrial jobs against 40 per cent of the European industrial jobs. Branch by branch, the comparison with the 12-Europe provides the following data: machine tools 33.1 per cent of the industrial jobs in Charleroi against 23.3 for Eur-12; metallurgy 25.3 per cent – Eur.12 5.3 per cent; building and public works 9.1 per cent – Eur. 12 5.3 per cent; transport – 8. 3 per cent; Eur. 12 6.0 per cent.
5. Calculated from the average of the 1989-1990-1991 data.
6. The average wealth per head, measured by the GDP per head, is 85.5 in Charleroi against an average European index of 100.
7. The 'Projet de Ville' rounds up all the local actors who seek to build up a real 'urban charter' on the eve of the 21st century. The Development Plan of the Charleroi region is called 'Charleroi Futura'. It was designed within the framework of the eligibility of the province of Hainaut to Objective 1 of the EU Structural Funds for the period 1994–9. This operation should not only allow the region of Charleroi to join the developed regions of Europe, but also to propel it as high as possible in the hierarchy of the high-GDP regions.
8. Sources: 'Charleroi Futura' and 'Projet de Ville' of the region of Charleroi.
9. Both the 'Projet de Ville' at the global level and the plan of regional development in relation to the eligibility to Objective 1 of the Structural Funds of the European Union.

References

Becattini, G. (1989), *Mercato e forze locali: il distretto industriale*. Bologna, Il Mulino.
Delapierre, M.M. (1990), 'Stratégies d'alliances face à un nouvel environnement', paper to the conference 'International strategies d'alliances : un nouveau défi pour les entreprises', Neuchâtel.

Gaffard, J.-L. (1993), 'Cohérence et diversité des systèmes d'innovation: le cas des systèmes d'innovation localisés en Europe', research report to Programme FAST.

Gordon, R. (1992), 'Réseau d'innovation et milieu technopolitan: La Silicon Valley', in Maillat, D. and Perrin, J.C. (eds), *Entreprises innovatrices et développement régional.* Neuchâtel, GREMI-EDES.

Maillat, D., Crevoisier, O., Vasserot, J.-Y., (1992), 'Innovation et district industriel de l'arc jurassien', in Maillat, D. and Perrin, J.C. (eds), *Entreprises innovatrices et développement régional.* Neuchâtel, GREMI-EDES.

Maillat, D., Quévit, M., Senn, L. (eds) (1993), *Réseaux d'innovation et milieux innovateurs: un pari pour le développement régional.* Neuchâtel, EDES.

Michalet, C.A., (1988), 'Les accords inter-firmes internationaux', in Arena, R. *et al.* (eds), *Traité d'économie industrielle.* Paris, Economica.

Planque, B. (1993), 'Réseau d'innovation et milieu régional: un cas méditerranéen', in Maillat, D., Quévit, M. and Senn, L. (eds), *Réseaux d'innovation et milieux innovateurs: un pari pour le développement régional.* Neuchâtel, GREMI-EDES.

Quévit, M. (1993a), 'Quelques repères pour la définition d'axes de coopérations transnationales et interégionales dans la perspective de l'Europe 2000', preparatory paper to the meeting of the EU member states Ministers in charge of spatial planning and regional development, 20 p.

—— (1993b), 'La problématique de la métropolisation de Charleroi: vers la création d'un bassin d'innovation', unpublished paper.

Quévit, M., Bodson, S., Van Doren, P. (1992), 'Analyse et anticipation de l'impact du Marché Unique sur le bassin économique de Charleroi', final report for IGRETEC.

Quévit, M., Houard, J., Bodson, S., Dangoisse, A. (1991), *Impact régional 1992: les Régions de Tradition Industrielle.* Brussels, De Boeck.

Quévit, M., Van Doren, P. (1993a), 'Stratégies d'innovation et référents territoriaux', *Revue d'Economie Industrielle,* 64: 38–53.

—— (1993b), 'Problématique des Milieux Innovateurs et politiques d'ajustements structurels territoriaux', paper presented to the GREMI IV conference 'Dynamiques d'ajustements structurels des milieux', Ascona, 29–31 October.

—— (1993c), 'Articulation des programmes d'infrastructures et des actions de développement local', final report to DGXVI, first volume.

Rozenblat, C. (1993), 'L'internationalisation des villes européennes par les réseaux des entreprises multinationales', *Revue d'Economie Régionale et Urbaine,* 4: 661–72.

6

Economic development in London in the context of national policy priorities
Conceptual, institutional and practical issues

IAIN BEGG AND ANNA WHYATT

Introduction

As well as being the administrative and political capital of the UK, London is a centre for tourism, retailing, transport, government and corporate activity (Brunet, 1989). As such, London plays a pivotal role in the UK economy, and is a leading international centre for financial and business services. Yet, despite its position as the hub of the British economy, London faces a number of challenges. It has been in almost continuous (relative) economic decline throughout the post-war period, a relative decline which has accelerated in the last decade. Although the 'South' came to be associated with economic success compared to the supposedly depressed 'North' during the 1980s, this dichotomy was never accurate. Instead, what has happened, in all parts of Britain, is that there has been a long-term relative decline of the large metropolitan areas in favour of smaller towns and rural areas (see Begg *et al.*, 1986). But the problems facing London are not just economic: its infrastructure is increasingly under pressure, especially the transport system; social cohesion is threatened by homelessness, racial division and crime; and it faces a crisis of governance (Thornley, 1992).

The aim of this chapter is to consider how the economic development effort in London can be improved in order to address London's predicament. This is shown to be part of the wider problem of fragmentation and diversity in the structures of government of the capital. The next section presents an overview of London's economic position, and attempts to identify the main strategic issues to be confronted. The second section (pages 118–122) outlines the policy framework within which economic development is formulated and implemented and is followed by a discussion of options for policy changes that would help to bring about a better future for London. Concluding remarks complete the chapter.

The London economy

'London' as an economic entity can be defined in a number of ways (Hall, 1989). The London metropolitan area is usually delineated by the boundaries of the former Greater London Council, and comprises the 33 London boroughs. The 'City' – the hub of the financial sector, is a relatively compact core, although its ambit does stretch to several adjoining boroughs, including the vast redevelopments now coming to fruition in Docklands. Much of the South-East planning region is, arguably, London's hinterland, and it can also be argued that parts of adjacent regions, such as Wiltshire to the West, or Cambridgeshire and Suffolk to the North East are also within the London sphere of influence.

Overview

There have been marked contrasts in the economic trends of these different areas. According to decennial censuses, London's population was growing steadily until World War II, but has been falling since then. The population loss has been more pronounced in inner London which, in forty years (Table 6.1), has lost over a third of its residents, while outer London was relatively stable until 1971. The fall in population was greatest in the decade from 1971 to 1981, with a particularly sharp drop in the inner London boroughs. The rest of the South East (ROSE) and the adjoining regions have consistently gained employment, while Greater London has lost jobs fairly steadily since the early 1960s. Between 1951 and 1981 total employment in London fell by 16.3 per cent.

Table 6.1 The population of Greater London, 1951–91

Area	1951	1961	1971 (thousands)	1981	1991	Change 1951–91 (%)
Inner London	3,679.4	3,492.9	3,031.9	2,496.8	2,343.1	−36.3
Outer London	4,517.6	4,499.7	4,420.6	4,199.4	4,050,4	−10.3
Greater London	8,197.0	7,992.6	7,452.5	6,696.2	6.393.6	−22.0

Source: OPCS

In the 1980s, the boom in financial services looked as though it might reverse this trend with increasing numbers of commuters travelling to jobs in London (Evans and Crampton, 1989), but the job exodus has resumed, especially in the recent recession. Between 1981 and 1993, 13.7 per cent of jobs have gone, and the three-year period from September 1990 to September 1993 saw a contraction in employment of nearly 300,000. Following the shakeout that occurred in the early 1980s, London has been by far the least successful region in the UK. It has lost jobs more than twice as fast as the three regions in the industrial heartland of England. Nor can recent trends provide any solace. As Figure 6.1 reveals, few net new jobs were created in the boom period of 1986–90, and the rate of job loss in the last recession (1990–93) was faster than in all other regions.

Figure 6.1 Employment change: all sectors (employees in employment)

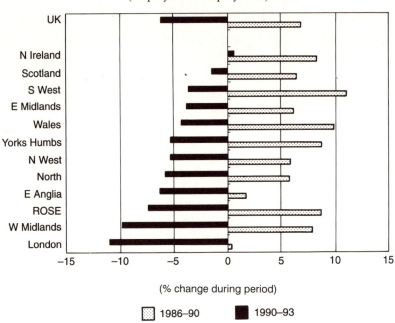

(% change during period)

▦ 1986–90   ■ 1990–93

Economic specialization is determined by a variety of factors which combine to influence competitiveness. One way to categorize this is according to the economic functions performed by the city following a hierarchy suggested by Noyelle and Stanback (1984). In their terms, London is a diversified service centre and a 'national nodal' centre which provides a wide range of services sold across the country and, indeed, internationally. It can also be portrayed as a 'global' city (Sassen, 1991; Kennedy, 1992) because it is prominent in international transport, communication and financial networks.

This global economic role is an important factor to bear in mind when considering its economic development and prospects. As Frost and Spence (1993) show, this is especially important for central London. This area supports over a million jobs which are, according to Frost and

Spence, expensive to support in terms of infrastructure, but depend to a growing extent on trends in the international economy, rather than domestic economic developments. Their analysis corroborates the work of Sassen (1991) who argues that this leads to specialized activity in a narrowing range of business services.

The London economy today is dominated by the service sector and this to a greater degree than the other major conurbations of the UK. Its manufacturing base has, however, contracted at a very rapid rate and this is reflected in the structural shift apparent in Table 6.2. Today, barely one job in ten is in manufacturing, whereas in 1975 it was over one in five. Even in financial services, London faces growing competition from other European cities, while on the global plane there are potential new entrants to the top-flight of financial services activity, such as Singapore or Toronto, which are striving to enhance their positions. Employment in services increased nationally by 16 per cent between 1981 and 1993, yet in contrast to all other regions it actually fell, by 3 per cent, in London. Nor has London fared well in the 'high-tech sectors', as can be seen from the analysis by Begg (1993), which shows that one in four jobs in high-tech was lost during the 1980s, the fastest rate of decline of any region.

Table 6.2 Structure of employment in London, 1981–93
(employees in employment, % of total)

Sector	1981	1986	1990	1993
Manufacturing	19.1	14.5	11.9	11.0
Services	74.8	80.2	83.1	84.6
Construction, utilities, etc	6.1	5.3	5.0	4.4
Total jobs (thousands)	3.567	3.448	3.460	3.079

Source: Department of Employment

These employment trends are mirrored in the steady increase in unemployment in London. In December 1993, the claimant count unemployment rate for London was 11.2, 1.5 percentage points above the GB average, whereas it had been below the average for most of the 1980s. The figures also reveal a worrying rise in long-term unemployment. London now has a higher unemployment rate than the other main urban regions of the EU, with the exception of Madrid.

Prospects for the London economy

Forecasts for the London economy (for example, Cambridge Econometrics, 1994) suggest that it will grow more slowly than any other British region in the next decade. Although such forecasts are subject to large margins of error because of uncertainty about the aggregate performance of the UK economy, the relative position of different regions is revealing. Thus, for the economy overall, GDP is forecast to grow by 2.9 per cent per annum, whereas it will grow by just 2.2 per cent per annum in London. Even if the outturn for national growth is different, this disparity would be expected to be maintained.

Forecasts based on econometric models are, however, conditional on assumptions about policy and on the persistence of existing trends. If policy changes in response to the problems facing the London economy, this could enable some improvement in the outturn. In the scenarios which follow, possible paths for the London economy based on alternative assumptions are explored.

Perhaps the most likely scenario for London's future is precisely the one that policy-makers will be least willing to embrace: continued decline. Many of the forces that have influenced the decline in jobs and population, particularly in inner London, can be expected to remain powerful (Robson, 1988). In addition, it appears probable that, for the foreseeable future, financial services will be shedding rather than creating jobs. Thus, unless there are significant shifts in the thrust of policy and in the resources deployed which begin to reverse past trends, further losses of economic activity and of employment, and more net emigration are all on the cards. The critical question then will be how such decline is managed in order to limit the adverse social consequences that already blight some areas of London, and which can often be the trigger for an aggravation of existing problems. The risks of an intensification of problems of crime, social exclusion and poverty are considerable. Up to now, decline has, by and large, been managed, though often by containment and 'fire-fighting' rather than strategic choices.

Hitherto, the very fact that decline has not been acknowledged to be the norm, and managed accordingly, has exacerbated its effects. Although management of the negative trends associated with decline is already happening, this has been predominantly at a localized level. The absence of a pan-London approach has not only accentuated some of the problems associated with decline, but has also resulted in a climate where collective decision-making has been based on fundamentally false prospects. The manifestly unpalatable consequences in terms of social exclusion, dereliction and lack of opportunity in major US cities serve as a warning of the risks of a failure to come to terms with relative economic decline. For London, the danger in this respect is that social polarization will become more pronounced and that this will be a drag on the economic attractiveness of substantial tracts of the city. This, in turn, would undermine the competitiveness of the London conurbation, overall, for activities such as tourism or financial services which are central to the economy and thus detract from its ability to fulfil its regional, national and international economic roles.

A second scenario is implicit in many of the policy documents that discuss London's future (Kennedy, 1992; LPAC, 1994), namely that a fresh dynamism and new economic specializations can be engendered in the economy which will stabilize employment and begin to reverse social problems. Stabilization will require progress in overcoming the many impediments to competitiveness. In transport, for instance, even if immediate action is taken to implement several of the major projects or initiatives already identified, it will be many years before the benefits from doing so materialize. This suggests that in the short term, the priority should be on fixes for some of the obvious but manageable problems. Realism is also needed on the planning of new developments, together with concerted support for such pan-London initiatives as inward investment. This is likely to need a cultural change in which the benefits for London as a whole are emphasized and demonstrated to transcend local or borough interests.

The key to this scenario must be wide-ranging action on the economic front, with physical planning as a complement to this, rather than the centrepiece as in the past. The quality of the physical environment, personal security and the rebuilding of social infrastructure (for example, good schools) are issues that need to be high on the agenda, but they will not enable London to turn the corner on their own. Since action on the requisite scale cannot be taken for granted, the stabilization scenario must, realistically, be regarded as one that will need radical improvements in policy, rather than being seen as the middle way. A further consideration is fiscal resources: unless the means are available to support economic development on a sufficient scale, the necessary momentum will be impossible to achieve.

A third scenario in which London makes a quantum leap from the decline of the post-war period to a renascent city of the twenty-first century can, of course, be envisaged. The difficulty is that too few of the obvious building blocks for such a scenario are in place. Unlike Paris, where a long-term and conurbation-wide plan has been the norm, London's development has long been piecemeal and, by and large, haphazard. Market realities also suggest that apart from financial and business services, it is not obvious what sectors can be expected to take the lead. One possibility might be tourism and leisure-related developments able to exploit available land in the East Thames corridor, particularly in the light of opportunities associated with the Channel tunnel. But such development would require implausible levels of investment from both public and private sources. Thus while a long-term vision of the 'phoenix' scenario can be contemplated, it cannot be regarded as plausible for the foreseeable future.

Strategic development issues

The multi-faceted character of London's economy and its sheer size as a centre of population and employment inevitably make it more difficult than for smaller, less heterogeneous cities to identify and prioritize strategic development issues. Strategic development has to be able to reconcile the competing aims of different groups and of distinctive economic functions. This requires not merely crude demographics or land-use planning, but a much more extensive appreciation of future trends in economic activity at the regional, national and international level, coupled with an analysis of social trends. A realistic appraisal of how London can and should develop is needed, rather than fanciful ideas that pay little heed to London's inherited physical, institutional and social make-up or the constraints imposed by its relationships with other parts of the British economy. For example, the transport system is so complex, and the population density so high, that a wholesale change in transport arrangements is not feasible, not least because of the need to respect environmental concerns in any development scenario.

Because London is the linchpin of the UK economy, its economic development has ramifications for the entire economy in a way that is much less true of other regions. Without the gravitational pull of London, many activities which prosper elsewhere in the country would lose ground. Tourism, financial and business services and international transport are all examples of industries for which London's global reach ensures that activity comes to the UK rather than being gained by another country. Nurturing this catalytic role is, in its own right, a key development issue for the UK economy.

This evolving role of an important component of the London economy calls for a reappraisal of policy in order to sustain and consolidate its leading position. Global competitors can be expected to look at the operating environment (widely defined), the available labour force and the infrastructure. London retains advantages stemming from its openness to international business and a reasonably transparent regulatory environment, but on several counts, London has been losing ground. Its transport system, once the envy of the world, has become increasingly run-down and inadequate. A comparison of transport in London and Paris (London Research Centre, 1992) concluded that recent and continuing transport investment in Paris will largely overcome the main congestion problems on public transport, and greatly improve the urban motorway network. In contrast, London has yet to agree plans to solve central area congestion.

London also suffered, in the 1980s, from high rents which have been identified as a dominant 'push' factor in the process of decentralization of offices (Jones Lang Wootton, 1992). Yet since the onset of recession in

1990, there has been a rapid increase in vacant office property, especially concentrated in a few areas, such as the City of London, where 15 per cent of 144 million square feet of property is unlet, and in Docklands where 40 per cent of 10 million square feet are vacant. Trends in residential preferences are also likely to have a bearing on the evolution of the economy. Frey (1993), in an analysis of trends in the USA (often a pointer to what will ensue in the UK), has noted that recent years have seen some reversal of the decline of major metropolitan areas, largely because of the upsurge of activity in producer services. However, this has been most apparent in suburban areas, which have also been favoured as residential locations. City cores have increasingly been populated by minority groups, especially in cities which serve as points of entry, and have witnessed growing concentrations of poverty. The indications are that London may well be following these trends, with the smaller urban centres in the Home Counties and East Anglia benefiting most from the expansion of producer services.

As a regional economy, London faces a number of competitive challenges. These include its ability to improve employment opportunities for residents and for commuters living in adjacent counties. In common with other UK conurbations London has witnessed increasing levels of poverty, deprivation and crime (criminal statistics show, for example, that the per capita value of property stolen in London is double the average for England and Wales, and higher than any other part of the country) which, in turn, have deterred economic activity. Rising unemployment, and its concentration amongst particular social groups and localities have exacerbated this problem and threaten a vicious circle of worsening social conditions allied to declining economic prospects. Avoiding such an outcome is an obvious priority for policy. A strategy for the city consequently has to take into account:

- London's multi-tiered economic role as a regional, national, European and international centre;
- The various pan-London, issue-based concerns, respectively, its industrial and business development; transport, infrastructure and the environment; housing, personal safety and other social issues; and labour market, training and employment.

The starting-point of any strategy for development is crucial, and it is our view that economic activity needs to be at the heart of the strategy. The strengths and weaknesses that will shape London's future are as much, if not more, human resource based as property based, especially from an economic perspective. Yet previous strategies have started from land-use considerations and have rarely been tailored to the enhancement of the competitiveness and viability of London's economy. Institutional fragmentation has, as we show in the next section, militated against effective solutions.

The policy framework

There have been substantial changes in the character of public administration in the UK since the 1970s and these have inevitably affected the context within which economic development policy is formulated and implemented. At the national level, a preference for market solutions has seen a reduction in direct industrial and regional policy support. This contrasts with recent trends in other countries, such as France and Spain where explicit decentralization has been enacted, and the USA where the state level has become much more active in local economic development. The changes have led to a weakened capacity for strategic development which is most acute in the major conurbations (Cheshire *et al.*, 1992).

The institutional context

Since the abolition of the Greater London Council (GLC) in 1986, there has been no ostensible regional government for the capital. At the point of abolition, a wide variety of powers and functions was initially vested within the 33 boroughs that make up the local government management of the inner and outer London area. Subsequently, other functions and powers have been transferred to a network of agencies and organizations, some of which are contained within borough boundaries, some of which cross borough boundaries while others operate on a pan-London basis. In addition to these formal arrangements, various private and public sector partnerships were created to carry through specific aims. The result is a matrix of activity, some of which operates well, some of which fails to carry through intended functions or objectives, while others are frustrated in their objectives because of the absence of any national or regional framework within which to operate. This last applies particularly to transport but also to other strategic issues. This gives rise to particular difficulties in the sense that major resourcing programmes and major strategic decisions are often based in or arise from the structures which have been formed rather than the needs and requirements of the capital and those who reside within it.

At the most local level, the responsibility for the widest range of public service and public administration still rests with individual boroughs, with average resident populations of just over 200,000. These currently hold responsibility for social and leisure services, housing, public highway, some transport functions, local planning matters, urban regeneration, inner city policy, environment, the servicing of direct work such as building works or refuse collection even where not carried out by the authority directly, and education. The borough administrations have a responsibility for rent collection, benefits administration, council tax collection and business tax collection. They are also, however, increasingly expected, within their own boundaries, to operate in partnership with other agencies, through precept or through either statutory or voluntary participation in bodies designed to deliver specific types of services.

A number of other organizations also attempt to operate forms of partnership. The most significant of these are the Training and Enterprise Councils (TECs) of which there are ten across the city. These were established by central government in 1990. They have responsibility (reporting directly to central government) for training and education for youths aged 16 and over, and for enterprise and employment work. However, in order to effect their youth training functions, they have to work in partnership with colleges of education and universities who now have a stand-alone existence and with local authorities. TECs are companies limited by guarantee with directors appointed by central government, principally from the private sector, but including two representatives from local government – from the executive, not the political level. Due to the varied nature of the remit with which TECs were entrusted, it has been difficult for them to do more within London than to establish and run the statutory training and education courses for which they have overall responsibility.

Although TECs were expected to prepare labour market analyses, few of them have actually prepared an audit of provision within their own boundary. As a result, programmes drawn up by TECs do not often relate to either the requirements of industry, either in the specific geographical area or in the wider London area. The fact that unitary development plans and economic development plans are drawn up on a statutory basis by boroughs, of which there may be four or five within a TEC area, complicates the situation still further.

As part of the programme to regenerate the docklands, the London Docklands Development Corporation (LDDC) was established. The LDDC covers a number of local authority areas and it was given wide powers to promote regeneration, including the final say over planning decisions. It is accountable directly to central government and does not have to answer to the local electorate. No other formal 'sub-regional' grouping of this sort exists. However, following the abolition of the GLC, boroughs recognized that they could not work exclusively on an individual borough basis on a range of issues, particularly with regard to transport. Some informal 'sub-regional' groupings were, therefore, set up to fill this gap. Although none has been statutorily established, nor have they in most cases sought government recognition, such recognition has been tacitly given. Example are groups established to promote the application for European regional development fund aid and the sub-regional group around the East Thames Corridor, for both of which government is a party to, and approves, the arrangements.

Such groups have come together primarily because of the absence of a pan-London authority in the capital, and of any strategic framework for the promotion of particular initiatives or proposals. It is arguable that the increased amount of work and activity involved in constructing this type of initiative would be unnecessary were there to be some overall frame-work for the development of London. Although few of these cross-borough organizations have explicit private sector involvement, there is a very high level of interaction between authorities within the groupings, both with individual private sector companies and organiza-tions of employers.

At the pan-London level there is a third series of partnerships and organizational arrangements. These include those with statutory arrangements such as the London Fire & Civil Defence Authority and the Metropolitan Police Authority, as well as the London Planning Advisory Committee (LPAC) which has a statutory responsibility for the drawing up of strategic guidance for London for land site planning. LPAC, in turn, is linked to a regional planning authority, SERPLAN (the South East Region Planning Authority), which has responsibility for overall strategic guidance for the South East Region including London.

These statutory areas of responsibility are complemented by a series of associations and informal arrangements which, although not having direct executive responsibility, influence policy development. Prominent ones include the London Boroughs Association, a grouping of Conservative-controlled boroughs, the Association of London Author-ities, a grouping of Labour-controlled boroughs, the Confederation of British Industry London region (representing the interests of business within the capital), and the London Chamber of Commerce. This last has decentralized with individual Chambers operating (with varying effect-iveness) in each of the London boroughs.

There are other less influential, but nonetheless, important associ-ations within the capital, notably the London Council for Voluntary Service and the Standing Conference of Churches. In 1992, a further major and pan-London grouping was established in the capital with the creation of London First. This arose out of two joint initiatives, one from central government and one from the private sector. Their aims, respect-ively, were to promote inward investment and to support the capital as a tourism and cultural centre; and to create 'a London which was capable of international promotion'. London First is primarily made up of private sector participants, with limited representation from local government, the churches, voluntary sector and from statutory organizations such as the health authority.

None of the organizations or groupings set out above has previously worked together on a totally joint basis, although some had previously worked with each other to promote specific partnership initiatives, for example in the East End. However, with the inception of a new national government programme to bring together all urban policy initiatives into a single regeneration budget and to create regional offices running across all central government departments to promote urban and regional development, a new imperative was placed on London-wide organizations to work together (by invitation from government) to establish a ten-year development plan for London. Accordingly, for the first time an informal steering committee has been established, on a pan-London basis, comprising the CBI, London Chamber of Commerce, London First, LBA, ALA, LPAC to oversee the production of a development plan. It will then have responsibility in the future for ensuring via the joint partners, that the plan is implemented.

These arrangements for London-wide development are intended to be reflected in the establishment of the new regional office of central government for London which, in a new departure, seeks to integrate the activities of several government departments. There is also a Minister for Transport in London and a new Cabinet Committee was established in 1993, comprising all the ministries to oversee London development at ministerial level. However, there have been few overt initiatives arising from either of these two government structures. The promotion of the East Thames Corridor is one such initiative, and there are also two major transport initiatives aimed at extending the underground system and capitalizing on the Channel Tunnel. The overall position with regard to future London development, therefore, remains uncertain. While there is no doubt that the acceptance on the ground and at government level of the need for integration of development programmes and the need for partnership between the private and public sector are two key elements of innovation, it is too early to say whether the other strategic fora will bring the benefits which might be expected of them. It must be better for the development of London to have cross-London co-operation, whether at the 'sub-regional' or pan-London level. In the same vein, improved relationships and partnerships between different sectors can only be beneficial.

However, the lack of any comprehensive strategic plan for London has severely hampered the operations of these fora. As a result, there is great discrepancy between areas where pan-London action has been taken and others where the approach continues to be fragmented. There have already been many instances of joint consultation and joint lobbying which have resulted in fairly wide consensual approach to transport in the city and agreements about the need for major projects and other changes in transport. In contrast, there has been almost no joint planning and no central approach towards matters such as housing policies, pan-London education and training requirements, nor a combined view on how to tackle polarization within the city. As this chapter demonstrates, the greatest area of strategic concern is the absence of a defined plan for the development of economic and industrial infrastructure for the capital.

Towards a more strategic approach

There is wide agreement amongst those with an interest in London on one thing: the need for a strategic London institution. Although opinions differ as to the nature of such an institution, there is a consensus that it should be streamlined. Many proposals for reform of London's system of government have been put forward. Hall (1989), for example, has called for a strategic planning body, while Cheshire and Gordon (1993), having investigated factors influencing the performance of urban regions in the European Union, assert that 'having a smaller number of authorities representing a functional economic region is helpful to the pursuit of competitive policies. It is significant in the contrast between London and Paris.' Hebbert (1992), similarly, argues that the London's difficulties are 'not in the structure of borough government, but in its superstructure'. Cheshire and Gordon argue that London has been handicapped by the conflicting interests of public agencies and inconsistency between the aims of the key manufacturing and banking and financial services sectors. This is exacerbated by conflict between central government departments concerned to promote sectional aims in competition both with other centrally controlled agencies and with local authorities.

Context

There can be little doubt that the next decade will see further major changes in the roles and performances of major cities. Looking at this question ten years ago, the OECD (1983) identified three major processes of structural change in the international economy of importance to the evolution of the urban system and hence London:

1   Broad movements in the international division of labour were a first factor, with much low-skilled assembly work being relocated to countries offering low labour costs.
2   In parallel, the OECD stressed the substitution of capital for labour as a fundamental structural change affecting city economies. In central business districts, office and leisure developments have tended to replace industrial and residential property.

3   The third factor cited by the OECD was the growth of the service
     sector, particularly of producer services and non-profit services
     which do not immediately serve local demand. Tourism has also
     emerged as a major growth sector.

The effects of these three broad processes are evident in the evolution of
London's economy in the last twenty years. Labour intensive manufacturing has declined substantially; other manufacturing has moved
away from inner city locations, and latterly also from the conurbations;
and the expansion of parts of the service sector has been the main source
of net new jobs. Now, however, a number of additional influences on
competitiveness are coming into play. Among these are:

- First, new communications technologies which can be expected not
  only to underpin the movement in the private sector towards
  decentralization in management, but also to increase the scope for
  fragmentation of the production process in services as well as
  manufacturing.
- The related phenomenon of the growing 'industrialization' of parts
  of the service sector, already evident in financial services. This is
  likely to reverse the trend of net employment creation of the 1980s
  and could mean that the structure of economic activity in London
  will be less favourable than in the past from the perspective of
  employment.
- Increasing concern from residents and businesses alike about the
  quality of the environment, in the widest sense of the term. Problems
  of social deprivation, congestion and degradation of the environment in parts of the city are reaching crisis proportions and it is
  particularly important in this regard to acknowledge the cumulative
  nature of these processes. These difficulties are exacerbated by fiscal
  pressures on local authorities arising from the increasing gap
  between public spending needs and a dwindling tax base, com-
  pounded by attempts by central government to cut public
  expenditure for macroeconomic policy reasons.
- The opening up of international competition in producer services,
  which is both an opportunity and a threat (Davis and Latter, 1989).

Until comparatively recently, London has also been on the wrong end of
UK spatial policy. Regional policy, traditionally, has been aimed at the
peripheral regions of Britain, and this has discriminated against the core.
New town and overspill policies actively sought to displace residents of
the major cities, especially London. Only in the last fifteen years or so has
policy been active in trying to regenerate inner urban areas, yet even this
belated shift has been beset by a lack of coherence and conflicts in
objectives, instruments and philosophies. In a memorable phrase, the

Audit Commission (1989) castigated urban policy thus: 'it is hard to escape the conclusion that at the level of the individual city there can be programme overkill within a strategic vacuum'.

Establishing priorities

The discussion above on strategic development highlighted a number of priorities that need consideration and showed how any strategy for London would need to operate at international/European, regional and local levels. It also emphasized the need to cross-reference pan-London strategic issues such as transport to other strategic considerations to have a full impact. This identifies economic and industrial strategy as the main issue, with land site development used as a resource to assist and support that strategy rather being its focus. It is too difficult within a single chapter such as this to set out all the issues on a comprehensive basis. What we attempt to do here is to draw together the primary horizontal and sectoral priorities.

If a strategy is to achieve more than the mere management of decline, then the two overarching priorities must be to improve the overall economic position and to address skill mismatch and access to jobs, particularly in those areas which have been most affected by increased unemployment. Even if such a two-fold strategy were to be exceptionally successful, it would still be insufficient to cope with the requirements of the long-term unemployed, and the sheer scale of unemployment in the London area. A further strategy would be needed to ensure greater mobility outside the capital as well as within it. This is not to deny the importance of many of the contextual horizontal issues such as transport infrastructure. What we argue, however, is that without a redressing of the economic position, efforts which are directed into these contextual areas will not yield the benefits expected.

We do not wish to suggest that there should be concentration in one area of the capital to the detriment of other areas. What we are arguing is that because there are considerable differences in the nature of problems in the different parts of the capital, policies to aid recovery and stabilization need to be tailored to them. The transport requirements, for example, of the east and south side of the capital are extensive due to historical lack of facilities in those areas, but it is also important to maintain and improve the transport infrastructure on the western and northern sides of the urban area to support business competitiveness.

The main problem with a business- and enterprise-led development strategy is that there is a dearth of material to inform such a strategy. No other city in the UK lacks a focused business and industrial development plan. Comparisons with other 'world cities' show that spatial redevelopment has been based upon a clear industrial and economic strategy which is linked (in the case of Germany or Japan) with an overall national economic framework. Both of these are absent in London.

A London strategy must recognize, but keep in perspective, the key role of the financial sector not only for the capital but also, as the findings of the *City Research Project* show (Brealey and Soria, 1993), for the UK economy overall. These sectors currently account for over 30 per cent of London's GDP and are, manifestly, central to London's prospects, but it must be open to question how much more they can expand given the overall size of the market for these services. It is important, therefore, not to have unrealistic expectations about how much more the financial and business services sectors can contribute to London's economy, especially, as noted above, in employment terms. At the same time, the complementarities between business services and manufacturing and the potential for enhancing links between the sectors deserve to be emphasized.

Tourism and leisure is the second largest sector of activity in London, and here a lack of information is a serious drawback. Although predicted growth is reasonable (16 per cent over the next 5 years – 14.8 million visitors projected in 2005), this is based simply on prior track record of 9–10 million visitors per year for the last 3 years and relies largely on projections of demand for extra hotel rooms within the capital. There is very little knowledge of the detail of the industry. This is particularly true of the areas south of the Thames area and in the East Thames Corridor which have not previously been much favoured by the industry. Consequently, although many high visibility flagship projects have been canvassed – London Thames Festival or even the Olympic Games – there is no strategic overview. In practice the main focus is on the provision of better transport facilities and signposting, or improved cleanliness overall in London. There is an urgent need to establish an in-depth assessment of the industry and all its assets and to develop a strategy for its growth. This would pick up, in particular, an already identified lack of training across industry as a whole. There is also a great need to understand the breadth of the industry, given that it cuts across conventional industrial classifications to embrace travel and accommodation, visual and performing arts, general leisure facilities, car sports, restaurants, museums, sightseeing etc.

The third key sector is manufacturing. The problem here is that while manufacturing accounts for barely 10 per cent of total employment in London, it is widely regarded as a critical part of the 'export base' through which income is earned. The scale of the decline in manufacturing has been rapid. Too little attention has been paid to knowledge- and technology-based manufacturing which ought to be a priority. What is most worrying is that links to financial services are not working as they might, especially in relation to high technology industry. Here again a lack of information is a barrier to development. An analysis of different types of manufacturing London-wide is required to look at those areas of business which have expansion potential, and in particular to promote innovation in manufacturing through partnership with academic and research organizations. Once these assessments have been made, there are several approaches which could be followed to assist the regeneration of manufacturing – development of technology parks, business support services, or collaboration between manufacturing and research institutes to promote innovation.

In each of these key industries, a similar lack of information and co-ordination of demand can be observed. This has led to shortcomings in the planning of developments of physical sites and potential regeneration areas within the capital. The projected uses of major sites bear little relationship to what the various industries, in aggregate, are able reasonably to support. Current plans show that the lesson has been learned with regard to oversupply of office space. However, much of site usage is in the 'general industry and warehousing use' category of land use. There is little development of industry-specific sites. This lack of connection with industrial and economic development showed itself most clearly in over-projection of office usage in the 1960s. It has began also to show itself in over-projection of housing provision within a certain market bracket within the major new developments in London Docklands. More recently, large-scale site clearances with prepared infrastructure and premium transport links in the Docklands have excited scarcely any interest. There is thus a pressing need for site usage and land site development to follow industrial and economic strategy and for some form of pan-London co-ordination of planning decisions that reflects overall demand for different uses.

The lack of developed industrial and economic strategic thinking is mirrored in the capital's performance in training and education. London region training provision is the lowest amongst UK regions. There is a poor level of under-fives provision leading to under-achievement throughout the school system and a substantial shortfall against pub-lished targets. Skill mismatch is clearly the primary problem. However, it is almost impossible to set provision in the capital against any projections that are required by industry, except on a very localized basis. Training and Enterprise Councils are required to produce a yearly assessment of their local labour market and a yearly business plan with targets, but as these are not produced on a pan-London basis, they can only relate to the localized area in which each of the ten Training and Enterprise Councils operate. In many areas, there has been no audit of provision such that it is extremely difficult to see whether the skill requirements are actually being matched to industrial and employment requirements and projec-tions for the future. It should be pointed out that TECs do not deliver the full range of programmes which might be promoted in any one area of the capital. They are relatively minor players compared for example with the London universities, the colleges of further and technical education and other providers of training both in the private and public sector.

Poor information on the labour market can lead to the development of ill-judged strategies. The question is whether the provision of training (which is increasingly based on market demand) really reflects the future needs of industry. Given that the universities and many of the colleges in the capital offer courses to students from outside London, a further question is whether the access of those resident in the capital to training provision is as developed as it might be. There is a need both for an immediate audit of provision and for a regular London-wide labour market analysis which has not been carried out for some time. Beyond this, there is a requirement to increase the number of organizations adopting quality training programmes or chartermark programmes; a need to establish a credit accumulation transfer scheme and to have a better integration of hiring education and business. These are very comprehensive requirements. However, we are convinced that were they to be put in place, radical changes could be made both to the provision of training in the capital and to the ability of the training system to meet the requirements of those seeking training. The ten Training and Enterprise Councils are the obvious focal points for such a shift to a proper and comprehensive training strategy. However, they would need to carry this out in tandem with a vast array of bodies and providers including the universities, colleges of further and technical education, local authorities and other providers. It is an undertaking which is substantial not simply in intellectual and strategic terms, but also in organizational terms.

The difficulties experienced by transport in the capital are very well documented and have long been a source of considerable anxiety and annoyance to visitors, residents and business alike. Although London has a well-developed transport system, it is not performing well. Average road traffic speeds are down to eleven miles per hour. There are poor intra-city connections and underuse of the river. Fare levels discourage use and the failure to modernize the underground system has been estimated to cost the UK 0.6 per cent of GDP per year. There are poor conditions for cycling and pedestrians. Observers from outside the UK might find the system of development somewhat bizarre – affected as it is by a constant lobby and representation system to central government rather than a clearly defined governmental plan for a strategy for the conurbation. The lobbying system has, however, resulted in a tremendous consensus both between the public and private sector on what is required. In addition, it is clear that a strategic integrated transport system is crucially needed with upgrading of key links and interchanges. Although the cost of these and other desirable measures is bound to be substantial, they are small set against the benefits which would accrue to the capital and the UK in terms of improved productivity and greater market competitiveness, attraction of increased visitors and improved visitor capacity.

There are a number of other contextual areas where improvement is needed but these are arguably less central to the development of the economic well-being of the capital than industrial development, training and transport. If the identified decline in specific areas in inner London is to be tackled and social polarization as seen in US cities is to be avoided, it is clear that there needs to be a retention of middle-income earners. This is further borne out by initial results from the 1991 census which show that, in general, there has been either no change in income levels or a fall in income levels. Thus, the retention of low- and middle-income earners is not simply a moral or social issue, it is also a market issue, as developers in Docklands during the late 1980s discovered when they were forced to lower purchase price, there being no market for the type of development originally envisaged. Similarly, there is no 'key workers' policy, leading to an unwillingness and an inability to locate within the capital. Although the severe recruitment problems experienced both by the public and private sectors in the mid-1980s show few signs of recurring, a key workers policy would enable a retention and attraction of middle-income earners. It would also potentially lower the number of those commuting into London.

House prices on average are as low as other world cities. The main housing problem is the mismatch between provision figures for dwellings between 1991 and 2006 and an estimate demand for 380,000 affordable dwellings. Social housing provision in other cities is much more comprehensive – in Tokyo for example it is 30 per cent, in Paris 40 per cent. The lack of affordable housing provision in London is due, in part, to the inflexibility of owner occupation but also reflects the need for a more integrated mix within public sector provision. There is therefore an urgent requirement to set need against capacity to reduce densities and achieve more integrated development activity and to forestall concentrations of disadvantage. Though not as acute as some other cities, it is clear that unemployment and poverty are rife in many large housing estates, rendering it very difficult to raise the level of activity within the local economy.

A major contextual area which is often raised by business and by residents is crime. Comprehensive efforts both by the Metropolitan Police and local government and local residents have resulted in some significant decreases in criminal activity – crime on the Underground for example has been reduced 15 per cent since 1987. In comparison to other world cities, London features extremely well in terms of safety. The perceptions of criminal activity in the capital are not helpful to London's overall image and this fear of crime needs to be tackled as well. Trends which gives rise to concern are crime inflicted on the poor by the poor and the high proportion of crime which is drug related. There is clearly a need to tackle drug trafficking (at present at a manageable level) before it begins to take over the inner areas of the capital.

Similarly, as with income and property, the health of inner city residents in the capital is giving rise to concern. There are poorly developed family doctor and community health services and inadequate premises for primary health care. There is a need for easier access to high quality cost-effective services, while accident and emergency services are badly located. There is a heavy cost of special care for the elderly and the mentally ill with insufficient residential provision. As with the role of universities in training, the national role carried out by the capital's hospital in specialist provision has been expanded at the expense of local secondary (general) hospital care. All of these matters are under review at present as part of a general health service review of services in the capital. Of primary importance must be the link between poor housing and inadequate diet and lack of adequate income – particularly in inner areas – a direct result both of unemployment, but also of low earning capacity.

The way forward

London's development has undoubtedly long been hindered by a lack of strategic vision of how the metropolis should develop. As Hall (1989) notes in contrasting the effectiveness of the 1944 Abercrombie *Greater London Plan* with the GLC's 1969 *Greater London Development Plan*, it is not the detail and the institutional framework which matter, but decisiveness in objectives and clarity in responsibility for implementation. He calls for 'a strong, slim strategic plan, Abercrombie-fashion, that will tell everyone what is going to happen and then allow them to get on and do it'.

London's position is far from irretrievable and there has been no shortage of proposals about how its economy and/or parts of it can be revitalized. The task for London as it looks towards the next century is to reconcile multiple development priorities and to find a way of assuaging competing sectional interests. This calls not merely for a means of co-ordinating the various economic actors and agencies with a remit to promote economic development, but also for a means of agreeing and implementing objectives. Such a function needs to go beyond the spatial planning or financial and administrative fora that are currently in place and which, in principle, already provide a pan-London framework, to give a full-blown and realistic plan for London. In particular, it has to encompass proposals for the economic development of London that are

both feasible and mutually consistent. Our view is that the main development priorities ought, therefore, to be:

Ensuring a strong economic base

This entails the consolidation of London's status as a 'world city' alongside development of its role as a UK and regional centre. It also calls
for sector-specific action to bolster key industries such as tourism,
financial services, or public administration, as well as a search for new
specializations.

High quality physical infrastructure and environment

The competitiveness of the economic base is inextricably linked to the
quality and efficiency of the infrastructure. This requires attention both
to basic physical sites and networks, and to enhancement of the environment. Natural assets such as the river frontage need to be preserved and
upgraded, transport systems have to be improved, and pollution reduced.
Equally, efforts must be made to ensure accessibility and to make the city
safe and pleasant to live in or visit.

Maximizing the human potential of residents

This too has several dimensions. Access to housing and amenities needs
to be complemented by effective policies to give individuals meaningful economic opportunities and to avoid social, ethnic, or economic
ghettos.

How can these be advanced? There is little nostalgia for the GLC, nor
any political likelihood that such a body could be reconstituted, but it is
hard to escape the conclusion that London badly needs an agency with a
remit to set policy strategically in a range of policy areas. This inevitably
opens a hornet's nest of awkward questions about the powers and
responsibilities that such a body should have, and how to ensure its
accountability. But such problems should not be allowed to obscure the
underlying need for it. There are already encouraging signs of institutional reform, such as the possibility of a merger between the Association
of London Authorities and the London Boroughs Association. The
development of the London prospectus and the need to implement it
have been a catalyst for unprecedented co-operation between the public
and private sectors and between political parties.
    It is useful to sketch out some characteristics and tasks that a strategic
authority should have, and how it might relate to other levels of public

administration. A first stipulation is that it should have sufficient authority both to arrive at decisions by mediating between different parties and to ensure that once the decision is taken, it is acted upon. This implies a direct relationship between such a body and borough-level government. Whether this power is vested in an elected mayor (as, for example, in Paris or New York) or takes the form of an appointed council (as is the case for the European Commission) is a matter for debate. It is, however, clear to us that the institutional form should be tailored to the tasks and functions to be carried out. In this regard, we see the primary task as being to manage the London economy. This entails a capacity for data gathering and analysis so as to identify priorities.

A further desirable feature is responsiveness allied to a capacity for strategic analysis. If the preceding assessment is accepted, London needs both a sense of direction that is apt to be lacking in some of the more woolly statements of 'vision' as well as flexibility to adapt to a rapidly changing national and international economic environment. To achieve this, what is needed is a body able to stand back from day-to-day concerns of government, yet also able to think through the consequences of change. This suggests that the executive powers vested in it should be limited in order to avoid it becoming embroiled in routine policy delivery. Nevertheless, once suitable consultations have been undertaken, a strategic body will need, when necessary, to exercise a power to override borough-level objections when the wider interest of the London economy is at stake. Making this palatable means that the ownership and commitment of different stakeholders are crucial, so that effective channels for such participation in the elaboration of plans are vital.

It is also essential that the many *ad hoc* forms of public–private partnership that have evolved in recent years be consolidated and extended. There is now sufficient positive experience of co-operation between local government, other agencies and the private sector, based on a variety of arrangements entered into in recent years, to suggest that this can be achieved. Accordingly, we advocate the creation of a strategic body able to draw on a wide range of expertise and commitment, but which ultimately has the executive power to ensure that key projects and developments take place. Experience shows that major reorganizations of service delivery are time-consuming, costly and often disruptive. London, as can be seen from the scale of the problems highlighted in this chapter, simply cannot afford an hiatus. We propose, consequently, to redirect existing efforts, rather than to seek wholesale change. For the most part, implementation can be carried out by existing agencies of public administration that have developed the necessary expertise and are, thus, the appropriate means of policy delivery. However, for major projects or initiatives, a seconded task force may be considered. If further institutional changes seem desirable, they can then be brought in incrementally and in the light of evaluation of existing procedures.

Conclusions

The long-run decline of the London economy and the particular difficulties which the conurbation has encountered in the downturn since 1990 are issues of concern not just for the residents of the capital, but also for the well-being of the UK economy. They point to a need for a strategic response in which full account is taken of the various facets of London. This must take a broad view of development priorities, and, in particular, lead to a strategy for the economy in conjunction with physical planning and other functions. In this chapter, we have advocated the creation of a new, overarching forum to guide the development of London. This body should, while working with other tiers of government, have effective executive powers and be capable of tough action when necessary. Unless meaningful changes of this sort are introduced, the likelihood is that many symptoms of decline in London will worsen with serious consequences for the UK economy.

The most striking conclusion from a cross-referencing of the strategic business and horizontal aims is that stabilization and development of the economy must be the first priority for the London of the future. To achieve this, there needs to be a growth of specific key sectors and a climate to enable this to happen. While consolidation of the service and finance sectors is very important and will give a leading edge, the need for a more diversified economic base is vital. In particularly, more efforts are needed to develop manufacturing and to ensure that it is encouraged to enhance innovation. Business success will be dependent on the development of growth sectors within a climate which ensures world city excellence in major areas such as transport, personal safety, housing, culture and leisure provision. However, the creation of such a climate should not be the be-all and end-all of development concern as it has been up to now. It is clear that there needs to be better management of the economy and more assistance and support given to industry to develop within the capital.

The future well-being of London will depend upon the realistic development of the different parts of the conurbation, targeted to make best use of the strengths of different localities. That a specific strategy is required for East London and the East Thames Corridor is without doubt. This has already been recognized in Objective 2 and Assisted Area Status for the capital. However, the land site development strategy needs to be linked to an industrial strategy. The retention of middle-income earners is extremely important particularly if they are key workers. Unemployment has occurred through skill mismatch, inappropriate and inadequate training and a lack of mobility intra city or outside the city. All of these major issues need to be addressed urgently. There is also a need to identify key geographic points in London for future development. It is clear that there are certain areas which strategically could help to change the nature of activity in London for the future – Stratford and the Channel Tunnel Rail Link is a prime example of such an area. These are the policy challenges.

References

Audit Commission (1989), *Urban Regeneration and Economic Development: the Local Government Dimension*. London, HMSO.

Begg, I.G. (1993), 'Industrial policy, high technology industry and the regions', in Harrison, R. and Hart, M. (eds), *Spatial Policy in a Divided Nation*. London, Jessica Kingsley.

Begg, I.G., Moore, B., Rhodes, J. (1986), 'Economic and social change in urban Britain and the inner cities', in Hausner, V. (ed.), *Critical Issues in Urban Economic Development*. Oxford, Clarendon Press.

Brealey, R.A., Soria, M. (1993), 'Revenues from the City's financial services', *City Research Project*, paper (mimeo).

Brunet, R. (1989), *Les Villes Européenes*. Paris, La Documentation Française.

Cambridge Econometrics (1994), *Regional Economic Prospects*. Cambridge, Cambridge Econometrics.

Cheshire, P.C., D'Arcy, E., Giussani, B. (1992), 'Purpose built for failure? Local, regional and national government in Britain', *Environment and Planning C*, 10.

Cheshire, P.C., Gordon, I.R. (1993), 'European integration: territorial competition in theory and practice', *Territorial Competition and the Single European Market*, working paper No. 2, CeSAER, University of Reading.

Davis, E.P., Latter, A.R. (1989), 'London as an International Financial centre', *Bank of England Quarterly Bulletin*, 29(4).

Evans, A.W., Crampton, G. (1989), 'Myth, reality and employment in London', *Journal of Transport Economics and Policy*, 23: 89–108.

Frey, W.H. (1993), 'The new urban revival in the US', *Urban Studies*, 30: 741–74.

Frost, M., Spence, N. (1993), 'Global city characteristics and central London's employment', *Urban Studies*, 30: 547–58.

Hall, P. (1989), *London 2001*. London, Unwin Hyman.

Hebbert, M. (1992), 'Governing the capital', in Thornley, A. (ed.), *The Crisis of London*. London, Routledge.

Jones Lang Wootton (1992), *Decentralisation of Offices from Central London*. London, JLW Research.

Kennedy, T. (1992), *London World City Moving into the 21st Century*. London, HMSO.

London Research Centre (1992), *Paris-London, A Comparison of Transport Systems*. London, HMSO.

LPAC (1994), *1994 Advice on Strategic Planning Guidance for London*. London, LPAC.

Noyelle, T.J., Stanback, T.M. (1984), *The Economic Transformation of American Cities*. Totowa, New Jersey, Rowman and Allanheld.

OECD (1983), *Managing Urban Change, Policies and Finance*. Paris, OECD.

Robson, B. (1988), *Those Inner Cities, Reconciling the Social and Economic Aims of Urban Policy*. Oxford, Oxford University Press.

Sassen, S. (1991), *London, New York, Tokyo*. Princeton, Princeton University Press.

Thornley, A. (1992), 'Introduction', in Thornley A. (ed.), *The Crisis of London*. London, Routledge.

Part III

The internationalization of local economic development strategies

7

The role of the European Union in local economic development

MICHAEL CHAPMAN

Introduction

The purpose of this chapter is to discuss the role of the European Union (EU) in local economic development. A key objective of the EU is to address all aspects of economic and social disadvantage at the European, national, regional and local level. European support for locally based development strategies includes rural and urban areas but in a period of growing European political and economic integration there is a growing awareness that the most acute forms of economic and social disadvantage are to be found in European towns and cities. Even in the relatively favourable economic circumstances of the late 1980s there appears to have been a continuation in the economic and social divisions between the rich and the poor in many urban areas. To understand this process Hall (1994) identifies seven major forces which have influenced the European urban hierarchy and these include: the globalization of the world economy and the formation of continental trading blocs; the transformation of Eastern Europe; the shift towards the informational economy; the impact of transport technology; the impact of information technology; the role of urban promotion and boosterism; and the impact of demographic and social change. Of fundamental importance in our understanding of European urban change has been the globalization of the world economy (see Chapter 1). The growth of the informational sector and the need for greater specialization within regions have brought about a new form of comparative advantage between cities leading, in Europe, to the deindustrialization of many older cities and the rise of a select group of information- and technology-rich cities.

The transformation and globalization affecting the economies of countries within the EU have not occurred in a vacuum. For the past twenty years, Europe has experienced rapid and complex changes to its economic and social situation. While the majority of European citizens have enjoyed the benefits of improved economic and social conditions there has been a significant and growing minority who have experienced unemployment, poverty and other forms of economic and social exclusion. Terms such as the excluded, the marginalized and the underclass have been increasingly used to draw attention to new patterns of inequality in the urban environment. At the same time and for various reasons policies have been developed which respond or react to the restructuring of the European economy. Among such policies are those specifically concerned with the promotion of economic and social cohesion at the European level (European Foundation for the Improvement of Living and Working Conditions, 1994).

Although the level of financial support available from the European Commission (EC) is relatively small compared to expenditure by individual member states on regional and urban policy, it is therefore unlikely that European funding alone would make any significant impact on the economic, environmental and social problems confronting urban areas.

Atkinson and Moon (1994) argue, in the case of the UK, that the European dimension is unlikely to make any significant impact on spatial disparities given the scale and nature of the urban and regional problem in the UK and the limited financial resources available from Europe. However, across the individual member states policy-makers increasingly recognize the importance of European policies and programmes and their benefit to the urban environment. As Robson (1994) notes, during a period of increasing economic, environmental and social stress in our cities many local authorities, especially in the larger metropolitan areas in the UK, have sought to utilize the European financial option.

The changing European urban environment

Although 80 per cent of the population of the EU live in urban areas, the EC has no direct competence for urban affairs. There is no integrated framework for urban policy at the European level as there is for transport, the environment or for the reduction in regional disparities. In keeping with the principle of subsidiarity, as outlined by the agreement of the European Council in Maastricht, December 1991, the responsibility for local economic development measures rests with the individual member states and corresponding regional and local authorities. But it is becoming increasingly apparent that the activities and policies of the EU do in fact either indirectly or directly impact on the urban environment. The recognition of the vital role to be played by cities and urban regions in the future integrated and expanded Europe is reflected in a series of reports published by the Commission (CEC, 1990; 1991 and 1992a). Of even far greater importance, however, is the development of recent EC legislation and research which has continued to identify new roles and spheres of activity for the EU in combating economic and social problems in European cities (CEC, 1992b, f).

Through the mid-1970s and 1980s policy-makers increasingly drew attention to the growing economic and social problems confronting urban areas (Cheshire and Hay, 1989). This led to the development and implementation of specific urban-based local economic development strategies at a national level. Accompanied also by the support from the EC via aspects of European economic and social policy; environmental policy, the anti-poverty programmes and initiatives are meant to combat social exclusion. All of these policies and programmes sought to address the emerging economic and social disparities between and within European cities. The EU has advanced through the introduction of the Single European Market (SEM), the creation of a single frontier-free market across the member states of the Community by 1992, the idea being that a large domestic market in Europe would not only strengthen the competitive position of European business but also lead to the improvement of the economic prospects for the Community as a whole. This process was intensified by the signing of the Treaty of Union (CEC, 1992c) which outlined a timetable for future economic, monetary and political integration. Through the process of continued integration and achieving economic and social cohesion across the Community, European cities have now established themselves on the political agenda. Although economic changes have made urban areas important centres of political power, in the post-Maastricht Europe, a debate is developing over the need for a more explicit Europe-wide urban policy. Currently almost all European cities have some areas or districts which have been run down or suffer from urban decay. Cities and city regions across Europe are arguing the case for a stronger leading role from the Commission in urban affairs. The challenge for the EU is how to address the needs of a significant and growing minority of European citizens who have been unable to benefit from the opportunities provided by the SEM and the moves towards economic and social cohesion. This minority of the urban population increasingly suffers from poverty, unemployment and other forms of economic and social disadvantage. As work published by the European Foundation for the Improvement of Living and Working Conditions suggests:

> In the late 1980s and 1990s change will be qualitatively very different from that of the last quarter of a century and the patterns and processes of urban growth and decline will in consequence be very different. Some shifts are already evident – counterurbanization and the growth of medium-sized or

small towns, return migration, long-term unemployment, major changes in patterns of family and household function. Living conditions in the 1990s will be a consequence of, and a reflection of the response to, these discontinuities and shifts in the direction of change. (European Foundation, 1986: 155)

Although there is no implicit European urban policy it is evident that urban areas are benefiting both directly and indirectly from European policies. Across Europe cities and metropolitan areas have received substantial levels of financial support from the Commission. This position has been even further strengthened with the introduction of the latest review of the Community Structural Funds (CEC, 1993a). Total population coverage under the Structural Funds has increased from 43 per cent to just under 52 per cent of the Community total, although half of this increase is due in part to the inclusion of the new German Länder since the unification of Germany in 1990.

Since the early 1980s the EC has been interested in urban change and monitoring the significant structural, demographic, economic and social changes that have taken place in many European cities. In 1990 the Commission produced its *Green Paper on the Urban Environment* (CEC, 1990), which identified the range of problems being experienced in European cities and suggested that the Community could take certain lines of action in areas such as transport, historical heritage, environmental heritage, industry, energy management, urban waste and urban planning. While the Green Paper was mainly concerned with urban environmental quality, nevertheless it represents an important step towards the establishment of an Europe-wide urban policy. This was the first time the Commission had broached the issue of whether the Community wanted to extend financial support for urban regeneration and environmental improvement over and above previous levels as allowed through the operation of the Structural Funds. The importance of understanding the impact of Europe-wide spatial change was further enhanced by the report *Europe 2000 – Outlook for the Development of the Community's Territory* (CEC, 1991). This report demonstrated that EC policies were having and would continue to have a significant impact on the land use and physical planning in urban areas of individual member states. As part of the work towards *Europe 2000* several other background reports were published by the Commission. One such report concentrated on the competitive position of European cities and was commissioned by DG XVI of the Commission. *Urbanisation and the Functions of Cities in the European Community* (CEC, 1992a) which identified, through the study of 24 European city case studies, several key problems associated with the European urban environment. The report argued that the function of European cities was changing and a key factor to explain this change was the importance given to the creation of the Single Market. The study clearly identified that successful cities would be those urban areas which had the ability to compete in the SEM through diversification of local economic structures, attracting inward investment and servicing new markets throughout the whole of the Community. Examples of these dynamic cities included Hamburg, Rotterdam, Dortmund, Montpellier and Seville. Those cities which failed to adapt to the competitive pressure would be those which, with severe structural weaknesses in their urban economies, have inadequate infrastructure and communications and would often be a branch-plant economy. Cities in this position included Marseilles, Dublin and Naples (CEC, 1992a).

Widening the debate: the social dimension to future urban integration and cohesion

Previous debates over the need for a European urban policy have tended to focus on the European urban system and how individual cities have coped with the economic restructuring, the implications of the globalization of production, the need for improved environmental awareness in the urban environment and the economic and social uncertainties caused by the introduction of the SEM (Cheshire and Hay, 1989; Hall, 1994). But more significant changes in policy direction can be identified in the wider context of economic and social cohesion. During a period of continuing European integration a question arises over the economic and social integration of disadvantaged groups in the population and in particular the integration of such groups in urban environments. The EU cannot be developed without internal cohesion and the future of European integration depends on the development of a social dimension to Community-wide policies. The growing risk for individual member states is that the economic, demographic and social pressures which are affecting European urban environments may continue and add to the polarization of the urban population. As Padraig Flynn, the Commissioner for Employment and Social Affairs, adequately states in the introduction to the text *Towards a Europe of Solidarity*:

> Europe faces many challenges, but one of the most difficult, which emerged in the 1970s and 1980s, is the changing nature and increasing incidence of poverty and deprivation. Whereas the Community entered the 1990s with a great deal of confidence, mainly on the foot of the prospects offered by the Single Market, at the same time, there were growing signs that the social situation of Europe's citizens might not be making equally positive progress. The effects of the world recession have intensified fears that social exclusion – a complex blend of interrelated factors – could become a persistent feature of the European Social Landscape. (CEC, 1992b)

The processes that have shaped the urban environments of many European cities are likely to persist for the foreseeable future (European Foundation for the Improvement of Living and Working Conditions, 1990). Industrial decline and economic restructuring in the inner city areas and the outer estates have resulted in the combination of physical and social decline with high concentrations of unemployment in specific urban areas.

> In the 60s and 70s complaints about the condition of old housing were in many areas dealt with by destroying whole neighbourhoods – 'clearing the slums' – and building 'high rise' blocks in their place or building new outer estates ... where the land was cheaper. Several forms of social damage were compounded in the worst of these schemes. Local networks and attachments were disrupted by the summary dispersal of residents to a variety of different and unfamiliar localities, the character of the new housing was often designed purely as a space for a few dwellings, not understood as needing to serve a variety of social functions calling for a variety of amenities. ... In addition these areas were characterised by a concentration of problem households, or households with a particular characteristic in common, such as single parent families, in particular estates or neighbourhoods. This has led to a compounding of the problems as there has not been a natural variety of ages, conditions and roles in the local population. (European Foundation, 1989)

As the EU develops a better understanding of urban change it has also developed a better understanding of the impacts of change and the effect change has had on urban areas and urban communities:

> The changing urban environment reflects the changing nature of national and international labour markets, changing fiscal priorities and changing life styles. For some groups this will enhance both living and working conditions. But for others, notably lower income, elderly and young single adults, single parent families and ethnic minorities, opportunities are likely to be constrained. A shrinking job market, the physical decay of the residential stock in many countries, public expenditure restraint and increased resources to market solutions, promise a more hostile urban environment for low income households. (European Foundation, 1986)

The term which is used to describe this problem is 'social exclusion'. The notion of social exclusion refers to the multiple and changing factors which result in people being excluded from the normal exchange, practices and rights of modern society. Poverty is one of the most obvious factors which can indicate social exclusion, but social exclusion also refers to inadequate rights in housing, education, health and access to services. Social exclusion affects individuals as well as certain groups in society. It can be identified in urban areas and rural areas alike, as people are in some way subject to discrimination or segregation. These conditions when combined with low income levels have produced a series of problems which can be summarized as follows;

(i) Lack of access to amenities, facilities and services which should be available;
(ii) Lack of mobility to jobs and career opportunities which would improve social position;
(iii) Lack of residential mobility to areas with better prospects;
(iv) Lack of choice in buying goods and services;
(v) Not receiving due health care, social support and education. (European Foundation for the Improvement of Living and Working Conditions, 1990: 95)

Data to illustrate these trends are problematic at the level of the EU. Each member state is affected by social exclusion but the attributes of the form of exclusion mirror the precise problems experienced by different countries and particular urban areas. The most recent comparable figures for the whole of the Community relate to 1985; since then most observers would comment that the position across the Community and in individual member states has become much worse. In 1985 in the twelve member states of the European Community it was estimated that over 50 million people were poor; 14 million people were unemployed, of which more than half were out of work for at least one year, and about a third were out of work for at least two years; 33 per cent of the long-term jobless had never worked; 35 per cent of the unemployed were less than 25 years old; 18 per cent of those aged under 25 were unemployed and 3 million people in the Community were homeless (CEC, 1993e).

The Treaty on European Union ratified in 1993 placed a strong emphasis on the need for the Community to achieve the necessary conditions to allow economic and social cohesion. Economic and social cohesion is seen as a prerequisite for the future enlargement as well as the economic, political and social development of the Community. This commitment was reflected in the provision for the establishment of a Cohesion Fund. The purpose of the Cohesion Fund, established under the Maastricht Treaty to work alongside existing European policy instruments, is to assist in the transition towards economic and monetary union for member states whose per capita GDP is under 90 per cent of the Community average. The Cohesion Fund will assist countries including Greece, Portugal, Ireland and Spain through supporting projects in the fields of environmental protection and trans-European networks. For the period 1993 to 1999 15.5 billion ECU have been earmarked for the fund.

Other significant policy documents which highlight the need for the Community to address barriers to cohesion include the 'Delors' *White Paper on Growth, Competitiveness and Employment* (CEC, 1993c). The

White Paper published at the end of 1993 outlines the proposals from the Commission that the Community itself should set a target of creating at least 15 million new jobs, thereby halving the present rate of unemployment by the year 2000. The level of European unemployment is the prime consideration behind the White Paper, but it does acknowledge the fact that no one single response could tackle these persistent levels of unemployment. Instead, responses and efforts towards providing new employment opportunities call for adaptation in behaviour and policies at Community, national and local levels. Each member state is encouraged to take from the document the element it regards as relevant for its own socio-economic situation. The need to address persistent levels of unemployment is also reflected in the Conclusions to the Belgium Presidency after the meeting of the European Council, in Brussels, on 10 and 11 December 1993. The European Council adopted an action plan which consists of a general framework for policies to be pursued at member state level to promote employment. The Green Paper on social policy was designed to encourage debate across Europe about the future direction and shape of European social policy (CEC, 1993b). The publication of the more recent White Paper on Social Policy – *A Way Forward for the Union* (CEC, 1994c) – establishes the main trends of European social policy. Although Europe requires a broad-based, innovative and forward-looking social policy, unemployment and the need for jobs are top of the policy agenda. The proposals on employment and training become an integral part of the policy response to unemployment initiated by the *White Paper on Growth, Competitiveness and Employment* (CEC, 1993c).

European policies to promote economic and social cohesion in the urban environment

European cities have been quick to realize the importance of access to EC policies and programmes. This does not mean that gaining financial support from the Commission is an easy option. Often obtaining funds requires well-thought-out planning, good quality bids which reflect an understanding of current European priorities and regulations, and the need for match funding from alternative and non-EC sources. The most significant source of European funding towards economic and social cohesion comes from the Community's Structural Funds. Other programmes with less financial resources offer opportunities for specific policy developments and include areas such as the Community Initiatives and the Human Resource Initiative which assists in employment training. There are also opportunities for cities and urban areas to participate in European networks and innovative measures, like the RECITE programme.

In the recent reform of Community's Structural Funds (CEC, 1993a) greater attention has been given to the problems experienced by urban areas. Cities across the EU have benefited from Community action in financial and policy terms during the period 1989–93. For the period 1994–99, a more ambitious and co-ordinated approach is being introduced by the EC which concentrates on the following areas;

- Continuation and strengthening of the financial support to cities which belong to regions or areas which are eligible under the Structural Funds, in particular for Objective 1 and 2 areas.
- Further research on issues linked to urban problems in particular through the new Fourth Research Framework Programme.
- Further introduction of the urban dimension in the formulation of various Community policies.
- A continuing dialogue with cities and their organizations, in particular through the newly established Committee of Regions.
- The launch of a new Community initiative for urban areas aiming to promote innovative actions which can be used as examples to be diffused in cities across the European Union and promotion of networks of exchange of experience and co-operation.

In order to understand the impact of the EU on local economic development policy in an urban context it is necessary to review the main European policy instruments and the implications they have for intervention in the urban environment as a mechanism to achieve economic and social cohesion.

The Structural Funds

In 1989, the per capita income of the ten lowest-ranking regions of the Community was less than a third of that of the ten highest-ranking regions, while unemployment for the ten worst hit regions was up to seven times greater than in the ten most fortunate regions in the Community. The reduction of regional disparities is considered to be one of the principal tasks for the EC and the chief mechanism used to achieve economic and social cohesion is collectively known as the Structural Funds. The Structural Funds are the principal policy instruments through which the Community supports the member states to achieve economic and social cohesion. The prime objective of these funds is to alleviate regional disparities between the most advanced and the less developed regions in the Community but it also implies a need to reduce disparities in living standards, infrastructure provision and employment opportunities.

The commitment to the Structural Funds was strengthened in 1988 with an agreed doubling (in real terms) of Structural Fund expenditure in order to tackle the regional imbalances posed by the Single European Act. In December 1992 at the European Council Meeting in Maastricht it was agreed that to ensure economic and political union then it would be necessary to strengthen the economic and social cohesion between the member states of the Community. As a response to the Maastricht debate the Commission published proposals for Structural Fund action after 1992. The principles underlying structural measures since 1989 were maintained. These principles centred on the need still to concentrate funding on the lagging regions in the Community and on the defined Community Objectives for development; to continue to implement a programme-based approach to regional problems; to emphasis the need for partnership in this process which involves close collaboration between the Commission and all the relevant and competent authorities and bodies; and additionality, which means that Community assistance complements the contributions of the member states rather than reducing them.

The new regulations governing the operation of the Structural Funds for the period 1994 to 1999 were introduced in 1993 (CEC, 1993a). The financial resources for the Structural Funds for the period 1994–9 will amount to 141.471 billion ECU. The Community's Structural Funds comprise the following:

- European Regional Development Fund (ERDF) which supports environmental and tourism projects, investment in infrastructure and assistance to small and medium-sized firms.
- European Social Fund (ESF) which supports training, retraining and vocational guidance with particular emphasis on young people and the long-term unemployed.
- European Agricultural Guidance and Guarantee Fund (EAGGF) which supports measures to speed up the adjustment of agricultural structures with a view to the reform of the Common Agricultural Policy.
- Financial Instrument for Fisheries Guidance (FIFG) which supports measures to speed up the adjustment of fisheries structures with a view to reforming the Common Fisheries policy.

It is not possible here to detail the mechanisms of each fund (for a presentation of the ERDF, see Chapter 9). The point is that they are to play an important role in the funding of local development initiatives. To give an example, the European Social Fund (ESF), in the context of eight million long-term unemployed in the EU and with many young people lacking the basic skills required by the labour market, has concentrated on retraining schemes for the long-term unemployed and special programmes to assist those under the age of twenty-five to get a job. Other groups that have benefited from the operation of the ESF include workers threatened with unemployment, women, migrants and workers in medium-sized enterprises. During the period 1989–93 the ESF devoted more than 21 billion ECU to these activities. These funds were distributed on the basis of operational programmes prepared by government departments of the member states in conjunction with competent authorities at the national, regional and local level. The ESF has been particularly important for urban areas as it performs an important role in influencing the urban labour market through training programmes and initiatives.

The Structural Funds are allocated to five priority Objectives for development and eligibility for funds is dependent on regions being classified in relation to these objectives. Table 7.1 illustrates the amendments to the priority Objectives in the revised regulations.

Other amendments to the Structural Funds apart from the priority Objectives concern eligibility criteria, programming periods and the simplification of administration procedures. Resources for the Structural Funds for the period 1994–9 will amount to 141.471 billion ECU at 1992 prices. This is roughly one third of the Community budget. This financial effort is only modest when viewed in terms of the resources deployed by the member states. However, it does signify the intent of the EC to pursue the goals of economic and social cohesion. Top priority for expenditure is still being given to regions whose development is lagging behind (Objective 1). These regions will receive about 96.346 billion ECU or about 70 per cent of the total budget. The remaining 45.125 billion ECU is divided among the other Objectives.

Community Initiatives

The major share or 90 per cent of the Structural Fund budget is used to support measures undertaken at the initiative of the member states. The EC also part-finances a series of measures which are proposed by the Commission itself, the Community Initiatives. The Community Initiatives provide the Commission with the opportunity to activate measures of special interest to the Community as a whole. Between 1989 and 1993 just under 10 per cent of Structural Fund commitment appropriations were allocated to the Community Initiatives, although they were criticized by the member states and the Commission itself due to the excessive number of initiatives, the administrative effort required to implement them and the restrictive geographical eligibility criteria surrounding their operation.

While acknowledging these criticisms the Commission has maintained that the Community Initiatives do perform a useful role as an instrument of Community policy, enabling measures to be undertaken which go beyond national boundaries. Following the publication of the Green

Table 7.1 Priority objectives for Structural Funds

Former Regulations 1989–1993	Revised Regulations 1994–1999
The 1988 reform had established five priority objectives for the Structural Funds.	
Objective 1: development and structural adjustment of the regions whose development is lagging behind.	The revised Regulations do not amend the definition of **Objectives 1 and 2**.
Objective 2: converting the regions or parts of regions seriously affected by industrial decline.	
Objective 3: combating long-term employment (more than twelve months).	The **new Objective 3** combines the tasks of the current Objectives 3 and 4 and also aims at 'facilitating the integration … of those threatened with exclusion from the labour market'.
	The **new Objective 4** must give effect to the new tasks laid down for the ESF in the Maastricht Treaty: 'to facilitate workers' adaptation to industrial changes and to changes in production systems'.
With a view to the reform of the common agricultural policy: **Objective 5a**: speeding up the adjustment of agricultural structures.	**Objective 5** aims to promote rural development: **Objective 5a** maintains its initial goal of speeding up the adjustment of agricultural structures as part of the CAP reform, but it also includes aid to modernize and restructure fisheries.
Objective 5b: development of rural areas.	**Objective 5b** facilitates the 'development and structural adjustment of rural areas'.
Objectives 1, 2 and 5b are specifically regional in nature; they involve measures restricted to certain eligible regions or parts of regions.	In accordance with the conclusions of the Edinburgh Council of 1992, the revised Regulations make provision to include areas which are suffering from a decline in **fishing activity** in regions or areas eligible under regional Objectives, by including appropriate new criteria for Objectives 2 and 5b.
Objectives 3, 4 and 5a cover the whole of the Community.	

Source: CEC (1993a).

Paper on the future of the Community Initiatives (1994a), the Commission has gone some way to address some of the criticisms levelled at the Initiatives. The Initiatives have been regrouped around five major priorities (Table 7.2), with greater transparency in budget allocations between the member states and the Commission and a more flexible approach towards the geographical eligibility criteria.

At the end of Autumn 1993, the Commission agreed that the financial framework for the period 1994–9 would total 13.45 billion ECU, 9 per cent of the Structural Fund commitment over this period. By June 1994 the Commission had adopted the final guidelines for each initiative. The programmes are to be proposed by the member states and these will then be adopted by the Commission. The programmes concentrate on seven themes:

- Cross Border Co-operation: INTERREG (3 billion ECU);
- Local Development in Rural Areas: LEADER (1.4 billion ECU);
- Support for the most Remote Regions: REGIS (600 million ECU);
- The Integration into the working life of Women, Young People and the Disadvantaged: EMPLOYMENT (1.4 billion ECU);
- Adaptation to Industrial change: ADAPT, SME, RECHAR, KONVER, RESIDER, RETEX etc. (3.8 billion ECU);
- Urban Policy: URBAN (600 million ECU);
- Restructuring the Fisheries Sector: PESCA (250 million ECU). (CEC, 1994d: 12)

Many European organizations including the European Parliament, made strong recommendations for expanding the current list of Community Initiatives. One measure to be established was the URBAN initiative which will specifically assist urban areas and tackle problems linked to social exclusion. The URBAN Community Initiative has been allocated 600 million ECU from the Structural Funds with 400 million ECU designated to towns situated in Objective 1 regions. Eligible areas will concentrate on urban neighbourhoods in cities in the Objective 1, 2 and 5b regions with a population of more than 100,000. There are some 350–400 cities in the EU which meet this criterion but only a limited number of cities will be assisted and the Commission are thinking of a maximum of 50 projects.

The target areas for the URBAN initiative will be identifiable geographical administrative units, within a densely populated area, minimum size of population, high level of unemployment, decayed urban fabric, bad housing conditions and a lack of social amenities. Programmes will have to be integrated, innovative and provide a basis for exchange of experience in the national and European context. Programmes supported by the initiative are expected to include measures

Table 7.2 Community initiatives: Regulations

Community Initiatives	(ECU million at 1989 prices)	Former Regulations 1989–93	Revised Regulations 1994–9
Envireg	500	Protection of the environment and development in the regions	On 16 June 1993 the Commission published a Green Paper on the Community Initiatives. This document is not an official proposal but a discussion paper on the future of these initiatives.
Interreg	800	Cross-border co-operation	
Rechar	300	Diversion in coal-mining regions	
Stride	400	Research, technology, development and innovation in the regions	The Green Paper has been submitted to all the parties concerned for their comments: the other Community institutions (European Parliament, Economic and Social Committee), the member states, plus the regions, local authorities and the two sides of industry. In the Green Paper, the Commission suggests five topics for future Community Initiatives:
Regen	400	Energy networks	
Telematique	200	Advanced telecommunication services	
Prisma	100	Services to businesses in connection with the single market	
Euroform	300	New skills and qualifications	•cross-border, transnational and inter-regional co-operation and networks (Interreg and Regen energy supply networks)
Now*	120	Equal opportunities for women on the labour market	
Horizon*	180	Access to the labour market for the handicapped and other disadvantaged groups	•rural development (Leader) •assistance to the outermost regions (Regis) •employment promotion and development of human resources (Now, Horizon and Euroform) •management of industrial change (Rechar, Resider, Retex, Konver, but also Prisma, Telematique and Stride in Objective 1 regions).
Leader	400	Rural development	
Total	3,800		
Retex*		Diversification in regions dependent on the textile industry	
Konver*		Diversification in regions dependent on the military sector	

Notes
*An additional sum of ECU 0.3 billion, available for Community Initiatives, was allocated to Retex and Konver – the subject of more recent decisions and for the purpose of increasing the funds earmarked for Now and Horizon.
Source: CEC (1993a).

relating economic development, the application of technology, environment improvement, transport, training and education, crime prevention and security, energy efficiency, infrastructure and social facilities.

The European anti-poverty programmes

Between 1975 and 1980 an initial Community programme of pilot schemes and studies to combat poverty were undertaken. Between 1985 and 1989 a further programme was introduced which focused on particular groups such as the unemployed, the elderly, single parent families and second generation migrants. The third anti-poverty programme from 1989 to 1994 was allocated a budget of 55 million ECU. The Poverty 3 programme extended and built on the experience gained from the previous two Community programmes but it was more ambitious as it emphasized the role of partnership, participation and a multi-dimensional approach to tackling social exclusion. The fight against social exclusion is considered to be one of the Commission's key economic and social priorities. The Poverty 3 programme finished in 1994 and the Commission has outlined proposals for a new five-year programme with a doubling of funding available. The Commission intends to allocate some 121 million ECU to the new programme which is likely to be known as the Exclusion 1 programme. The reasons for such an increase in funding reflects the Commission's concern about the 15 per cent of the European population who live below the poverty line while more than three million Europeans have no fixed accommodation.

Innovative measures and European networks

One of the important roles that the EC has developed over the years has been the promotion of innovative measures through the regulations governing the operation of the Structural Funds. Innovative measures which are adopted by the Commission are the only exception to the principle of programming through partnership which is one of key components of the operation of the Structural Funds. The EC can on its own initiative introduce new measures such as pilot projects, networks for co-operation, studies and the exchange of experience, which through a Community–wide experimental approach aim to result in the development of new Community policies.

Article 3 of Regulation (EEC) No 2052/88 and Article 10 of Regulation (EEC) No 4254/88 of the 1988 European Regional Development Fund Regulation provide the basis for the Community to initiate and pilot studies which promote regional development at the Community level. According to the Regulations these actions should relate to measures which are seen to outline the utilization of the Community's territory and the spatial consequences of major infrastructure projects. Second, the work should develop an understanding of the problems confronting border regions and measures which promote the exchange of experience and co-operation between regions. Measures under Article 10 can be applied across the Community and thereby provide an important link between regions which are covered by the geographical Objectives of the Structural Funds and other regions which are not eligible. By the end of 1992 a total of 275 million ECU had been committed to studies and pilot projects under Article 10 (CEC, 1994b: 40). Most of the resources were committed to measures which improved Community knowledge about European spatial planning and policy, cross-border co-operation, co-operation between regions and cities and measures which focused on urban issues.

The EC also contributes funds to assist the financing of European networks between cities under the framework of the RECITE inter-regional co-operation programme. The regional network programme started on an experimental basis in 1990 with twelve network pilot projects. Following a review of these networks, the RECITE programme which was launched in the summer of 1991 aimed at the promotion of co-operation between regions and cities throughout the whole of the Community. The RECITE programme provides the EC with a solid base to develop experimental measures which help to assess which forms of interregional co-operation are most effective in contributing towards the overall objectives of economic and social cohesion. The RECITE programme is open to any local or regional authority with responsibility for a population of more than 50,000. Examples include the Eurocities network which was established in 1986 and the *Quartiers en Crise* network which began in 1989 as a means to foster exchange and co-operation in towns and cities experimenting with integrated approaches to urban development.

The Commission sees an important role to be played in facilitating the exchange of ideas between cities and member states on how to improve the effectiveness of their urban policies. Through Article 10 of the ERDF Regulation, the Commission has co-financed 32 urban pilot projects over the period 1990–4. These projects are designed to test out new ideas in the delivery of urban policy within the Community. Although the projects under the scheme would contribute to the economic functioning and well-being of a city rather than directly dealing with housing or social problems. Three areas for policy intervention were identified:

1   Peripheral and inner city housing problem areas, where access to jobs and training excludes many from the economic mainstream.
2   Projects geared to bring together economic and environmental goals.

3   Economic and commercial life can be brought back to the historic centres of cities where for various reasons the inner city fabric has been allowed to decay.

These pilot actions can be used to identify existing types of measures included for areas eligible for Structural Fund support, especially for the new programmes to be adopted for the period 1994–7. Cities which have gained support for projects concerned with economic development in urban areas with social problems include: London, Marseilles, Rotterdam, Brussels, Lyon, Copenhagen, Alborg, Paisley, Groningen and Bremen. Cities involved with environmental actions linked to economic goals include: Belfast, Athens, Neunkirchen, Madrid, Gibralter and Stoke-on-Trent. Finally, the urban pilot projects have been used to assist in the revitalization of the historic centres of European cities which include work undertaken in Lisbon, Thessaloniki, Dublin, Berlin and Genoa.

Conclusions

The completion of the Single Market has been the driving force behind the moves towards further European economic integration. As Europe takes steps towards laying the foundations for economic, political and monetary union it is evident that the process of integration implies that Europe has to confront several new challenges:

- the uncertainty and scepticism felt after the ratification of the Maastricht Treaty;
- the perceived need for European institutions to regain a sense of legitimacy and to improve their decision-making capabilities, thereby enhancing the somewhat tarnished image of policy processes for many European citizens;
- to improve economic co-operation throughout the EU and with other non-Union European countries;
- to actively engage in the tackling of the problems associated with unemployment and combat social exclusion as persistent high levels of unemployment across Europe are now considered to be both politically and economically unacceptable to the Community.

The EC has increasingly concentrated its efforts to ensure that measures which are implemented at either the European, national, regional or local levels contribute towards achieving the conditions necessary for economic and social cohesion. The importance of cohesion at every level of the Community raises important debates over the way in which European policy is being developed. For many individuals who live and work in the communities and areas which are the target for EU action, concerns are mounting over the real level of power entrusted at local level. Is it the case that ordinary people in these communities do have the ability to decide the best way to use and spend European funds in their own localities, or is it still very much a top-down approach to local economic development? In the end as the need to address these economic, social and environmental problems at the neighbourhood and community level becomes more apparent, Europe has to ensure that partnership at the local level really means empowerment for local people to improve the conditions in which they live and work.

Although the Treaties of the EU do not give any mandate for the development of a Europe-wide urban policy, it is clearly evident that the numerous policies and activities of the EU impact on urban areas and urban communities. The EU has increasingly concerned itself with the future prosperity and development of European urban areas and it is apparent that it will continue to strengthen policies which improve the economic and social conditions in European cities as well as to develop networks of experience and interregional co-operation across the Community. The significance of the Community's influence on urban policy must be examined in the wider context of the European policy agenda and the moves towards further economic, monetary and political integration. Although experience has been uneven, it is still the case that many European cities have benefited from the application of the Community's Structural Funds and other funded programmes. As Europe enters a new era of development it is apparent that European cities will continue to benefit from the activities of the Commission.

References

Archer, C. (1994), *Organizing Europe: The Institutions of Integration*. London, Edward Arnold.

Atkinson, R., Moon, G. (1994), *Urban Policy in Britain, the City, the State and the Market*. London, Macmillan.

Bidwell, C. (1993), *Maastricht and the UK*. Public Affairs Consultants Europe Limited.

CEC (1990), *Green Paper on the Urban Environment*. Brussels.

—— (1991), *Europe 2000 – Outlook for the Development of the Community's Territory*. Brussels.

—— (1992a), *Urbanisation and the Functions of Cities in the European Community*. Centre for Urban Studies, University of Liverpool.

—— (1992b), *Towards a Europe of Solidarity. Intensifying the Fight Against Social Exclusion, Fostering Integration*. Brussels.

—— (1992c), *Treaty on European Union*. Luxembourg.

—— (1992d), *Towards a Europe of Solidarity*. Communication from the Commission, COM(92) 542 final. Brussels.

—— (1992e), *From Single Market to European Union*. Luxembourg.

—— (1992f), *Reform of the Structural Funds: A Tool to Promote Economic and Social Exclusion*. Brussels.

—— (1993a), *Community Structural Funds 1994–99: Regulations and Commentary*. Luxembourg.

—— (1993b), *Green Paper: European Social Policy Options for the Union*. Brussels.

—— (1993c), *White Paper on Growth, Competitiveness and Employment*. Brussels.

—— (1993d), *Medium-Term Action Programme to Combat Exclusion and Promote Solidarity: A New Programme to Support and Stimulate Innovation (1994–1999)*. COM(93) 435 final, Brussels.

—— (1993e), *Background Report. Social Exclusion – Poverty and Other Social Problems in the European Community*. Jean Monnet House, London.

—— (1994a), *The Future of Community Initiatives under the Structural Funds*. Com (94) 46 Final, Brussels.

—— (1994b), *Community Initiatives Concerning Urban Areas (URBAN)*. COM(94) 61 final 2, Brussels.

—— (1994c), *European Social Policy. A Way Forward for the Union*. A White Paper. Com (94) Final, Brussels.

—— (1994d), *Europe at the Service of Regional Development*. DG XVI, Brussels.

Cheshire, P. C., Hay, D. G. (1989), *Urban Problems in Western Europe: An Economic Analysis*. London, Unwin Hyman.

European Council (1993), *Presidency Conclusions*. Brussels.

European Foundation for the Improvement of Living and Working Conditions (1986), *Living Conditions in Urban Areas*. Dublin.

—— (1989), *Social Change and Local Action: Coping with Disadvantaged in Urban Areas*. Dublin.

—— (1990), *Mobility and Social Cohesion in the European Community – A Forward Look*. Dublin.

—— (1994), *Bridging The Gulf*. Dublin.

Hall, P. (1994), 'Forces shaping urban Europe', *Urban Studies*, 30: 883–98.

Lawless, P. (1992), 'Social integration and new urban activities', in *The Improvement of the Built Environment and Social Integration in Cities*. Dublin, European Foundation for the Improvement of Living and Working Conditions.

Robson, B. T. (1994), 'No city, no civilization', *Transactions of the Institute of the British Geographers*, 19: 131–41.

8

New forms of local economic development in the global economy
Transfrontier co-operation and internationalization

PETER REID AND ANDREW
CHURCH

Introduction – local authorities and globalization

'Globalization or the Global Economy are terms often applied loosely or indiscriminately to imply a totally pervasive set of forces and changes with all-embracing effects on countries, regions and localities' (Dicken, 1993). This view reflects concern that the phenomenon of globalization is an accepted norm which lacks debate over its nature and extent. The general rhetoric of globalization has started to appear in local authority economic development strategies that are seeking to develop policy responses at the international scale. This chapter considers the evolution of local authorities' policy initiatives that involve action at the international scale and it is argued that one well-established and increasingly common response to globalization by local authorities is international cross-border co-operation. The development of these responses is examined in a series of case studies and the key influences on the nature of the policy initiatives are discussed. The implications, problems and advantages of co-operation are also identified. Some of the examples used involve co-operation across problematic frontiers where the border relationship has changed markedly in recent years and the policy initiatives are relatively recent.

The need for financial assistance is revealed as one of the key driving forces behind the internationalization of policy at local level and in many cases the globalization of local economic development policies. The problems of unemployment and declining base industries are a common factor across Europe and in many other parts of the developed world and this has led many local authorities to develop strategies which will attract funds from international organizations such as the European Commission. For many of the international agencies the encouragement of such co-operation is one of their key aims.

Goldsmith (1993) considers that internationalization and globalization of local authority activity are the result of a number of worldwide trends. These include increasing interdependence of the world economy, changes in the balance of economic power and shifts in the location of industrial and manufacturing activities. There is also a changing balance in economic activities and increasingly important financial and service sectors of many of the developed countries' economies. All these factors have, according to Goldsmith (1993), been aided by the dramatic change in communications during the last twenty years.

In Europe, Parkinson *et al.* (1992) identify the importance of city networks in the development of local government international co-operation. These networks occur in old core, new core and peripheral areas and the authors suggest that, along with global economic restructuring, a number of other broad processes encourage this co-operation including political and administrative decentralization within states, the failure of traditional regional policies and a growing awareness of economic competition between cities in an increasingly integrated Europe. Despite the emergence of these networks Parkinson *et al.* conclude that globalization and global interdependence will still mean that international economic policies are increasingly concentrated in the hands of the European Union organizations.

City networks by their nature cover a wide geographical area compared to the more localized transfrontier co-operation, but as will be shown in this chapter the co-operative groupings that have developed around certain borders cover very large areas and can involve regions from more than two countries. Cappellin (1992) argues that cross-border co-operation is mainly the outcome of European integration and economic internationalization, with the latter process viewed as paramount as local authorities respond to the increasingly flexible, networked, global economy. Joint initiatives are thus seen as an economic response by the public sector to generate network economies, reduce transaction costs, control and limit competition, and create economies of scale through shared resources (Cappellin, 1992). While these economic factors are undoubtedly important in the emergence of international local authority policy, state agencies have played an active role and a diverse range of political considerations have contributed to the globalization of policy. In Europe the EU has played a considerable role in the internationalization process both nationally and locally; because of the shift of power to Brussels most local authorities are affected both directly and indirectly by the EU in many areas of service provision as part of the progression towards integration. The move towards a Single European Market and the subsequent removal of trade barriers has speeded up the process of European integration and cross-border co-operation is seen by the EU as a precursor to further integration. Despite the diversity of the administrative and political structures in each EU country the availability of EU funding has resulted in a broader view by many of the smaller local authorities on co-operation and cross-border co-operative ventures. This is hardly surprising in regions where deindustrialization has created communities with significant levels of unemployment. Local authorities across Europe have been faced with the problems of dealing with these difficulties with limited injections of resources from national governments. The result has been the search by local authorities for funding locally, nationally and internationally and from multi-agency sources in collaboration with other local authorities, the private and voluntary sectors. A further stimulus to such international co-operation is the belief amongst many local authorities that the formation of a credible regional grouping is considered essential in order to compete with other parts of Europe that are also acting jointly to attract mobile international investment (Church and Reid, 1994). Co-operation between regions in the north-east of Spain through southern France and into northern Italy conveniently balances some of the international initiatives in north-west Europe.

Other political issues that have prompted international economic co-operation include an increasing concern with foreign policy issues in some US cities (Hobbs, 1994) and concerns for environmental issues that so often pay no attention to national boundaries . In the latter case local community politics as opposed to class-based politics have played a role in the development of cross-border co-operation on environmental issues (Church and Reid, 1994). Generally in Europe, however, the internationalization of local authority economic policy is as much a response to international political structures as it is to the nature of the globalized economy. The aim of the case studies will be to examine the different economic and political influences on one example of international local authority policy, transfrontier co-operation and to consider the organizational and political consequences of these new local economic initiatives. The internationalization of local economic policy can take a number of forms from town twinning schemes which encourage links between firms in specific areas to large-scale international promotional exercises; cross-border co-operation is part of this more general trend. The two main study areas used in this chapter are first the co-operative grouping of Kent County Council in England and Nord Pas-de-Calais in France who are partners in the Transmanche Region, and second, the members of the Transmanche Metropole who are Portsmouth, Southampton, Poole and Bournemouth in England and Caen, Rouen and Le Havre in France. These provide interesting comparisons since each grouping contains partners who are diverse politically but share a common agenda. The Transmanche Metropole is primarily concerned with obtaining funding from the EU. The Transmanche

Region is a broader and more mature co-operative grouping initially growing out of the co-operation between Kent and Nord Pas-de-Calais that was stimulated by the new Channel Tunnel link.

For comparison, a number of other cross-border relationships are also considered briefly in order to indicate the variety of initiatives and the diverse processes that encourage co-operation. These include Poland/ Germany, Italy/Slovenia, Sweden/Finland and Israel/Lebanon. The borders between some of these are geographically or politically difficult but they highlight the range of such co-operative initiatives and their possible future developments. They also serve to show that the development of cross-border co-operation is a continuing process throughout the world and as such its impact on national, regional and local government is increasing.

Borders and the background to transfrontier co-operation

There have been many studies of border regions from a number of perspectives. Brocker (1980) and Perschel (1985) undertook trade flow studies while the examination by Evers and Oosterhaven (1988) of passenger flows argues that national frontiers reduce trade flows and income levels in border regions. House (1981) developed an operational economic model for examining the effect of frontiers on regional development in border areas. Measures of perceived or actual distance/decay effects from the boundary line were used as the conceptual basis for defining border zones in terms of measurable or perceived (House, 1981). An adaptation of this approach based on core/periphery concepts and the transactional flow analysis was used by Minghi (1991) who sought to examine borders where political conflict had given way to co-operative ventures. The main case study was the Alpes Maritime border between Italy and France and Minghi argues that improvements in political relationships in this border area are a result of increased economic exchanges and extended co-operative ventures which thus improve the overall political relationships.

Balassa (1989) suggests that co-operation and the removal of customs barriers between states could potentially benefit border regions either by reducing the peripherality of the area or by accentuating any comparative advantage. Alternatively, non-frontier regions may find that the economic differences between core and periphery are maintained or even increased (Balassa, 1989). Cappellin's (1992) analysis of customs barriers argues that their removal has an 'ambiguous effect' leading either to economic dispersal or concentration. Border region conflict and tension, it is argued, emphasize political peripherality since they heighten the relevance of centre–periphery conflict. Transfrontier co-operation which encourages the integration of peripheral regions into Europe and their respective nation states thus has the potential to reduce core–periphery disparities (Cappellin, 1992).

A less optimistic view is taken by Camagni (1992) who argues that such co-operation, especially if it involves regions with similar problems, may project a 'club of the poor' image to international investors. He acknowledges, however, that transfrontier initiatives between regions with differing levels of economic activity may have more potential to alter existing patterns of economic development. The Kent and Nord Pas-de-Calais case study used in this chapter is based on two areas with very regional economic experiences. Kent, apart from the coastal resorts in the east of the county, is certainly a core region of the UK, while Nord Pas-de-Calais, despite its position close to the economic centre of Europe, has many of the features of a declining peripheral industrial region. Also in this area the ambiguous effects of changes to borders highlighted by Cappellin (1992) is emphasized by Vickerman's (1990) crossroads or corridor scenario for the impact of the Channel Tunnel. The crossroad effect would see expansion of growth nodes around the terminal areas with an opposite scenario created for the coastal areas of Kent and Nord Pas-de-Calais by the corridor effect. Cappellin (1992) suggests this latter outcome is more likely if the link provides direct access to capital cities, as is the case with the CT and TGV. Other research in this area, however, merely serves to highlight the problems of predicting the local economic outcomes of changes to borders. Holliday and Vickerman (1990) and Begg (1990) have argued that the impact of the Channel Tunnel and Single European Market may well have a centralizing effect in the economic process. This will benefit the core regions of north-west Europe. Chisholm (1992) is more sceptical, arguing that such impacts will be uneven and may not lead to the growth in core areas which others predict. His study of ports in the south and east of England concluded that local differences in factor costs mean that proximity to Europe does not seem to have a clear net influence on port performance and that other processes determine the performance of ports on the English borders (Chisholm, 1992). Whatever the final outcome of border changes in Kent and Nord Pas-de-Calais it is clear that economic change in border regions will be subject to a diverse and changeable range of economic processes and it is in this uncertain environment that local authorities have been developing co-operative policies.

The evolution of the Transmanche Region

In Kent and Nord Pas-de-Calais the construction of the Channel Tunnel is clearly a key factor in explaining the evolution of the co-operative Transmanche Region and the availability of EU Interreg 1 funding provided the impetus for the development of a formalized Transfrontier Development Programme (TDP). A number of other processes, however, have also encouraged these two quite different regions to enter into co-operative policy initiatives. Central government in both France and the UK are now involved in this initiative, but its initial evolution was the outcome of local and regional government activity and despite the particular circumstances of the Channel Tunnel the TDP illustrates a number of the features of internationalized local authority economic policy. Changes to EU border regulations have been accompanied by similar examples of transfrontier co-operation in Europe during the last few years (Capellin, 1992), but the nature of co-operation across different land and sea borders of European countries is not just a response to broad international economic and political forces but is also the outcome of physical, economic, political, cultural and social factors particular to each border.

The contrasts in the economies of Kent and Nord Pas-de-Calais are well known. While both have substantial agricultural areas, Nord Pas-de-Calais differs from Kent in having its economic base firmly in restructuring manufacturing and extractive industries which have been in decline since the 1980s (Flockton and Kofman, 1989). Consequently, Nord Pas-de-Calais is recognized by the EC as an assisted area under Objectives 1 and 2 of the European Regional Development Fund. Kent, however, is situated in the South East region and despite the recent recession is a relatively prosperous English county based on service sector employment. In 1991, manufacturing only accounted for 17 per cent of Kent's total employment (NOMIS, 1993) compared to 33 per cent in Nord Pas-de-Calais which has a higher proportion of employment in large establishments (INSEE, 1990). The unemployment figures in Nord Pas-de-Calais had risen to 11.5 per cent in 1992, whereas in Kent the figure was 7.9 per cent (Eurostat, 1993). The scale of the unemployment problem is greater in Nord Pas-de-Calais since it had a population in 1991 of 3.9 million compared to 1.5 million in Kent (Eurostat, 1993). Nevertheless, in some of the coastal areas of east Kent, such as Folkestone and Thanet, unemployment is high due to the decline in tourism and port-related industries; the potential threat to existing jobs from the Channel Tunnel has resulted in certain districts becoming eligible for national regional aid and related EU Objective 2 funds.

The coastal local authorities on both sides of the Channel have a common problem, namely the potential negative effects of the Channel Tunnel on their localities and the port industry in particular. At Dover and Ramsgate the ferry operators are gearing up to compete with the Channel Tunnel and they anticipate that their improved super ferries will prove effective. It is very much a case of what proportion of the cross-Channel trade will be diverted to using the CT. There is likely to be the novelty factor which could boost initial take up of crossings by Le Shuttle. The total operation with freight and through trains to European capitals will clearly impact on the ferry trade. There is considerable pressure, therefore, on the economies of both Kent and Nord Pas-de-Calais and concern regarding the effects of the Channel Tunnel on the high unemployment levels already evident in these two areas. The removal of cross-border controls as a result of the SEM have already played a part in exacerbating the unemployment problems (Reid, 1993). Furthermore, the recession in Britain which is now increasingly evident in France and the rest of Europe has also exacerbated the problems of both areas. The reluctance of developers to commit funds during the last two years has increased the difficulties for local authorities trying to attract commercial and industrial businesses to their areas. With these problems local authorities such as Kent and Nord Pas-de-Calais and the other tiers of local government have been forced to take any action they can to attract investment. It is the potential negative effects of the CT and SEM that have really been the catalyst for Kent and Nord Pas-de-Calais (Reid, 1993) to develop the co-operative ventures of TDP which have been particularly aimed at this border regional area.

In 1987 Kent County Council and Nord Pas-de-Calais regional council signed a joint accord which set out a number of policy areas where co-operative relationships could be developed. These included transportation, economic and commercial links, education and tourism. The broad aim was to reduce the barriers created by national boundaries and in particular to maximize the benefits stemming from the Channel Tunnel and the SEM. This was the first such agreement between a French and UK region and was initially typified by activities involving the exchange of information (Church and Reid, 1994). Under the joint accord it was decided that future initiatives would be targeted at the coastal areas of Nord Pas-de-Calais and Kent. In the latter this included the five East Kent districts of Shepway, Dover, Thanet, Ashford and Canterbury. By September 1990 the joint accord had led to the development of the Transfrontier Development Programme (TDP) which was submitted to the EC for funding under Interreg 1. This bid for resources was given formal approval by the EC in May 1992. Intense lobbying by Kent County Council of both the EC and the UK government had been required since the Interreg programme was initially only developed for land borders and for a period this region was the only non-land border in Europe to receive support from Interreg 1.

While the bid for support was with the EC the larger Euroregion was formed. In June 1991 a joint declaration promoting transfrontier co-operation was signed between the five regions of Kent, Nord Pas-de-Calais, Wallonia, Brussels Capital and Flanders. The Transmanche region maintains its separate identity within the larger grouping and as with the original two regional agreements there are marked political differences between the Euroregion areas. There are now five working groups of Transport and Telecommunications, Land Management and Environment, Economic Development, Education and Training, and Tourism Development which are designed to relate to the sub-programmes in the TDP.

The overall budget of the TDP involving Kent and Nord Pas-de-Calais between May 1992 and the end of 1993 was 54 million ECU (38 million), of which only 40 per cent comes from Interreg 1 with the remainder coming from national and local government in France and the UK. These funds were focused on particular sub-programmes so that 39 per cent of expenditure went to the Land Management and the Environment sub-programme and 37 per cent to Tourism Development; whereas the Education and Training sub-programme received 13 per cent, Economic Development 7 per cent and Transport and Infrastructure 4 per cent. Under Interreg 2 the TDP has received a further 88 million ECU for the years 1994–9. Again half of these funds are from national governments as match funding for EU expenditure. The sub-programmes that make up the TDP for this second period have been altered slightly to reflect a greater concern for strategic planning issues and environmental priorities. The Strategic Planning and Communications sub-programme will receive 25 per cent, Tourism 23 per cent, Economic Development 20 per cent, the Environment sub-programme 19 per cent and Human Resource Development 11 per cent. The emergence of a separate Environment sub-programme indicates the influence of local community politics we have noted before (Church and Reid, 1994). Nevertheless, the key influences on the emergence of this co-operative initiative are clearly the Channel Tunnel and the availability of EU funds, but the Economic Development sub-programme is also a clear reaction to the impacts of economic restructuring and globalization. Interestingly this internationalization of local economic development policy has not stopped at neighbouring border regions. Kent County Council are now in contact with authorities in Hungary and are collaborating with them on a number of initiatives. The experience of internationalization of local policy through the TDP has encouraged further development of this phenomenon.

The emergence of the Transmanche Metropole

The existence of the smaller Transmanche region within the larger Euroregion creates a complex organizational context to the cross-border co-operation between Kent and Nord Pas-de-Calais. These new structures appear relatively simple in comparison to the complexity of organizational networks surrounding internationalization and co-operation elsewhere along the Channel. The Transmanche Metropole is an emerging co-operative strategy between the English local authorities of Southampton, Portsmouth, Bournemouth and Poole and the city authorities of Caen, Le Havre and Rouen in France. The four authorities in the UK have varying economic bases and political persuasions, however, they formed the South Coast Metropole which was constituted in May 1993. The local economic policy agendas of each of the authorities in the UK are different. Southampton and Portsmouth are concerned to maintain industrial and port activities, whereas Bournemouth and Poole promote a local economy based on tourism and specialist activities such as language schools. The original South Coast Metropole evolved partly as a result of concerns expressed by the four English towns that they did not have a clear regional identity. The area is on the border of the standard regions of South East and South West England, but does not feel a strong affinity with either. In addition, the French towns of Rouen, Caen and Le Havre already had an informal partnership. The two existing urban groupings provided the basis for potential cross-border co-operation. Of course, the possibility of EU funding was a further stimulus to joint initiatives between these seven urban areas. Currently, however, the Transmanche Metropole is based upon a loose local economic accord which seeks to promote co-operative ventures. The initiative has not been deemed eligible for grants from Interreg II which will start in 1995. Competition, for such funding is of course highly competitive and the scramble for EU support has had important implications for the future development of the Transmanche Metropole.

On 1 July 1994 the EC announced the list of border regions that will be eligible for funding under Interreg II (Michie and Bachtler, 1994). This included a significant number of maritime border areas that were not eligible in the draft regulations for Interreg 2 issued in February 1993. A number of coastal regions, including some from both sides of the Channel, undertook intense lobbying of the Assembly of European Regions, the Regional Policy Committee of the European Parliament, the European Parliament and the Management Committee of the EC with the aim of adding their names to the list. In the UK eligibility for Interreg funding was dependent on support from central government and a lack of central backing was one reason why a number of the Channel coastal areas in the UK were not included on the revised list. The English county of Essex was seeking to co-operate with the Picardie region in Northern France and the constituent regions of the Transmanche Metropole were also seeking Interreg II funding for their co-operative initiative. Neither Essex nor the English towns in the Transmanche Metropole were on the final Interreg II eligibility list, but on the French side the Somme department within Picardie was included with the English county of East Sussex as its partner. The towns of Le Havre and Rouen are also now eligible for Interreg II funding since they are in the department of Seine-Maritime which is also co-operating with East Sussex.The four UK maritime border areas and their partners now eligible to receive support under Interreg II are Kent and Nord-Pas de Calais, Gwynedd/Clwyd and the Republic of Ireland, Gibraltar and Morocco, and East Sussex and the Department of Somme and Seine-Maritime, which are in Picardie and Haute-Normandy regions respectively. Oddly, one of these French departments was not initially aware of its inclusion on the final list since most of the application had been dealt with by its constituent region and the French regional agency DATAR.

By late 1995 central government in the UK will have submitted to the EC a Single Programme document for Interreg II setting out the priority themes for these four cross-border initiatives. In some cases the sums of money involved will be quite small due to the allocation procedure. The global allocation for Interreg II for each member state is set in Brussels and this is shared out by national governments. The Interreg II funding for the four projects involving UK regions may total approximately 99 million ECU over 4–5 years which will be match funded. Of this 75 per cent will go to border regions which are also Objective 1 regions and the remaining 25 per cent is allocated in order of priority to Objective 2 regions, Objective 5b regions and unclassified regions. East Sussex will fall into the unclassified group and expects only to receive approximately 1 million ECU per annum for five years. As with Kent and Nord Pas-de-Calais the projects that receive support will be catalyst infrastructure, training, environmental and tourism initiatives designed to stimulate the existing economy and attract inward investment. The sums available, however, may not even be sufficient to pay for the main local economic policy priority which is the major infrastructure project of the outer harbour at Newhaven that East Sussex hoped Interreg II would enable. Dieppe has recently opened a new outer harbour to accommodate bigger and faster ferries and at the moment this ferry link lacks 'half of the bridge'. Nevertheless, the inclusion of East Sussex on the Interreg II list was viewed locally as a considerable achievement. A local economic accord to promote joint initiatives had been signed by East Sussex and the Department of Seine-Maritime in September 1993, but at one point it seemed likely that the application to Interreg II for the Channel border areas would be dominated by the Transmanche region and the Trans-manche Metropole. One argument that East Sussex employed in its favour was that the county's coastal strip was an extension of the depressed coastal areas in Kent and should also receive funding. Indeed, in the longer term it is possible that the existing co-operative initiatives could expand and be the basis of an embryonic larger Channel region, called the Arc Transmanche, which contains a unique type of regional problem based on depressed resort towns, restructuring ports and a rural hinterland with marginal agricultural activities. In the shorter term it is clear that internationalization and cross-border initiatives have led to intense competition for EU funding and the emergence of tensions between neighbouring regions in one country as they seek to form links across the same border. Towns or regions may even find that the nature of competition requires them to switch partners. City government in Le Havre is keen to maintain its links with the Transmanche Metropole but may also be required by its constituent Department of Seine-Maritime to co-operate with East Sussex. At a more general level the aim of co-operation in these coastal areas goes beyond gaining EU grants and is designed to develop local economic initiatives which by their cross-border nature contribute to the general process of local economic policy internationalization. In the uncertain global economy the international-ization of policy based on cross-border co-operation and EU funding is clearly an appealing option for local authorities.

Further examples of cross-border co-operation and internationalization

The development of cross-border co-operation in the EU has taken place at varying rates and with differing degrees of success over the last twenty years. The two case studies presented so far have been influenced by a wide range of economic and political processes some of which are quite particular to the European Union. Similar examples of international co-operation between local authorities are also developing in very different circumstances. EU legislative changes to borders were an important political stimulus to the initiatives in the two case studies, but in many border regions political and legislative changes to frontiers have been even more marked. The fall of communism in Eastern Europe together with the reunification of Germany have allowed local government in countries such as Poland to pursue policies which promote and develop international economic and cultural relationships. This type of co-operation was not entirely new since the former COMECON trading bloc did lead to the development of cross-border co-operation but more recently East European countries have been able to develop trans-frontier initiatives with EU countries. In recent years the EU has only been prepared to fund co-operative policies amongst regions within the Union. However, this has not prevented authorities in neighbouring borderland zones from establishing contacts.

The development of new political and economic environments in Eastern Europe has enabled local authorities to explore a wide range of local economic policies and in many cases they have chosen to develop Euroregion-style co-operative networks. There are a number of such transfrontier ventures along the border from the Baltic to the Carpathian mountains in the Ukraine. In a study by Koter (1994) he indicates that the individual co-operative units have their own specific agendas, although all have technological, economic and cultural exchanges as key central themes. In the case of the Polish/German borderland the aim of Polish local authorities is to improve economic links with the core regions of Europe and central government is supportive of such initiatives since they provide evidence of a commitment to full EU membership (Koter, 1994). Ossenbrugge (1994) is slightly more critical of these measures and argues that while recognizing they are significant for future integration with the EU, the marked differences in economic wealth between the regions involved may result in uneven power relations in the political alliances which may hinder the development of useful co-operative measures.

At the southern end of the former iron curtain, cross-border relationships on the Italian/Slovenian border has been the subject of a number of recent studies. Bufon (1994) and Minghi (1991, 1994) both point out that despite long-standing disagreements over this border after World War II and the problems caused by the Balkan conflict, border relations have improved and certain limited co-operative economic initiatives have started to develop. For Minghi this is not an isolated example, however, and many other European borders have recently moved from a situation of conflict to one of relative harmony (Minghi, 1991).

The Israel/Lebanon border, however, is still very much typified by conflict and tension. Nevertheless, Soffer (1994) notes that informal cross-border co-operation can still occur even in this hostile environment. The borders separated by the security zone are still used by workers, tourists and others on a daily basis and 30,000 workers commute across each day to jobs within Israel. In addition, ethnic groups and families have developed regular trade links both openly and secretly. Thus, informal and small-scale, cross-border economic co-operation occurs despite the tension between the national governments (Soffer, 1994). This suggests that even in quite unlikely situations there may still be existing processes that can form the basis for local economic development policies based on co-operation.

Similarities and differences in the case studies

There is, of course, immense variety in the operation and reasoning behind the cross-border relationships and initiatives. Those regions operating within the EU see the opportunity for co-operation and internationalization as one which will enable them to access EU funding whether through the ERDF Objective system or in the case of cross-border regions through the Interreg I and II programmes. In addition, the economic basis for action is to form groupings that can establish a credible profile in the globalized economy. The examples outside the EU such as Poland and Slovenia have a clear economic motivation, but with slightly different specific intentions. Co-operation and internationalization are seen as methods of creating a relationship which will in the long run produce either admission to the EU or increased market and economic opportunities. In addition, the Polish regions are also seeking to learn from the free market expertise and technological skills of neighbouring German regions (Koter, 1994). In all the cases, however, there is a realization of the importance of external co-operation for developing effective local economic strategies that take account of the effects of globalization.

There are, of course, a number of marked differences between the international co-operative strategies developed in each of the study areas. The Transmanche Region is the only co-operative venture of the group which has developed as a direct result of a major construction project, namely the Channel Tunnel. The Eastern European cross border co-operation is the result of a major political change as is the Italy/Slovenian area. In all the cases the level and degree of co-operation are at different stages of development. The TDP between Kent and Nord Pas-de-Calais has established a formal organizational structure involving both central and local government. Furthermore, the TDP has a strong emphasis on both economic and environmental issues whereas many of the other case studies are primarily concerned with economic development. By contrast, with the continuing tension between Israel and Lebanon economic co-operation across the border is likely to remain of an informal nature between ethnic and family groups. The examples of Germany/Poland and Italy/Slovenia do indicate how quick the change can be from hostile to co-operative cross-border activity in the aftermath of major political changes at the national and international level.

Conclusion – problems and advantages of internationalization and co-operation

Transfrontier initiatives highlight a number of the potential difficulties and benefits of the internationalization of local economic policy. Within individual authorities the commitment to international co-operation of limited public funds may conflict with elected representatives' more local economic concerns. Bids for funds from international organizations like the EU can demand increasing amounts of the time of local economic policy officers. In Kent concern has emerged recently over the possibility that in future the availability of match funding from the EU rather than local needs may drive the allocation of limited local funds (Church and Reid, 1994). At a broader institutional level internationalization and co-operation will clearly require that potential political conflicts within a grouping of regions are resolved. The former Conservative-controlled county of Kent and the socialist regional council of Nord Pas-de-Calais clearly had different ideological commitments and yet in this case difficulties based on different political ideologies never really emerged. Due to recent political changes both councils have moved towards the centre but the larger Euroregion may contain extra tensions due to the diverse nature of the participating French, Belgian and English regions. In the department of the Seine-Maritime co-operation with East Sussex has already created certain tensions since the major towns of Rouen and Le Havre still have an involvement with the Transmanche Metropole.

Some of the transfrontier co-operation case studies were preceded by small scale co-operative schemes, such as town twinning, and in the case of the Israeli/Lebanon border co-operation is still very limited and informal. The expansion of small-scale initiatives into a major project will often require the involvement of other tiers of government. For example, central government appointees are now involved in the administration of some of the case studies in order to oversee expenditure. In such a situation local authorities may feel that their sense of ownership of a programme is weakened. Martin and Pearce (1993) noted how in the UK central government often adopts a 'gatekeeper' role in respect to EU funding. In all these transfrontier initiatives it will also be necessary to maintain a balance between more localized operational schemes and strategic aims. In the more diverse transfrontier co-operative ventures preserving a strategic direction may prove problematic as participating regions aim to extract funds for localized initiatives that benefit their area. The TDP for Kent and Nord Pas-de-Calais is trying to avoid this problem by establishing a specific strategic sub-programme for 1994–9. Elsewhere along the Channel external political factors have created a number of difficulties for co-operative ventures due to the competition which has arisen between neighbouring authorities.

Of course it is quite possible to view the problems that arise from internationalization and co-operation in a more positive manner. Beneficial information exchange and network economies may arise from the time spent by government officers developing international, as opposed to local, initiatives. Competition with neighbouring authorities and within co-operative groupings may result in more dynamic local economic policies with each region. For East Sussex the fear that it might be crowded out of co-operative initiatives by the Transmanche Region and Transmanche Metropole led it to develop an innovative co-operative economic strategy that secured Interreg II funding. International co-operation may also be useful for local authorities in countries with little regional government. In Europe as a whole existing regional élites will be seeking to gain from the political institutionalization of regions, but co-operative initiatives may allow local authorities in nations with a weak or virtually non-existent tier of regional government to construct alliances and thus develop a role at the regional level. Indeed, both Kent and Nord Pas-de-Calais argue that a key benefit of the TDP and Euroregion is that they allow them to maintain international relations and operate more effectively in the competitive global arena (Church and Reid, 1994). For some commentators co-operation and internationalization play an important role in developing 'meso-government' and establishing a more decentralized, pluralist model of government in highly centralized countries like the UK (Martin and Pearce, 1993). It is unclear yet, however, whether co-operative groupings can provide the political basis for constructing spatial development policies that will match those of more established regional agencies. A critical perspective on co-operation and internationalization is still necessary since the impact of such initiatives on spatial economic variation is still unclear and may be hard to separate from other developments such as the SEM and large frontier infrastructure projects like the Channel Tunnel. Indeed, even major initiatives may have only a limited impact on the distribution of economic activity. The Kent Impact Study 1991 (PACEC, 1991) considered the potential impact of the Channel Tunnel, SEM and high-speed rail link on firms in the area. Of the 200 firms interviewed 43 per cent considered that these events would have no impact on their company. When considering the Channel Tunnel alone 90 per cent of the firms gave the response that it would have either a slight effect or no effect (PACEC, 1991). In Nord Pas-de-Calais there appears to be more optimism than in Kent that the Channel Tunnel may benefit companies in the medium to long term. In a smaller survey carried out in Nord Pas-de-Calais, only 30 per cent of firms interviewed considered that the Channel Tunnel, SEM and TGV would have no impact on their company (Reid, 1993). In this situation of uncertainty the expenditure occurring on a cost-sharing basis through EU-sponsored programmes such as the TDP may play a minor but important role. The scale of this type of public investment is similar to certain urban policy measures elsewhere in the UK that have managed to attract private investment. EU funding through Interreg can be viewed as pump-priming initiatives in a rapidly changing regional economic environment.

The potential economic benefits of co-operation and internationalization must be counterbalanced by a recognition of their impact on the process of policy evolution. The individual projects that are part of these cross-border programmes are typified by environmental improvements, training provision, tourism promotion and infrastructure projects which are standard elements of current local economic policy. Co-operation and internationalization may, therefore, simply encourage a conformity of local policy at the expense of innovative community-based strategies that are more concerned with limiting the negative effects of globalization. Furthermore, transfrontier co-operation and international networks serve to focus local governments' attention on the international scale which may facilitate the activities of large-scale corporations who will benefit directly from the global awareness of local and regional government while distancing these state agencies from the demands of local communities. Such a scenario may not actually emerge but clearly there are a number of potential problems associated with international co-operation on local economic policy. Nevertheless, the involvement of local and regional authorities in co-operative programmes is likely to expand as the need for mutual assistance and the constant search for solutions to continuing labour market problems will ensure the continuance of such co-operation at least in the medium term.

References

Balassa, B. (1989), *Comparative Advantage: Trade Policy and Economic Development*. Hemel Hempstead, Wheatsheaf.

Begg, I. (1990), 'The Single European Market and the UK regions', *Cambridge Journal Economic Review*.

Brocker, J. (1980), *Measuring Trade – Impeding Effects of Distance by Log-Linear Interaction Analysis*, DP-16. Kiel, Institut für Regionalforschung, Universität Kiel.

Bufon, M. (1994), 'Local aspects of transborder co-operation: a case study in the Italo-Slovene border landscape', in Gallusser, W. (ed.), *Political Boundaries and Co-existence*. Berne, Peter Lang.

Camagni, R.P. (1992), 'Development scenarios and policy guidelines for the lagging regions in the 1990s', *Regional Studies*, 26: 361–74.

Cappellin, R. (1992), 'Theories of local endogenous development and international co-operation', in Tykkylainen, M. (ed.), *Development Issues and Strategies in the New Europe*. Aldershot, Avebury.

Chisholm, M. (1992), 'Britain, the European Community and the centralisation of production: theory and evidence, freight movements', *Environment and Planning A*, 24: 551–71.

Church, A., Reid, P. J. (1994), 'Anglo-French co-operation: the effect of the Channel Tunnel', in Gibb, R. (ed.), *The Channel Tunnel: Geographical Perspective*. London, John Wiley.

Dicken, P. (1993), 'The changing organisation of the global economy', in Johnston, R. (ed.), *The Changing Geography, the Changing Discipline*. Oxford, Blackwell.

Eurostat (1993), *Basic Statistics for the European Community*. London, Eurostat.

Evers, G.H.M., Oosterhaven, J. (1988), 'Transportation, frontier effects and regional development in the Common Market', *Papers and Proceedings of the Regional Science Association*, 64: 37– 51.

Flockton, C., Kofman, E. (1989), *France*. London, Paul Chapman.

Gallusser, W. (ed.), *Political Boundaries and Co-existence*. Berne, Peter Lang.

Goldsmith, M. (1993), 'The internationalisation of local authority policy', *Urban Studies*, 30: 683–708.

Hobbs, H. H. (1994), *City Hall Goes Abroad: The Foreign Policy of Local Politics*. London, Sage.

Holliday, I., Vickerman, R.W. (1990), 'The Channel Tunnel and regional development: policy responses in Britain and France', *Regional Studies*, 24: 455–66.

House, J. (1981), 'Frontier studies: an applied approach', in Burnett, A.D. and Taylor, P. (eds), *Boundary Studies in Political Geography*. Association of American Geographers.

INSEE (1990), *Profils de l'économie Nord Pas-de-Calais*. Lille, INSEE.

Koter, M. (1994), 'Transborder "Euroregions" round Polish border zones as an example of a new form of political coexistence', in Gallusser, W. (ed.), *Political Boundaries and Co-existence*. Berne, Peter Lang.

Maillot, D. (1990), 'Transborder regions between members of the European Community and non-member countries', *Built Environment*, 16: 25–37.

Martin, S., Pearce, G. (1993) 'European Development Strategies: Strengthening Meso-Government in the UK?' *Regional Studies*, 27: 681–5.

Michie, R., Bachtler, J. (1994), 'EU regional policy: community initiatives 1994–9', *The Newsletter of the Regional Studies Association*, 194: 10–11.

Minghi, J. (1991), 'From conflict to harmony in border landscapes', in Rumley, D. and Minghi, J.V. (eds), *The Geography of Border Landscapes*. London, Routledge.

—— (1994), 'The impact of Slovenian independence on the Italo-Slovene borderland: an assessment of the first three years', in Gallusser, W. (ed.) *Political Boundaries and Co-existence*. Berne, Peter Lang.

NOMIS (1993), *1991 Census of Employment*. Durham University, NOMIS.

Ossenbrugge, J. (1994), 'Economic interaction and co-operation along the German-Polish border in comparative perspective', in Gallusser, W. (ed.) *Political Boundaries and Co-existence*. Berne, Peter Lang.

PACEC (1991), *Kent Impact Study 1991 Review*. Cambridge, PA Cambridge Economic Consultants.

Parkinson, M., Bianchini, F., Dawson, J., Evans, R., Harding, A. (1992), *Urbanisation and the Function of Cities in the European Community*. Brussels, European Commission.

Perschel, K. (1985), 'Spatial structure in international trade', *Papers and Proceedings of the Regional Science Association*, 58: 97–111.

Reid, P.J. (1993), 'Calais, the red city: its position in economic development in Nord Pas-de-Calais', *Modern and Contemporary France*, NSI (4): 397–408.

Soffer, A. (1994) 'Forms of co-existence and transborder co-operation in a hostile area: the Israeli case', in Gallusser, W. (ed.), *Political Boundaries and Co-existence*. Berne, Peter Lang.

Vickerman, R.W. (1990), 'Whither the core of Europe in the 1990s', paper presented to a 'Seminar on Land Use Planning in Europe', PTRC 18th Annual Meeting, Brighton.

9

Euregions: springboard to regional economic development?

Innovation policy and cross-border co-operation in the Euregion Maas-Rhine

FABIENNE CORVERS, BEN
DANKBAAR AND ROBERT HASSINK

Introduction

Borders – symbol of the nation-state – have impeded the natural cohesion of border regions for centuries and have caused therefore countless border problems. The Single European Market, created by the Single European Act in 1986, is expected to have a large impact on the economic development of border regions. Although more economic integration may lead to a decrease of regional economic inequalities, large economic divergences between regions, on the other hand, may very well hinder the economic integration process. The European Union (EU) has therefore implemented a regional policy to stimulate regional development in economically disadvantaged regions.

In border regions cross-border co-operation is stimulated by the European Commission in order to solve common border-related problems and take advantage of the possibilities of the border region as a whole (e.g. joint planning, production and provision of public goods and services). By the end of the 1980s this had led to the existence of about forty 'Euregions', an abbreviation of European region, geographically located along the internal borders of the European Union and indicating some form of cross-border co-operation between (semi-)public organizations. A 'Euregion' can be considered as an organized border region.

Firms located in border regions are traditionally confronted with an incomplete market since half their hinterland is on the other side of the national border, whether it concerns their customers, their employees, their suppliers, 'knowledge institutes' or their competitors. The opening up of the internal European market in 1993 is expected to have considerable impact on firms in border regions, since economic integration will take place in their backyard. The future development of the border regions has a particular importance for the Union since they represent both a potential impediment to and a potential model for the integrated development of the EU in political as well as in economic terms. The hypothesis of this chapter is that a 'Euregion' can become a springboard for regional economic development. The question this chapter will try to answer is how cross-border co-operation between (semi-)public authorities can stimulate regional economic development.

In order to answer this question the chapter is organized as follows. The second section, pages 174–176, tries to clarify the relationship between the European economic integration process and the regional policy of the European Union. Both aspects will have a considerable impact on the future development of border regions in the EU. The third section, pages 176–178, elaborates on the term 'Europe of the Regions' since this implies a new geo-economic order in Europe and a change in the hierarchical relationships between the various regional and urban production systems. The fourth section, pages 178–180, examines one of the economically disadvantaged regions the European Commission has distinguished in its regional policy, namely border regions. Border regions are regions that can benefit substantially from the European integration process. This also applies to firms located in border regions, clarified in the fifth section, pages 180–181, since economic integration is taking place in their backyard. The sixth section, pages 182–189, will then take a look at one border region in particular, namely the Euregion Maas-Rhine along the Dutch-Belgian-German border. After some statistical inquiries, the seventh section, pages 189–193, is interested in the way firms located in this border region perceive the opportunities of the Euregion. Are they taking advantage of the economic integration process which is said to be taking place in their backyard? The eighth section, pages 193–195, answers the question of this chapter.

The chapter is based on a research project called 'New Chances for Firms in Border Regions'. This project has been commissioned for MERIT by the Dutch Social Economic Council, an advisory board of employers' organizations and trade unions that advise the national government.

The relationship between European economic integration and EU regional policy

Throughout the history of the European Union, starting with the Treaty of Rome in 1957 and stressed again in the Single European Act of 1986 and the Treaty of Maastricht in 1992, strong emphasis has been put on the reduction of economic divergences between regions of the EU. The decisions to create a customs union (1957), a common market (1986) and an economic and monetary union (1992) were taken in the conviction that more economic integration in the Union will lead to a decrease of regional economic inequalities. However, what the effect of greater economic integration will be on regional economic disparities in the EU is by no means an easy task to verify (Armstrong and Taylor, 1993). The gap between the richer and poorer regions of the EU has not shown much reduction relatively since the early 1970s, even though the total GDP of the Union has increased considerably (Cole and Cole, 1993). On the other hand, it was presumed that large economic divergences between regions would hinder the economic integration process.[1]

Since the beginning of the European Union, therefore, activities have been undertaken to stimulate regional development. Although no European regional policy was pursued before 1975, the EU did finance activities that created important regional effects (Van Run and Verheij, 1991). In 1975 the European Regional Development Fund (ERDF) was created, marking the official beginning of a European regional policy. The European Commission was of the opinion that regional policy is 'not only desirable, it is ... one of the conditions for continuing European integration' (CEC, 1977:4 as quoted in: Armstrong and Taylor, 1993: 289). One of the criteria for regional assistance from the ERDF was (and still is) that GDP is lower than 75 per cent of the EU average. In 1992 the Treaty of Maastricht introduced the Cohesion Fund to assist the poorer countries of the EU, namely Spain, Portugal, Greece and Ireland, in particular. It is argued that without this financial assistance it will be very difficult for these countries to meet the criteria of the EMU, since their economic development still lags behind the other countries of the EU. Without this Fund, it is argued, the EU could very well turn into a 'Europe of two speeds' which is totally contrary to the idea of a more united Europe, hence the name 'Cohesion' Fund.

One could ask the question whether the economic divergences between regions in the EU are really so large that they could actually form an impediment to the economic integration process. One look at the European regions teaches us that this could very well be true, since they not only differ widely on economic performance indicators (such as GDP per capita), but they also make up a wide variety of different types of depressed areas. In 1989, GDP per capita ranged from 173 per cent of the EU average in Hamburg (Germany) to only 50 per cent in Nisia (Greece) (Armstrong and Taylor, 1993). Similar disparities are revealed when other indicators of regional disadvantage are examined, such as unemployment rate, annual growth of employment and average annual household income (Corvers *et al.*, 1994a, b). The large economic disparities between regions in the EU greatly exceed those inside the United States (Boltho, 1989). Considering the different types of economically disadvantaged areas in the EU, one can distinguish (CEC, 1991; Armstrong and Taylor, 1993):

1   Urban areas
    - depressed industrial areas (e.g. South Limburg, the Nether-lands);
    - areas of severe urban poverty and decline (e.g. Birmingham, UK).
2   Rural areas
    - depressed agricultural areas under pressure from modern development, near or easily accessible from large conurbations (e.g. Picardie, France);
    - depressed agricultural areas in decline whose survival is threatened (e.g. Calabria, Italy);
    - depressed agricultural areas which are remote, isolated and depopulated (e.g. west Ireland).
3   Border areas
    - along the internal borders of the EU (e.g. Saar-Lor-Lux, along the German-French-Belgian-Luxembourg border);
    - along the external borders of the EU (e.g. northern Greece).

In general, there is a distinct tendency for the poorest regions to be located on the geographical periphery of the EU (especially Ireland, southern Italy, Spain, Portugal, East Germany, Greece) and for the most prosperous regions to be centrally located.

Europe of the Regions

After the signing of the Single European Act (1986) the term 'Europe of the Regions' emerged and was widely known and discussed by the time the Treaty of Maastricht (1992) was signed. The effect of a Single European Market would not only be increased competition between firms, but also between regions. Considering the big differences in economic development between the European regions (around 200), business – no longer hindered by trade barriers – will locate where the locational advantages are best. Therefore, it is believed that previously unknown competition will break out between the European regions (especially between the economically more viable ones) if they want to attract firms to their region.

If a 'Europe of the Regions' is equal to a survival of the fittest regions on the Single European Market there is a real danger of polarized regional development after 1992. Echoing the arguments of the critics of the neo-liberal view which asserts that the 'free market' will favour all types of regions, the European Commission recognized this danger. Higher transport and communication costs in the geographically peripheral regions are likely to put industry in these regions at a disadvantage

(Amin, 1993: 279). In addition to this, a centralization of resources towards the core regions will take place because of their proximity to markets, their superior agglomeration economies, and their established strengths in reaping the scale benefits of market integration in the EU (Amin, 1993: 280). The European Commission's proposed solution to this danger has been the implementation of a more pro-active EU regional policy and the doubling of the budget, in real terms, of the Structural Funds in 1993.

The Treaty of Maastricht introduced a second and from a political point of view interesting definition of a 'Europe of the Regions', when it supplemented the 'economic foundation of federalism' (Cappellin and Batey, 1993: 8) with the principle of subsidiarity as one of the fundamental features of the European Union. The principle of subsidiarity means that each function should be attributed to the lowest efficient decision level within the hierarchical system of relationships between regions, nation-states and the EU. Therefore, functions should not be transferred to a superior level when they can be efficiently exercised at a lower level.[2]

More regional independence from national governments and stronger local representation at the European level is encouraged by Brussels. The core argument is that some degree of regional financial autonomy, coupled with strengthened local governance structures (e.g. regional government, regional assemblies, and regional development agencies) will empower the regions to pursue their own development goals.

Some believe that the 1990s will see a further shift in influence and powers from the national level within the EU 'upwards' towards the EU institutions and in influence 'downwards' towards the regions (Cole and Cole, 1993). The role of the regions will certainly become more explicit, as the extent of regional autonomy according to the principle of subsidiarity depends on criteria of efficiency. However, the actual solution may be rather ambiguous, since the principle is a mere guideline, and depends on the specific country and region concerned, and especially on the different approaches adopted in the specific policy fields considered (Cappellin and Batey, 1993). The Treaty of Maastricht and its principle of subsidiarity represent an important development in the further integration of the EU. Key policy areas, nevertheless, will remain in the hands of the twelve member states.

Besides the economic and political definition of a 'Europe of the Regions', a third definition can be discerned from the work of the European Parliamentary Committee for the Study of Economy and Monetary Union (1989). 'Europe of the Regions' is an explicit recognition of the desirability of preserving and encouraging regional cultural diversity after 1992, so as to allay fears of the potential loss of local identity as a result of the economic and monetary integration of the EU (Amin, 1993: 279).

Border regions: model for or impediment to economic integration?

Considering the different types of economically disadvantaged areas in the EU, three types were distinguished: urban, rural and border regions. Since more economic integration in the Union is expected to lead to a decrease in regional economic inequalities, these regions could benefit significantly from the common market initiative. This is especially true in the case of the border regions. Border regions face a backward regional economic development because of their peripheral location within the nation-state. Historically, border regions have never played an important role in the industrial development of a country. The few times they were integrated in the process of industrialization occurred because of their natural resources, for example, coal. In most cases border regions are economically underdeveloped because of the danger of a military con-flict, the agglomeration tendency of industry elsewhere and the impossibility of market expansion (Mikus, 1986). To their peripheral location can be added the lopsided production structure (either agri-culture or declining industries) and the lack of basic (let alone cross-border) infrastructure (Corvers, 1992).

With increasing economic integration, the Union's internal frontiers will lose much of their previous significance, thereby creating enormous opportunities for border regions. The peripheral location from a national viewpoint, will change into a central location from a European viewpoint which is considered to be a critical locational advantage. For the first time in their existence, border regions can achieve economies of scale and improved efficiency through the joint planning, production and provision of public goods and services (e.g. the linking up of missing infrastructure, the organization of common transport and communication systems, the joint promotion of industry and services). The future development of the border regions has a particular importance for the Union since they represent both a potential impediment to and a potential model for the integrated development of the EU in economic as well as in political terms (CEC, 1991).

One could ask the question whether the importance attached to border regions is reasonable. Consideration of the fact that the EU has almost 10,000 kilometres of land frontier shows that it is. The internal borders make up roughly 60 per cent of this, the remainder being borders between the EU and its neighbours in Central and Eastern Europe. The regions along these borders account for around 15 per cent of the total land area of the Union and some 10 per cent of its population (CEC, 1991).

The European Commission is convinced that the border region is the ultimate place where the success of European integration will be proved. Large differences in production structure and production milieu between areas on either side of the border are considered to hinder that success. The European Union has therefore put a lot of (financial) effort into promoting cross-border co-operation between these regions in order to solve border-related problems. The INTERREG initiative, launched in 1990, stimulates cross-border co-operation in seven areas,[3] is based on projects and finances up to 50 per cent of the project costs. For the first INTERREG period (1991–3) 800 million ECU was made available for all European border regions for a period of three years. Although the negotiations between the European Commission and the member states are still in progress, it is estimated that the budget for the second INTERREG period (1994–9) will be around 3 billion ECU for a period of six years. The launching of this initiative led to the emergence of a new phenomenon, the so-called 'Euregion'. Euregion is an abbreviation of European region, and in most cases is geographically located along the borders of the European Union and indicates some form of cross-border co-operation between (semi-)public organizations. The European Commission was willing to finance cross-border co-operation on condition that border regions have some kind of organization (ranging from gentlemen's agreement to civil and public law) in view of the accountability. Therefore, a Euregion can be seen as an organized border region.

Although the impression could be given that border regions are homogeneous areas and share the same characteristics all over Europe, this is not true. On the contrary, they can be quite diverse in terms of their geographical size, physical characteristics, population density, language, culture, economic characteristics and degree of development (Martinos and Caspari, 1990; CEC, 1991; Corvers *et al.*, 1994a, b). Moreover, there are also significant differences in the bodies that have been set up to initiate, plan or implement cross-border co-operation and the degree of formal co-operation that has been established (Martinos and Caspari, 1990). Differences in level of co-operation (local or regional), in administrative structure (*de facto* or according to civil or public law), in goals to be achieved as well as ways to finance cross-border co-operation make this diversity even more varied (Kessen, 1992). Research on the regional economic profiles of 'Dutch' Euregions showed the reality of this diversity to exist even in a country as small as the Netherlands (Corvers *et al.*, 1994a).

Besides these differences, there also exists a north–south divide between the more developed border regions in the north of the Union and the less developed border areas on the southern and western periphery of the EU (CEC, 1991). These border regions, in Ireland and the south of the Union along the borders between Spain and Portugal, Spain and France, France and Italy and along the external borders of Greece, are largely mountainous areas with underdeveloped economies. Population density in these regions varies from just over 40 people to just under 100 people per km^2, compared to the EU average of 145 (CEC, 1991). By contrast, most border regions in the north of the Union, such as those along the Dutch-German, French-German and Dutch-Belgian frontiers, are densely populated in the range of 240 to 780 people per km^2 (CEC, 1991; Corvers, 1992). These border regions are not divided by any dominant physical features and their economies are developed, yet divided by historical events.

Firms in border regions: economic integration in the backyard?

Firms located in border regions are traditionally confronted with an incomplete market since half of their natural hinterland is on the other side of the national border. This incompleteness refers not only to the firms' sales potential (its customers), but also to the labour market (its employees), the suppliers of its capital goods, its raw materials or semi-manufactured articles and the supply of knowledge by commercial, non-commercial and intermediary organizations. At the same time this incompleteness means that half of the firms' potential competitors are also on the other side of the border. The Single European Market will generate an increase in competition between firms. Being confronted with competitors that used to be invisible behind the national border, firms in border regions will be forced to be more alert concerning possibilities to improve their products in terms of price, quality, speed of delivery and after-sales service. In the 'survival of the fittest firms' it will be necessary to develop faster and more often new or improved products and processes. The availability of technological knowledge in order to put this into practice within a firm becomes crucial to survive on the common market. Besides these threats, the single market initiative will offer previously unknown opportunities for firms located in border regions. These opportunities, however, differ widely between border regions along the external and those along the internal borders of the EU.

The single market opportunities for firms located in the southern and eastern border regions – along the external borders of the EU – are more difficult to predict than for firms along the internal border regions. First, because the external borders of the EU are likely to be replaced by a whole set of new borders by the end of the decade (enlargement discussion). Second, the lack of economic integration between regions on either side of the European eastern border (due to the former Iron Curtain) is likely to hinder development efforts. Third, as a result of that, the administrative, legal and economic systems on either side of this border are much more divergent than those between EU countries. The ability to share public services (health, education, police) and public utilities (electricity, gas, telecommunications) in order to achieve economies of scale and efficient delivery will therefore continue to be severely limited because of these differences. Fourth, the conditions for the free movement of goods, services, labour and capital across the southern and western borders of the EU are rather different from those within the Union (where you have intra-EU trade and cross-border infrastructure). Fifth, border regions in the east will face (and are already facing) significant immigration flows from the East European countries, including flows from the former Soviet Union. These flows are likely to concentrate, at least initially, in areas such as northern Greece, southern Italy, north-eastern Italy, Austria and Germany. Greece and Italy in particular, face an uncertain future as a result of the conflict in Yugoslavia. All these events do not induce an economic and politically stable climate for firms.

The single market opportunities for firms located along the internal borders of the EU seem more obvious, such as an increase in sales potential, a larger supply of labour, cheaper purchasing possibilities and a larger number of knowledge suppliers, all within a radius of 100 kilometres (their natural hinterland). Whether these opportunities (and threats) are indeed seized by firms, nevertheless, depends on three factors.

The first factor is the level of economic development on either side of the border in terms of GDP per capita, unemployment rate, annual growth of employment and average annual household income. Large differences in economic development on either side of the border do not facilitate regional economic integration. A second important factor, besides the level of economic development, is the economic characteristics of the border region – in terms of production structure and production milieu. Opportunities occur when such a region shares complementary sectors, e.g. steel industry on one side of the border and mechanical engineering on the other.

A third factor is the role of the Euregion and particularly what local and regional governments make of it. Cross-border co-operation between (semi-)public organizations in various policy areas can create favourable conditions for regional economic development. For the first time in the existence of border regions, cross-border planning, production and provision of public goods and services will become possible and create unprecedented opportunities for the region as a whole.

The Euregion Maas-Rhine: some statistics

One of the border regions along the internal borders of the EU that will be dealt with in more detail here is the Euregion Maas-Rhine along the Dutch-Belgian-German border (see Figure 9.1). If border regions represent both a potential impediment to and a potential model for the economic integration process of the European Union, this Euregion can be considered an ideal test-case. Compared with other border regions, the Euregion Maas-Rhine has a rather complex setting since it consists of:

- five regions: South Limburg in the Netherlands (NL), Belgian Limburg, the province of Liège and the German-speaking community in Belgium (B) and the Aachen region in Germany (D);
- five cities: Maastricht and Heerlen in the Netherlands, Hasselt and Liège in Belgium and Aachen in Germany;
- four regional authorities: Province of Limburg (NL), Province of Limburg (B), Province of Liège (B) and Regierungsbezirk Köln (D);
- four cultures: Dutch, Flemish, Walloon and German;
- three countries: the Netherlands, Belgium and Germany;
- three languages: Dutch/Flemish, French and German.

Almost 3.6 million people live in the Euregion Maas-Rhine on an area of 10,745 km^2; half of this population lives in the five major cities. The population density of the region is 335 inhabitants per km^2 (the EU average is 145). The Dutch part of the Euregion Maas-Rhine is the most highly populated area per km^2, 787 inhabitants per km^2. The Aachen region has the largest number of inhabitants, over one million.

Organization of cross-border co-operation

The Euregion Maas-Rhine was established in 1976. In this so-called area (see Figure 9.1) it was agreed that cross-border co-operation would take place on a regional level between the Dutch Province Limburg, the Belgian Provinces Limburg and Liège and the German region Aachen (which is located in the Regierungsbezirk Köln and consists of the Stadt Aachen, Kreis Aachen, Kreis Düren, Kreis Euskirchen and Kreis Heinsberg). Their goal is 'to improve the social-economic development of the region by strengthening its advantages and solving its cross-border related problems' (GAP, 1986: 117). In 1990 around sixty projects were submitted for the INTERREG programme by the co-operating provinces. The two policy areas that cover most projects are environment (V) and recreation and tourism (III).

In 1988 the Dutch national government published a White Paper on Spatial Planning ('*Vierde Nota over de Ruimtelijke Ordening*') forecasting the changes in society and their spatial effects to be expected in the next thirty years. One project that was launched in this White Paper was the so-called MHAL project. The goal of this project was to improve the cross-border infrastructure in the area around the cities Maastricht/ Heerlen, Hasselt/Genk, Aachen and Liège (MHAL). The actors who participated in this cross-border co-operation were: the Dutch Ministry of Spatial Planning, the Dutch Ministry of Economic Affairs, the Province of Dutch Limburg and the cities Maastricht and Heerlen. Succeeding in the improvement of cross-border infrastructure cannot be

Figure 9.1 The Euregion Maas-Rhine

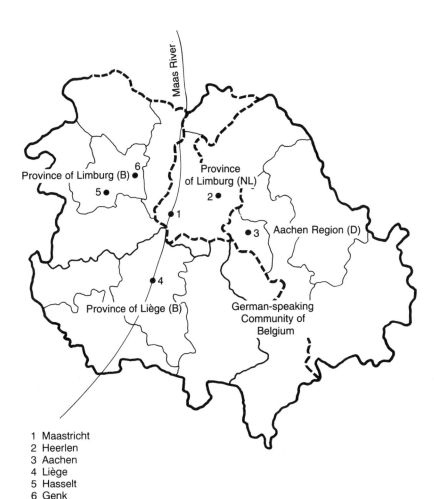

1 Maastricht
2 Heerlen
3 Aachen
4 Liège
5 Hasselt
6 Genk

accomplished by the Dutch Ministry of Spatial Planning alone. Therefore, in December 1989 the Ministers of Spatial Planning of the
Netherlands, Flanders, Wallonia and North Rhine-Westphalia signed a
declaration of intent to co-operate together on this pilot project and
develop the cross-border infrastructure in the Euregion Maas-Rhine
jointly.

In 1989 a third form of cross-border co-operation in the Euregion
Maas-Rhine was established by the five major cities, the so-called MHAL
cities. This local level of co-operation can be considered a spin-off from
the national MHAL project and a reaction to the meagre results of the
provincial co-operation since 1976. The MHAL city co-operation concentrates on specific topics such as knowledge infrastructure, tourism,
environment and transport, in order to develop the potentials of this (in
their view) coherent urban area. Unlike the provincial cross-border co-
operation, where the individual border problem is the starting-point, the
urban co-operation takes the high degree of urban cohesion in the area as
its starting-point. The cities have developed a joint physical planning
policy with a clear cross-border dimension in which each city will pursue
a certain functional specialization.[4]

Economic history

Although the Euregion Maas-Rhine is now divided by three national
borders, it has shared a similar economic history based on a long tradition
of industrialization on the basis of coal and iron, which goes back to the
middle of the nineteenth century. The Euregion Maas-Rhine forms one
of the rare examples of a border region that has played a crucial role in
the industrial development of its country. Early industrialization is still
visible in the presence of a large number of traditional industries (metal,
paper, ceramics, glass and chemical industry). From the second half of
this century coal- and steel-based activities could no longer ensure
sufficient economic growth and since the 1960s all parts of the Euregion
have been struggling with problems of economic conversion. Over
100,000 people lost their jobs in mining and national governments have
pursued different restructuring policies to solve the enormous unemployment problem. Common to these restructuring policies is the emphasis
on improving basic infrastructure (road, rail, water, industrial estates),
attracting new firms (often branch plants) and establishing knowledge
institutes (the University of Maastricht was founded in 1974 and formed
a significant part of Dutch restructuring policy).

The mines in the Dutch part of the Euregion were the first to close,
starting twenty-five years ago. Conversion has been largely completed by
transforming the Dutch State Mines into one of the largest chemical
enterprises in the world (DSM, net sales in 1991 FFr9.347 billion). Before

the end of this century the mines in the Aachen area will be closed and Aachen will no doubt base its conversion on the presence of the largest European technical university, which has already led to the establishment of hundreds of small engineering and consultancy firms. The prominent position of manufacturing in the Belgian parts of the Euregion has lost considerable ground to services in the past decade, much more than in the rest of the Euregion, as a result of economic conversion policies.

The problematic economic development of the Euregion has also attracted (financial) attention from the EC. Being a border region and consisting of depressed industrial and agricultural areas, the Euregion embodies three types of economically disadvantaged areas which have been distinguished by the European Commission in its regional policy. Economic indicators such as unemployment rate and gross regional product show that all parts of the Euregion Maas-Rhine, despite the national restructuring policies, still lag slightly behind average figures of the national state or 'Land' (see Table 9.1).

Table 9.1 Economic indicators per sub-region in the Euregion Maas-Rhine

Area	Unemployment rate 1992 (%)	Gross regional product per inhabitant 1990 (ECU)
The Netherlands	8.7	14,705
South Limburg	8.9	12,918
Belgium	7.6	15,200
Limburg	7.8	15,034
Liège	10.8	13,971
North Rhine-Westphalia	5.7	17,641
Aachen region	5.8	13,197

Sources: Eurostat (1992); ETIL (1993)

Production structure

The whole Euregion Maas-Rhine can be regarded as a manufacturing area (see Knapp *et al.*, 1988), although employment in the service sector has been growing rapidly during the 1980s and agriculture is still important in certain parts of the Euregion (see Table 9.2). In all sub-regions, except for the western part of South Limburg, many people work in the manufacturing industry compared with national or 'Land' figures. The Belgian parts of the Euregion are more characterized by a concentration of manufacturing industry in a few branches than the Dutch and German parts of the Euregion. In Liège 44 per cent of the manufacturing employees work in the metal industry. In Belgian Limburg the metal and car industries are by far most important (49.9 per cent of manufacturing employment) (Allaert, 1992: 69). In the Aachen region, 45 per cent of the employees in the ten largest manufacturing industries work in mechanical engineering, electrical engineering and coalmining (Fromhold-Eisebith, 1992: 95). The three largest industries in the manufacturing sector in South Limburg are chemicals, wood/paper and stone/ceramics/glass, employing 43 per cent of the manufacturing workers. The chemical industry is much more important in South Limburg than in the Netherlands as a whole (28.5 per cent of the total manufacturing workforce in South Limburg compared with 10 per cent of the total Dutch workforce in manufacturing industry) (Dassen *et al.*, 1992: 12).

Firms in the Euregion Maas-Rhine tend to employ a large number of employees compared with national figures. Apart from the Aachen region, where firms have an average size (Fromhold-Eisebith, 1992: 94), in all other sub-regions in the Belgian and Dutch part of the Euregion the number of large firms (500 and more employees) are over-represented (Knapp *et al.*, 1988: 40). Manufacturing industry in South Limburg is little dependent on decisions from outside the region compared with national figures and foreign neighbouring regions, such as Belgian Limburg. In South Limburg 85.7 per cent of manufacturing firms are independent (in the Netherlands 73.0 per cent), 9.4 per cent are branches of a Dutch company (in the Netherlands 17.7 per cent) and 4.9 per cent are branches of a foreign company (in the Netherlands 9.3 per cent) (Kleinknecht and Poot, 1990: 74). In contrast with the other parts of the Euregion, Belgian Limburg has attracted many foreign 'branch plants' in order to compensate for the job losses in coalmining (Swyngedouw, 1990). More than 50 per cent of the manufacturing employment in Belgian Limburg belongs to foreign companies (such as Ford, Philips, Volvo Car, KNP, Siemens), whereas in Dutch Limburg 20 per cent of the employment belongs to foreign companies, in the Aachen Region 25–30 per cent and in the Province of Liège 25–30 per cent (BCI, 1990).

Public research establishments and policies to stimulate technology transfer

Public research establishments consist of those public or semi-public organizations that either carry out research exclusively to serve government or that partly carry out market-oriented research (Charles and Howells, 1992: 24), for example the Fraunhofer Institutes or Max Planck Institutes in Germany, the laboratories of the Centre National de la Recherche Scientifique (CNRS) in France and TNO in the Netherlands. Although South Limburg has many higher education institutes, there are almost no public research establishments that could be used by firms to solve technological problems (Ter Haar and Vermeulen, 1991). Technical subjects are not unrepresented at the University of Limburg in Maastricht (7,000 students). The polytechnic at Heerlen (1,700 students) offers technical subjects, but has no research facilities. Public research establishments that could be used by firms in South Limburg are located just on the other side of the border in the Aachen region. This region is extremely well equipped with higher education institutes (RWTH with 37,000 students and Polytechnic Aachen with10,600 students) and public research establishments (Federal Research Centre Jülich and Fraunhofer Institutes for Laser Technology and Production Technology in

Table 9.2 Production structure of the Euregion Maas-Rhine in terms of sectors

	30 June 1982	30 June 1989
South Limburg (NL)		
Agriculture	3.0	2.9
Manufacturing/energy	26.9	27.6
Building	9.2	7.5
Services	46.3	48.0
Public sector	14.6	14.0
Total	100.0	100.0
Belgian Limburg (B)		
Agriculture	0.4	0.6
Manufacturing/energy	41.2	34.0
Building	8.0	7.7
Services	27.8	36.4
Public sector	22.6	21.3
Total	100.0	100.0
Liège (B)		
Agriculture	0.3	0.3
Manufacturing/energy	31.3	24.6
Building	7.5	6.2
Services	36.4	44.5
Public sector	24.5	24.4
Total	100.0	100.0
Aachen region (D)		
Agriculture	0.7	0.9
Manufacturing/energy	44.5	42.0
Building	8.0	6.3
Services	40.1	44.0
Public sector	6.7	6.8
Total	100.0	100.0

Source: EMR (1991: 8)

Aachen). Belgian Limburg has only a small university in Diepenbeek (LUC, 1,400 students) and lacks important public research establishments. Liège has a full university (ULg, 12,000 students), and several specialized research centres, such as the Centre de Recherches de Metallurgiques. Although the variety in public research supply in the Euregion is large, cross-border technology transfer is at a low level in general (Beerts, 1988; Fromhold-Eisebith, 1992).

In all parts of the Euregion, Maas-Rhine initiatives have been set up to foster technology transfer. This can be seen in the framework of the shift from traditional regional policy (the attraction of inward investment) to the development of regional endogenous potential in which technology transfer and support for small and medium-sized enterprises play an important role (Hassink, 1992). In the Aachen region, the Aachener Gesellschaft für Innovation und Technologietransfer (AGIT) is a powerful regional body which is responsible for all activities in the field of regional technology transfer, consultancy and marketing of the Aachen region (inward investment). In South Limburg there is more overlap. Two nationally initiated organizations, the Innovation Centre and the Industriebank LIOF, are the two main organizations engaged in technology transfer and consultancy. In Belgian Limburg, the Gewestelijke Ontwikkelings Maatschappij (GOM) is the main regional development body. The GOM focuses mainly on attracting inward investment, although it also has some technology-related consultancy tasks for endogenous firms. The regional development organization in Liège, the Société Provinciale d'Industrialisation (SPI), fully concentrates on real estate management in order to offer inward investors a proper site. The technology transfer agency of the University of Liège, Interface, can be considered the main technology transfer body in this sub-region. Unlike the transfer agencies of the other universities in the Euregion, Interface has a pro-active attitude towards SMEs, as it visits some 200 of these enterprises each year.

The above-mentioned organizations differ considerably with regard to their tasks, their financial sources and their organization. Cross-border co-operation between these bodies in order to foster Euregional technology transfer and networking is undertaken, but has proved to be rather difficult. Unlike the technology transfer organization in the Aachen region, the Dutch and Belgian 'regional development organizations' are not regionally initiated, but are installed by national policy to induce regional economic growth. Therefore, they are confined to national tasks and less interested in cross-border co-operation. In addition to this, simultaneous co-operation and competition between the regional development agencies obviously make for an uneasy alliance. The technology transfer agencies of the universities in the Euregion, however, are now in the middle of a co-operation process, as they have established the Euregional TRansfer Agency (ETRA).

Firms in the Euregion Maas-Rhine: results of a questionnaire

In order to find out whether the opportunities of the Single European Market are being seized by the firms located in the Euregion, a questionnaire was sent to almost 2,200 manufacturing firms with 10 or more employees in the Euregion Maas-Rhine between September 1992 and April 1993. One of the questions asked what business partners (nine in total) were considered to be the most important for the development or introduction of technically improved or new products or production methods. A second question asked where the business partners that were considered 'most important' were geographically located. The response rate was 22.3 per cent (483 firms out of 2,163 filled in and returned the questionnaire). South Limburg had the highest response rate (30.0 per cent) whereas the Aachen region had the lowest (19.7 per cent) (see Table 9.3).

Table 9.3 Analysis of response in the Euregion Maas-Rhine

	Number of firms contacted	Number of questionnaires received	Response rate (%)
Dutch part (South Limburg)	483	145	30.0
Belgian part (provinces of Limburg and Liège)	866	178	20.5
German part (Aachen region)	814	160	19.7
Euregion Maas-Rhine	2,163	483	22.3

Source: MERIT, ISI, Namur

According to one contemporary influential body of thought the existence of bottom-up developed networks between small and medium-sized enterprises as well as between SMEs and institutions attached to SMEs, such as research centres and training facilities, is considered to be an important factor in enhancing regional economic growth (Piore and Sabel, 1989; Porter, 1990). These networks can perform as an ideal mechanism for the absorption and diffusion of new technologies because they link up all the activities that are important in one specific industry in one region. Research done by the Fraunhofer-Institut für Systemtechnik und Innovationsforschung (FhG-ISI) in Karlsruhe, Germany, showed that firms which were innovative and developing well economically tend to have many external relations with research centres and other firms.

Our questionnaire was therefore interested in the business partners that firms considered to be important for the development or introduction of technically improved or new products or production methods. From the nine categories of business partners, customers and suppliers were considered most important by all enterprises in the Euregion Maas-Rhine. Among the business partners regarded as least important for generating new technological ideas were the universities, chambers of commerce, industry associations and other intermediary organizations (Figure 9.2).

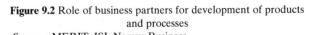

Figure 9.2 Role of business partners for development of products and processes
Sources: MERIT, ISI, Namur Business

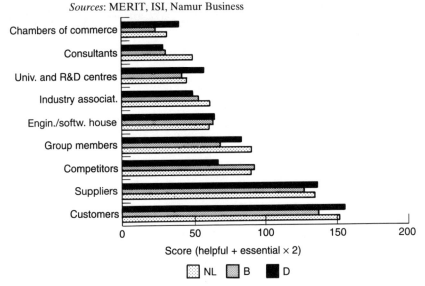

The geographical location of the most important business partners – mostly in the region or further away in their own country – confirms the national orientation of firms. Although there may be cheaper purchasing possibilities just across the border or markets to be discovered, the orientation of firms in all three parts of the Euregion Maas-Rhine is primarily national. However, we have found some differences between the three sub-regions. Enterprises in South Limburg have more customers, suppliers and competitors they consider an important business partner in the foreign parts of the Euregion than enterprises in the Belgian and German parts (compare Figure 9.3 with Figures 9.4 and 9.5).

German enterprises are noteworthy because they have the lowest orientation on the Euregion in terms of customers, suppliers and competitors (see Figure 9.4). Belgian enterprises take up a middle position:

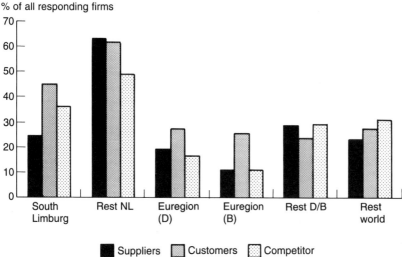

Figure 9.3 Location of important business partners of Dutch firms in
the Euregion Maas-Rhine
Sources: MERIT, ISI, Namur Business

important customers and suppliers are located in the region and in the rest of the country, but they also have some of these business partners in the foreign parts of the Euregion (see Figure 9.5).

Besides differences between sub-regions, the geographical location of important business partners is also related to the size of firms in the Euregion Maas-Rhine. Small and medium-sized enterprises are more regionally oriented whereas large enterprises have more suppliers from outside the Netherlands, Belgium and Germany. The same applies to the customers and competitors of large enterprises: they operate on a global market. About 50 per cent of the small and medium-sized enterprises indicated that an important source of technological knowledge could be found among their customers and competitors in the region.

Not only networking between firms, SMEs in particular, is seen as an important factor in enhancing regional economic growth, but also net-working between SMEs and universities and research institutes. Although enterprises in all parts of the Euregion Maas-Rhine consider universities and research institutes less important in generating new technological ideas, there are some differences.

Enterprises in the Aachen region have more contacts with universities and research institutes (36.6 per cent) in order to attract technological knowledge than the Belgian (22.6 per cent) and Dutch enterprises (21.0 per cent). Although there is a traditional difference between SMEs and large enterprises in attracting technological knowledge from universities and research institutes, this difference is much less apparent in the

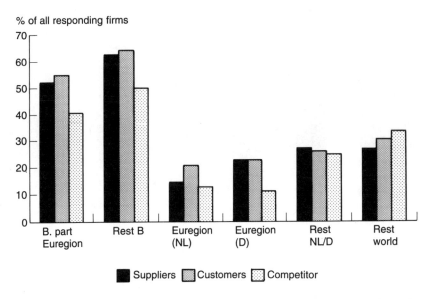

Figure 9.4 Location of important business partners of Belgian firms
in the Euregion Maas-Rhine
Sources: MERIT, ISI Namur Business

Aachen region compared with the foreign parts of the Euregion. A reason for this could be the vast supply of knowledge institutes in the

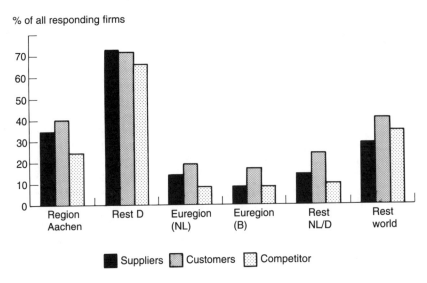

Figure 9.5 Location of important business partners of German firms
in the Euregion Mass-Rhine
Sources: MERIT, ISI, Namur Business

Aachen region and the more intense relationships between firms, including SMEs, and universities and research institutes via former students and former supervisors. The existence of these personal technology transfer relationships could indicate a higher level of innovativeness of firms in the Aachen region.

Of all the enterprises in the Euregion, firms located in South Limburg have the most Euregional contacts with universities across the border, whereas German firms have no Euregional university orientation at all. This is less surprising when you consider that the university located in the Aachen region, the RWTH, is Europe's largest technical university. Again, Belgian enterprises take up a middle position: they have some contacts with Euregional universities, but most of the mentioned international contacts are with the Technical University Eindhoven, which is located just outside the Euregion Maas-Rhine.

Conclusion

The emergence of a 'Europe of the Regions' could become real for some regions – the economically most viable – and due to the subsidiarity principle might empower them to pursue their own economic development goals. However, there is a likely danger that the economically more disadvantaged regions will find themselves worse off. In this respect, border regions form an interesting case, since their economic performance could go either way. The fact that the cause of their backward economic development, namely an incomplete hinterland due to the existence of a national border, is abolished certainly opens up new opportunities as well as new threats for their future economic development.

One such border region where new opportunities for regional economic development are emerging is the Euregion Maas-Rhine situated along the Dutch-Belgian-German border region. The opportunities seem rather obvious, considering the level of economic development of the Euregion Maas-Rhine in terms of economic indicators and the economic characteristics in terms of production structure and production milieu. Cross-border co-operation has existed in the Euregion Maas-Rhine since 1976 on the provincial level and since 1989 on the urban level. Although both forms of cross-border co-operation aim at stimulating the Euregional economic development in the light of the 'Europe of the Regions', one can ask whether the formula chosen is the best way to overcome border problems. Should the starting-point have been the firms in the region, since they are the engine of regional economic growth? Is there not a real danger that the border problems which are solved by the provincial and urban authorities are completely different from those encountered by firms located in a border region?

Cross-border co-operation between (semi-)public organizations in various policy areas can create favourable conditions to stimulate or at least facilitate economic growth. The question addressed by this chapter is how? Starting from the hypotheses that a prosperous region is built upon prosperous firms and that the prosperity of firms nowadays depends increasingly on their ability to innovate, we investigated what firms in the Euregion consider to be the most important business partners for the 'development or introduction of technically improved or new products or production methods' and where these business partners are located geographically. A questionnaire was sent to almost 2,200 manufacturing firms with 10 or more employees in the Euregion. The almost unanimous outcome was that customers, suppliers and competitors were considered to be the most important business partners by firms in all parts of the Euregion Maas-Rhine. A more striking result was that, despite the common industrial history and heritage of the Euregion based on coal, these important business partners were located either in the firm's region or in the rest of the country. This was true for firms in all parts of the Euregion. SMEs in all parts of the Euregion are more regionally oriented, whereas large enterprises are more likely to operate on a global market, beyond the nation-state.

If governments really want to 'use' the instrument of cross-border co-operation to stimulate or at least facilitate economic growth in the region, regular or (even better) institutionalized contacts between governments on either side of the border are useful, but not sufficient. Since economic growth is produced by firms and since the competitive potential of a firm depends increasingly on its technological knowledge and practical application, cross-border co-operation should focus more on firms and facilitate technology transfer across the border. Many sources of technological know-how in border regions are still untapped, whether they concern customers, suppliers of capital goods, raw materials or semi-manufactured articles, competitors, employees or universities and research institutions. Research done by the Fraunhofer-Institut für Systemtechnik und Innovationsforschung (FhG-ISI) in Karlsruhe, Germany, showed that innovative firms which were developing well economically tend to have many external relations with research centres and other firms.

If it is possible for public actors to intervene in the relationships between firms and their business partners, the question is how to facilitate this cross-border networking. A well-thought-out Euregional innovation policy (including a well thought out cast of actors most suited to implement it) might just provide the answer. Elements of an 'Euregional innovation policy' could be:

1. Regional and urban as well as semi-public authorities such as chambers of commerce and regional development agencies could co-operate together in order to supply 'high quality' information on aspects such as export opportunities in the Euregion Maas-Rhine, potential suppliers, useful research institutions and the possibilities of co-operation with complementing firms.
2. Since firms, especially small and medium-sized firms, regard their customers and suppliers as the two most important sources for technological ideas, chambers of commerce and regional development agencies should take this relationship as the starting-point. This could be achieved by organizing Euregional industrial fora, trade and industry 'contact days', partner match conferences, workshops and information gatherings (for example on specific technologies).
3. Employers are also a source of (technological) knowledge, but neither firms nor (semi-)public organizations have yet exploited the possibilities of the Euregional labour market. More co-operation between technology transfer agencies in the Euregion could help here. Other activities could include exchanges between schools (secondary level), cross-border vocational training, profession-oriented language courses for employees, stimulating students to take courses at the other universities in the Euregion Maas-Rhine (and certifying them) and cross-border apprenticeships.
4. Finally, one has the impression that the governments – both provincial and urban – participating in cross-border co-operation are very keen on emphasizing the advantages of closer co-operation in the Euregion Maas-Rhine (e.g. a market of almost 3.6 million consumers opening up), but avoid addressing the typical border-related problems that can only solved by closer co-operation.

Notes

1. 'In order to promote its overall harmonious development, the Community shall develop and pursue its actions leading to the strengthening of its economic and social cohesion. In particular, the Community shall aim at reducing disparities between the various regions and the backwardness of the least-favoured regions' (Art.130a EEC Treaty 1986 as quoted in: Cole and Cole, 1993: 224).
2. 'This Treaty marks a new stage in the process creating an ever closer Union among the peoples of Europe, where decisions are taken as closely as possible to the citizens ... The Community shall take action ... only if ... the objectives of the proposed action cannot be sufficiently achieved by the Member States' (Art.1 Treaty on European Union as quoted in: Cole and Cole, 1993: 277).
3. These seven areas are: I networking, information exchange and communication; II traffic, transport and infrastructure; III recreation and tourism; IV

education and labour market; V environment; VI technology transfer and innovation; VII research and project management.
4. Aachen: strong technological knowledge infrastructure.
Liège: transport sector, international commercial services.
Maastricht: conference city, international knowledge institutes, non-commercial services.
Hasselt/Genk: industrial position (strong automotive sector).
Heerlen: chemical industry.

References

Allaert, G. (1992), *De regionaal-economische dynamiek van Limburg: een verkenning en aanzet tot strategische planning voor de jaren '90*. Hasselt, Stalmans and Gen, SSRG/Universiteit Gent.

Amin, A. (1993), 'The globalization of the economy. An erosion of regional networks?', in Grabher, G. (ed.), *The Embedded Firm. On the Socio-Economics of Industrial Networks*. London, Routledge.

Armstrong, H., Taylor, J. (1993), *Regional Economics and Policy*, 2nd edn. New York, Harvester Wheatsheaf.

BCI (1990), *Waar liggen de grenzen? Een visie op Limburg, 25 jaar verder*. Nijmegen, Buck Consultants International.

Beerts, L. (1988), *Het produktiemilieu van Limburg in grensoverschrijdend perspectief*. Maastricht, Economisch Technologisch Instituut Limburg.

Boltho, A. (1989), 'European and United States regional differentials: a note', *Oxford Review of Economic Policy*, Summer.

Cappellin, R., Batey, P.W.J. (eds) (1993), *Regional Networks, Border Regions and European Integration*. London, Pion.

CEC (1977), *Guidelines for Community Regional Policy*. COM (77) 195 final, Brussels.

—— (1991), *Europe 2000; Outlook for the Development of the Community's Territory*. Brussels/Luxembourg, CEL, DG XVI.

Charles, D., Howells, J.(1992), *Technology Transfer in Europe: Public and Private Networks*. London, Belhaven Press.

Cole, J., Cole, F. (1993), *The Geography of the European Community*. London, Routledge.

Corvers, F.B.J.A. (1992), 'Grensregionale samenwerking als institutioneel arragement. De Nederlandse grensregio Euregio Maas-Rijn als voorbeeld'. MA thesis, University of Leiden, Faculty of Social Science, Department of Public Administration.

Corvers, F., Dankbaar, B., Hassink R. (1994a), *Euregio's in Nederland. Een inventarisatie van economische ontwikkelingen en beleid*. Den Haag, COB/ SER.

—— (1994b), *Nieuwe kansen voor bedrijven grensregio's, eindrapport*. Den Haag, COB/SER.

Dassen, H., Derks, W., Hanraets, P., Vermeulen, W. (1992), *Zuidlimburgse Ekonomie, Sterkte en zwakte, kansen en bedreigingen*. Maastricht, Economisch Technologisch Instituut Limburg.

DSM N.V. *Annual Report 1991*.

EMR (1991), *Operationeel INTERREG-programma 1991-1993 voor de Euregio Maas-Rijn.*

ETIL (1993), *Limburgse Sociaal Ekonomische Verkenning.* Maastricht, Economisch Technologisch Instituut Limburg.

Eurostat (1992), Regional statistical data. Luxembourg.

Fromhold-Eisebith, M. (1992), *Wissenschaft und Forschung als regionalwirtschaftliches Potential? Das Beispiel von Rheinisch-Westfälischer Technischer Hochschule und Region Aachen.* Aachen, Informationen und Materialien zur Geographie der Euregio Maas-Rhein, Beiheft Nr. 4.

GAP (1986), *Grensoverschrijdend Actieprogramma van de Euregio Maas-Rijn.* Euregio Maas-Rijn Bureau.

Hassink, R. (1992), 'Regional innovation policy: case-studies from the Ruhr Area, Baden-Württemberg and the North East of England'. PhD thesis at the University of Utrecht, Faculty of Geographical Sciences (Netherlands Geographical Studies 145).

INTERREG (1990), Explanatory Memorandum, XVI/66/90A, Notice C(90) to the Member States, XVI/66/90B. CEC, Brussels.

Kessen, A.A.L.G.M. (1992), 'Bestuurlijke vernieuwing in grensgebieden; intergemeentelijke grensoverschrijdende samenwerking'. PhD thesis at the University of Nijmegen, Faculty of Policy Sciences.

Kleinknecht, A.H., Poot, A.P. (1990), *De regionale dimensie van innovatie in de Nederlandse industrie en dienstverlening.* Amsterdam, Stichting voor Economisch Onderzoek der Universiteit van Amsterdam.

Knapp, W., Mielke, B., Weber, R. (1988), *Strukturanalyse für die Euregio Maas-Rhein.* Dortmund, Institut für Landes- und Stadtentwicklungsforschung des Landes Nordrhein-Westfalen.

Martinos, H., Caspari, A. (1990), *Co-operation between Border Regions for Local and Regional Development.* The Innovation Development Planning Group, prepared for the CEC, DG XVI.

MHAL (1993), *Ruimtelijk Ontwikkelingsperspectief Ontwerp.* Internationale Coördinatiecommissie MHAL.

Mikus, W. (1986), 'Industrial systems and change in the economies of border regions: cross cultural comparisons', in Hamilton, I., (ed.), *Industrialization in Developing and Peripheral Regions.* London, Croom Helm.

Piore, M.J., Sabel, C.F. (1989), *Das Ende der Massenproduktion.* Frankfurt am Main, Fischer Taschenbuch Verlag.

Porter, M.E. (1990), *The Competitive Advantage of Nations.* London, Macmillan.

Swyngedouw, E.A. (1990), 'Limburg en de wereldeconomie: het Belgische Fordisme op zijn best', in Kesteloot, C. (ed.), *Barsten in België.* Berchem, EPO.

Ter Haar, J.G., Vermeulen, W.C.M. (1991), *Industrie en innovatie in Limburg. Een aktuele schets.* Maastricht, Economisch Technologisch Instituut Limburg.

Van Run, P.L.J.M., Verheij, A.H. (1991), 'Regio's in Europa / Europese Fondsen', in Roest, N.F., Mortelmans, K.J.M., Oele, A.P., Boone, J.H. (eds), *Europa binnen het bestuur.* Den Haag, SDU Uitgeverij.

Part IV

Community-based economic development in the Americas

10

Community-based economic development in the USA and Latin America

PATRICIA A. WILSON

Introduction

Privatization, decentralization, cost recovery, free trade, and flexible production – the key words of the hegemonic paradigm reflect a fascinating
change in the correlation of forces. Over the last fifteen years a diminishing
role for the nation-state has left greater responsibility to local actors to
address local needs for jobs and income, and the changing global economy
has made it imperative to do so in most cities and communities. Local civil
society has blossomed into an array of organizations aimed at local
economic development (LED). They have created partnerships among
themselves, between community and business groups and with the local
public sector, and they have networked nationally and internationally.
Community economic development is no longer either localist or naive.
Yet with its increasing sophistication, it has not lost the ultimate source of
its strength and wisdom: the community itself.

This chapter first reviews the diminishing role of the nation-state in
both North America and Latin America, where striking similarities and
interlocked trends are found. It then describes the rise of civil society's
involvement in local economic development, through the community
development corporation (CDC) movement in the USA and the proliferation of community-oriented NGOs (non-governmental organizations) in Latin America.

The public sector and LED

Urban economic development in the USA

US inner city unrest in the 1960s roughly paralleled the rise of urban
populist demands in Latin America. Like many national governments in

Latin America, the US government responded with nationally funded
community development programmes. President Johnson's Model Cities
programme was designed to address urban poverty through federal
spending for community services and housing – not jobs and income.
Urban economic development did not get on the federal government's
agenda until the late 1970s, except for the introduction of federal loans to
small minority-owned businesses – Nixon's 'black capitalism' approach.

The Carter administration in the late 1970s saw the end was near for
large-scale federal spending programmes for urban poverty. It was time
for government to work with the private sector to alleviate urban poverty
through job creation. The federal government began to fund local
governments to hire economic development planners. It made existing
federal revenue sharing money eligible for local economic development
activities. It provided funds to cities for lending to private companies
willing to invest in low income areas (the recapitalized fund would
become the city's to continue to lend).

Federal funds for urban economic development were allocated in part
on the basis of need – e.g. poverty and unemployment indicators – and
partly on the basis of the local government's ability to leverage private
sector investment. Measuring private/public investment ratios and public
cost of private job created became the trendy thing to compete for grants.
So local governments, with federal government funding, plunged into the
business of 'deal making' – gap financing, finding just that amount of
private investor subsidy required to make the bottom line interesting to
the investor. Federal incentives to promote local strategic planning for
economic development resulted only in perfunctory responses seen as a
hurdle to get federal funds. Local economic development planning
remained little more than individual deal making, often with outside
investors pitting one community against another in a zero-sum game.

Then came the Reagan–Bush years, with a redefinition of the term
entrepreneurial government. It no longer meant deal making, it meant
efficient, downsized, and lean. Local government was not to get involved
in private investment, but to provide whatever public services it was
supposed to as efficiently as possible, hopefully through private con-
tractors. Federal grant and loan programmes for urban economic
development were decimated. Local 'deal making' was decried as inefficient subsidies to the private sector. Industrial revenue bonds, the
popular local recruitment tool that provided below-market money to
developers at the expense of foregone federal tax revenue, were sharply
curtailed as an example of inefficient place competition based on private
sector subsidies. Despite free market rhetoric, the defensive posture of
communities in the global economy made the zero-sum game of luring
outside companies with local subsidies the major economic development
game in town.

The Clinton administration has inherited the conservative (now bi-partisan) mantle of dismantling the welfare system, replacing it with incentives to work. But the rhetoric behind the administration's efforts is distinctly different from the conservative rhetoric of efficiency and free market. During the presidential campaign Clinton framed the debate on urban poverty and the role of the state in terms of empowerment, not in the 1960s' sense of the have-nots against the system, but in the sense of individual transformation encouraged by the state. The state must never again undermine the self-respect, self-esteem, inner strength of the individual as it has through welfare. It must empower each individual to develop his/her full potential as a human being. This was the media message that the election campaign put across and that the public largely bought into willingly and excitedly.

Now in practice, the empowerment rhetoric has been battered down in Congress to a combination of training programmes tied into limited welfare funds, a few 'empowerment zone' showcases, several dozen urban 'enterprise communities', and support for development banking.

While the proposed empowerment zones and enterprise communities do not look qualitatively much different from prior enterprise zones, there is one new ingredient: consensus building among the local organized civil society, the local state and the business sector. To be granted an empowerment zone, a city must show that it has devised an economic development strategy that reflects a consensus among the stakeholders. The strategy must reflect the principles of equal opportunity, sustainable community development, community-based partnerships, and strategic planning. An important goal is to ensure that grassroots groups and the NGOs that work with them will be brought to the table, thus helping to legitimate and empower them and forge consensus rather than confrontation. The administration is counting on the small probability of a city's being selected as one of only six urban empowerment zones to motivate cities across the nation to engage in this horizontal planning process. Of course, the administration's effort to involve community groups in consensus building around local economic development is not original, in that grassroots groups and their NGOs have been learning since the late 1970s the need for, and art of, consensus building and co-operation with the private sector. (See section on CDCs, pages 207–209.) What the strategic planning requirement in the empowerment zone legislation could do is give the local public sector a more pivotal role at the table.

The other Clinton initiative is development banking. The 1980s witnessed a spontaneous growth in third sector development banking – i.e. private for profit or non-profit financial intermediaries with social objectives. They include large intermediaries such as the Ford Foundation's Local Initiatives Support Corporation, South Shore Bank, and the

Lakota Fund, as well as many small funds operated by community development corporations and community credit unions. They finance community-based enterprises ranging from sizeable land developments to micro-enterprises (see section on CDCs, pages 207–209). Commercial banks have also been creating non-profit community development banks to satisfy the requirements of the Community Reinvestment Act, federal legislation lobbied for and monitored by grassroots initiative to reduce redlining in low income and minority areas.

Thus, the proposed federal support for development banking is building on an existing movement, not introducing a new tool. Through the 1980s development banks were capitalized primarily by philanthropic foundations and socially minded individuals. In the 1990s, development banking gained support from state and local governments. Some observers question the advisability of federal involvement, as Clinton plans, because of the controls and standards that are tied to the funding (see Chapter 14).

Most of the Clinton initiatives for urban economic development are intended to be funded by redirecting existing programmes. For example, the Federal Department of Housing and Urban Development, headed by former San Antonio mayor and one-time CDC staffer, Henry Cisneros, is targeting existing work-study money to encourage minority and low income students to study community development planning and do paid internships with community-based NGOs involved in local community and economic development.

Decentralization and municipal strengthening in Latin America

Neo-liberal, or free market, discourse started in Chile in the mid-1970s and, with the economic crisis of the early 1980s spread throughout most of Latin America. In many countries military governments began dismantling populist reforms, lifting protectionist trade barriers, and privatizing state-owned industries. With the resurgence of civilian governments throughout the region in the 1980s, decentralization to the hitherto ignored municipal level became the clarion call.

Yet among the 'competences' being decentralized to the municipal level, economic development did not figure. Local government in Latin America never got involved in deal making with the local private sector as it had in the USA. The neo-liberal shift more directly paralleled the Reagan years in the USA. With the support of international lenders, municipal strengthening focused on efficient management, revenue generation (through streamlining tax collection), cost recovery in municipal service provision, privatizing even long-standing municipal enterprises and services such as slaughterhouses, central markets, and garbage collection. By and large, neither international lenders nor central governments have considered economic development an appropriate function for local government.

Nevertheless, some municipalities, now with greater autonomy and resources, have been promoting local economic development in the informal sector – e.g. organizing grassroots micro-enterprises to provide low-cost public services for marginal neighbourhoods such as garbage collection and street paving. A number of municipalities have awakened to the fact that the informal sector can be an economic resource to be encouraged rather than an obstacle to orderly development. Local government involvement in economic development is still incipient, however, in Latin America.

Civil society and LED

The 1980s and 1990s witnessed a new vitality in civil society and the increasing involvement of grassroots groups and NGOs in local economic development in both the USA and Latin America.

NGOs and LED in Latin America

Since the early 1970s more than 100,000 NGOs have been founded in the Third World, over 10,000 of which have been in Latin America (Breslin, 1991; Fisher, 1993). The grassroots NGO movement took off in Latin America in the 1970s, when the region was covered by military governments that allowed no political expression through parties. International donor money, side-stepping the authoritarian governments, gave generously to the NGOs. They continued to give generously in the 1980s, as Latin American governments offered very little in the way of social programmes to address the inequities of neo-liberal development. NGOs that support grassroots groups are typically founded either by the grassroots groups themselves, by local academics or professionals, or by international or national organizations. It is commonplace now to find intellectuals and technically trained professionals in Latin America seeking to work with grassroots organizations and NGOs.

While many of the urban NGOs started out to support local self-help efforts to meet specific community needs, a second generation of NGOs has taken on developmental aims. Drawing on the strength of the growing informal sector, they arc helping grassroots organizations to develop income-generating activities – e.g. micro-enterprises, producer co-operatives, credit unions and lending circles (Korten, 1987). Many NGOs have taken on ecological and gender concerns as well, seeing them as an integral part of their development concerns (Fisher, 1993). Grassroots NGOs in Latin America sometimes use an empowering verbal consciousness-raising method popularized by Paolo Freire, a student of

Foucault. This method allows community members to see the inter-relatedness between problems by drawing on their own self-knowledge (see Chapter 13).

Three generations of NGOs in Latin America
1   Oriented towards specific community needs
2   Involved in income-generating activities
3   Broader strategies, networks and institution building

International donors of all political stripes have been supportive of NGO efforts in micro-enterprise development. The right sees it as relying on the market to address social problems. The left identifies it as a means for organizing the community. But increasingly the left–right dichotomy is giving way to the view that micro-enterprise development is simply a way of recognizing the reality of the growing informal sector and improving the well-being of its members. Many NGOs integrate micro-enterprise development with other aspects of community development.

A third generation of NGOs in Latin America is integrating specific local interests into broader strategies, networks and consortia, and institution building. They are networking micro-enterprises to achieve economies of scale, as in the case of Villa El Salvador, Peru.[1] They are building spatial networks across neighbourhoods, cities, regions, countries and internationally. Such networks include citywide federations of *barrio* organizations, as in Brazil and Venezuela; national sectoral organizations of micro-producers, such as the *tricicleros* in the Dominican Republic, and gender-based organizations, such as the nationwide federation of women's textile co-operatives in Bolivia. Many grassroots NGOs are linked to each other through international NGOs, and are linked with specialized international NGOs that provide training, technical assistance, financing, and other services. Increasing communication through international seminars and personal computers with modems has further strengthened the grassroots NGO movement in Latin America.

Third-generation NGOs are using their strength to challenge governmental policies, expand civil society, and ultimately work with government to address the needs of the poor. NGO activists who might have been revolutionaries in the 1970s now address 'the need to meld liberal democratic values with social justice through the growth of civil society' (Fisher, 1993: xiii).

In the 1990s international donors have been requiring NGOs to become more accountable, efficient, strategic, and entrepreneurial. A recent study of popular economic organizations in Chile, composed primarily of members of the informal sector, shows increasing financial independence from initial donors through profit-making activities (Downs *et al.*, 1989). Without losing their idealism, grassroots NGOs are showing a pragmatic awareness of the need for cost recovery to sustain them economically.

CDCs and LED in the USA

NGO involvement in local economic development in the USA spans three decades, from the confrontational 1960s to the entrepreneurial 1990s, characterized now by an impressive level of sophistication and institutional maturing. Community-based economic development in the USA traces its roots to confrontational community organizing started in Chicago in the 1950s by community organizer extraordinary Saul Alinsky, and to black inner city church efforts to mobilize corporate donations to address social service needs, like Philadelphia Reverend Leon Sullivan's youth training service founded in the 1950s. It was galvanized by the civil rights movement. It fed on inner city dissatisfaction with both urban renewal from the l950s and Johnson's War on Poverty in the 1960s. Political enfranchisement was not enough. Social programmes were not enough. Inner city residents wanted economic enfranchisement, and that meant community control and jobs (Peirce and Steinbach, 1987).

Inner city riots beginning in Watts in 1965 prompted the federal government to modify the War on Poverty legislation. Robert Kennedy introduced legislation to fund community-based NGOs called community development corporations (CDCs). It created several dozen CDCs around the country who wanted to build and rehabilitate housing and create jobs for their inner city communities. Civil rights organizers became the 'technical' staff for many of the CDCs. The Ford Foundation provided additional funding for CDCs, and by 1970 there were about 100 of them (sometimes known as economic development corporations, neighbourhood development organizations, etc.).

Flush with federal funding, the early CDCs hired large staffs and undertook massive housing projects, commercial land development ventures, social service programmes, and even started their own for-profit enterprises. But many of these early efforts ran into trouble. They did not have the managerial or technical capacity to handle the funds. In the 1970s hundreds of new CDCs emerged, a second generation of CDCs that did not have the large-scale public funding. They were supported by a dozen smaller federal programmes and a growing number of private philanthropies. Many of these second-generation CDCs started as community organizations formed around protest movements (redlining, freeway intrusions, demolitions, inadequate public service delivery); some evolved out of social service organizations set up by the federal government as part of the War on Poverty. The technical sophistication of these CDCs grew as they learned during the 'let's make a deal' era (see above) how to leverage public and private resources. By the end of the 1970s there were about 1,000 CDCs and a variety of specialized NGOs providing technical assistance to them. Yet few businesses started by the CDCs were very successful (Peirce and Steinbach, 1987: 31).

Table 10.1 Thirty years of Community Development Corporations in the USA

Years		No.
1960s	Extensive federal subsidies	100
	Housing rehabilitation	
	Retail/service business development	
1970s	Leveraging public and private resources	1,000
	Commercial land development	
	Value-added business development	
1980s	Entrepreneurial	3–5,000
	Rise of 'third sector' lending	
	CDCs become lenders rather than owners	
1990s	Maturation of institutional support networks	

The Reagan administration all but eliminated federal support for CDCs in the 1980s, prompting them to become more entrepreneurial and efficient. Corporations, commercial banks, and insurance companies became major partners in hundreds of CDC projects. A new institution arose in the 1980s that became a major source of project financing for CDCs: development banks. As of 1987 there were an estimated 3,000 to 5,000 CDCs in the USA (Peirce and Steinbach, 1987: 8).

A successful example of a private for-profit development bank is the South Shore Bank in Chicago whose investors willingly forego a certain amount of return in order to make investments in inner city neighbour-hoods. Another example of a private for-profit development bank is the Community Loan Fund, started in 1979 by the Institute for Community Economics, an NGO that assists CDCs. The Local Initiatives Support Corporation (LISC) is an example of a private non-profit development bank whose purpose is to lend to CDCs. Capitalized in 1980 by the Ford Foundation and six corporate investors, LISC concentrates CDC invest-ments in target areas to promote synergy among them. In the late 1980s LISC created a secondary market for CDC loans in order to generate additional capital (Peirce and Steinbach, 1987).

Development banking also includes loan funds for micro-enterprise development. Lisa Servon (Chapter 14) documents the growth of micro-credit in the US Accion International and other NGOs experienced in Third World micro-enterprise lending started to lend to micro-enterprises in the USA in the mid-1980s, following the Grameen Bank model from Bangladesh. In the 1990s federal government funds started to become available for micro-enterprise lending and a few local governments began micro-enterprise loan programmes.

Most of the micro-lending programmes are aimed at low income US citizens. However, community-based micro-enterprise development efforts are also occurring in the undocumented immigrant community in the USA. The level of Third World immigration accompanying global restructuring is of such magnitude that significant portions of the urban population in the USA are both politically and economically disenfranchised. Stephanie Pincetl's sensitive case study documents organizing efforts in the Latino community of Los Angeles that have begun to include loan programmes and saving circles for undocumented women street vendors (Pincetl, 1994: 13–14).

As the CDC movement has matured in the United States, it has created its own umbrella organizations. With corporate and foundation funding, the Development Training Institute provides one-year training programmes to CDC directors and senior managers across the country in business and real estate development, finance, organization and management, and strategic planning at the neighbourhood level. CDCs often have their own umbrella organization at the state level. They also have their own national membership organization – the National Congress for Community Economic Development. Community development assistance providers also have their own national membership organization, the National Neighborhood Coalition.

Other national organizations have special programmes to assist CDCs. The National Urban Coalition, for example, has a spin-off non-profit called the Community Information Exchange, which offers technical assistance to CDCs and maintains a computerized database of community-based development ventures. A few NGOs provide legal advice to CDCs, such as the National Economic Development and Law Center in Berkeley, California. A number of NGOs provide policy and research assistance to CDCs: e.g. the Center for Community Change, the Institute for Local Self Reliance, and the National Center for Policy Alternatives. Also a number of universities provide free or low-cost technical and research support and student interns. Local and nationwide electronic mail networks are also flowering in support of community-based development.

Conclusion

The community-based economic development movement in both the USA and Latin America has reached a level of maturity and consolidation involving third sector networks and institutional development. A growing synergy between NGOs, the informal economy, and the 'third sector' underlies the movement. Of course, individual grassroots NGOs are not without their problems: they may be top-down; may respond to funding sources indiscriminately; may be stifled by requirements of donors; may not be entrepreneurial or efficient; may suffer from ego trips by the professional activists; may be insensitive to gender, indigenous, or environmental issues; may be reluctant to co-operate with the local government; or may internalize the values of the 'oppressors' (see Chapter 15). Nevertheless, the grassroots NGO movement in Latin America and the USA has become a sophisticated, internationally connected force that has not lost the original source of its strength and wisdom: the community.

Notes

1. In Villa El Salvador, a low income settlement on the outskirts of Lima, 'every block and every activity is intensely organized through crisscrossing neighborhood associations, women's groups, youth groups, artisan associations, and production coops. An estimated 2,000 organizations are nestled within federations of larger federations, and these confederations largely control the democratically elected local government. Its mayor, in turn, represents Villa El Salvador to the (metropolitan government) of Lima and to the national government' (Fisher, 1993: 64).

References

Breslin, P. (1991), 'Democracy in the Rest of the Americas', *Grassroots Development*, 15: 3–7.

Downs, C. *et al.* (1989), *Social Policy from the Grassroots, Nongovernmental Organizations in Chile*. Boulder, Westview Press.

Fisher, J. (1993), *The Road from Rio, Sustainable Development and the Nongovernmental Movement in the Third World*. Westport, Praeger.

Korten, D. (1987), 'Third Generation NGO strategies, a key to people-centered development', *World Development*, 15: 145–59.

Peirce, N, Steinbach, C. (1987), *Corrective Capitalism: The Rise of America's Community Development Corporations*. New York, Ford Foundation.

Pincetl, S. (1994), 'Challenges to Citizenship. Latino Immigrants and Political Organizing in the Los Angeles Area', paper presented at the International Conference 'Cities, Enterprises and Society at the Eve of the XXIst Century', Lille, 16–18 March.

11

Strategies for local economic development

The experience of Montreal and Quebec

DIANE-GABRIELLE TREMBLAY

Introduction

The increasing affirmation over the last fifteen years of the local field as an area of economic intervention is changing the mode of intervention adopted by the different levels of government (municipal, provincial and national) which are taking an ever greater interest in this field in Quebec and in Canada. On the one hand, autonomous organizations are appearing, supported for the most part by particular levels of government (provincial or national) for socio-economic intervention on the micro-territorial scale. On the other hand, the municipal level is tending to broaden its economic action for a more effective intervention by the different key actors upon its territory.

In Canada, several types of local development organizations have appeared over the last decade. They have in common the comprehensive development of micro-territories, and a responsibility for bringing together different groups in the community into new partnerships. In general, these new partnerships join together the state (federal or provincial), municipalities or specific neighbourhoods or *arrondissements*, organizations in the community sector, and sometimes representatives of trade unions or employers' organizations. In this chapter, we shall be concerned more specifically with the situation in Quebec,[1] although several types of organization and modes of intervention are to be found elsewhere in Canada.

In the first part of this chapter, we will attempt briefly to distinguish the different approaches in the area of local development initiatives in a North American local environment, in comparison with Europe. Subsequently, we will introduce the different types of organization active in Quebec, and, to a lesser extent, in Canada. Last, by way of conclusion, we

will discuss the main issues and challenges which confront local development in the North American context.

Local development: what do we mean?

In this first section, we will discuss overall definitions and the main points
of convergence and divergence between local development and
community economic development, as well as the central issues in this
'matrix'.

Definition of local development

Amongst European and North American writings we find two expressions to describe efforts to bring about improvements through the
medium of resources found at the local level. These are local development and community economic development. However, some writers or
organizations use hybrid expressions based on these two terms. It is
sometimes difficult to distinguish between the different perspectives
where specific initiatives are concerned, and it is for this reason that many
writers do not dwell on definitions. Nevertheless, it seems to us to be
important to query these concepts and the meanings they contain.[2]

Local development and community economic development

For several writers, amongst them Newman *et al.* (1986), local development and community economic development have their origin in one and
the same established fact: the exclusion of certain population groups
from employment and socio-economic development.[3] The development
model encouraged, from the mid-nineteenth century on, by the major
firms and the Canadian government, often described as 'development
from the top', is not adequate to ensure a fair distribution of wealth
between the different regions of the country, and the different population groups. In fact, the vulnerability of urban or rural communities to
phenomena such as concentration of capital, lack of investment, industrial decline, the depletion of natural resources, the spread of tertiary
activity or the obsolescence of methods of production, has given rise to a
new concept of development within these communities, both in Canada
and in the majority of developed countries (Newman *et al.*, 1986). Local
or community economic development, which we are discussing in this
section, is essentially a manifestation of this new way of thinking about
development and making it happen.

Local development of a free market or a progressive type

In contradiction to this progressive local development, some people put forward a local development of a free-market type.[4] Blakely (1989) holds that local economic development falls within the process whereby local government or community organizations stimulate economic activity and employment. The main aim of local economic development consists in increasing job opportunities in sectors which improve the community's situation, by drawing on existing human, natural and institutional resources.

This type of local development emphasizes job creation without any particular social concern. According to Blakely, this type of vision has existed since the last century. It falls within the terms of free-market action aiming first and foremost at growth, and encourages neither social alternatives nor social change which could be described as instituting reform.

This strategy is put forward as a route for the recovery of local economies by means of job generation. This is something like the vision to be found in the Community Development Program run by Employment and Immigration Canada, which has since become the Canadian Department of Human Resources:

> Local development aims to increase the community's ability to adapt to change, and to encourage and support private enterprise. That includes the identification of market opportunities which can be used competitively by these localities.
> The underlying principle of community-oriented economic development is action taken by people at a local level in order to improve economic, social and environmental conditions. Job creation, in the context of local economic development, is a key element in this process which brings together at a local level those who have decided to take action and innovate, in order to fight unemployment. (Employment and Immigration Canada, 1990: 24–5)

We will come across the same palpable divide – progressive versus free-market attitudes within the implementation of community economic development. Numerous writers distinguish the two basic forms of community economic development. The first is oriented towards the development of businesses, whereas the second aims as a priority at the empowerment of the community (McCormick *et al.*, 1987: 2).

In this way, Swack and Mason (1987) emphasize this very Anglo-Saxon dimension of empowerment, which has implicit in itself the building up of autonomy as well as the assumption of power or the extension of it. The authors (1987: 237) define community economic development as an effective strategy, allowing solutions to be found to the problems of poor and powerless groups, and also those of underdeveloped communities. In their opinion, what is needed is not to make the situation more palatable, but to transform it, and set up permanent institutions within the community. The community itself therefore plays an important part with regard to external institutions, and residents manage to take better control of their community's resources.

In contrast, for the Economic Council of Canada (Conseil économique du Canada), the definition is centred rather on the improvement of employment and income, and, following from this, on the revitalization of the economy:

> Community economic development is the improvement of job prospects, income, and other aspects of the economy, not only for our local people, but by our local people. (Economic Council of Canada, 1990: 3)

The Economic Council of Canada (1990) also underlines the importance placed on the fact that activities should be carried out by the populations which are to reap the advantages of these improvements. Some writers describe this action on the part of the local people themselves as 'development from the bottom'. The concept of community economic development put forward by the Council links up with the most commonly held idea of local economic development.[5] The aim of improvements in jobs, income and the socio-cultural environment of the neighbourhood or the city is in fact the one most commonly advanced, together with achievement of this 'by and for' the people.

Taking into account the specific geographical and linguistic characteristics of Quebec, the local development movement in Quebec draws its inspiration both from 'community development' in the United States, and *'le développement local'* in France. It may be useful to discuss here the different sources of inspiration. As for the concept of *'développement local'* in Quebec , we can define it as follows: local development is a strategy for economic intervention through which local representatives of the private and public sectors, or co-operative groups, work towards the development of a community's human, technical or financial resources by joining together within a private or public, sector-based work structure, or one which crosses boundaries between sectors, and which has the central aim of developing employment.

Local development in America and in Europe

In the American context, community initiatives, or 'community development' as it is called, refer to all activities organized by the key actors in a community in order to satisfy that community's needs. Since the 1960s, it has been linked above all with projects involving urban and rural redevelopment, neighbourhood revitalization, and the development of the communal aspects of the living environment (public housing and housing co-operatives). Over the course of recent years, however, more and more experiments have been oriented towards jobs, on account of the unemployment problems increasingly felt by cities and regions in the United States following reductions in military spending. In Quebec, local initiatives have been mainly oriented towards jobs, as Quebec has had important unemployment problems for over two decades.[6]

In the United States and English-speaking Canada, people generally use the term community economic development to refer to a process whereby a community, through the work of its leaders, creates a range of socio-economic organizations, with a view to achieving the following aims:

1   To attract capital to the community on terms it can accept.
2   To improve the immediate physical environment by using local or external resources, for example through government action on the level of infrastructure (roads, schools, housing), and so on.
3   To increase job opportunities and set up businesses for community residents by providing training or directly setting up collectivized businesses.
4   To encourage businessmen or deciders to offer services, or make services accessible to members of the community (priority for local people in employment, for instance).

If Europeans place more importance on locality, it is doubtless to express a reality – a decentralization at decision-making level, and within institutions. Americans more often talk about the action of a social entity, a community, as the agency for securing the machinery to make development possible. The two visions conjure up two somewhat different realities before our eyes. Both in Europe and in North America, we do in fact find both forms of economic development. Nevertheless, they will not be viewed in the same way. North American approaches based on locality more often involve traditional key actors, large key actors – the state in all its forms, and medium- or large-scale private capital. Projects are generally implemented without reference to community development, but rather to partnerships at a local level.

European community-based approaches tend to involve collective agencies which have developed a regional identity (Breton, Basque, etc.). Reference is more often made to regional development, with slogans like 'living in the country', developing 'the hinterland'.

Local economic development initiatives in Quebec

In the Montreal region, CEDCs or Community Economic Development Corporations (Corporations de Développement Economique Communautaire) are concentrated in the city centre, where the municipal authorities have demonstrated leadership by putting together a local development policy. The stated aim of the municipality is to see CEDCs set up in each of the nine *arrondissements* of the City of Montreal. A wider consultatory framework, with the avowed purpose of developing the greater Montreal region, is, moreover, in the process of being set up. This raises questions concerning the specific role of the city as distinct from the wider region of Montreal. The latter includes the suburbs which have an utterly different economic dynamic from that of Montreal, and, in particular, that of the former industrialized districts, where the dynamic of local development is strongest.

Outside Montreal, Quebec's regions have been given Regional Councils with a mandate from the provincial government to plan for and define a development strategy for their territories. Within the regions, the local development organizations, such as the CFCs or Community Futures Committees (Comités d'Aide au Développement des Collectivités), or the municipalities and RCMs (Regional County Municipalities or Municipalités Régionales de Comtés) are increasingly seen as major players on the level of micro-territorial development. In addition to local development structures or community economic development structures, there exist a multitude of more or less formal consultative centres, which bring together key actors of one or a number of types on issues affecting local development or other specific aspects. Mention should be made of consultation between all sides of industry (employers, trade unions, other groups from different areas) for job creation in the context of the jobs forums which have been held in the different regions of Quebec, the CDCs or Community Development Corporations (Corporations de Développement Communautaire) which form part of the approach towards development from the standpoint of the community sector; or again, the ACs or Adjustment Committees (Comités d'Adaptation de la Main d'Œuvre), set up by the federal employment ministry, which bring together employers' and union representatives in order to give a boost to a particular firm or sector of economic activity, and which often are clearly well fitted for local development. In this part of the chapter, we shall concentrate on introducing the main organizations involved in local development in Quebec.[7]

Local economic development organizations

In Quebec, the first organizations dedicated to the economic development of local areas were set up on the basis of the administrative regions. Thus, from the end of the 1960s, we find the Regional Development Councils or RDCs (Conseils Régionaux de Développement). Socio-economic intervention on a micro-territorial scale became more structured, particularly from the middle of the 1980s, with the emergence of two types of organization, the Community Futures Committees (Comités d'Aide au Développement des Collectivités) in rural environments or on the fringes of the major urban centres, and the Community Economic Development Corporations (CEDCs) in urban environments. These organizations have a general consultative role for those involved in development. They act within a perspective of comprehensive development, and aim to be representative of their community, while being set up on a basis specific to themselves.

Regional Development Councils

As early as the start of the 1960s, several regions in Quebec set up Regional Economic Councils (Conseils Economiques Régionaux); in 1967–8, there were around fifteen in the province. They sometimes acted at regional level, and sometimes within smaller territories. At the very beginning of the 1970s they were brought into regional planning by the provincial government, under the name of Regional Development Councils (RDCs). Councils were then set up in the majority of administrative regions, the borders of which had been drawn several years previously by the government. The new Regional Councils were given a consultative and representative mandate for the region in the area of regional development. They were accountable to the Quebec Planning and Development Office (Office de Planification et de Développement du Quebec, QPDO) which represented the government in the area of regional development.

The Councils kept a consultative role for an entire decade, and then they received a mandate oriented even more towards consultation and the promotion of regional development. The consultative activities took shape from 1983 on, with the holding of the regional socio-economic conferences, also known as socio-economic summits. In 1986 the conference process was formalized by the government. The machinery and the stages to be followed, and also the participants and the responsibilities of each of them, were laid down. From now on they were to be known as Regional Consultative and Development Organizations (Organismes Régionaux de Concertation et de Développement).

The socio-economic conferences constituted a huge exercise, whereby the regional players determined the overall directions for regional development which would be given preference, and the strategies and projects to be implemented in order to give concrete shape to development. The exercise, which lasts for several months, culminates in a regional summit, where a four-year framework agreement is reached between regional and government representatives. This agreement records the projects chosen as priorities for the region, and undertakings by the government and the region's key actors with regard to these projects. Several stages precede the summit meeting. They take place within a local consultation process: discussion groups bringing together local people, and sector-based consultation schedules aimed at identifying development projects, and forums for the choice of regional priorities, etc. Biennial conferences are also organized to provide a check-up on undertakings.

From 1983 to 1991, fifteen summits took place in the different regions of Quebec. In 1991 the government imposed a moratorium on socio-economic conferences in anticipation of a rethink on government participation in the area of regional development. At the end of 1991 the government put forward the document *Developing Quebec's Regions* (*Développer les régions du Québec*), or the guidelines for its new policy on regional development. Development was looked upon as comprehensive action, which aimed not only at the economic aspect, but which embodied the results of measures taken for the advancement of the economic, social and cultural improvements to make development possible. The policy was calculated on an increased responsibility for the regions. These were looked upon as partners with the government in regional development. The regional authority responsible for development was defined as the organization for co-ordinating and planning regional development. The council was to lay down the overall directions and priorities for regional development for a period of five years into the future. Strategic planning was the working tool. Overall strategy thus defined was the subject of an agreement with the government. The mandate to consult with the regional agencies remained, together with an increased role on the level of negotiations with the government, and the management of a regional development fund in conjunction with the government.

In tandem with the setting up of the Regional Councils, the Quebec government proceeded to dismantle the Quebec Planning and Development Office, together with its regional branches. In its place, it set up the Secretariat for Regional Affairs. This has the responsibility of preparing policies and an overall direction for the government in the area of regional development. Regional delegates act as spokespersons for the Regional Councils; they have the job of ensuring consistency in government actions in the regions. The regional development organizations have therefore seen their role change to a considerable extent since their setting up in 1970. From being consultative organizations offering advice to the government on planning and regional development, they have become orchestrators of consultation between regional agencies. From the 1980s onwards, the government has defined itself less as the driving force in development, and more as a partner in the regional dynamic. The region has increasingly become the place where priorities and strategies for regional development are worked out and managed. These changes are part of the policy of regionalization begun by the Quebec government, notably with the health and social service administrations, which have also been set up on a regional scale.

There are fourteen Regional Councils in the administrative regions of Quebec, excluding the Montreal region. These organizations have the job of co-ordinating and planning development in partnership with the government. They employ between three and five people and have an operating budget of CAN$300,000 and a development budget of around 3 million Canadian dollars. The mandate handed down to the Regional Councils in 1992 included the following responsibilities: to facilitate consultation between the regions' agencies; to advise the government on the various issues affecting the region; to define a development strategy which identifies priorities and overall directions for regional develop-ment; to provide co-ordination and follow-up for initiatives and development programmes across the region.

Committees for Assistance in Community Development

The Community Futures Committees (CFCs) were set up in the context of the federal government programme Community Development (Développement des Collectivités). This programme contains several constituent parts, amongst them the CFCs, which were founded as the organizations responsible for economic development. The Community Development programme was run by Employment and Immigration Canada, which shortly afterwards became the Canadian Department of Human Resources.[8] This programme was designed with a view to local development. Generally speaking, its aim is to offer to small localities the support and necessary means to solve their long-term employment problems by being the labour force for their development.

The originality of this scheme lay in dealing with a community rather than businesses or individuals. The community is defined as the group of localities which encompass one and the same labour market. In Quebec, this definition of community usually means the regional county municip-ality (RCM). Quebec is divided into 99 RCMs.

The communities aimed at by the programme are located outside the urban areas, and often experience more marked deficiencies than are found on average in their respective regions or provinces. In general, these deficiencies manifest themselves in a very weak labour market and are characteristic of regions in decline. There might be a high rate of chronic unemployment, a marked dependence by local people on social security income programmes, and a low retention rate of the population of working age. Communities which may take advantage of the pro-gramme must also demonstrate their ability to organize, and 'take their development in hand' as the accepted expression puts it.

The Community Futures Committee, as the body responsible for economic development, constitutes the first stage in the implementation of the Community Development programme. It is made up of the main socio-economic players in the community: representatives of trade unions, educational establishments, economic development corporations, municipal authorities, social and community groups, etc. Depending on the number of players present, the composition of each CFC may vary perceptibly from one region to another. There are 55 CFCs in Quebec and over 200 in the whole of Canada.

The Community Development programme does not fix the composition of the CFCs either regarding number or type of the members. Nevertheless, the composition must be representative of the community. Participation is on a voluntary basis. In their current form, the CFCs have boards of trustees which vary between twenty and thirty members. On them are to be found representatives of business, commerce, trade unions, educational establishments, community development organizations, municipal administrations and any other group which is representative of the community.[9]

The role of the CFCs consists in assessing the community's needs with regard to adaptations in the local economy, and in working out a development strategy in accordance with these needs. In order for the community to implement strategies appropriate for creating and retaining jobs, what is needed is a contribution towards an improvement in training and in workforce skills through the adoption of a comprehensive approach to development, oriented towards a local tackling of the issues. To achieve these aims the priority should be given to strategic planning and local partnership. Rather than intervening directly by offering these services, the CFC should encourage partnership and consultation, support initiatives and co-ordinate development at a local level.

The CFCs may call upon other constituent parts of the Community Development programme in order to carry out their development strategy. Three main options are on offer. The Community Initiatives Fund or CIF (Fonds pour les Initiatives Communautaires) may be used for the reorganization of infrastructures linked to the development of new economic activities within the community. A Business Development Centre or BDC (Centre d'Aide aux Entreprises) can also be called upon for support to small businesses. A non-profit-making organization, the BDC's aim is to provide technical back-up and advisory services for local small businesses which are already established or just starting up. In addition it has a capital fund for development which allows it to give repayable loans, seed money, or loan guarantees. Last, the option Self-Employment Assistance (Aide au Travail Indépendant) is devised to stimulate enterprise. It allows the unemployed, or social security claimants, to build up self-employed work while continuing to receive their benefits.

The CFCs were not necessarily designed as permanent fixtures in a community. The programme is in force for a period of five years. After this period, the programme may be renewed if the community still needs it, and if the CFC shows that it is fulfilling the need effectively. The federal government has asked that CFCs and BDCs unite to form only one organization; this process is to be completed during 1994.

The CFCs' mandate includes the following: to call upon the private sector together with other sections of public administration to assess the community's problems and develop the necessary solutions; to prepare a comprehensive development plan for the local economy and recommend short- and long-term solutions to the problems of the labour market; to co-ordinate mutual aid initiatives at a local level; to monitor the effectiveness of the strategic plan while it is being implemented and to make an annual update of the strategic plan.

Community Economic Development Corporations

In Quebec, the Community Economic Development Corporations (CEDCs) are involved with intervention in urban environments, and originate in the field of community organizations. These structures have a responsibility for consultation and intervention for neighbourhood socio-economic revitalization. Hitherto, it was an essentially Montreal structure which first appeared in de-industrialized districts which were grappling with a range of social and economic problems. Originally set up on a neighbourhood basis, their field of activity is currently spread over the nine *arrondissements* recently drawn up by the City of Montreal. These municipal sub-divisions generally amalgamate two or more neighbourhoods, with a population varying between 68,000 and 152,000 inhabitants. Seven CEDCs have been set up since the mid-1980s, and the city's past administration (RCM) wanted them to cover the whole of the nine *arrondissements*; the new administration elected in November 1994 has not yet announced its position on this issue.

The CEDCs, at least the first ones, were structures that sprang directly from the neighbourhood. They were involved in consultation, partnership and direct intervention between the marginalized inhabitants and companies on their territory. Two stages feature in the setting up and development of CEDCs. The first is the search for adequate solutions to the problems of the locality by those actively involved in the community; the second is the consolidation of activities and the widening of the representative structures and the territory covered.

It was in the Pointe-Saint-Charles district that the first CEDC (the PEP) was set up in the mid-1980s. In 1984, community organizations, facing up to the limits of their action in a difficult economic climate, formed a committee to examine, and to try to resolve, the different socio-economic problems which persisted in their neighbourhood: a deterioration in living conditions, job shortages, low achievement in schools, heavy dependence on government income support schemes, gentrification, etc. The working party placed the jobs issue at the centre of its remit. Local people rapidly took action to demand support from the government for this initiative. Following an enquiry, those actively involved identified community economic development as a means of revitalizing the district, particularly on account of its comprehensive approach, the development of local resources, and the democratic control which are its characteristics. The model was inspired by American CEDCs, but the activities advocated were oriented towards job creation, training and urban development, rather than housing, as was most often the case in the United States. Since the vacant accommodation rate is around 5–7 per cent in Montreal, depending on type, and prices are relatively low, this issue was less important in Montreal CEDC activities.

In 1985, two other CEDCs were set up in old districts of Montreal: Centre-Sud and Hochelaga-Maisonneuve. With the PEP, these other two CEDCs were able to launch their activities on receiving three-year funding from the Quebec Office of Planning and Development (Office de Planification et de Développement du Québec, QPDO) in the context of a pilot experiment. During this period, each of the CEDCs developed specific tools to give a new boost to its district. In Pointe-Saint-Charles, the overall direction was first towards the creation of small businesses by local people, then an employment skills service was developed, following an enquiry into local people's needs. In the Centre-Sud district, small businesses were targeted as a means for revival. The CEDC developed technical support and training services appropriate to small businesses, together with an annual enterprise competition. In Hochelaga-Maisonneuve, a one-stop help desk was set up for the unemployed, bringing together bodies from the three layers of government involved in training and employment.[10]

At the end of the 1980s, the setting up of the two ACs (Adjustment Committees, set up by Canadian Employment and Immigration) for the east and south-east of Montreal paved the way for an enhanced role for the CEDCs. This was the recognition of intervention of this type as a means of neighbourhood revitalization, whether in consultation work, or strategies developed. The adoption of a policy of support for local development by the City of Montreal was another step in the same direction. This policy, entitled Partners in Neighbourhood Economic Development, recognized the CEDCs as promoters of consultation between partners in the *arrondissement* with the aims of developing job skills and opportunities for the unemployed, and also support for creating and retaining jobs. It was around these aims that CEDC involvement centred from 1990 on. Though involvement took different forms depending on the different experiments, previously organized strategies, and resources available, these overall working directions will serve as models for CEDCs yet to be set up.

CEDC activities are targeted at one and the same time towards consultation, local partnership, and direct intervention between marginalized populations and local businesses. The majority of CEDCs include an employment skills development service and a service for businesses. Some have developed a community development service, aimed more towards social and community activities. Activities vary from one CEDC to another. In employment skills and community development, what is involved might be the provision of a job search support service, or setting up training in keeping with local needs (adult literacy, technical training, enterprise training, etc), supporting job generation initiatives that originate in the locality, etc. Where the service to business is concerned, intervention is equally varied: setting up links with local businesses, technical support, funding for small businesses, visits to prevent closures, enterprise training, etc. The services undertaken by CEDCs also vary from one to the other depending on organization in the *arrondissement*. Some, for instance, undertake services that are lacking in the area; others encourage the emergence of new initiatives, building on resources already in place.

The CEDC boards of trustees are made up of thirteen to eighteen members drawn from the community, trade unions, public bodies, financial institutions, business, commerce and the ethnocultural field. Some offer individual membership. Composition varies from one organization to another, but in general ensures a balance between representatives from the social sector, and representatives of business.[11]

Since 1990, the three layers of government have taken part in the funding of CEDCs within a written agreement. Funding is therefore agreed for intervention on the basis of the *arrondissements*, and this requires a wide input from the various socio-economic players. These arrangements have made a fair difference to the CEDCs which had operated hitherto with an almost entirely community representation, on a smaller, neighbourhood scale. The City of Montreal contributes to the basic CEDC funding in accordance with its plan of action in the field of local development. The Secretariat of Regional Affairs (formerly the QPDO) also supports the running of the CEDCs on the basis of its Plan of Action for the Economic Development of Disadvantaged Districts of Montreal. Supplementary funding comes from different ministries or government organizations in the context of specific plans of action, policies, or again, particular programmes or aims. Overall CEDC funding is not an integral part of any of the government's community or local economic development policies.

There are now seven CEDCs in operation in Montreal *arrondissements* and the Montreal CEDC model is gaining ground in other urban centres in Quebec. Promotional committees are active in Hull, Quebec, and Lanaudière.

Community Development Corporations

Community Development Corporations or CDCs (Corporations de Développement Communautaire) bring together community and people's organizations with a general aim of developing the community sector, making it better known, and establishing it as a partner in community development. They have a range of aims, first on the level of social development, but sometimes on the economic level too – strengthening the community network, providing support for collective service groups, encouraging consultation between groups, setting up community resources (base groups, community co-operatives, and other co-operatives) promoting the active participation of the community network in the various decision-making authorities, contributing to the improvement of the community's social fabric, etc. The CDCs base their action on being democratically run, on individual and collective empowerment, and direct links with the community.

The first CDC, the Bois-Francs Community Development Corporation, was set up in 1984. At the outset, the Corporation's mandate was to consolidate the development of community co-operatives within its territory. One of the CDC's first acts in this direction was to acquire a building to house community organizations, and also to allow it to share out resources. Later, the CDC widened its mandate to include political activities to represent its members.

There are now a dozen CDCs in Quebec. For the most part, they were set up at the end of the 1980s, mainly as a tool for consultation with community organizations on a local basis. It seems that the regionalization of the social services and regional development, which began several years ago, has created a context that favoured the emergence of CDCs by further triggering the participation of community organizations. The CDCs are mainly to be found outside the large urban centres, generally within a Regional County Municipality (RCM) (Municipalités Régionales de Comtés). Since they receive no regular funding from any layer of government, the majority of CDCs have few resources at their disposal.

Municipal initiatives

As we mentioned earlier, the key municipal actors are increasingly to be found in the area of local or community development. More specifically, this section discusses their activities in Quebec, and, in particular, the City of Montreal and the Quebec metropolitan area, where these activities are more important.

The role traditionally assumed by municipal authorities in the area of economic development reveals more and more gaps when it comes to solving the problems connected with the economic and social dislocation experienced by some urban areas. The same is true of traditional economic and social intervention on the part of the higher reaches of government, which are usually applied uniformly to all regions, but the failures of which are increasingly recognized, precisely because of this uniformity of application, whereas the socio-economic conditions in the different regions of Canada differ markedly. Increasingly, municipalities are attempting to attack the underdevelopment of city districts or localities by trying to ensure that interventions have an impact on the populations which need them.

Small municipalities tend to act jointly in order to develop economic and social initiatives appropriate to the area. In Quebec it is becoming increasingly common for Regional County Municipalities (RCMs) to assume responsibilities of this kind. The large municipalities, Montreal for example, encourage the development of partnership at neighbourhood level for social and economic revitalization.

As well as the usual tools of developing urban infrastructure, planning and urban development, the promotion of industry and support for business, the municipalities are encouraging an approach based on consultation between partners, aimed at job creation and the integration of marginalized populations. Consultation brings together key actors from different groups depending on the initiative. As is the case for oganizations described earlier, partnership will in general call in equal measure upon the more traditional key actors in economic development – chambers of commerce, industrial commissions, representatives of government economic organizations, local businessmen, etc – and upon those involved in the social or socio-economic field: community organizations, trade unions, community workers, representatives of government social agencies, etc.

An analysis of strategies for revitalization and local development adopted during the 1970s and 1980s has allowed us to highlight several types of initiative aimed at creating and retaining jobs, training, and urban and rural planning. The cities studied by Lemelin and Morin (1989) all adopted a partnership approach to achieve the aims of revitalizing neighbourhoods in decline, and stimulating employment. The

initiatives which arose from these partnerships inspired the City of
Montreal's intervention. Intervention took numerous forms, but these
can basically be summarized under the following broad headings:[12]

- initiatives for creating and retaining jobs;
- initiatives for the development of employment skills;
- initiatives in the area of urban and rural development, including
  protection of industrial zones by revitalization measures.

The participation of the City of Montreal in local development

In 1989–90, the City of Montreal drew up a document which defined its
vision of local development. This document, *Partners in Neighbourhood
Economic Development* (*Partenaires dans le développement économique
des quartiers*), was designed to serve as the basis for its interventions. A
new municipal government was elected in Montreal in November 1994
and it remains to be seen whether this interest in community local
development will remain alive in future years.

Several factors have led the city to study the possible ways ahead for
neighbourhood development. On the one hand, in spite of positive
indicators of economic performance during the 1980s, it had to be
accepted that the spin-offs from growth did not benefit the whole of the
population. The unemployment and poverty levels rose throughout the
decade, and keenly affected some Montreal neighbourhoods. At the end
of the 1980s the unemployment rate exceeded 20 per cent in some areas
surveyed. Like several major North American cities, Montreal under-
went the combined consequences of a number of trends: an exodus of
people and businesses from the city centre to outlying areas, the effects of
de-industrialization and industrial restructuring, and in addition, the
effects of the slump. Low academic achievement and the lack of vocational qualifications across a large part of the workforce had the effect of
hindering the adjustment of the labour market to new situations. On the
other hand, traditional methods of intervention turned out to be severely
limited when it came to encouraging across-the-board improvements for
neighbourhoods or populations in difficulties. On the lookout for innovative solutions to supplement more traditional action, Montreal drew
inspiration from approaches developed in other cities, and also from
efforts already undertaken by the Montreal community sector, in order
to define its intervention in the area of local development.

A consensus seemed to form on the choices to be given priority: very
decentralized action, projects and programmes arising locally, meeting
the specific needs of different groups seemed to be the vital and necessary
complement to government programmes. In this way the city chose an
approach which supported community organizations already active in

neighbourhood revitalization and job creation. This approach was based on consultation between partners in order to find solutions, and on implementing projects likely to mitigate the effects of underemployment and poverty.

The plan of action put forward by the City of Montreal contained several planks, one of which was directed more specifically towards the CEDCs and the different community groups active in job creation. It took the form of a programme of financial support to which the city allocated a 6 million dollar budget, spread over five years reckoned from 1990. This programme was designed with a view towards a substantial input from the provincial and federal levels, which would enhance the city's contribution.

The support offered to the CEDCs was to help these organizations to continue and develop their function as magnets for integration at the local level. Municipal financial support was based on a role of consultation between partners in the *arrondissements* for projects with the unemployed, and job creation. The other local organizations targeted by the programme obtained financial support for projects allowing the people to develop employment skills, or which helped the unemployed to find job opportunities. This could be projects such as enterprise schools, business incubators, external labour services, projects aimed at finding a place in the labour market for target groups – women or cultural minorities, for instance.

The other actions advocated by the City of Montreal are based on partners in the three layers of government and the private sector working together to retain a strong manufacturing base, and on consultation over training the workforce, and for job generation. Last, the plan envisages an effort on the part of the city to take on to the city payroll those with specific difficulties in finding employment.

The Montreal Urban Community's Economic Development Office (Commission d'Initiative et de Développement Economiques de Montréal, CIDEM) is the municipal organization with general responsibility for the action plan. CIDEM is responsible for policies encouraging economic development and for co-ordinating government action in this field, and, through this plan, takes on an enhanced role with regard to promoting employment and action for local economic development. Again it remains to be seen whether this will continue in spite of the change of government in Montreal.

The Regional County Municipalities

The Regional County Municipalities (Municipalités Régionales de Comtés, RCMs) are supra-municipal administrative structures which bring together representatives of all the municipalities across a given territory.

It was with the adoption in November 1979 of the Law on development and town planning (Law 125, *Loi sur l'aménagement et l'urbanisme*) that these new structures came into being. This provincial law set up 95 RCMs which at that time numbered between 6,500 and 300,000 inhabitants. They replaced the County Municipalities (Municipalités de comté), a similar division of the territory, but one which excluded Urban Municipalities (Municipalités urbaines). Thus, with the exception of the municipalities that were already included in the urban communities of Montreal and Quebec, and in the regional community of Outaouais, all the municipalities in Quebec were brought within an RCM. Over the last few years, some borders have been redrawn, with the effect that the RCMs are currently 99 in number.[13]

Originally the central function which was devolved to the RCMs was that of drawing up a development plan for their area. The development plan is a planning document which lays down authoritative guidelines for the organization of the area by bringing consistency to the choices and decisions affecting all municipalities, and reconciling local policies with those of the government. The RCMs had three years from the time the law came into force to draw up the plans, and seven years to implement them. Subsequently, the RCMs must undertake a revision of their plan every five years.

The main function of the RCMs was achieved several years ago and gave rise to an ongoing debate about the role of the RCMs in the future. The question mainly affects the sharing out of responsibilities between the municipalities and the RCMs, and between the provincial government and the RCMs. It seems that the habits of consultation acquired during the drawing up of the development plans have led the RCMs progressively to assume new responsibilities previously held by the provincial government, or again, through intermunicipal agreements, responsibilities belonging to its constituent municipalities. Thus, during the course of the 1980s, several RCMs have taken over services in the areas of surveying, waste management, highway maintenance, economic and tourist promotion, cartography, municipal civil engineering, etc.[14]

A recent study on the commitments of RCMs (Audette, 1992) has also shown that several of them have gone beyond the framework of the development plan to become involved on other levels, such as the joint provision of services and regional development. There does not seem to be a typical RCM profile, as their activities vary in accordance with local needs and dynamics. For several observers, the RCM automatically occupies the appropriate stratum for social and economic development. It is seen as a place of participation where the habit of consultation has developed, a place of mutual commitment where mediation is possible between territories of unequal development, a place that fosters a sense of belonging, a more sensitive reading of the distinctive characteristics of micro-territories, and which has, moreover, democratic legitimacy since it is made up of elected representatives.

Conclusion

Several types of local development organization have appeared over the decade. They have in common the aims of the overall development of the micro-territory and the responsibility of uniting all the forces of the community within the framework of partnerships.

Outside Montreal, the regions have Regional Councils with a mandate from the provincial government to plan for and lay down a development strategy for their territory. Within the regions, the local development organizations such as the CFCs, the municipalities and the RCMs are increasingly seen as major agencies at the level of micro-territorial development.

In the Montreal region, the CEDCs are concentrated in the city centre where the municipal authorities have shown a degree of leadership by drawing up a local development policy. A wider consultatory framework charged with the development of the region of greater Montreal is in the course of being defined.

In addition to the local development structures or the community economic development structures discussed in this chapter, there currently exist a multitude of places for consultation, more or less formal, which bring together key actors of one or more kinds on issues affecting local development or other specific aspects. We are thinking, for example, of the consultation between partners from different areas for job creation through the Forums for Jobs (*Forum pour l'emploi*), the CDCs which are part of the approach to development from the standpoint of the community sector, or again the Adjustment Committees (ACs) which bring together representatives of employers and trade unions to give a boost to a particular business or sector of economic activity. All of this consultation activity and these partnerships are part of a new vision of economic development. However, a large number of issues arise from these new forms of intervention, issues which we will attempt to summarize briefly in conclusion.

The main issues in local or community economic development consist in showing that this form of intervention is a viable response to social or regional marginalization; as Nancy Neamtan has put it:[15]

> The traditional levers of our economy have not been able to respond to the needs of increasingly marginalized populations and regions. Left to themselves, these populations have refused to be victims, and have built up movements of mutual commitment locally to promote the development of their areas. They have given themselves means which are appropriate to both wider realities and wider markets. And these initiatives have not only

proved themselves on the economic level, they have also opened doors to
the development of more comprehensive strategies, in national, regional
and municipal terms, which are being recognised by more and more
governments. (Neamtan, 1989: 16)

The groups involved in local economic development must therefore
show that we are dealing here with an adequate model for providing
answers to the contemporary problems of social and regional exclusion.
Although they have been actively supported by municipal administrations, and also by the governments of Ottawa and Quebec over the
course of the last few years, the legitimacy of these interventions and
groups has not yet been thoroughly established. The organizations must
constantly try to give proof of their contribution to the economic development of the communities they claim to serve, all the more so in that the
funding of certain organizations depends on it.

It is of paramount importance for the local or community economic
development movement, in particular the CEDCs and CFCs, to win
recognition for their economic force, but also the achievements in terms
of the reduction in social costs, of their intervention strategy. These
organizations should ensure that their action takes concrete form in a
positive spin-off for the communities which implement it (Neamtan,
1989: 16), and also visible benefits for the governments which fund it. The
vindication of social practices often looked upon as marginal, but which
nonetheless constitute a movement of international scope, which bring
concrete answers to the recession and to the problems of unemployment
and poverty brought about by the actions of traditional key actors,[16] is
therefore at the heart of the future of the local or community development movement in Quebec.

Community economic development is a fledgling movement, but it is
increasingly recognized, all the more so, as over the last few years, it has
scored points both on the economic and political levels. In fact, as the
experience of the Montreal economic development corporations has
shown, it is increasingly influencing the modes of intervention of the
traditional key actors.[17] However, these same traditional key actors are
borrowing the philosophy of community development more and more, so
that the borderlines between the different types of organization are
increasingly blurred. In contrast, the traditional agencies (municipalities,
RCMs and other traditional local key actors) have the advantage of not
having to prove their legitimacy, or to seek out sources of finance (or not
as much).

The future apparently lies in a partnership between the two types of
organization, but for some people, there is then the risk of seeing the
traditional key actors – more strongly inclined towards the economic
than the social – decide and plan, while the 'new social key actors'

represented by those involved in community economic development (often arising more from social and community intervention than from the field of economics) will see themselves relegated to implementation. Certainly these latter groups are attempting to avoid this, and attach great importance to perfecting their contribution, but much is yet to be decided, certainly in these times of budgetary rationalization, when many organizations have found themselves having to make compromises in order to survive.

When discussing the issues at stake, we observe different perceptions, and as a result, we must contemplate a compromise. Society is not a monolithic block; thus, problems and their solutions are not analysed in the same way by all. Consequently, the concept of a local answer to a local problem will take a different form depending on whether it is broached by key actors from the business or the community environment.

Traditionally, the key actors in economic development work separately, each from their angle. Now, this situation is yielding to a new dynamic, that of consultation and partnership. It is no longer possible or desirable to envisage a continuation of the centralizing and authoritarian model for taking decisions which affect community issues.

Local development rests on the premise of the participation of all the key actors, and on these grounds, organizations are investing a great deal of energy in activities designed to establish or strengthen dialogue between different groups. This dialogue may encourage a compromise to be reached on the issues of revitalization, fairness, the spread of democracy and the viability of development. Nevertheless, it will not necessarily be easy to arrive at it.

Notes

1. This chapter is based on research carried out for Tremblay and Fontan (1994). The completion of this research and this book, which is used as a foundation document for a course on local development, was made possible by financial support from the Télé-université, the Secretary of State for Canada and the University of Quebec Fund for the Development of Distance Teaching (Fonds pour le développement du télé-enseignement de l'Université du Québec); we would very much like to thank these organizations here. This chapter has been written by Diane-Gabrielle Tremblay from material put together by Andrée Lévesque and Jean-Marc Fontan, who have worked under contract with the Télé-université to put together the book and the course. However, I assume responsibility for the opinions expressed here.

2. This will be done very briefly here, as the chapter had to be reduced in length; see Tremblay and Fontan (1994) for details.

3. See the introduction to Newman *et al.* (1986: 1–5). It is to be noted that the findings put forward by the authors are the outcome of a review of the literature on the question.

4. We use the term 'free market' with the economic meaning borne by the word 'liberal' in French and British tradition.

5. In any event, this is the idea which occurs most commonly in both the written material and the interviews conducted for the television series accompanying the book.

6. Unemployment there has been 11% on average from 1982 to the present.

7. This second part of the chapter has largely been compiled on the basis of research work by Andrée Lévesque, who was employed as a research assistant in the context of my research and coursework project on local development.

8. The federal ministries have all been undergoing reorganization since the election of a Liberal government in October 1993. The CFC programme remains for the present, but it is not known how it might develop and what its new administrative connections will be.

9. Examples of CFC intervention are given in Tremblay and Fontan (1994).

10. The television series which accompanies course ECO 3007 on local development, and is broadcast by the Open University includes detailed interviews on the CEDCs, their origin, the overall directions of their intervention, and their achievements, etc.

11. Examples and CEDC case histories are given in Tremblay and Fontan (1994).

12. Incubators refer to facilities where small local businesses and startups can enjoy below-market rent, shared services and access to consultants.

13. Details from Statistics Canada.

14. The Union of Quebec Municipalities (Union des municipalités du Québec), Report of the Study Commission on Municipalities (1986).

15. In her inaugural speech at the symposium 'Le Local en Action'.

16. This idea of a movement is also present with Newman *et al.* (1986: 25), who depict community economic development as being at one and the same time a movement and a process.

17. On the history and development of the Montreal CEDCs, see Fontan (1991). For the influence of the CEDCs on the layers of government, see Deland (1992).

References

Audette, R. (1992), *Les MRC dix ans après : un bilan de leur engagement*. Quebec Council for Social Affairs.

Blakely, E.J. (1989), *Planning Local Economic Development*. London, Sage, Library of Social Research.

Conseil économique du Canada (1990), *La relance locale, pour une approche communautaire du développement économique*. Ottawa, CEC.

Deland, P. (1992), *Les interventions du gouvernement du Québec dans les quartiers défavorisés et la stratégie gouvernementale en matière de développement régional*. Quebec, Office de planification et de développement du Québec.

Fontan, J.-M. (1991), 'Les corporations de développement économique communautaire montréalaises. Du développement économique communautaire au développement local de l'économie'. Montreal, Thèse de doctorat en sociologie, University of Montreal.

IFDEC, ANDLP (1989), *Le Local en Action*. Paris, Editions de l'Epargne.

Lemelin, A., Morin. R. (1989), 'Le développement économique local et communautaire: éléments d'analyse et pistes de réflexion pour une stratégie municipale', *INRS-Urbanisation*, May.

McCormick, L. *et al.* (1987), *Community Economic Development Strategies; A Manual for Local Action*, Chicago, University of Illinois, Center for Urban Economic Development.

Neamtan, N. (1989), 'Discours de Madame Nancy Neamtan', in IFDEC, ANDLP, *Le Local en Action*, Paris, Editions de l'Epargne.

Newman, L.H., Lyon D. M., Philp, W. B. (1986), *Community Economic Development: An Approach for Urban-based Economies*. Report 16, Winnipeg, Institute of Urban Studies.

Pellegrin, J. (1987), 'Initiatives locales, promotion de l'emploi et développement', in Chassagne. M.E. and de Romefort, A. (eds) *Initiatives et solidarités pour le développement local: l'affaire de tous*. Paris, Syros/Adels.

Swack, M., Mason, D. (1987), 'Community economic development as a strategy for social intervention', in Bennett, E.M. (ed.), *Social Intervention: Theory and Practice*. Lewiston, N.Y., Edwin Mellin Press.

Tremblay, D.-G., Fontan, J.-M. (1994), *Le développement économique local: la théorie, les pratiques, les expériences*. Paris/Montreal, Presses de l'Université du Québec et Télé-université.

Part V

Progressive local economic development strategies and their effects on social exclusion

12

Packaging the place

Development strategies in Tampa and Orlando, Florida

KEVIN ARCHER

Introduction

There has been much recent discussion in the literature about the rise of 'urban entrepreneurialism' as the dominant form of urban development policy (Frieden and Sagalyn, 1989; Judd and Parkinson, 1989; Leitner and Garner, 1993). While local boosterism has long been a part of US urban policy, such entrepreneurialism has intensified greatly since Goodman (1979) first called attention to it (Logan and Molotch, 1987; Squires, 1989). For the present purposes, such entrepreneurialism involves the attempt to reconstruct the built and social environments of cities in order to market them to increasingly footloose capital and people (Harvey, 1989a,b; Swyngedouw, 1989; Logan and Swanstrom, 1990; Paddison, 1993). Private sector groups most attached to place work together with the public sector – what Molotch (1988) calls the local 'growth élite' – to redevelop and package their respective place commodities. Decisions about development are made on the basis of private business criteria as urban policy becomes the purview of specialists with only indirect public accountability and a narrow, 'bottom-line' focus to their efforts.

According to Leitner and Garner (1993), how this trend in urban development policy is assessed depends on what is considered important in terms of urban governance. Those most taken by urban entrepreneurialism underscore efficiencies achieved by relying less on politicians and more on development 'experts'. Privatizing urban development policy streamlines the process, making it less likely that deal making with developers will be impeded as a result of public scrutiny. In Tampa, for example, even the more progressive growth élite of recent years considers public participation an obstacle to effective deal making.

Others, however, suggest that this depoliticization of urban development policy has enormous implications in terms of what are considered appropriate development goals, who should benefit from growth, and who should have a say in the process (Gottdiener, 1987; Smith and Feagin, 1987). Privatizing urban policy merely assures that the local growth élite will benefit disproportionately in the development process at the expense of other groups in the city. As local government assumes the role of private entrepreneur, public control of the development process is severely curtailed. Even though public funds continue to be essential to urban development – particularly in much hailed public–private partnerships – public accountability has virtually disappeared (Levine, 1987; Squires, 1989; Kearns and Philo, 1993).

The global context of urban entrepreneurialism

Despite such criticism, the growth of urban entrepreneurialism continues apace, largely as a result of two main processes. The first is the movement towards information-based, service economies in urban areas as a part of the more general trend towards flexible, post-Fordist regimes of accumulation in advanced industrialized countries (Harvey, 1989a; Moulaert and Swyngedouw, 1991). The economic viability of cities is now contingent on the attraction and retention of increasingly footloose economic activities, either in the form of services production or that of the 'consumption' of place amenities in the form of conventions, festival markets, and other tourist activities (Castells, 1989).

The second process involves central state withdrawal from the responsibility for the economic and social well-being of urban areas. What Helm (1989) calls the 'borders of state activity' have been steadily rolled back in advanced industrialized countries. Cities have been left to fend for themselves in terms of economic development and, in most instances, the funding of local social services (Liner, 1989; Archer and Morici, 1993). Within this context, urban entrepreneurialism should be considered an economic necessity rather than a policy choice (Goldsmith and Blakely, 1992).

These general contextual processes have rendered cities increasingly alike as a result of what Harvey (1989a,c) calls the 'serial reproduction' of office towers, convention centres, festival markets, and arts centres. This is certainly true of the built environment, but it is also true of the social environment as urban projects are developed to cater to the needs and desires of only 'the right sort of people' (young, professional and affluent). In most cases, this serial gentrification of the built and social environments of cities has occurred in spite of immediately adjacent areas of decline and blight where the 'wrong' sort of people remain (Levine, 1987). As in any other capitalist market, urban place commodities are being produced to meet only effective, not social, demand. The serial reproduction of urban built and social environments is merely a specific manifestation of the capitalist accumulation process with its cycle of innovation and high profit, mass reproduction, and eventual crisis of overproduction (Harvey, 1982).

This view of cities as commodities is not, of course, new. The discussion over Logan and Molotch's (1986) analysis of the 'political economy of place' has made it clear that treating urban places literally as commodities involves some significant definitional innovation (Harvey, 1989a). The emphasis here, however, is on an important implication of the mass production of capitalist cities. As in any other mature capitalist market, competition among similar place commodities is based increasingly on the production of images. As cities have become more alike, adequate effective demand must be created on the basis of some consciously constructed difference. What Paddison (1993) calls 'image reconstruction' is now of crucial importance in the urban development process.

Packaging and marketing the urban place commodity

Constructing an image of difference necessitates projecting some attribute of the place that distinguishes it in the market. This is done in two clearly interrelated ways. First, place difference can be constructed on the basis of some pre-existing historical, cultural, or natural attribute of the place. Urban entrepreneurs in Tampa, for example, waver between an emphasis on the Latin heritage of the Ybor City district or that of the downtown docklands prime for redevelopment (Mormino and Pozzetta, 1990). In the same way that beer is marketed for its unique constitutive qualities, places are packaged on the basis of some inherent attribute.

The second way place difference can be constructed is by what Disney engineers call imagineering (Fjellman, 1992). Places are packaged on the basis of some entirely imaginary attribute. Mega-malls in West Edmonton and Minneapolis certainly fill this role as do other downtown arts and entertainment districts and festival markets. Orlando is perhaps the best example of such marketing as the city's image is entirely intertwined with that of Disney World. The attraction of Orlando is the safe, controlled, sanitized image that Disney projects as much as the attraction of Marlboro cigarettes is the rugged frontier image of the Marlboro Man.

These two ways of constructing difference are not always, of course, as distinguishable as they are in the case of Tampa and Orlando. Nor are they entirely separate in practice. It is not a matter of the first marketing strategy being somehow more real or authentic than the second. In fact, both methods of packaging places are exercises in imagineering. Urban place commodities are being developed and marketed by entrepreneurs catering to what can be called the 'global gentry' of post-industrial

producers and consumers. In the process, place attributes become sanitized built and social facades much like the 'World Showcase' of cultures
at Disney World's Epcot Center.

Both ways of constructing place difference thus involve constructing a
'difference' that is not too different. The key, as Relph (1987: 252–3)
points out, is to 'integrate into the existing order' everything that has to
do with difference. This necessitates imagineering history, culture, and
even nature to fit the discourse of this order by rendering invisible the
potentially unsafe social relations of really different ethnicity and class.
The privatization of urban development policy simply ensures that this
gentrification of urban built and social environments in advanced industrialized countries will continue. Success at packaging the place is now as
important as providing the standard built amenities. As a result, precisely
how the place is packaged has become a new terrain of potential social
conflict at the local level (Boyle and Hughes, 1992; Paddison, 1993).

Orlando: the quintessential post-industrial place-commodity

The attempt by the local growth élite to gentrify the environment and
image of Tampa's downtown docklands has indeed been impeded by
public opposition. Before examining this, however, some context to the
politics of urban development in Tampa is necessary. The attempted
reconversion of the local economy from port-related industrial activity to
services is taking place in the shadow of what can be considered the
quintessence of post-industrial urban development. Orlando, located
about 130 km northeast of Tampa, has grown extremely rapidly since the
opening of Disney World in 1971. From a sleepy agricultural centre
before the Disney onslaught, Orlando has become one of the best-known
cities in the world. Orlando has not only been gentrified physically and
socially, it has been completely remade in the Disney mode (Fjellman,
1992).

Orlando's pre-Disney history as a small agricultural centre is not one
of diversity, either in economic or social terms. Unlike Tampa with its
industrial port and strong Latin and African-American working-class
heritage, Orlando's economy revolved around the local citrus and cattle
industries. Aside from a small population of African-American and
other, seasonal, largely Hispanic, farmworkers, Orlando was a typical
rural, white US farming community. Disney was able literally to remake
the area in its image because Orlando was a relative greenfield site. There
was no real opposition to Disney's plans for the area and, in this respect,
the urban development process of Orlando was privatized from the start
(Shafner, 1984).

The Disney effect on Orlando's growth has been nothing short of spectacular. The population of the Orlando metropolitan area, spanning Orange, Osceola, and Seminole counties, has grown 218 per cent since 1960, from a total of 337,516 to 1,072,748 in 1990. After increasing 34.3 per cent between 1960 and 1970, the population of the metropolitan area skyrocketed during the next two decades after the opening of Disney World in 1971, increasing 54.4 per cent between 1970 and 1980 and a further 53.3 per cent between 1980 and 1990. By contrast, the total population of Florida increased 37.2 per cent between 1960 and 1970, 43.5 per cent between 1970 and 1980, and 32.7 per cent between 1980 and 1990 (Shermyen *et al.*, 1991).

With this rapid increase in population has come a corresponding boom in the local economy. In the first year after the opening of Disney World, the value of building permits shot up 131 per cent and employment increased by 12 per cent (Fjellman, 1992: 131). As Judge (1973) relates, Orlando became a boomtown after Disney arrived, including the more nefarious problems that come with overly rapid development. While some of these problems have subsided, those critical of the Disney boom consider problems of congestion and transiency the very essence of contemporary Orlando (Fjellman, 1992).

The story of Orlando's Disney-induced boom has been recounted in detail elsewhere (Shafner, 1984; Presti, 1991; Fjellman, 1992). Of interest here are the general characteristics of this boom. Disneyesque Orlando, perhaps like no other city of its size, has been struck directly in the mould of the global gentry. The main cause of Orlando's growth success is its overwhelmingly post-industrial orientation at a time when less specialized cities are competing for the same activities. This certainly is a problem for nearby Tampa. As Tampa literally begs developers to construct an adequately sized convention centre hotel, new hotel building continues at a rapid rate in Orlando. In 1971, for example, Orlando's almost 7,000 hotel rooms were 66 per cent occupied and 301 conventions were booked in the area. By 1990, there were almost 78,000 rooms, about 80 per cent occupied, and as many as 1,500 conventions booked in Orlando (Presti, 1991). Orlando's convention facilities are actually a multiple of those of Tampa, even though Tampa has almost twice the population. In short, Orlando has developed to be what Sanders (1992) calls the 'convention city' of the 1990s (see also Braun, 1992).

Urban entrepreneurialism in Orlando is thus very much based on what Presti (1991) calls the 'Disney difference'. Association with Disney has greatly facilitated Orlando's attraction of international firms such as Tupperware, Harcourt-Brace-Janovich, General Electric, United Technologies, and Stromberg Carlson (Fjellman, 1992; *Tampa Tribune*, various issues). The Disney difference was also crucial in attracting a National Basketball League franchise and in Orlando becoming the site of national ice-skating championships and 1994 World Cup soccer matches (Hooper, 1992). The arrival of Disney has also produced significant agglomeration effects in the tourist industry as other theme parks such as Anheiser Busch's SeaWorld and Universal Studio's fantasy movie production lot have located in the direct vicinity. Disney itself is set to open two more theme parks in the near future in addition to the Magic Kingdom, MGM-Studios, and Epcot Centre. This tourist-based development has generated more than a critical mass of such activity as many other, smaller attractions have opened to profit from the influx of people to the major theme parks.

More recently, Disney announced its plans to enter directly into residential real estate development in the Orlando area by constructing a wholly new 4,000 acre (1,619 hectare), futuristic community on its property. This community, to be called 'Celebration', will include almost 9,000 housing units, a major shopping mall, an educational centre, several hotels and millions of square feet of additional office space (Wilson, 1992; Associated Press, 1993). This new 'edge city' (Garreau, 1991) will be constructed completely in the safe, sanitized, and controlled Disney mode, thereby assuring its success in attracting the global gentry. However successfully Tampa gentrifies its core, it will never be able to match such a complete gentrification of urban space.

On the basis of such private sector-led development, it is no wonder that Orlando has come to be what one major US accounting firm, Ernst and Young, labels the second-best growth market in the nation, both in terms of tourist and business activities. While downtown office space remains only 65–70 per cent occupied in Tampa, it is over 80 per cent occupied in Orlando. In 1992, the *Wall Street Journal* considered Orlando fourth in the country in terms of job growth in small businesses and *Fortune* magazine named it one of the top ten cities for business (*Tampa Tribune*, 3 May 1992). In short, development policy in Orlando has been merely the attempt to catch the private sector tiger by the tail without holding on too tight.

Orlando is thus a post-industrial urban entrepreneur's dream. Development policy is driven by one dominant private sector actor whose strategies and objectives precisely mirror those of the global gentry. While it is true, as Turner (1992) points out, that Orlando politicians have been able to redirect some development benefits towards needed housing rehabilitation and downtown services, this activity will only continue as long as it does not affect Orlando's boom. Indeed, by labelling Orlando's 'downtown politics' as 'progressive' in this respect, Turner (1992: 13–14) underscores the paradoxical nature of this term (e.g. Clavel, 1986). That is, the capacity for instituting progressive policies at the local level is really contingent on the rate of economic growth. The point at which progressive public policies impact private costs and benefits in adverse ways is the point at which such policies are curtailed in order to retain or attract developers.

The whole history of Disney's presence in Florida is a testament to this last assertion. Disney actually changed the state's legal framework for development by privatizing a huge chunk (68 sq km) of central Florida territory where it could be safe from public regulation and development impact fees (the Reedy Creek Improvement District). Florida was faced with the familiar choice of Disney or no Disney in the original negotiations over this concession in the same way that local governments are faced with it today as Disney expands (Fjellman, 1992). Whatever good intentions Orlando's politicians may have, the ball is clearly in Disney's court when it comes to local development.

In the shadow of Mickey: redeveloping and marketing Tampa

It is within this regional context that Tampa's urban entrepreneurs are operating. In the attempted reconversion of Tampa into a post-industrial city, it is clearly Orlando that is the main competitor for development. Once the economic centre of the region, Tampa now finds itself taking a backseat to its smaller neighbour. The strategy of Tampa entrepreneurs in the face of such competition has been to attempt to reconstruct and market the city's cultural and historical diversity. Orlando is disparaged by the local growth élite, for example, as being artificial, a fantasy land with no substance. As Tampa's current mayor, Sandy Freedman, puts it: 'I don't want to live in Orlando I don't want to live in a community that is a series of theme parks.' 'Bore-lando' is the term for the area according to the local press in the sense that it is strictly 'dull and white bread'. According to this view, Orlando simply does not have a history, nor any real cultural attributes (*Tampa Tribune*, 3 May 1992).

What seems to be lost on local place entrepreneurs is that it is precisely this 'dull and white bread' image that is attractive to a similarly white bread global gentry. The precise characteristics of Tampa's effort to merchandize local culture and history are worth exploring in more depth, then, as a specific example of the growing need to construct some 'difference' that is not too different in the highly competitive place commodity market. As a south Florida city, for example, Tampa has a history that dates essentially from the turn of the century. The city's early settlement was as a military port and the population of the area only began to grow in the 1920s and 1930s. Of interest in this early history is that Tampa developed on the basis of cigar manufacturing which was, in turn, introduced to the area by Cuban immigrants. Revolving around this one industry, Tampa emerged as an atypical multi-cultural southern city, particularly as Spanish and Italian immigrants came to the cigar-making district – Ybor City — to join their Cuban, and increasingly South American, counterparts (Mormino and Pizzo, 1983; Mormino and Pozzetta, 1990). With its Spanish colonial architecture and what is left of its Latin ambiance, Ybor City is still an attraction for visitors to the area.

The early African-American community of Tampa was made up of former slaves, some of whom found work in the cigar factories or as domestic servants. As in other southern cities, African-Americans were residentially confined to areas that continue today to be the poorest districts of Tampa (Robinson, 1993). The city remained segregated in this way well into the 1960s as Jim Crow segregation laws were strictly enforced. Regardless of such outright discrimination, however, the African-American community grew steadily reaching about 25 per cent of the current population of Tampa (City of Tampa, 1993). Significantly, African-Americans were able eventually to secure jobs at the growing industrial port. After World War II, Tampa's port evolved into one of the leading industrial ports in the nation, specializing in the export of locally mined phosphates and the import of petroleum products and automobiles (Bane and Moore, 1981). By securing jobs on the docks, African-Americans became active participants in the working-class politics of industrializing Tampa. The first black city councilman elected in this century (Perry Harvey, Jr.) comes from a district near the port and is heavily backed by the longshoreman's union of which he was an official.

These brief glimpses of Tampa's cultural history are meant merely to indicate what are considered by local entrepreneurs as the two main attractions of the area. While Orlando's agricultural past was rapidly overwhelmed by the Disney invasion, Tampa's history can still be read in the Latin heritage of Ybor City and the downtown industrial docklands. For the local growth élite, it is this heritage that is considered the all-important Tampa difference in the place commodity market (Mormino and Pizzo, 1983).

Unfortunately, packaging Tampa's Latin heritage for consumption by the global gentry has proven difficult. The reason for this is twofold. First, the heyday of cigar manufacturing occurred before World War II. The original factories, workforce, mutual aid societies, and related Latin businesses that had developed around the cigar industry were already in decline by the 1950s. Those most successful, both capitalists and workers, joined the general post-war movement to the suburbs (Mormino and Pozetta, 1990). As indicated in Table 12.1, the suburban trend was manifest in Tampa. This movement to the suburbs included many from Ybor City, particularly as urban renewal policies in the 1960s destroyed much of Ybor's built environment. Such urban renewal policies resulted in what has been called the 'sterilization of Ybor City' (Mormino and Pizzo, 1983: 183). As those of Latin heritage continued to move out of Ybor City, African-Americans began moving into one of the few areas of the central city in which they were allowed to reside. This, in turn, eventually transformed the cultural flavour of the area.

Table 12.1 Population growth in Tampa and Hillsborough County

Year	Tampa	County	Percent of County
1950	124,682	249,894	50
1960	274,970	397,788	69
1970	277,753	484,490	57
1980	271,577	646,939	42
1990	280,015	834,054	34

Sources: *Florida Statistical Abstract*, various years

The increasingly WASPish élite of Tampa also actively discriminated against the Latin community of Ybor City. As the population of Tampa more than doubled in the 1950s, the growing white professional class of Tampa was loath to characterize their city as 'Latin' or to preserve the built environment of Ybor City. As a local paper put it in 1961 with clear reference to Ybor City's industrial and cultural heritage: 'practically every tourist of any sense by-passes Tampa now because they think of Tampa as a grimy factory town' (Mormino and Pozzetta, 1990: 301). It was during this time that 'many leading downtown businessmen' came to feel 'that the public linkage between cigars and Tampa hindered urban development' by connecting Tampa directly to the dreaded 'Latin ethos and life-style' (Mormino and Pozzetta, 1990: 300). The most concrete result of this backlash against Tampa's Latin heritage remains, of course, the destruction of much of Ybor City in the name of 'urban renewal'.

The attempt to disassociate Tampa from the Latin lifestyle was a common strategy of the local growth élite well into the 1970s. As a result, the inner city district of Ybor City is quite literally a facade of Latin heritage, existing only in bricks and mortar, some of which constitute merely reconstructed 'authenticity'. With its gutted core area, small, now ethnically diverse population, and blocks of vacant lots left as a legacy of urban renewal, the Latin heritage of Ybor City seems destined to play only a minor role in Tampa's post-industrial reconversion. The major role has been given instead to what the current growth élite believes will allow Tampa to follow the successful lead of other historic port cities: the redevelopment and packaging of the downtown docklands.

Tampa's initial growth spurt and downtown redevelopment

Through the 1970s, Tampa's growth élite consisted of a very small, homogeneous group of powerful businessmen and politicians. This élite was so exclusive that two local historians have characterized the rebuilding of the central business district in the 1970s as the direct result of private discussions between the mayor and only 'two distinguished and most influential businessmen' who agreed to invest downtown (Bane and Moore, 1981: 92). Tampa's economic structure consisted of a few large-scale industrial firms connected to phosphate mining, processing, and shipping. Like the growth élite of other cities, the powerful, white businessmen who headed such firms were joined by their similarly few counterparts heading local utility firms. As a result of this specialized economic structure, and unlike other south Florida cities linked more to sun and fun, Tampa's social environment was, and largely remains, working class. The 'grimy factory and working port' ambiance of the area assured that Tampa was not considered a final tourist destination nor even a good place to reside for those flocking to the sunbelt in the 1960s (Bane and Moore, 1981; Mormino and Pizzo, 1983).

As it became clear that Tampa was being bypassed in this early Florida boom, a more visible, if still only *ad hoc*, growth strategy began to emerge. The focus of Tampa's élite was placed specifically on what Bane and Moore (1981: 74) call 'the downtown dream'. Since the Latin heritage of Ybor City already had been gutted, reconverting the central business district and downtown docklands seemed the answer to Tampa's marketing problem. The general suburbanization trend of the post-war period had left the downtown area in serious decay, 'straddled by warehouses, rail tracks, skid-row streets, and one-acre blocks abandoned in the urban exodus' (Mormino and Pizzo, 1983: 188). If Tampa was to attract new development, something had to be done about this growing black hole in the centre of the city.

In what was to become the general pattern of Tampa's redevelopment process, a small number of 'distinguished and powerful' businessmen eventually developed a major office, hotel, and conference complex downtown only after federal funds were made available in 1979 to construct a parking garage. This initial public–private partnership in turn spurred further investment in the downtown area eventually totalling an estimated $800 million and involving as many as 55 major projects by 1983 (Mormino and Pizzo, 1983: 187). Such a large-scale influx of private capital downtown was also facilitated by the rapid population growth of the Tampa area in 1970s and 1980s as a result of another wave of migration to the sunbelt. While population within the city limits actually decreased between 1970 and 1980 – from 277,753 to 271,577 – the population of the metropolitan area as a whole increased by as much as 46 per cent – from 1,105,553 to 1,613,600. Public participation may have been crucial to start the downtown redevelopment process but this process was kept going by private entrepreneurs. The rapid growth of the area resulted in both a real estate boom and a significant change in the local social mix, as more young professionals came to the city that Naisbitt (1982) prominently promoted as one of the top ten 'megatrend' areas of the country. While most residential growth took place in sub-urban areas, private developers fell over themselves in attempting to supply office space in the downtown area for the relocating financial and real estate firms that were coming to dominate the local economy. In this context, Tampa's downtown reconversion was less the result of a con-scious growth strategy than that of highly favourable market trends.

Not surprisingly, there was little disagreement among Tampa's growth élite over development policy. Both because of its very exclusive, 'good ole boy' constitution and because public sector members fashioned their strategies directly to fit the needs of the private sector, Tampa's growth élite was easily able to act in unison. What Kerstein (1991) calls a 'privatist-corporatist regime' of urban governance existed in Tampa well into the 1980s. Best exemplified during the 1979–86 term of Tampa mayor Bob Martinez, who later served as governor of Florida and eventually Ronald Reagan's 'Drug Czar', this regime prompted private investment by virtually deregulating the development process. Private developers were given the main role in determining what, where, and how downtown development was to occur. The key strategy was to allow private developers the maximum room to manoeuvre while, at the same time, cutting local property taxes almost in half. By doing this, Martinez had the reputation of someone who could 'finish the deal', usually behind closed doors with little or no public scrutiny (Kerstein, 1991: 64).

Unlike Orlando, which at least attempted to co-ordinate rapid growth by means of a centralized, downtown development authority, Tampa's redevelopment process was undertaken in a strictly *ad hoc* fashion. Success at fostering office development as a result of this approach prompted the Martinez administration to take the final step towards urban entrepreneurialism – the aggressive marketing of place – in the early 1980s. The idea was to complete the post-industrial redevelopment of the downtown area by concentrating on consumption after the model of other former industrial port cities like Baltimore, Philadelphia and Seattle. The two major results of this strategy were the construction of new, state-of-the-art performing arts and convention centres downtown (Kerstein, 1991). The key was to build and market what local advertise-ment executives dubbed 'America's Next Great City' on the basis of cleaning up the last remnants of Tampa's heritage of manufacturing and port-related industry. Tampa's entrepreneurs thus did their part to further the trend towards the serial reproduction of post-industrial urban environments.

'America's next great city' stagnates

The favourable growth context of Tampa's redevelopment, however, did not last. By the mid-1980s, growth had slowed considerably. Unlike Orlando, Tampa experienced much difficulty in maintaining a profitable occupancy rate in its new office towers downtown. Similarly, the hotel and convention market remained soft at best. Tampa hotels, as late in the redevelopment process as 1988, maintained an occupancy rate of only 56 per cent in a market that measures minimum profitability at the 65 per cent and higher range (Albright, 1989). In this context, Tampa's urban entrepreneurs had trouble attracting new development to the downtown core. Mayor Martinez even found it impossible to 'finish the deal' with private developers to finance Tampa's convention centre which was to be a cornerstone of Tampa's urban renaissance.

In the context of much slower growth, the public role in the public–private partnership was greatly expanded. Martinez's administration took the lead, actively directing and committing public funds to the redevelopment process. After failing to find a private developer for the convention centre, Martinez had the city borrow $156 million to build the centre itself. Combined with the $39 million in public bond debt incurred in the construction of a $57 million performing arts centre, this new commitment by the city was to increase dramatically the tax-supported debt load of the citizens of Tampa. As indicated in Table 12.2, the net long-term debt per capita in Tampa has increased over tenfold since 1975, with the most dramatic increase occurring between 1985 and 1986. The vast majority of funds accrued from the original downtown tax increment finance district (TIF) are now earmarked exclusively to paying this debt, particularly since property taxes remain close to the much lower levels set by Martinez.

By the late-1980s, then, 'America's Next Great City' was looking like every other economically struggling, mid-size US city. Martinez was at least opportunistic enough to run in, and eventually win, the Florida gubernatorial race in 1987 on the basis of his earlier 'success' at redeveloping Tampa while lowering taxes. The downside of redevelopment in terms of public debt and unprofitably low office and hotel occupancy rates were not yet apparent, particularly because of the then commonly held belief that the growth cycle was merely in a lull before the next upward spurt. Unfortunately, as of 1994, Tampa remains in this growth lull.

Table 12.2 Net general long-term public debt per capita, Tampa

Year	Per Capita Debt ($US)
1975	78.60
1980	176.78
1985	260.55
1986	699.08
1988	839.94
1991	868.06

Sources: City of Tampa (1981, 1988, 1992)

This is the context in which Tampa's first female mayor, Sandy Freedman, was elected by a landslide in March 1987. While committed to finishing the previous administration's convention centre project (including finding a hotel developer to ensure the centre's actual use), Freedman declared that her administration would be less development and more socially oriented. Significantly, Freedman's administration put debt repayment, low income housing, race relations, and crime at the top of its policy agenda, reaching out particularly to Tampa's African-American population. The new local politics was to be one of 'inclusion', not the narrow domain of the powerful, highly exclusive, 'good ole boy' network (Sutton, 1989b; Kerstein, 1991).

The growing contradiction between the commodification of place and progressive politics of inclusion

Mayor Freedman eventually accomplished parts of her agenda, even receiving a favourable look from the new Clinton administration for her success in developing low income housing programmes with the local financial sector. Freedman is also given high marks for having the political courage to raise property taxes to service the debt and to pressure the local Chamber of Commerce to be more gender and racially inclusive in its programming. Of interest here, however, is that this attempt to be more socially progressive was occurring at a time when the attraction of economic activity to Tampa was becoming quite difficult. Whatever her social agenda, this increasingly unfavourable economic context meant that Freedman would have to pay considerably more attention to selling Tampa to potential developers than she had originally thought.

Mayor Freedman's attempt to engender a local politics of inclusion appeared to the old guard growth élite as folly. After Freedman raised local property taxes, the development community made it clear that they considered her administration to be 'anti-economic growth'. As this label filtered into the press, the blame for the continuing lull in Tampa's redevelopment process shifted from the private to the public sector. The press repeatedly spoke of Freedman's 'lack of vision' and her inability to provide strong leadership for the redevelopment process. Unlike Martinez, Freedman not only did not come across as someone who could 'finish the deal', she was increasingly portrayed as someone who was not even interested in the deal. Unlike still booming Orlando with its solidly pro-growth élite, Tampa was now considered floundering, with a newly forming élite more interested in social inclusion than in much needed development (Sutton, 1989a).

For Freedman's administration, this was an unenviable position to be in. As Tampa's growth continued to stagnate, the perception that the city was anti-growth served only to exacerbate an already bad situation. Freedman continually had to reassure the development community about her policy agenda. By assuming the public commitment to the convention centre and agreeing to another downtown TIF district, Freedman hoped to combine pro-growth policies with her progressive social agenda (Kerstein, 1991: 66–7). In the end, however, this attempt to balance the two interests has succeeded merely in reinforcing the image of the new, more inclusive élite as having no clear vision or capacity for community leadership.

The Freedman administration is also regarded with scepticism from the other side of the political divide. While the old guard growth élite considers the politics of inclusion an obstacle to redevelopment, those to be 'included' in local policy-making question Freedman's commitment to her social agenda. A good part of this scepticism comes from a consideration of Freedman's own background as a long-time member of Tampa's élite. Before becoming mayor, Freedman was a member and then chair of the city council and thus very connected, in many people's minds, to Tampa's 'good ole boy' network. This perception seemed corroborated by the fact that Freedman's initial run for mayor in 1987 was the best financed in the city's history with campaign funds of over $500,000 donated by the private sector (Samek *et al.*, 1988).

Whatever her true intentions, Freedman's ability to complete her progressive social agenda was severely limited by the local economic context. With a stagnating local economy and already riddled with a high public debt load, a more sympathetic view would be that the Freedman administration's balancing act is the only viable course of action. Again, this is most often the context in which 'progressive' urban policies are likely to founder. Rather than attempt to determine Freedman's true intent, however, of more interest is the way in which this growing contradiction between the commodification of Tampa and the politics of inclusion has manifested itself in attempts by the new urban entrepreneurs to package the place.

Myth and reality in the packaging of Tampa's nautical past

By the early 1990s, the need to market Tampa more aggressively was clear, particularly since Orlando was more successful in attracting the natural inflow of people and firms to the Florida sunbelt. Tampa's performing arts and convention centres were in place and considered attractive, even if the latter was still without an adjoining hotel of appropriate dimension. Yet Tampa has yet to shake its industrial working-class image, rendering it difficult to attract the type of 'higher value added' development even the more inclusive local growth élite desires (*Tampa Tribune*, 14 January 1991). Reconstructing and marketing a difference that is not too different, then, is now of utmost importance for Tampa's development prospects.

Because the Latin heritage card is largely unplayable, Tampa's current urban entrepreneurs hope to tie downtown redevelopment more directly to the docklands. The waterfront warehouses, petroleum storage tanks, railway lines, and phosphate terminals are now considered a crucial part of 'downtown' reconversion as Tampa's entrepreneurs hope to showcase the area's traditional link to the water. This enhanced focus on the docklands has resulted in several projects either proposed or in the process of development along Tampa's waterfront. The first major initiative, now under construction, involves a waterfront aquarium project destined, according to the local press, to be the 'largest and most elaborate' in the country (Pease, 1993). Continuing to take the lead in the downtown redevelopment process, the city is financing $84 million of the total $94 million project on the basis of long-term bonds (Fleming, 1993). Similarly, the city was recently able to get the local National Hockey League team to commit to building an arena at a nearby waterfront site by assuring an approximately 60 per cent public–40 per cent private $110 million deal. The city is donating land, building a $13 million parking garage, guaranteeing the team at least $1 million a year in parking fees plus the use of office space built into the garage, and eliminating the local transportation impact fee usually levied on downtown developers. In addition to these contributions from the city, the arena project will also benefit from some $5.5 million a year in subsidies from the county and the state (Lowitt, 1993). When combined with the possibility of another huge commitment by the city to the proposed $137 million convention centre hotel, such public largesse seems to belie the Freedman administration's stated goal to be less growth and more socially oriented.

This disciplining of the local regime by the place commodity market is even more apparent in the struggle over the market image of Tampa. The attempt to convert the industrial docklands into a tourist attraction has necessarily included an attempt to invent a more appropriate nautical heritage. The still 'grimy', heavy industrial, working-class ambiance of

Tampa's docklands is as little appropriate for the present purposes as was the Latin ethos of Ybor City in times past. The key now is to invent and market a nautical past that is as white bread and Disneyesque as the global gentry it is designed to attract. While it was possible to construct such an image out of the nothing that was Orlando, in Tampa this necessitates the conscious deconstruction of a wholly different sort of history.

Fortunately, Tampa has another nautical tradition that can be put to use in packaging the docklands. Since 1905, Tampa's white élite has cultivated a highly public, if completely mythical, link to the pirate tradition of the Caribbean and the Gulf of Mexico by celebrating a fictitious buccaneer named José Gaspar. The 'Gasparilla Days' festival includes a mock invasion of the city by these élite 'pirates' and an eventual distribution of the 'booty' with the locals, in terms, presently, of public feasts and local arts events. The festivities are organized by a private men's club of the rich and powerful known as Ye Mystic Krewe of Gasparilla, modelled after the Mardi Gras Krewes of New Orleans.

Continuing the tradition today, the Gasparilla Days festival is held at the beginning of each year and is considered Tampa's most important civic celebration. The symbolism of the festival is what is important here. According to D'Ans (1980), the celebration originally served two purposes. Created by the emerging white élite at the turn of the century, the pirate legend served both to announce and to legitimize the transfer of power from Tampa's original Latin élite. Powerful white men, disguised in pseudo-ethnic pirate attire, both sacked the city and yet seemingly redistributed the booty to the ethnic working classes. Such festivities were intended to bring the community together by apparently bridging the then widening class and ethnic divides.

The Gasparilla festivities also allowed the emerging white élite to flaunt their wealth and, more importantly, their power to control local society. As D'Ans (1980: 26) points out, Tampa's lower classes were not only spectators of the invasion and parade, they were also an integral part of the spectacle itself. They were 'local actors' in a 'grand spectacle staged for outside businessmen' who were 'invited to witness a happy city cheer its élite' creating 'the publicity that would attract new customers to Tampa'. The key was to portray a newly Anglo-ized Tampa as both prosperous and safe for whites, the Latin ethos now fully domesticated and under control.

The mythical linkage to the pirate tradition remains today in the self-image of white Tampans. Tampa's National Football League (NFL) team is called the 'Buccaneers', thus announcing Tampa's arrival as a 'big-league' city in locally symbolic terms. Similarly, Ye Mystic Krewe of Gasparilla is still considered to be the most important private men's club in the city. Until very recently, it was the club where Tampa's growth élite quite literally was formed and made plans. As one of Mayor Freedman's top aides put it in 1990, the Krewe, 'by their very position set the moral tone for this community. They set the tone for the quality of life' of Tampa (*Tampa Tribune*, 28 August 1990).

Throughout the Martinez administration, urban development policy was formulated in this exclusive, private club context. The people and goals of the Freedman administration, however, seemed to suggest that times had changed. As a woman, Mayor Freedman herself could not become a member of the all-male Krewe. As we shall see, the first major event signalling that times had changed in the governance of Tampa was the controversy that arose during the planning of the 1991 NFL Super-bowl festivities. Hosting the Superbowl was to render Tampa immediately more attractive to potential investors and urban tourists. This was the outcome of the first Superbowl Tampa hosted in 1984 and it was a much hoped-for outcome in 1991, particularly given the economic doldrums that the city was then experiencing.

The 1991 Superbowl festivities were to play a major role in hastening the redevelopment of Tampa's downtown docklands. Not surprisingly, Ye Mystic Krewe of Gasparilla was called on to organize the main Superbowl parade and linked events. The pirate motif was especially appropriate, not only because of the hometown 'Buccaneers', but also because of the new emphasis on Tampa's docklands. Unlike in 1984, however, this attempt to market Tampa was severely criticized by groups, particularly African-Americans, traditionally excluded from Tampa's power structure but now empowered, symbolically if not thoroughly, by the Freedman administration.

From ending the pirate charade to sinking the Whydah slaveship

The deconstruction of the working-class heritage of Tampa in the process of inventing a more appropriate one for the place commodity market is therefore not taking place without conflict. The industrial tradition of the docklands has been especially hard to tame as inventing a more appropriate dockland tradition means necessarily gentrifying both a class and an ethnic heritage. As mentioned, the economic viability of Tampa's African-American community traditionally was linked directly to that of the port as one of the few places where blacks were allowed to work. It was also adjacent to the port that blacks were allowed to live in what continue to be overwhelmingly poor, black, residential neighbourhoods (City of Tampa, 1993).

Like in most US cities, Tampa's black population remains at the lowest end of the socio-economic scale. The unemployment rate among local African-Americans in 1990 was 11.6 per cent while that of whites was 5.3.

Between 1980 and 1990, the income of black households actually dropped, from 59 to only 55 per cent of that of whites. In those districts of the
city considered 'minority concentrated' (over 40 per cent minority), over
50 per cent of the residents over age 25 did not have high school diplomas
in 1990. Racial minorities, mostly blacks, now comprise over 91 per cent
of all households receiving public assistance. Significantly, according to
the city's own documents, while Tampa 'has recently experienced a wave
of new growth. The development nodes that have been targeted by the
City all border minority-concentrated areas' and yet have not stimulated
any development in 'the cores of these areas' (City of Tampa, 1993: 3). As
a result, the 'greatest concentration of very low income minority population of Tampa was in those census tracts immediately adjacent to the
Central Business District' both in 1979 and 1989 (ibid., 195–6).

The attempt to package Tampa's docklands on the basis of the pirate
motif is being made in this context of severe social, ethnic, and internal
place disparities. Empowered by the new rhetoric of inclusion, it is no
wonder that the attempt to imagineer and package this part of the
African-American heritage of Tampa has met with significant popular
resistance. During the planning of 1991 Superbowl festivities, for
example, a newly formed Coalition of Black Organizations revealed to
the nation's media that the reinvention of Tampa's heritage was not
taking place without a struggle. While, in 1984, the black population of
Tampa was largely unseen and accrued very little benefit from the
Superbowl, black groups this time were demanding equity (Rimer,
1991).

Significantly in both economic and symbolic terms, the focus of the
Coalition's efforts was on the role of Ye Mystic Krewe in organizing
Tampa's Superbowl parade and linked festivities. The Coalition, made
up of prominent black clergy, civil rights groups, academics, and business
leaders, threatened publicly to boycott selected white businesses if the
Krewe did not allow black members into their ranks (*Tampa Tribune*, 28
August 1990). The economic significance of this gesture was that blacks
were demanding a much expanded role in Tampa's still exclusively white
growth élite. The symbolic significance of the gesture, however, was that
blacks, constituting a quarter of the population, were no longer willing to
be ignored in the marketing of Tampa. The traditional white élite,
dressed in pirate garb, were no longer going to be able to capture and
control the new, inclusive Tampa, either for their own benefit or for that
of 'visiting businessmen'.

The results of the Coalition's campaign were an urban entrepreneur's
nightmare. The national media focused on Tampa's racial strife, particularly since Ye Mystic Krewe merely withdrew from the Superbowl
festivities rather than allow minorities to join the club. The Freedman
administration was also directly implicated in the local strife because,

even though the major parade would have been funded by the private Krewe, the city was to support it by providing security, traffic control, and eventual clean-up services. To both the local and national media, the Coalition wondered how the progressive, 'inclusionary' Freedman administration could have even pondered this endorsement of such an exclusionary group (*Tampa Tribune*, 10 September 1990). Again, it appeared that the place market had disciplined Freedman's social agenda.

An even better example of the contradiction between market discipline and social agenda in the packaging of Tampa was to occur just two years later. In 1992, two developers from New York began preliminary discussions with urban entrepreneurs in Tampa to construct a large-scale $70 million nautical museum on the waterfront. The main attraction of the museum was to be artefacts from a recently rediscovered pirate ship that had sunk off the coast of Cape Cod, Massachusetts in the early 1700s. For Tampa, such a project would provide a major impetus to the gentrification of the docklands. The museum, to be named after the pirate ship – the Whydah – and including a full-scale model that would simulate its sinking, would particularly complement the nearby aquarium as an urban tourist attraction. To Tampa's urban entrepreneurs, such a proposition could hardly have been a better fit, especially given the prominent pirate motif.

Not surprisingly, all the 'movers and shakers' of Tampa supported the project from the start. Ye Mystic Krewe assumed a major role in advocating the Whydah museum and, again, as a local newspaper puts it in retrospect, 'no one noticed' that the group negotiating for the city 'included few blacks' even though 'only two years earlier business leaders publicly committed to include blacks in key economic decisions' in the aftermath of the Superbowl controversy (*Tampa Tribune*, 21 April 1993). Getting the deal finished was considered more important than bickering about inclusion, especially given the economic as well as symbolic potential of the pirate ship project for the redevelopment of Tampa's docklands.

In the process of getting the deal finished the fact that the Whydah was first used as a slave ship was simply overlooked. When the Coalition of African-American Groups finally got wind of it, however, this apparently minor detail became the centre of dispute. Tampa's growth élite again had ignored the African-American experience in its attempt to package the place. That the proposed development was to be located in the docklands and that it was to reinforce the mythical pirate tradition of the area merely caused the Coalition to redouble its efforts against the museum. Even after the developers promised to add a wing to detail the ship's former slaver status, the Coalition demanded that the city withdraw its support for the museum. Significantly, the Coalition argued that, far from being similar to a Holocaust museum, the slave experience could hardly be given its proper due in the same building that housed a Disneyesque simulation of a ship sinking in high seas. In short, the proposed juxtaposition of history and fantasy was more likely in the Coalition's eyes to be a merging and, because of the very role of the museum as an urban tourist attraction, it was not likely that the tragic history of slavery would be the dominant discourse experienced (*Tampa Tribune*, 26 February 1993).

After much public debate, the potential developers of the Whydah museum withdrew their offer to Tampa in July 1993. The local social environment seemed much too hostile, particularly along the black–white divide. To the local and national press, Tampa again seemed to be driven by racial strife, neither safe nor very attractive as a place to visit or to do business. Of interest here is that the scuttled Whydah project can be considered a microcosm of the attempt to package Tampa for the global gentry. Like the museum developers, Tampa's urban entrepreneurs are mixing fantasy with history in the redevelopment of the docklands. To finish the deal in the highly competitive place commodity market necessitates an emphasis on the invented pirate tradition, even though the élitist and racist (and sexist) pirate motif is in complete contradiction with the rhetoric of the progressive Freedman regime. In this case, as in that of the pirate museum, fantasy and not history continues to be the dominant discourse in the packaging of Tampa.

The leaders of the African-American community deserve the credit for successfully challenging the attempt to imagineer Tampa's heritage by lifting the veil of the pirate fantasy. It remains to be seen, however, whether the campaign to stop the Whydah museum project will have any more lasting effects on Tampa's governance than the earlier campaign to integrate Ye Mystic Krewe. The discipline of the place commodity market makes success in this regard very difficult to attain. If Tampa cannot get the deal finished because of political uncertainties, already gentrified Orlando certainly will accomplish the feat.

Urban entrepreneurialism and the disciplining of progressive politics on the eve of the twenty-first century

Mayor Freedman's administration was as implicated in the Whydah museum fiasco as it was in the earlier dispute over the Superbowl festivities. 'No one noticed' that blacks were not involved in the city's negotiations with the museum developers and this included the mayor herself. Again, in spite of the rhetoric of political and social inclusion, local politicians were proceeding with getting the urban deal finished much like they always had: with a few, well-chosen local élite, behind closed doors, and wholly driven by private sector criteria. Indeed, this has been the style of urban entrepreneurialism throughout Freedman's term of office leading, finally, to an actual lawsuit brought against the Mayor's office by the local firefighters' union in 1993 charging the city with unconstitutional secrecy in negotiating with potential convention hotel developers. Since the city intends to back the hotel with significant public debt, the union reasoned, the negotiations should be open to the public (*Tampa Tribune*, 5 September 1993).

Regardless of Freedman's true intentions, her attempt to construct a more democratic local politics has been severely disciplined by the place commodity market. The contradictory demands of urban entrepreneurialism and inclusionary politics have rendered the Freedman administration unable to be successful at either endeavour. Hence, to the old guard growth élite, Freedman appears to be indecisive, lacking vision, and incapable of finishing the urban deal (Szymanski and Gilpin, 1993). Similarly, for Tampa's African-American community, Freedman's rhetoric of inclusion appears to be a ploy aimed more at political co-optation than actual participation.

In the end, the lessons to be learned from the fate of the Freedman regime are essentially threefold. First, the discipline of the place commodity market is severe, particularly for mid-sized cities like Tampa just now gentrifying their physical and social environments. As more cities attempt to capture post-industrial development, competition among places will only increase. In this context, progressive public policy must be formulated, from the start, with an explicit understanding of the goals of local 'development'. Such goals should not be assumed, as is largely the case with the Freedman regime, but should be discussed openly with local inhabitants. Questions that must be addressed include: what kind of city should Tampa be?; what local physical and social assets should policy-makers emphasize and what sort of emphasis should be placed on such assets? Inhabitants must be included in this process of creating a 'vision' of the local future. Continuing to privatize local development policy will merely hasten the serial overproduction of imagineered convention cities.

The second lesson to be drawn from Tampa's experience follows directly from the first. In order for inhabitants to be involved in creating a vision for the local future, policy-makers must ensure that the process of local development is rendered much more inclusionary. In Tampa's case, the rhetoric of inclusion hides a policy process that still excludes important segments of the population. Development deals continue to be made behind closed doors by essentially the same individuals as before the Freedman regime. Ensuring an inclusionary development process necessitates much more effort on the part of policy-makers to facilitate public participation in deciding not only what development deals should be made, but also how such deals are to be made – for example, what precisely the public role is to be in public–private deals and whether deals involving public funds include explicit provisions for payback or linkages for parallel investments in public goods.

The third lesson is that progressive regimes need to ensure that the greater public participation resulting from a more open discussion of development goals and process explicitly includes groups which traditionally have been excluded. This will involve much critical missionary work on the part of policy-makers because, as we have seen with regard to Tampa's African-American community, such groups have a healthy cynicism about the public process. It cannot be assumed that a general invitation to all local citizen groups will elicit their participation. Representatives from traditionally excluded groups must be asked directly to participate in the policy process. A local politics of inclusion must be actively constructed, in this regard, as such a politics will not simply arise from general calls for public participation.

In short, a progressive, democratic politics of local development will not be easily achieved. An actively constructed politics of inclusion necessarily will engender significant differences in opinion over local development goals, how such goals should be achieved, and who should be involved in the decision-making process. A politics of inclusion, in other words, is inherently a politics of difference. To the extent that this is fully understood, the key for local policy-makers is to render the procedures of participation as open and as fair as possible. As long as all involved continue, legitimately, to feel some ownership of the local development process, significant differences in opinion can be managed without being co-opted in a prematurely forced consensus. While constructing such an inclusionary local politics may be hard work, it is a far cry better than leaving local development to public–private 'experts' whose decisions are based solely on bottom-line, market criteria.

References

Albright, M. (1989), 'The center of attention – lack of hotels may hurt convention hall', *St. Petersburg Times*, 11 September.

Archer, K., Morici, P. (1993), 'State-export promotion policies', in Brown, D.M., Fry, E.H. (eds), *States and Provinces in the International Economy*. Berkeley Institute of Governmental Studies, University of California.

Associated Press (1993), 'Disney plans futuristic city', *St. Petersburg Times*, 23 January.

Bane, M., Moore, M.E. (1981), *Tampa: Yesterday, Today, and Tomorrow*. Tampa, Mishler Consulting Group.

Boyer, M.C. (1992), 'Cities for sale: merchandising history at South Street Seaport', in Sorkin, M. (ed.), *Variations on a Theme Park: The New American City and the End of Public Space*. New York, Hill and Wang.

Boyle, M., Hughes, G. (1992), 'The politics of the representation of "the Real": discourses from the left on Glasgow's role as European City of Culture, 1990', *Area*, 23: 217–28.

Braun, B.M. (1992), 'The economic contribution of conventions: the case of Orlando', *Florida Journal of Travel Research*, Winter: 32–7.

Castells, M. (1989), *The Informational City*. Oxford, Basil Blackwell.

City of Tampa (1981, 1988, 1992), *Comprehensive Annual Financial Reports*. Tampa, City Hall.

—— (1993), *Minority Affairs Addendum: Tampa Comprehensive Plan*. Tampa, City Hall.

Clavel, P. (1986), *The Progressive City*. New Brunswick, Rutgers University Press.

D'Ans, A-M. (1980), 'The Legend of Gasparilla', *Tampa Bay History*, 12: 5–29.

Fjellman, S.M. (1992), *Vinyl Leaves: Walt Disney World and America*. Boulder, Westview Press.

Fleming, J. (1993), 'Aquarium lures fund-raiser', *St. Petersburg Times*, 22 July.

Frieden, B.J., Sagalyn, L.B. (1989), *Downtown, Inc. How America Rebuilds Cities*. Cambridge, The MIT Press.

Garreau, J. (1991), *Edge City: Life on the New Frontier*. New York, Double-Day.

Goldsmith, W.W., Blakely, E.J. (1992), *Separate Societies: Poverty and Inequality in US Cities*. Philadelphia, Temple University Press.

Goodman, R. (1979), *The Last Entrepreneurs: America's Regional Wars for Jobs and Dollars*. New York, Simon and Schuster.

Gottdiener, M. (1987), *The Decline of Urban Politics*. Beverly Hills, Sage.

Harvey, D. (1982), *The Limits to Capital*. Oxford, Basil Blackwell.

—— (1989a), *The Condition of PostModernity: An Enquiry into the Origins of Cultural Change*. Oxford, Basil Blackwell.

—— (1989b), 'From managerialism to entrepreneurialism: the transformation in urban governance in late capitalism', *Geografiska Annaler*, 71B: 3–17.

—— (1989c), 'Flexible accumulation through urbanization: reflections on post-modernism in the American city', in Harvey, D., *Urban Experience*. Baltimore, Johns Hopkins University Press.

Helm, D. (1989), *The Economic Borders of the State*. Oxford, Oxford University Press.

Hooper, E. (1992), 'Orlando pursues future pro bowls and more', *St. Petersburg Times*, 4 August.

Judd, D.R., Parkinson, M. (1989), 'Urban revitalization in the United States and the United Kingdom', in Parkinson, M., Foley, B., Judd, D., (eds), *Regenerating the Cities: The U.K. Crisis and the US Experience*. Glenview, Scott, Foresman, and Company.

Judge, J. (1973), 'Florida's booming – and beleaguered heartland: the mouse gets the blame', *National Geographic Magazine*, November: 585–621.

Kearns, G., Philo C. (eds) (1993), *Selling Places: The City as Cultural Capital, Past and Present*. Oxford, Pergamon Press.

Kerstein, R. (1991), 'Growth politics in Tampa and Hillsborough County: strains in the privatistic regimes', *Journal of Urban Affairs*, 13: 55–75.

Leitner, H., Garner, M. (1993), 'The limits of local initiatives: a reassessment of urban entrepreneurialism for urban development', *Urban Geography*, 14: 57–77.

Levine, M. (1987), 'Downtown redevelopment as an urban growth strategy: a critical appraisal of the Baltimore renaissance', *Journal of Urban Affairs*, 9: 102–23.

Liner, E.B. (ed.) (1989), *A Decade of Devolution: Perspectives on State-Local Relations*. Washington D.C., The Urban Institute.

Logan, J., Molotch, H. (1987), *Urban Fortunes: The Political Economy of Place*. Berkeley, University of California Press.

Logan, J., Swanstrom, T. (eds) (1990), *Beyond City Limits*. Philadelphia, Temple University Press.

Lowitt, B. (1993), 'The lightening: Q and A', *St. Petersburg Times*, 24 November.

Molotch, H. (1988), 'Strategies and constraints of growth élites', in Cummings, S. (ed.), *Business Elites and Urban Development: Case Studies and Critical Perspectives*. Albany, State University of New York Press.

Mormino, G.R., Pizzo, A.P. (1983), *Tampa: The Treasure City*. Tulsa, Continental Heritage Press.

Mormino, G.R., Pozzetta, G.E. (1990), *The Immigrant World of Ybor City*. Urbana, University of Illinois Press.

Moulaert, F., Swyngedouw, E. (1991), 'Regional development and the geography of the flexible production system', in Hilpert, U., (ed.), *Regional Innovation and Decentralization*. London, Routledge.

Naisbitt, J. (1982), *Megatrends*. New York, Warner Books.

Paddison, R. (1993), 'City marketing, image reconstruction and urban regeneration', *Urban Studies*, 30: 339–50.

Pease, M. (1993), 'Florida aquarium begins to take shape', *St. Petersburg Times*, 26 June.

Presti, K. (1991), 'The Disney difference', *Florida Trend*, December: 28-41.

Relph, E. (1987), *The Modern Urban Landscape*. Baltimore, Johns Hopkins University Press.

Rimer, S. (1991), 'Big game revealing a city's changes', *The New York Times*, 22 January.

Robinson, P. (1993), 'Isolated deprivation in Tampa, Florida'. Unpublished master's thesis, Department of Geography, University of South Florida.

Samek, R., Dolan, M., Good, J. (1988), 'The year in review: a year of pride and protest', *St. Petersburg Times*, 1 January.

Sanders, H.T. (1992), 'Building the convention city: politics, finance, and public investment in urban America', *Journal of Urban Affairs*, 14: 135–59.

Shafner, J.H. (1984), *Orlando: The City Beautiful*. Orlando, Walsworth Publishing.

Shermyen, A.H., Floyd, S.S., Thompson, G.H., Evans, D.A. (1991), *1991 Florida Statistical Abstract*. Gainesville, University Press of Florida.

Smith, M.P., Feagin, J.R. (eds) (1987), *The Capitalist City*. Oxford, Basil Blackwell.

Squires, G.D. (ed.), (1989), *Unequal Partnerships*. New Brunswick, Rutgers University Press.

Sutton, C. (1989a), 'Lacking vision, Tampa's growth plan merely presents . . . the statistics of decline', *St. Petersburg Times*, 25 June.

—— (1989b), 'Tampa mayor emerges from past shadows', *St. Petersburg Times*, 16 April.

Swyngedouw, E.A. (1989), 'The heart of the place: the resurrection of locality in the age of hyperspace', *Geografiska Annaler*, 71B: 31–42.

Szymanski, D., Gilpin, F. (1993), 'A vanishing breed: an energetic group of activists led Tampa's growth. Now they wonder who is in charge', *Tampa Tribune*, 25 July.

Tampa Tribune (1990), 'Black group shifts focus to economics', 28 August.

—— (1990) 'Mayor takes gloves off on Gasparilla', 10 September.

—— (1991), 'The future of Tampa', 4 January.

—— (1991), 'The future of Tampa', 14 January.

—— (1992), 'Orlando', 3 May.

—— (1993), 'Excerpts from the coalition statement', 26 February.

—— (1993), 'Tampa's movers and shakers overlook racism issue', 21 April.

—— (1993), 'Dealing under the table', 5 September.

Turner, R.S. (1992), 'Growth politics and downtown development: the economic imperative in sunbelt cities', *Urban Affairs Quarterly*, 28: 3–21.

Wilson, C. (1992), 'Orlando poised for 2nd surge', *St. Petersburg Times*, 22 February.

13

Conversations of power
Community organizing strategies of the St Thomas Resident Council, New Orleans

ALMA H. YOUNG AND JYAPHIA
CHRISTOS-RODGERS

Introduction

In this chapter we look at the holistic approach developed by a community of African-American women who live in public housing in New Orleans to resist the impacts of urban restructuring on their lives. We first provide the national and urban context by deconstructing the strategies for economic development which unreflectively assume privilege and drain low-income communities of resources. We show how access to resources in the corporate city is organized for low-income African-American communities. We then look more specifically at the effects of economic restructuring on New Orleans in general and the neighbourhood where these women live in particular.

We analyse the work these women do as members of the St Thomas Resident Council (STRC). The work is analysed in terms of four 'conversations' in which the Council is involved that challenge the dominant societal discourses from many different angles. These are a conversation about institutionalized racism and community power, a conversation about youth and family well-being, one about economic development, and one about land use.

French philosopher Michel Foucault (1980) has suggested that social life is organized around discourse, a form of 'power/knowledge' that circulates within the social field and can attach itself to strategies of domination and its acceptance and to those of resistance. Discourse, which may be likened to a conversation, is expressed through language in the form of text and narrative, and through practices (Diamond and Quinby, 1988). In critiquing Foucault and developing a more sociological approach to discourse analysis, called 'institutional ethnography', Dorothy Smith (1987) points out that what Foucault calls 'power/knowledge' is a mystification of the actual social relations underlying the concerted activities of individuals across the institutional world. If we wish to understand how the social world is organized for people, that is, how ruling and governance are accomplished, enquiry must begin in people's actual experience in their everyday worlds. This first level of enquiry must seek the ruptures, the places where consciousness is bifurcated, between the everyday world and the institutional world which organizes local experience at many extralocal levels (Smith, 1987). If we wish to understand how people bring about social change we must examine how, with awareness of these ruptures, those engaged in resistance generate alternative discourses which enter into conversations with the dominant societal discourse.

This 'conversational' approach to making social change is supported by the social theory of authors like Smith and Foucault. However, the St Thomas community did not discover this strategy in academic literature. Rather, it has unfolded from a history of local and national community organizing practice as community leaders and professional organizers have, over the last fifteen to twenty years, struggled to address the intersection of racism and poverty in communities of colour. This work within the St Thomas community has taken a holistic approach to community development. By this we mean that the strategies go beyond piecemeal practices and analyses. This work seeks to integrate marginalized neighbourhoods within the fabric of the city and to reintegrate marginalized people within families and communities.

Historically, black women have carried on this kind of community work (Hooks, 1990; Gilkes, 1994). In this instance we look at the STRC primarily through the eyes of black women who, because of public housing policy, are lessees and therefore eligible to sit on the official resident council board. However, one important aspect of their work is their awareness that the spaces they inhabit are racially gendered in a manner that marginalizes black males within families and the community (Young and Christos-Rodgers, 1994). This recognition means that part of their work to make the community whole is challenging non-inclusive policies and affirming their solidarity with black males.

Economic restructuring and the dominant discourse

Economic restructuring, caused largely by the global change from a goods-producing to a service-producing economy, has profound implications for cities around the world. Generally, these cities reflect a regime of flexible accumulation with its emphasis on flexible labour, depressed wages and the dismantling of the welfare state (see Logan and Swanstrom, 1990). To cope with the changes wrought by economic restructuring, many cities adopt the 'corporate center approach' (see Hill, 1983; Feagin, 1986; Logan and Molotch, 1987; and Robinson, 1989), which stresses growth and real estate development, especially in the central business district. The goals of the approach are increased economic growth and tax base expansion, with little concern about the distribution of benefits. Thus, according to Goetz (1992: 540):

> In many cities the recent transformation of the central business district (CBD) into a centre of finance and real estate capital housed in skyscraping office towers has been matched by the continued deterioration of working-class neighbourhoods and the elimination of poor neighbourhoods that had encircled the downtown area and threatened its expansion.

This uneven development leads to class recomposition and social polarization, as the growth of high-wage jobs is accompanied by the rapid expansion of low-wage jobs and the informal economy, in which work remains undocumented and unprotected (Sassen, 1988). As a result, there is much inequality among individual wages, as well as family income. Margrit Mayer (1991: l09) speaks of this as the 'dual city', which is 'determined by two equally dynamic sectors: the advanced services and high-tech sector and its unregulated, labor-intensive sector'.

This dual city is reinforced by residential separation, with both residential and economic patterns responding to a legacy of racial segregation in the United States. What few public areas there were historically in cities are being replaced by the development of closed communities of consumption: gated residential communities, enclosed downtown malls, and entertainment areas presented as urban spectacle. The focus in all of these privatized spaces is upon a safe and sterile enclave in which the unpleasantries of inner city decay are invisible to the residents, consumers and office workers who fill them (see Crawford, 1992).

This focus has specific consequences for women of colour and their families. In these safe enclaves, it is women of colour who tend to work the lower end service sector jobs that keep the places running. At the same time, these women often live in communities which have been left to decay, while public resources are put into these glitzy private enclaves. These women and their children experience first hand the changes in the welfare system – the retrenchment in material benefits and the increase in social regulation. For example, in 1973, nearly 85 per cent of children living in poor families collected welfare (i.e. Aid to Families with Dependent Children, AFDC); by 1986, less than 60 per cent received benefits. Also, the purchasing power of AFDC benefits fell by one third between 1970 and 1986 (Amott, 1990: 290–2).

The state's regulation of poor people and people of colour is seen most dramatically in the growth of the prison and jail population, from 350,000 in 1980 to 1,200,000 in 1990, and the number of black men who fill those cells. As of 1990, 23 per cent of black men between the ages of 18 and 30 in the United States were in prison, in jail or on probation, compared to

6 per cent of white men in the same category (Dumm, 1993: 190). With many poor men of colour in prison, central city neighbourhoods are left to be headed by women. These women find themselves in racially gendered spaces as a result of policies, both direct and default, that impact their ability to create resources that would be beneficial to themselves and their families (Spain, 1993; Young and Christos-Rodgers, 1994). Thus, the development pursued by many cities as a result of economic restructuring works to the disadvantage of low-income women of colour and their families.

Like other cities around the world, New Orleans felt the impact of economic restructuring and in response enacted policies which it hoped would help it to compete more successfully. In the process, New Orleans experienced uneven development, with some areas benefiting from growth while others suffered from neglect. Between 1960 and 1990, New Orleans lost almost 21 per cent of its population, going from 627,525 people in 1960 to 496,938 in 1990. On the other hand, the metropolitan area had a population gain of about 43 per cent (from 868,480 in 1960 to 1,238,216 in 1990) (Mumphrey and Akundi, 1994).

During that thirty-year period, the racial-ethnic composition of the city changed dramatically, going from 62.6 per cent white in 1960 to 61.4 per cent black in 1990. The city's median family income grew between 1960 and 1970, but has been in decline since then. In 1990, the median family income was $22,987 (compared with median family income for the metropolitan area of $30,493). In 1960, 24 per cent of New Orleans families were below the poverty level. By 1980, that number was 21.8 per cent. Yet, when compared to the 25 largest cities in the United States, New Orleans had a greater proportion of its population earning less than $10,000 for the years between 1960 and 1980. However, a smaller proportion earned between $10,000 and $25,000 in these years (Mumphrey and Pinell, 1992; Mumphrey and Akundi, 1994).

Since the 1960s the New Orleans economy has relied on three major bases: the port, oil and related industries, and tourism (see Whelan, 1989). Increasingly, these sectors of the economy are controlled by outside interests and are highly subject to swings in the national and international economy. Historically, the port has been central to the city's growth. More recently, the port faced problems of competition from other cities, and decreases in tonnage passing through and workers employed followed. Since most of this dock labour is black, the effects on the black community are especially severe, as blacks have lost relatively high-paying unionized jobs (Whelan, 1989). Under new port leadership, the volume of cargo (but not the number of jobs) has increased. To become more competitive, the public port authority is constructing new facilities away from downtown and towards impoverished black neighbourhoods (Young and Whelan, 1993).

The oil industry became an important part of the New Orleans economy after World War II with the discovery and drilling of oil off the Louisiana coast. The initial expansion of the city's central business district was largely as a result of the construction of regional oil and gas headquarters. With the drop in the price of petroleum and related products in the 1980s, the city's economy was devastated. The city had double-digit unemployment for three years, and the collapse of the industry led to a population out-migration, of mostly young, well-educated professionals. The out-migration had a negative effect on the housing market, city taxes and the subsequent delivery of services (Whelan, 1989).

By 1987 there was some recovery in the oil and gas industry, but by that time tourism had displaced petroleum as the mainstay of the local economy. The number of hotels, conventions, and tourists has increased substantially since 1975. By the mid-1980s tourism was seen as a $2.5 billion business for the metropolitan area, with much of the industry located in downtown New Orleans (Brooks and Young, 1993: 262). To maintain an attractive and secure environment for tourists and conventioneers, the city (through its quasi-public Downtown Development District) spends additional funds in the downtown area on police, sanitation and removing the remnants of Skid Row. While many jobs have been created in the tourist industry, most of them are low-paying service positions, with high turnover rates and little opportunity for career mobility, an employment sector in which blacks are overrepresented.

Since the late 1960s the city of New Orleans has pursued a corporate centre strategy that emphasizes revitalization of the central business district and promotion of tourism. Relatively few redevelopment efforts have centred on the city's neighbourhoods. Historic neighbourhoods, or those with architecturally significant structures have been protected to some extent by the strong preservationist movement in New Orleans. Other neighbourhoods have been left to deteriorate. Today there are 37,000 blighted or vacant housing units in the city. Earlier, some low-income black neighbourhoods were devastated due to displacement caused by the completion of public projects (a civic centre in the 1960s, an interstate highway in the 1970s, and a park in the 1970s). For blacks, such displacement led to doubling up in private housing, most of which is rental in New Orleans, and to living in public housing. In New Orleans, one resident in ten (or approximately 50,000 people) lives in public housing. This makes the Housing Authority of New Orleans (HANO) the sixth largest in the United States. The city's oldest public housing developments were built close to downtown and to transit lines; today, they are close to viable residential neighbourhoods. Thus public housing in these locations is often seen as a threat to urban regeneration efforts, and plans are underway to minimize its impact, generally by making the housing developments smaller (see Cook and Lauria, 1993).

The St Thomas Resident Council

One such public housing development that has been the subject of particular interest among local developers, businesses and city officials is St Thomas. This public housing development is located about two miles from downtown (once out of the development, one is on a major thoroughfare which is a direct route to the CBD). It is also only a couple of blocks from the uptown riverfront, which is receiving increased attention from public officials and developers alike.

The St Thomas housing development, which opened in 1941, is one of the oldest public housing developments in the United States. In the days of officially segregated public housing, St Thomas was built for whites. Originally St Thomas blended into its neighbourhood, but with the extension built in 1949, the massiveness of the development overtook the neighbourhood. The entire development is 49.33 acres and consists of 1,510 units. After desegregation, the first black family moved into St Thomas in 1965; today St Thomas is 96 per cent African-American (Calvert, 1990).

As of May 1990 there were 4,772 persons living in St Thomas. The population of St Thomas is very young: only 7 per cent of the population is over 20 years old; 70 per cent is under 14. Of the householders 90 per cent are female. Those with incomes below $15,000 comprise 85 per cent and 61 per cent have incomes lower than $5,000 a year. Those receiving some form of public assistance comprise 85 per cent (Jones, 1993).

St Thomas is a part of the St Thomas/Irish Channel neighbourhood. This is a neighbourhood of vast contrasts: whites and blacks live side by side; wealthy homeowners and poor tenants live in the shadow of each other; urban gentrification and renewal coexist with decaying housing. Of the neighbourhood residents 34 per cent have incomes under $5,000, while 7 per cent have incomes between $50,000–$100,000, and 2 per cent have incomes over $100,000. A variety of social service agencies and homeowner and business associations coexist in the area (Urban Land Institute, 1993).

Since the late 1950s the St Thomas development has been system-atically cut off from the rest of the community in which it sits. What were originally through streets have been closed; escalating crime rates in the area have been used to stigmatize the residents as deviant; and social service delivery has largely been contained within the community. In more recent years, because of its prime location, St Thomas has begun to

experience the impact of encroaching development. First gentrification
of the adjoining neighbourhood, then riverfront development – from
both the port, which is moving more of its terminals and warehouses
away from the central business district and towards the St Thomas area,
and commercial development, especially as a result of pressures from
riverboat gambling and the planned land-based casino (due to open in
1996).

These development pressures are being experienced within a context
which calls for the scaling back of public housing developments throughout the city, including St Thomas (see Cook and Lauria, 1993). There is
much less discussion about where public housing residents would live,
should the scale back occur. It is as a result of these kinds of encroach-
ments that the women of St Thomas have organized to resist urban
development and maintain a space for themselves and their families.

The residents of St Thomas originally incorporated as a council in
1975; in 1989 they reincorporated as the St Thomas Development Resident Council, Incorporated (STRC). The STRC is an eleven member
board of duly elected representatives of the tenants of the St Thomas
public housing development. The council is composed exclusively of
women; this reflects public housing policy which makes women the
official lessees of the housing units. One of the purposes of the council is
to 'expand opportunities for residents to participate in the development
management [sic] affairs and in programs designed to strengthen self-
sufficiency and foster upward mobility among its residents' (Jones, 1993:
187).

Because of its ability to organize and mobilize its members, the St
Thomas Resident Council is recognized as one of the strongest councils
in the city. For example, in 1982, to protest against poor living conditions
in the city's public housing, the council organized a four-day takeover of
the local HANO main office. After the takeover, St Thomas residents
organized an eleven-month rent strike. As a result of the rent strike, St
Thomas was awarded a $21 million rehabilitation grant from the Depart-
ment of Housing and Urban Development (Jones, 1993: 187).

The strength of the St Thomas Resident Council, and subsequently of
the community, lies in the holistic approach to community development
which has unfolded over time. The continuity of the organizing effort in
St Thomas over the last fifteen years has allowed the STRC to develop an
understanding of the ways that the issues of race, economics and housing
are inseparable. At the heart of the strengths of this community of
resistance are three principles: leadership development, accountability,
and self-determination. This understanding and these principles came
out of a relationship with the People's Institute for Survival and Beyond,
which we introduce in the next section.

Conversations

Conversation I : Institutional racism and community power

The STRC is linked to the broader movement of people of colour through its collaboration with the People's Institute for Survival and Beyond. The People's Institute, founded in 1980, is a national, multi-racial, anti-racist collective of organizers and educators dedicated to building an effective movement for social change. The team of trainers are men and women who are veterans of community organizing for social justice over the past twenty years. The Institute grew out of a rupture between the everyday organizing experiences of the two African-American men who founded it and what they were being formally taught as community organizers.

During the 1970s Ron Chisom and the late Dr Jim Dunn were trained in a variety of 'state-of-the-art' community organizing models. Both found that their experience in being of and working in specifically African-American communities was never addressed in their training. Their work evolved around this recognition that analyses of race and racism were curiously absent from the dominant discourse on community organizing. Thus, the People's Institute training focuses on the import-ance of history, culture and power in undoing the racist policies and practices that affect poor communities of colour by keeping the inter-section of race and poverty in place.

Through the Institute the experiential knowledge of organizers and leaders from around the country is brought together, synthesized and refined. This oral theorizing, sometimes called the 'organic theories' of community development (see Rubin, 1993), constitutes an intellectual discourse that occurs in meetings, conferences and other group activities. Through conversation, holistic analyses of the workings of power on communities are woven together to articulate a cohesive social theory which informs praxis.

The Institute's training offers an 'institutional power analysis' of racism which asserts that interlocking systems of social institutions sur-round poor communities and operate in a manner in which the accountability of institutional actors is to the institutions, rather than to the communities they serve. These institutions, it is argued, have been organized around implicit and explicit assumptions of white skin priv-ilege and it is these assumptions which must be challenged if social and cultural change are to occur.

Crystal Jones, former resident and long-time activist and organizer of St Thomas, is also board president of the People's Institute. Jones (1993) recently completed a comprehensive study of the STRC and its pro-grammes, principles and processes. According to her, leadership development means that the organizing efforts make resources available to nurture the abilities of individual members of the community who, thus empowered, move the collective forward. This strategy seeks to support the next principle, self-determination. As leaders develop and the community becomes stronger and wiser, the collective is not willing to allow agencies and institutions external to it to make all the decisions. For a people to empower themselves to the point of self-determination means that those who have had the power must let go of some control. For STRC, this has meant that professionals working in the community must do so in collaboration with, and accountability to, the indigenous leadership. Together these three principles form the basis upon which the collective and the individuals that compose it wield power that previously was wielded only by agencies and institutions.

With the assistance of organizers from the People's Institute, the St Thomas Resident Council (STRC) began to question the role of social service providers in their community. The STRC observed that while a great deal of money is spent servicing and studying poor people, the practitioners who work inside or in relation with poor communities answer to their agencies and institutions and rarely have any accountability to the communities they serve. Fannie McKnight, the Vice-President of the STRC, explains why they began to look at social service agencies:

> We kept saying that people were putting money for services in the community but things didn't get better for *my* people. There were people getting rich off of us. We had been so busy fighting the Housing Authority [we had forgotten that] we had to look at services. [emphasis added]

Because so many families in St Thomas depend upon the state and social service agencies for economic support, their first front of struggle on economic issues was with these institutions. For this reason the STRC worked to develop strategies for obtaining accountability from the institutions which surrounded the neighbourhood. According to Barbara Major, one of the principal organizers in the community:

> We began by saying to the social service agencies in the geographical area, 'If you are in our community and you are, and you're getting money to provide services for us and you're using us as the statistical base to provide those services, then we surely have a right to say what those services will be and how they will be offered. We are now in our own growth and development ready to be in true partnership in all programs developed on our behalf.' It's very difficult for the agencies and so what we said was, 'If you're not willing to be our partner then we are willing to go to the funding sources and say, keep your money because it doesn't impact our lives or to the point of making us self-sufficient.'

Building an organizational structure that brings the various institutions together with the residents of the community they service is a long-term process, currently in its fifth year. In 1989, the STRC sent a letter to all social service agencies operating in the St Thomas area, inviting them to 'come to the table', to discuss how they might work in partnership with the community. After a number of meetings, the group formed the St Thomas/Irish Channel Consortium. The Consortium is a community board of twelve member agencies, including health, social service, advocacy and religious organizations, along with the People's Institute and the St Thomas Resident Council. The Resident Council has veto power over all Consortium decisions.

For agency organizations, 'coming to the table' requires a commitment to address issues of racism and its impact on the residents of the St Thomas area, and to accept the leadership of the Resident Council. Barbara Major outlines the difficulties experienced by the group, but also the promise provided by the Consortium:

> We were multi-racial and historically multi-racial groups have never been able to work together because you still go into the group with an imbalance in power ... As the agencies got involved they realized that what we were saying is not that we want you to leave but that we want a different relationship with you. We've had our struggles but we've done real good because we're still at the table .... Because we are not willing to leave the table, we struggle with each other, we've come up with another model for mediation.

During its existence the Consortium has been a forum for struggle and consciousness raising. It has also been a place to build a sense of community and extended family across race and class lines without ignoring the histories of oppression and privilege that underlie such relationships. We see here that the group has focused, as many other women-centred community development groups have, on developing workable processes for building partnership. By this, we observe that the focus of the group is not exclusively on building oppositional power to leverage or force accountability, but to build long-term relationships through committed struggle, even when the struggle is prolonged. The philosophy undergirding the group is that the 'consortium is a family and no one is prepared to leave'.

The Consortium and the collection of strategies implemented through it are part of the Resident Council's overall holistic approach to organizing which focuses upon process as political, and upon empowering individual members of the community as it addresses specific issues. At its most basic level, holistic organizing means reintegrating the members of the community who have been isolated from each other by, for example, service delivery practices which treat the well-being of the elders or the youth as separable from that of the other age groups within the community. If programmes are to address effectively the troubles of low-income communities, then practitioners must understand the community as a collective and work with the indigenous leadership in its efforts towards reintegration.

Conversation II : Youth and family well-being

To these women it is clear that organizing their community requires work that is multi-faceted and ongoing. They have had to find ways to challenge the systems of power relations which provided for and regulated the community. Beyond that, their work has had to reach into the fabric of the community to address internalized oppression as well as external control, exploitation, and paternalism. This work is expressed through a second set of conversations that centre around the needs of youth and families. These conversations have led to the creation of two specific programmes, both under the umbrella of the Consortium. The Kuji Center and the Plain Talk Initiative are community based and seek to strengthen families so that they can better support their youth. The Kuji Center is a year-round, after-school programme that seeks to improve and expand the life options available to teenagers in St Thomas, and thus prevent teenage pregnancy. According to Demetria Farve, who is one of the mothers in St Thomas and also the President of the Resident Council, 'When I was a teenager sex seemed like the only recreation available to me. Now I'm 24 and I got four children. If there was Kuji when I was coming up I might have made different choices.'

The Kuji Center was created in 1990, after the Consortium applied for and received a million dollar grant from a local foundation to create a community-based comprehensive service programme that met the needs of the youth of St Thomas. The Kuji Center responds to the needs of the teenagers by providing cultural, educational and recreational programmes, as well as entrepreneurship, leadership training and peer counselling. The centre's name is a shortened version of the Swahili word, Kujichagulia, which means 'self-determination'.

The Plain Talk Initiative is funded by a national foundation to develop a community strategy for reaching sexually active teenagers. The foundation leaves specific programming to the community, but requires substantial ownership of the programme among the residents. The St Thomas leadership decided to use 'home health parties' as a way of beginning a conversation in the community about how to protect sexually active youth. During the first year, over ninety parties were held, giving adults and youth an opportunity to explore in familiar surroundings issues of sexuality in general, as well as issues of domestic violence and child abuse. According to Petrice Sams-Abiodun, a former resident of public housing who has completed a master's degree and is now co-ordinating Plain Talk:

> Through Plain Talk residents of St Thomas, along with service providers, churches, schools, policy-makers and other community representatives came together to build community consensus and a collective strategy for the protection of sexually active youth from unplanned pregnancy and sexually transmitted diseases including HIV. Through these community conversations a Health Care Partnership emerged which challenged health and social service providers to develop cultural and age-appropriate services to youth in St Thomas.

Both the Kuji Center and Plain Talk include men in their programming, and the efforts are paying off. For instance, at Plain Talk's initial retreat, no men showed up. At the retreat the following year, after a number of house parties during the year at which men were encouraged to take part in the discussions on sexuality, twelve men attended. Recently a 'manhood co-ordinator' was hired from within the community to expand the men's participation in these community conversations.

The residents have also used this time together to begin a discussion on street and domestic violence in the community. Fannie McKnight expresses how the community is beginning to grapple with the issue of violence:

> Our young men are talking about wanting to stop the violence in our community. They say they're tired of it … . We're taking a spiritual approach to dealing with all this violence. We're not crying and complaining, we're pulling ourselves up to fight. There's a spiritual grieving process going on. This city was dead but the people in this community is not. Shame can't be used against them anymore.

Recently a series of conversations has begun between professionals and community members that is being called the Child and Family Safety Partnership. A central topic was that of the ways violence affects children and the interconnections between domestic and street violence. The agencies are coming to realize that many of their strategies for addressing violence pit community members against each other. The community is also talking about ways that members of the community perpetuate violence on the streets and within their homes. According to Reverend David Billings, another organizer within St Thomas:

> Previously the community could not risk having this discussion. When intimidation goes on within the home, the temptation is to give up or give over. But external brutality is working on the sons of the community and the bond and knowledge of family is still there underneath this wounded tyrant.

Through programmes like the Kuji Center and Plain Talk the community is creating safe spaces in which to examine how it perpetuates violence against itself and how it can heal. Other issues on the table at the Child and Family Safety Partnership include problems of community policing, creating child abuse reporting procedures that are culturally sensitive, and developing a holistic, Afrocentric system of healthcare delivery and wellness within the community. At the heart of the discussion is the recognition that policies that invisibilize black males destabilize whole families and perpetuate violence and poverty in the community.

Conversation III : Economic development

A third conversation centres around the residents' economic development strategies. According to Brenda Dillon, a resident who is currently the co-ordinator for the St Thomas Economic Development Corporation (STEDC), which was incorporated by the Resident Council in 1987:

> When we started talking about economic development we knew we spent money already and we wanted to know what our purchasing power was. We did a survey of the development where we found out how much everyone spent when they made groceries and what kinds of things they bought. We found out we spent nine million dollars a year at two grocery stores.

From that knowledge came the decision to open a dry goods store in the neighbourhood. The store is to sell such items as household cleaning supplies, housekeeping supplies and other essential things at a reasonable price. It will be operated by Ms Dillon and will provide part-time employment for children of residents. The concept of the store was borrowed from another local community group which consulted with STRC as the Council developed its proposals and then sought the resources to implement them. The Council struggled successfully with the Housing Authority for it to turn over to them a site for use as the store. Many of the needed resources are now in place for the store to open later this year.

Because the whole organizing effort has many fronts, and is focused on process and the balancing of individual and collective empowerment, slow progress does not concern the organizer. Speaking of the store, Barbara Major says:

> Somebody might say, why did it take so long to open a store or why did the store only make ten thousand dollars its first year, but then [ten] thousand dollars doesn't mean as much to us as the value of that community having its consciousness raised to know that they can own their own economic

development corporation. And see this one woman, to me, to see that she can run her own store, that means more than anything.

The STEDC, made up of residents from St Thomas, is accountable to the Resident Council. The STEDC has secured $167,000 from a citywide development corporation to renovate several houses near St Thomas. They started renovations on two vacant houses this summer and the idea is to sell them to low- and moderate-income buyers. Restoring vacant houses is seen as a major way not only to enhance the neighbourhood but to encourage homeownership by those with family and community ties to St Thomas residents, as well as to diversify the homeowner pool. The Resident Council has also negotiated with the Housing Authority to renovate 120 substandard and abandoned apartments in 13 buildings in St Thomas. The contract that was awarded for this work also included a commitment to hire as many residents of St Thomas as possible (Jones, 1993: 126–7).

In 1992 the New Orleans Legal Assistance Corporation (NOLAC) entered into a contract agreement with the STEDC to conduct door-to-door canvassing to approximately 10,000 households in the city's public housing developments and scattered site apartment complexes to determine eligibility for SSI benefits. The canvassing was first pretested in St Thomas because in the purchasing power research, 15 residents had already gained experience in surveying their community. NOLAC provided additional training to the survey team. Eventually, STEDC surveyors formed the nucleus of the surveying teams that conducted the outreach to the housing developments citywide. After this door-to-door project was completed, the survey team trained other residents living in public housing citywide (Jones, 1993: 124–5).

Through these Economic Development Corporation activities, the STRC has developed its own professional indigenous survey team. This was important because the community had for so many years been 'assessed, monitored and evaluated to death' by outside sources that had little or no sensitivity to the culture of the community. This survey team is trained in community organizing and data collection. The primary data that the team produces have been used to inform the conversations around programme initiatives and the monitoring of programme performance. For example, the national consulting firm contracted by funders to evaluate the Plain Talk Initiative has engaged the St Thomas Survey Team to collect primary data. Another national evaluator has stated that the STEDC survey team has created a national model for data collection by indigenous leaders within their communities (Jones, 1993: 125).

The survey team activities have been informed by and inform the work of the People's Institute. For example, throughout their workshops, trainers call on participants to 'be social scientists' as they analyse the power relationships which systematically work on people in low-income communities. Using the concepts and empirical tools of sociological analysis, the Institute encourages communities to learn to assess their own strengths and needs and economic resources.

Conversation IV : Land use

Another set of conversations within the community centres around the issue of the changing land use in the area. Land use practices in St Thomas are at the threshold of great flux. As Fannie McKnight has said, 'Everybody over the years has been taking pieces of St Thomas.' In response to the encroachment by a variety of urban interests, especially tourism, the STRC over the last two years helped to organize the Community Resource Partnership (CRP). The aim of the CRP is to achieve rehabilitation and restoration of St Thomas and the surrounding area. In the CRP, St Thomas residents have allied themselves with unlikely partners from within the community, including preservationists, upper-middle-class homeowners and developers. CRP was formed because of the concern with gentrification and land speculation by St Thomas residents. This conversation and the strategic plans which are emerging from it are viewed within a broad context. According to Barbara Major, 'We are addressing the inaccessibility of land to low-income people by addressing national land use policy.'

As part of its strategy the CRP has enlisted the assistance of the Urban Land Institute (ULI), a national non-profit consulting firm. ULI conducted an intensive study of the St Thomas/Irish Channel area and developed a set of designs and recommendations aimed at revitalizing the entire neighbourhood. Most importantly, ULI recommended that St Thomas be turned over to its residents to be owned and managed in partnership with a private firm in which the Resident Council would hold 51 per cent of the ownership.

Among other recommendations specific to St Thomas were opening up the now closed thoroughfares which segregate St Thomas from the rest of the neighbourhood, renovating the development, and turning it into a development with a mixture of residents from different socioeconomic levels. In other words, some renovated units would be rented to working-class families while others would continue to be leased to families on public assistance. At this time the CRP is involved in studying ULI's recommendations and in building the relational base to sustain the partnership and arrive at consensus in the STRC itself.

The question that remains is that it is one thing to demand accountability from social service agencies but quite another to demand accountability from city hall and developers. From STRC's past experience with a developer who came into their community in the mid-1980s, they know how difficult and frustrating it can be. At the heart of STRC's work in CRP is the relationship they have built with another prominent developer who owns a large tract of riverfront land that lies between St Thomas and downtown.

Central to this relationship is that the process began with a 'straight up' acknowledgement of his goals and intentions. As Barbara Major describes it, what impressed the STRC was the developer's forthright statement that he wanted to make money. STRC could live with that, as long as the developer accepted the fact that the community was not going to be acted upon but wanted to be a player in what happened to their neighbourhood.

As with the Consortium, this relationship has been built over time and is itself still evolving. What seems to be making this relationship work is the developer's willingness to accept the residents' understanding of the issues and to discuss race and class differences. According to Barbara Major, this relationship is centred around trust:

> Trust has to be earned. This is not to say that things won't fall apart. You are always in a very vulnerable and tenuous relationship across such diverse lines but the trust has been earned in that he has worked with us in a respectful way. He has acknowledged the differences first of all. And has not tried to pretend that they are not there. He's come to also see that there is a wisdom in [our] community that warrants listening to and following a lot of times. So far he's been honest and forthright about that and until he does otherwise we have no reason not to trust him. We're always wondering and I'm sure they're always wondering. People think that you just walk in and say 'trust me'. *But trust is an earned jewel and it comes through interacting and relationship building.* [emphasis added]

This trust was not built only through the developer's rhetoric. He also brought the principles of STRC into practice in the course of his business. He has raised critical questions about a number of projects going on in the vicinity, questions that others in business would not expect a developer to raise. Such questions and other comments he has made lead the STRC to believe that he understands that his development plans will be more viable if their community is developed, too. Because of this record the mayor has recently appointed him to the board of commissioners of the local housing authority.

Through the CRP the St Thomas community and its allies are taking the neighbourhood's future into their own hands. According to the Urban Land Institute, what they are doing is expected to serve as a model for other communities in New Orleans and across the nation. The strength of this model, then, is that public housing residents are at the table as full partners in the conversation about ways that land is used.

Conclusion

Here we have illustrated a holistic approach to community development undertaken within the context of urban economic restructuring. The STRC is engaging simultaneously in four distinct 'conversations' which, taken together, are uplifting the whole community. Traditionally, piecemeal approaches to development have failed to bring about true social change in low-income communities of colour. At the root of the strategy pursued by STRC is an analysis of racism and community power that steers all other conversations.

An important set of principles and practices has emerged from the dialogue on racism and community power. These include self-determination, accountability, and leadership development which give rise to varying forms of collaboration such as the Consortium and CRP. The goal is to move beyond relationships based on domination and subordination to relations based on collaboration and mutual accountability. Authentic collaboration means that institutional partners must have decision-making representatives at the table taking direction from indigenous leadership. 'In this view,' says Reverend David Billings, 'institutional change must be strategically linked to the community's process of self-determination.'

Most traditional approaches to social service programming and research isolate target groups within communities in ways that fail to represent the complexity of specific issues. These practices also alienate community members from each other. If programmes are to address effectively the concerns of low-income communities and if research is to describe accurately what goes on inside communities they must not merely work on isolated aggregates of individuals. Rather, practitioners must understand the community as a collective and work with the indigenous leadership in its efforts to reintegrate members of the community who have been isolated from each other.

Through its relationship with the People's Institute for Survival and Beyond, the St Thomas community is connected to a national network of anti-racist community organizing and educating. At the same time, the St Thomas community is informing the social theorizing of this national network. Just as the cutting edge of sociological theory lies in the synthesis of micro-level and macro-level theorizing, the praxis which is unfolding at the cutting edge of community organizing practice weaves together micro-level and macro-level analyses and practices. The analyses developed here attend to institutional policies and practices that perpetuate poverty and racism, as well as internalized racism born of centuries of oppression. This analysis is powerful because, while some researchers such as Williams *et al.* (1994) have defined measures of institutionalized racism, few strategies for dismantling it have been developed, let alone tested out in practice.

Through the Consortium and its programming and the Survey Team the community is involving itself in the practice of lay social science. The practice of social science is being recreated and the community is developing a sense of ownership of these practices. The knowledge generated in the work of the STRC provides the community and the professions with authentic, community-based analyses of the social organization of a low-income black community. Such analyses are vital tools with which to meet the challenges of urban economic restructuring, such as class and income polarization, large-scale unemployment, and urban decay.

The ongoing conversations about economic development, youth and family well-being, and land use all complement one another. This holistic approach strengthens the possibility that social changes instituted in this community will run deep into the community's consciousness and will affect institutional practice. Numerous professionals and community leaders and organizers from around the country are watching the St Thomas community to learn from its experience. The conversations we have analysed here allow us to see how the members of STRC work to maintain their space. In so doing they recreate the relationships among themselves and their families, with service providers, and with developers who encroach upon the fabric of the community. They are thus redefining what it means to be black women living in public housing.

References

Amott, T. L. (1990), 'Black women and AFDC, making entitlement out of necessity', in Gordon, L. (ed.), *Women, the State and Welfare*. Madison, University of Wisconsin Press.

Brooks, J. S., Young, A. H. (1993), 'Revitalising the central business district in the face of decline, the case of New Orleans, 1973–1993', *Town Planning Review*, 64: 251–71.

Calvert, L. (1990), 'An inquiry into the feasibility of community-based housing strategies for the St Thomas Neighborhood', master's thesis presented to the faculty of the College of Urban and Public Affairs, University of New Orleans.

Cook, Ch. C., Lauria, M. (1993), *Urban Regeneration and Public Housing in New Orleans*. DURPS Working Paper 17, New Orleans, Division of Urban Research and Policy Studies, University of New Orleans.

Crawford, M. (1992), 'The world in a shopping mall', in Sorkin, M. (ed.), *Variations on a Theme Park, The New American City and the End of Public Space*. New York, Hill and Wang.

Diamond, I., Quinby, L. (1988), *Feminism and Foucault, Reflections on Resistance*. Boston, Northeastern University Press.

Dumm, T. L. (1993), 'The new enclosures, racism in the normalized community', in Gooding-Williams, R. (ed.), *Reading Rodney King/Reading Urban Uprising*. New York, Routledge.

Feagin, J. R. (1986), 'Corporate center strategy, the state in central cities', *Urban Affairs Quarterly*, 21: 617–28.

Foucault, M. (1980), *Power/Knowledge, Selected Interviews and Other Writings, 1972–1977*, Gordon, C. (ed.), Brighton, Harvester Press.

Gilkes, C. T. (1994), 'If it wasn't for the women..., African American women, community work, and social change', in Baca Zinn, M. and Thornton, B. (eds), *Women of Color in US Society*. Philadelphia, Temple University.

Goetz, E. G. (1992), 'Land use and homeless policy in Los Angeles', *International Journal of Urban and Regional Research*, 16: 540–54.

Hill, R. C. (1983), 'Crisis in the motor city', in Fainstein, S. *et al.* (eds), *Restructuring the City: The Political Economy of Urban Development*. New York, Longman.

Hooks, B. (1990), *Yearning, Race, Gender and Cultural Politics*. Boston, South End Press.

Jones, C. H. (1993), 'The bottom-up approach to collaboration for social change, a case study of the St Thomas/Irish Channel Consortium', master's thesis presented to the faculty of the College of Urban and Public Affairs, University of New Orleans.

Logan, J. R., Molotch, H. (1987), *Urban Fortunes: The Political Economy of Place*. Berkeley, CA, University of California Press.

Logan, J. R., Swanstrom, T. (1990), *Beyond the City Limits, Urban Policy and Economic Restructuring in Comparative Perspective*. Philadelphia, Temple University Press.

Mayer, M. (1991), 'Politics in the post-Fordist city', *Socialist Review*, 21: 105–24.

Mumphrey, A. J., Akundi, K. (1994), *City-Suburb Interdependencies in the Urban Mosaic*. NCRCC Working Paper 11, New Orleans, National Center for the Revitalization of Central Cities, University of New Orleans.

Mumphrey, A. J., Pinell, K. (1992), *New Orleans and the Top 25 Cities, Central City and Metropolitan Dualities*. DURPS/NCRCC Working Paper 1, New Orleans, National Center for the Revitalization of Central Cities, University of New Orleans.

Robinson, C. J. (1989), 'Municipal approaches to economic development, growth and distribution policy', *Journal of the American Planning Association*, Summer, 55: 283–95.

Rubin, H. J. (1993), 'There aren't going to be any bakeries here if there is no money to afford jelly-rolls, the organic theory of community-based development', paper presented to the 23rd Annual Meeting of the Urban Affairs Association, Indianapolis, 21–24 April.

Sassen, S. (1988), *The Mobility of Labor and Capital: A Study in International Investment and Capital Flow*. New York, Cambridge University Press.

Smith, D. (1987), *The Everyday World as Problematic: A Feminist Sociology*. Boston, Northeastern University Press.

Spain, D. (1993), 'Built to last, public housing as an urban public space', paper presented to the 23rd Annual Meeting of the Urban Affairs Association, Indianapolis, April 1993.

Urban Land Institute (1993), 'A presentation by the Urban Land Institute to the St Thomas/Irish Channel Consortium', New Orleans, 10 December.

Whelan, R. K. (1989), 'New Orleans, public-private partnerships and uneven development', in Squires, G. D. (ed.), *Unequal Partnerships: The Political Economy of Urban Redevelopment in Postwar America*. New Brunswick, N.J., Rutgers University Press.

Williams, D. R., Lavizzo-Mouey, R., Warren, R. C. (1994), 'The concept of race and health status in America', *Public Health Reports*, 109: 26–41.

Young, A. H., Christos-Rodgers, J. (1994), 'Women's resistance to gendered space in the urban environment, the case of the St Thomas Resident Council, New Orleans', paper presented to the International Conference on Cities, Enterprises and Society at the Eve of the XXIst Century, Lille, France, 16–18 March.

Young, A. H., Whelan, R. K. (1993), 'Strategic planning for the Port of New Orleans', in Meyer, P.B. (ed.), *Comparative Studies in Local Economic Development: Problems in Policy Implementation*. Westport, CO, Greenwood Publishers.

14

The economic development potential of Microcredit
Myths and misconceptions

LISA J. SERVON

Introduction

Microenterprise programmes have received a great deal of attention in the USA over the last two years, largely because of the Clinton administration's stated plan to provide $382 million to support microenterprise programmes and community development banks. The popularity of these programmes stems from their foundation of bipartisan support, the high payback rates of existing lending programmes, and the ease with which they tap into both poverty alleviation and economic development rhetorics.

Thus far, little work has been done to study how, specifically, these programmes work, where they fit into the context and history of programmes designed to promote economic development and alleviate urban poverty, and who (broadly defined) these programmes serve. This work is warranted for several reasons. First, microenterprise programmes are representative of a new breed of economic development strategies that have emerged as a result of recent shifts in both the poverty alleviation and economic development fields. Second, existing research on microenterprise programmes has been largely funder driven and has focused on narrow and often inappropriate definitions of success without adequate discussion about the process through which these outcomes are achieved. Marrying a fine-grained description of how these programmes work – from the perspective of borrowers, programme staff, and field organizers – with existing data on the outcomes they produce, will lead to policy that is much better informed. Third, the lack of research about these programmes has fed debates that have become polarized by dichotomous positions based on insufficient information. Existing research presents one-dimensional 'snapshot' data of borrowers at a given point in time, which tend to miss the range of people that use these strategies and the circumstances that led them to view self-employment in general and microcredit in particular as an economic option. Fourth, a core group of US microenterprise programmes has been in existence for between five and ten years, long enough for these programmes to have established a history that enables them to be studied. Finally, public resources at all levels are increasingly being used to fund these programmes, making the need for better information even more pressing.

This chapter presents findings from case studies of three urban microenterprise programmes in the USA: Women's Initiative for Self-Employment (WISE) in San Francisco; ACCION New York in Brooklyn; and Working Capital, based in Cambridge, MA. The research begins from the recognition that debates on the microenterprise strategy have become polarized. Supporters of these programmes claim that microenterprise programmes provide disenfranchised populations with an entry point into the mainstream economy through self-employment and may further operate to revitalize low-income communities. Critics, on the other hand, argue that microenterprise programmes perpetuate existing power structures that operate to maintain the marginalization of these groups, getting them off public support but keeping them among the working poor in the fringe economy. These dichotomous positions tend to obscure the complex nature of these programmes, the life situations of the populations they serve, and the relationships formed between lenders and borrowers within these programmes. I argue that a closer examination of these complexities is needed in order to determine how these programmes actually work and where they fit in along the economic development/urban poverty policy continuum.

This chapter both answers and raises questions based on the case study findings. The second section, which follows, presents a brief description of the microenterprise strategy including a cursory portrayal of the three programmes that form the core of the project. The third section, pages 286–291, places the microenterprise strategy into the context of economic development and poverty alleviation theory and practice, recognizing that the emergence of strategies like microenterprise results in part from recent shifts in both of these fields. The fourth section, pages 291–294, outlines the characteristics of the emergent breed of strategies to which microenterprise programmes belong. The fifth section, pages 294–300, lays out and debunks several of the myths that have arisen from attempts to fit microenterprise programmes neatly into either the economic development or poverty alleviation sphere. Policy recommendations following from sections form the basis of the sixth section, pages 300–301.

The microenterprise strategy[1]

Recent research claims that access to credit and training are two of the ingredients most lacking in US urban areas with persistently high poverty levels (see especially Bates, 1993). Microenterprise programmes, which provide these two ingredients, have quickly multiplied in response to this need. The Aspen Institute's *1994 Directory of US Microenterprise Programmes* (Clark *et al.*, 1994) profiles 195 programmes in 44 states that have assisted in the creation and growth of over 50,000 businesses, mostly among low-income people. Of these programmes, 131, or 67 per cent, do some kind of lending. Microenterprise programmes exist in both rural and urban settings, target diverse populations, and maintain different criteria for lending. Their single common denominator is that they all serve as 'lenders of last resort', providing credit to people who want to be self-employed but who cannot obtain credit through traditional channels (McLenighan and Pogge, 1991). Microlenders make it their mission to take risks that fall outside of the standards of traditional banks. These programmes seek to combat the idea that the poor are poor because they are lazy or otherwise deserving of their economic status.

In explicit recognition of the fact that access to resources such as credit and training is further obstructed along race/ethnicity and gender lines, nearly 50 per cent of programmes documented in the Aspen Institute's Directory target women, and many others target a specific racial or ethnic group. Many programmes, including two of those studied here, model themselves on alternative credit institutions in the developing world, which is where this strategy originated.[2] ACCION New York is part of ACCION International, which began working with informal economies in Latin America in the 1960s. Cambridge, MA-based Working Capital is modelled on the Foundation for International Community Assistance (FINCA), which also operates throughout Latin America. These alternative foci have led to the creation of lending institutions that differ radically, both methodologically and philosophically, from traditional financial institutions.

Methodologically, microenterprise programmes differ from mainstream financial institutions in several ways. First, many programmes use some form of group lending, in which group members guarantee each other's loans, and peer pressure substitutes for collateral. Second, when evaluating a potential borrower's loan application, programme officials or borrower group members look beyond traditional criteria of collateral and cash investment, incorporating such factors as sweat equity and experience into their decisions. Third, most programme methodologies reflect the recognition that the borrowers served require both credit and training by combining both elements in a single programme.

Microenterprise programmes further differentiate themselves from traditional financial institutions by operating with specific goals of individual empowerment and community development. This key difference is rooted largely in the fact that these programmes are not profit driven, as are banks and venture capitalists. These other incentives allow microenterprise programmes to make loans to people that banks do not consider creditworthy. Many microenterprise borrowers have problematic credit histories, for example. Programme officials and borrower groups look beyond credit histories in order to learn the particulars of these ratings and often provide these people with a second chance. Traditional financial institutions have also been shown to base lending practices on unfounded assumptions about where people live. These practices have resulted in widespread perceptions that the poor are not creditworthy. Microenterprise programmes combat these perceptions by making loans that traditional financial institutions consider too small or too risky.

Programmes studied

Beyond the similarities that allow programmes to be grouped together under the same label, important differences exist that distinguish one programme from another. Critical variables include loan size, target population, and type of business served. Each of the three programmes studied approaches the problem of access to credit among the urban poor in a different way. The choice to look at programmes that differ in significant areas reflects the objective of documenting the variety of ways in which this strategy has emerged and been implemented across the country. Table 14.1 below, which illuminates the variables that distinguish one programme from another, provides some insight into the variety that exists among programmes.

Each programme has structured its lending policy somewhat differently. WISE does only individual lending, while ACCION does both group and individual lending, and Working Capital lends solely through groups. Each programme also targets a different client base. WISE serves low- and moderate-income women, while ACCION serves Latinos. Working Capital targets less than the other two programmes, serving a mixed community of urban and rural self-employed people. While Working Capital directs its resources towards the creation of strategies that will help the low-income self-employed, the programme does not exclude others who believe they can benefit from these services. WISE serves women who are in the process of starting businesses as well as those who have existing businesses. ACCION serves only those entrepreneurs who have been running a business for at least one year.

Table 14.1 Characteristics of programmes studied

	WISE	ACCION	Working Capital
City	San Francisco/Oakland	New York City	Boston
Type of lending	Individual	Group and individual	Group
Target population	Low- and moderate-income women	Latinos	Low-income
Type of business served	Start-ups and existing	Existing (1 year or more)	Start-ups and existing
Type of technical assistance	Classes and individual consulting	Individual consulting	Training within groups
Average loan size	$3,255	$1,500	$824
Average loans made per year	10	21	162

Source: Clark *et al.* (1994)

Working Capital targets those who are already self-employed but allows individual groups to decide whether or not to lend to start-ups.

The balance that each programme has struck between training and lending also distinguishes them. WISE requires potential borrowers to take twelve weeks of classes before they can apply for a loan. ACCION has no formal training, although business consultants learn about client businesses during the loan process and often advise them on an individual basis. Working Capital borrower groups proceed through training exercises with the help of an enterprise agent upon the formation of the group; the decision of whether or not they complete the training manual provided by Working Capital is left up to individual groups, however.

Microenterprise in context

The characteristics that define the microenterprise strategy derive from a philosophy that blurs the lines between the traditional fields of economic development, which is based on working with economic conditions, and poverty alleviation, which is often based on 'reforming' individual and family characteristics. This integration of what are generally thought of as separate spheres makes it difficult to evaluate microenterprise programmes. Indicators used to evaluate economic development programmes are generally quantitative and include categories such as: changes in jobs created; changes in income; changes in the number of businesses within a given area. Indicators used to evaluate poverty alleviation strategies or social welfare programmes, on the other hand, often consist of more qualitative categories such as: changes in self-esteem and changes in family stability.

Microenterprise programmes are particularly difficult to evaluate because they tend to incorporate both kinds of goals. In addition, the weight that programme missions accord one function as opposed to the other, which is often manifested by the resources it devotes to training versus lending, differ greatly from one programme to the next. Delma Soto, executive director of ACCION New York, explains that in her programme, 'Every decision that's made is based on a business implication as opposed to a social .... The social aspect happens as a result of making the right business decisions .... We're providing people with an opportunity to grow their business. And by growing their business and earning more income, there's a whole list of things that result from that. Empowerment is just one of them.' This stance results partly from the fact that ACCION works only with businesses that have been established for at least one year. WISE, on the other hand, works with any woman who meets the income criteria and wants to explore self-employment. According to Miriam Walden, the WISE loan fund director, this means that, 'WISE has chosen to work with a group of people who, in general, require assistance in preparing their ability to argue for a loan and their ability to repay it. So that means you have to take on the training challenge in order to do it. And then training is a big and expensive thing ... so naturally it looks like the organization is mostly training ... And the other side of the question is that I think it's always been an expressed belief of this organization that ... training is actually more important than lending, and that our primary mission is to do training and not lending.'

To some extent, the philosophies of ACCION and WISE represent opposite ends of a spectrum. The position that each holds is dynamic rather than static, however. ACCION is currently exploring ways to incorporate more training into its programme, and WISE has begun to generate additional loan products. The explanation for the creation and rise in popularity of microenterprise programmes lies partly in this integration of social welfare and economic development goals. Microenterprise programmes encapsulate critical shifts that have occurred in both areas. The remainder of this section will look more closely at the specific changes in the economic development and poverty alleviation fields that have created space for strategies like microenterprise to emerge.

Shifts in economic development theory and practice

Urban economic development strategy and policy have undergone a shift over the last five years in the USA. One of the primary manifestations of this alteration is the treatment of business within urban economic development. While the decade of the 1980s was characterized by business attraction strategies, with cities and regions competing with each other to lure businesses, by the end of the decade the strategy had begun to shift to business generation. In the 1990s, several practical responses to theoretical advances supporting business generation over business attraction have grown increasingly popular. These responses generally consist of local level strategies that focus on people rather than places, make increasing use of public/private partnerships, and target specific populations. New strategies include microenterprise development programmes and a number of primarily state-based initiatives that I group together under the term 'technology transfer programmes'.[3]

The shift in the manner in which economic development problems are attacked comes partly as a result of the increased attention accorded economic development across the range of policy-making arenas, and especially at the local level. One of the primary elements of this shift is an inward-looking orientation as opposed to one that looks outward. This inward focus could also be described as investing rather than spending. In the case of business, this means building on existing capacity rather than spending to attract corporate capital from somewhere else.

A second element involves a decentralization of the responsibility for economic development. Once the primary province of federal agencies, economic development is increasingly created, funded, and managed by state and local governments along with a critical cadre of private non-profit organizations, which are responsible for much of the innovation in the field, including the microenterprise strategy. To some extent, this shift has been a matter of necessity rather than of choice, responding as it did to severe cutbacks in allocations to federal agencies responsible for economic development in the early 1980s under Reagan. Despite its roots, however, many economic development theorists have applauded the results of this shift, which is based on the recognition that economic development is a local phenomenon generated by local actors, and that the scale of state and local government is often the most appropriate one in which to generate approaches to economic development problems.[4] For one thing, the local focus opens up the potential for creating meaningful partnerships with the private for profit and non-profit sectors, and with existing community organizations and institutions.

The third element, which involves increasing the creativity of government, derives partly from this increase in public/private partnerships. Peter Eisinger talks about this change in economic development policy and strategy as a shift from a 'supply-side' focus to a 'demand-side' focus. Increased attention to the demand-side of the economic growth equation has operated to create what Eisinger calls 'the entrepreneurial state'. Eisinger is not alone in documenting this change. Like Eisinger, David Osborne and Ted Gaebler, in their 1992 book *Reinventing Government*, use the term 'entrepreneurial' to modify government; they argue that entrepreneurial government should meet five conditions. First, it should act as a catalyst – it should 'steer rather than row'. Second, it should base itself in communities – 'empowering rather than serving'. Third, it should operate competitively rather than through a single delivery structure. Fourth, it should be 'decentralized' and 'market-oriented'. Fifth, it should focus on leverage of public funds and activities – 'earning rather than spending'. Susan Clarke and Gary Gaile (1992: 189) use the term 'market-based' to describe policy strategies distinguished by: '1) the focus on value-creating processes by private investors and 2) the investment and risk-taking role adopted by local officials'. John Herbers calls this new breed of programmes the 'third wave'. The third wave is characterized by a new role for government that involves 'meet[ing] economic development needs by creating working marketplaces, where citizens can articulate demands and select from multiple suppliers'.[5]

Given the new orientation of urban economic development, the logic by which the microenterprise strategy has emerged and gained in popularity seems relatively straightforward. Microenterprise programmes focus on business generation rather than business attraction. In addition, programmes are usually generated and operated at the local level.[6] Finally most microenterprise programmes began as private non-profit organizations, bringing in local, state, and/or federal government partners at a later stage. This structure has enabled both the programmes and their public partners to behave in a more entrepreneurial fashion.

Shifts in approaches to poverty alleviation

Shifts in approaches to poverty alleviation are currently more theoretical than practical. The fact that policy has not kept pace with theory reflects both political and economic conditions. While the Clinton Administration's working group on welfare reform has demonstrated a desire to experiment with new ideas, the process of obtaining the necessary mandate and implementing new policy is time-consuming. Further, the legacy of the Reagan/Bush era looms large and is difficult to overcome. Finally, the kinds of policies that poverty experts are currently recommending are expensive and have long time horizons. These factors make them difficult choices during the current economic climate, particularly for a president who will be seeking re-election facing the anti-big government signal sent to the Administration in the 1994 elections.

For the majority of voters, the poor continue to be perceived as 'them', or as 'the other'. In order to organize the kind of long-term support that these policies will require to be effective, popular thinking will have to be re-oriented so that the poor are seen as part of a larger 'us', as poor rather than deviant. Current conservative rhetoric holds part of the responsibility for this problem. In a recent *New York Times* editorial, Bob Herbert (1994) stated that, 'The Republican Party, delirious with its recent successes but lacking any solutions to the very serious problems that underlie the voters' unease, has accelerated its cruel tactic of demonizing people on welfare ... Welfare recipients have become the official national scapegoats.'

One way of shifting from a 'them' to an 'us' orientation involves increasing the use of universally available social programmes (like Social Security) as opposed to those available only to the poor (such as AFDC). The logic for a framework of universal programmes within which selective targeting could be implemented as needed was introduced in Chapter 13. This concept stems from a recognition that the working and middle classes also need many of the benefits generally sought only for poorer groups.[7] The wider availability of these programmes would operate not only to build long-term political support but also to enable people to see their common interests regarding 'unemployment and job security, declining real wages, escalating medical and housing costs, child care programmes, the sharp decline in the quality of public education, and crime and drug trafficking in neighborhoods' (Wilson, 1994: 268). While theorists such as Wilson focus primarily on policies with a universal structure, most also recognize that, at least over the short term, certain groups will require extra help in order to exit poverty. Rather than maintaining the current system of targeted programmes, however, the push is for a welfare reform strategy that would address 'the current problems of public assistance, including lack of provisions for poor two-parent families, inadequate levels of support, inequities between different states, and work disincentives' (Wilson, 1987: 152).

A second shift in poverty alleviation theory and strategy involves increasing the use of asset-based strategies (such as Earned Income Tax Credits) as opposed to income-based strategies (such as Unemployment Insurance). According to Michael Sherraden (1991), anti-poverty policy has historically concerned flows of income: 'Whether in health care, housing, direct financial assistance, education, or any other area of welfare, the emphasis has been on levels of goods and services received and, presumably, consumed.' This focus implies that income is the most important, if not the only, measure of poverty. Sherraden urges a restructuring of social welfare policy that would include an emphasis on asset accumulation. The rationale underlying this call for a shift is that, 'income only maintains consumption, but assets change the way people think and interact in the world. With assets, people begin to think in the long-term and pursue long-term goals' (1991: 6). Indeed, education has been widely cited as the single best predictor of who will escape poverty.

In recent years, both policy-makers and researchers have begun to explore the potential of asset-based programmes, which often take the form of tax and credit mechanisms, as a component of poverty alleviation strategy. The Clinton administration has already begun to work on some of these strategies including expanding the Earned Income Tax Credit and reforming AFDC. These strategies do three things that poverty alleviation strategies have failed to do historically. First, they recognize and support survival strategies already practised by the working and welfare poor, such as income packaging. Second, they combine goals of income redistribution and asset accumulation. Third, they combine economic development and social welfare goals to a greater degree than before.

The microenterprise strategy clearly makes sense in light of these changes in thinking about how best to alleviate poverty. Programmes exist in both targeted (WISE, ACCION) and universal forms (Working Capital). Some, like WISE, provide training to any woman who needs it, but make the loan fund available only to those who meet income criteria. This structure, which is similar to Working Capital's, is a kind of targeting within universalism. In addition, the microenterprise strategy is clearly based on a philosophy of asset building. The goal of most microenterprise programmes is to provide people with access to the resources they need in order to attain economic self-sufficiency.

Characteristics of new strategies

The new strategies that arise from these trends follow rather directly from the 'hand up rather than a handout' mentality. At the same time, they do not attempt to replace redistributive programmes but rather to complement them. While most include an assistance component, they are primarily incentive based rather than assistance based. The emphasis in these new programmes is similar to the War on Poverty's focus on work and skill building. The new piece has to do with fostering entrepreneurialism among the disenfranchised.

Blending economic development and poverty alleviation

The new strategies that have emerged are characterized by an effort to combine technique and philosophy from both the economic development and poverty alleviation fields. Drawing on these two fields simultaneously allows policy-makers to address both the material and human/institutional dimension of the urban poverty problem at once, a necessary first step towards breaking the economic and psychological dependency of impoverished inner cities (Haberfeld, 1981: 14).

Broad-based political support

This new strain of programmes also has broad political appeal. Con-
servatives respond positively to the notion that these programmes push
people to be productive rather than allowing them to sit back and collect
benefits. In the case of lending programmes, the idea that loans will be
repaid is also attractive. Liberals tend to support these programmes
because they attempt to equalize opportunity over the long term by
providing disenfranchised populations with access to critical resources,
such as credit and training, that translate into asset building. In addition,
they tend to provide a more empowering alternative to traditional
welfare.

Creative use of public/private partnerships

The increasing use of public/private partnerships also distinguishes these
strategies from former ones. While these kinds of arrangements have
resided in the economic development practitioner's toolkit for a long
time, their current configuration shows that they can be markedly different than they were in the past. In the 1980s, a public/private partnership
generally meant that state or local government was luring a business to a
place using subsidies and tax incentives. While that kind of activity still
occurs, the medium of the public–private partnership has also begun to
be employed with greater creativity.

Focus on small business

Many of the new strategies that favour business generation over business
attraction and which represent the fallout of the shift towards an entrepreneurial state focus on small business.[8] Why is this? Some research
maintains that small businesses constitute the most efficient means for
creating net new jobs and for fostering economic growth within impoverished areas. If this is true, then the focus on small business may operate
to address the uneven development engendered by smokestack chasing.
According to the SBA, small firm employment rose by over four million
between 1977 and 1987, the same period that large firm employment in
the leading ten industries dropped by nearly two million jobs.[9] In addition, the corporations and branch plant facilities that have constituted the
prizes in the business attraction game are more footloose than home-
grown businesses. They may be less inclined to reinvest profits in the
local economy, channelling them away to distant headquarters instead.
Similarly, if a good incentive package enticed Corporation A to locate in
City X in the first place, a slightly better package may be all that City Y
needs to create in order to lure the company away.

Greater risk

Encouraging entrepreneurialism is risky business, particularly when undertaken with disenfranchised populations. Many of the new strategies are characterized by a greater willingness, both on the part of government and within the private, non-profit sector, to take these risks. Whether a state technology transfer programme is helping an existing business to expand into a more technical sector or a microenterprise programme is working to transition a woman from welfare to self-employment, the service provider is placed in a new and higher risk role. The relationships required to succeed require trust, the pay-off is long term rather than short term, and the potential for failure is always present. However, the potential return on investment is great. Fostering entrepreneurship not only helps people to exit welfare, it may also create jobs for others, provide necessary services in impoverished communities, and turn people into community role models.

Changing role of the non-profit sector

Non-profit organizations play a bigger role in the emergent breed of strategies than they did before. This expanded role has mostly to do with the federal government's severe cuts in social services beginning in the early 1980s. Jennifer Wolch (1990: 15) calls this strengthening of the non-profit sector 'the emergence of the shadow state', which she claims is 'fundamentally linked to recent transformations in the welfare state'. As a result of these cuts, state and local governments were left to cover the costs of a whole range of programmes. However, the incentives were not in place to encourage city and state officials to replace lost federal funds. Rather, the combined effects of federal cuts and the process of de-industrialization led many local governments to adopt practices such as business attraction that supposedly would work to expand the tax base (Sclar and Hook, 1993: 62). The residual demand for services not provided by the market or by government increased, and the role of non-profits grew. Some of this growth was also fuelled by the federal government opting to contract out to the non-profit sector for services, which simultaneously filled the need of maintaining some level of provision and creating the illusion of compliance with calls for less bureaucracy.

Emergence at state and local level

Another feature of these new strategies is that most have emerged at the local level. The entrepreneurial behaviour necessary to generate these programmes was in large part a response to cutbacks in federal aid to cities that peaked in the 1980s. Perhaps, in this case, necessity is the mother of invention. Pierre Clavel (1986) demonstrates the extent to which cities have created and implemented successful reforms in the face of adverse larger level economic conditions. This local level creativity should come as no surprise, since that is where theorists have been placing their bets on where change is most likely to occur. At the local level, there simply seems to be more room to manoeuvre.

Several states have begun to experiment with programmes that consist of a mix of new strategies. The term 'technology transfer programmes' is used somewhat loosely here to describe an entire constellation of techniques – reinvigorating manufacturing, stimulating new firm investment, filling capital market gaps, improving labour-management co-operation, and upgrading education and training. Programmes of this kind in Michigan and Pennsylvania have been quite successful. Other states have experimented with welfare reform, encouraging beneficiaries to pursue education and business ownership. Iowa's Human Investment Policy, for example, includes rewriting the welfare programme to assist progress towards economic independence, an asset-building strategy which would create 10,000 Individual Development Accounts, a system of Family Development and Workforce Development centres operating with decategorized funding, and a high-wage development strategy (Friedman, 1993: 10).

Microenterprise in practice: what it can and can't do

The microenterprise strategy is to some extent an outgrowth of the shifts in orientation in the economic development and poverty alleviation fields, described above. Attempts to fit microenterprise neatly into either the economic development or the poverty alleviation field, however, is the equivalent of trying to push a square peg into a round hole – it tends to obscure the complexities of what microenterprise programmes attempt to accomplish, the variety of reasons why poor people consider starting businesses in the first place, and the realities of using self-employment as a route with which to escape poverty. This section lays out several myths that have surfaced as a result of, first, trying to make microenterprise conform to old models; and, second, making inaccurate assumptions about what it means to be poor and what it means to operate a very small business.

Myth 1: Access to credit is the biggest need facing poor entrepreneurs

Many loan funds have been started and funded based on the assumption that lack of access to credit is the biggest barrier for poor people who want to become self-employed. This may be true for some, but is rarely the case for the poor urbanites that programmes often target. In reality, these potential entrepreneurs often come to microcredit programmes needing much more than just credit. As a result, many of these programmes have shifted their activities and now do much more training than lending. One example is Women's Initiative for Self Employment (WISE) in San Francisco/Oakland, which has always viewed its loan fund as 'grease for the wheel'. While business planning classes are consistently oversubscribed, the loan fund is underutilized. The goals of the WISE programme emphasize empowerment, economic literacy, and learning to make informed life decisions. Looked at in this way, starting a business is only one of many positive programme outcomes.

Many microcredit programmes employ a strategy called group lending, which also illustrates this point. Group lending, or peer lending as it is sometimes called, operates as follows: a small group of people (usually 4–6) who currently or desire to operate their own business form a group, receive training together, and decide who will receive the first loan. The trust of fellow members serves as collateral. Other members receive loans and achieve eligibility for additional loans only as long as all members maintain current payments. Both in developing and developed countries, groups of women comprise the vast majority of peer lending groups. Recent literature in development economics suggests that the primary reason for employing the peer lending strategy is that it operates as the conduit to the information the banks lack – the bank delegates monitoring responsibility to the group, the members of which know each other, thereby lowering the risk undertaken by the bank. The drawback, as Stiglitz (1990) sees it, is that this system, which creates an 'artificial' interdependence among group members, induces members to bear more risk than they otherwise would have.

What these theorists fail to recognize is that credit is only the most obvious resource provided by the majority of alternative financial institutions that employ a peer lending system, and that both lenders and borrowers invest in these relationships seeking a different kind of relationship than that constructed within traditional financial institutions. Women who belong to the Chicago-based Women's Self Employment Project (WSEP) groups acknowledge that the opportunity to network and talk about ideas is as important as the more formalized meeting purposes. In addition, this structured meeting time precipitates discussion of other issues, such as housing and childcare, that do not form part of the official agenda. Working Capital borrowers in Boston have formed a Borrowers Council that is starting a mentoring programme for urban youth. The Council has also created a directory of Working Capital borrowers and their businesses, which will enable borrowers and other community members to support each other's businesses. While these positive outgrowths are perhaps more visible in programmes that do group lending, they are not confined to these programmes. Julia, a WISE borrower who owns a dance studio, claims that 'one of my goals in my [business] mission is community ... And with that the goals would be employing more dancers, and getting more arts into the community, because schools are just dropping them ... I would like to fill some of that gap, because that's our future right there.'

The microenterprise strategy therefore works towards social as well as economic goals. In addition, the communities in which group lending typically takes place are often characterized by the presence of other kinds of support networks. One largely unexplored factor that probably contributes to the amenability of poor, urban, US women to working with the peer group structure is the already entrenched system of women-centred support networks which operate as survival strategies in impoverished urban areas (see Stack, 1974).

Myth 2: Given capital and training, most microentrepreneurs can become self-employed in less than a year

The path that begins with walking in the door of a microcredit pro-gramme and ends with self-employment is longer and more complex than programme organizers and funders originally thought. An intermediary step of asset creation is often needed before income generation is possible. After learning about the realities and demands of self-employment, the potential entrepreneur often realizes that she must do other things, such as acquire more education, leave a bad home situation, or save to buy a car, before starting a business. Many of those who effectively 'drop out' of programmes at some point, or go through programmes without starting a business right away, return to them after having amassed the necessary resources to re-enter the process. In another scenario, those who leave programmes may never start businesses. However, many credit their participation in microenterprise programmes with their success in attaining jobs in the mainstream economy that they would not have been able to obtain prior to pro-gramme involvement.

The qualitative outcomes that programmes produce, such as economic literacy and increased self-esteem, often enable participants to access a wider range of options that includes but is not limited to self-employment. Walden of WISE looks at the role self-employment can play as follows: 'Tangling with the idea [of becoming self-employed] can lead to another stage. While we might have only a 10 per cent level of success at turning people into borrowers, or a 15 per cent success at turning people into business owners, and a lot of those businesses may not last longer than 3 years, we probably have more like a 70 per cent or a 75 per cent rate of success at turning people into more effective people.' In a recent survey, approximately 50 per cent of WISE clients reported increases in self-esteem, career skills, work options, potential for success, and decision-making ability, which they attributed directly to the programme. In a similar evaluation conducted for Working Capital, 40 per cent of participants reported that the programme had 'a lot' of impact on their self-confidence; 20 per cent reported that it had 'a lot' of impact on their participation in civic or social activities outside the group; and 15 per cent reported that it had 'a lot' of impact on their family relationships.

Myth 3: All poor entrepreneurs start businesses in order to grow them

Women's businesses in particular are often discredited for not growing in the same way or at the same rate as men's. In many cultures and sub-cultures, women have little or no control over their earnings; they are used either for basic immediate needs such as food or become part of a family pool to which the women often have no access (see Noponen, 1977). Under these circumstances, women cannot reinvest their earnings into their businesses. When women do have control over family finances, they often invest surplus income into their families rather than using it to grow their business. Irene Tinker asserts that:

> For economists who consider profit-making and growth the very essence of entrepreneurship, alternative behavior is dismissed as pre-entrepreneurial; [women's] enterprises are not deemed worthy of inclusion in credit and other support programmes designed to assist micro and small scale enterprises ... the problem lies with the dominant economic value system, not the micro-entrepreneurs; the solution is for a paradigm shift to a more human economy. (Tinker, 1989)

The concept of human economy acknowledges the legitimacy of valuing people and community welfare over individual avarice. It builds on data that show women continuing to 'invest in their children's food or education despite accusations that this is not rational economic behavior'.[10]

Alternative growth paths apply most often to women, but not exclusively. Howard, a retired mail carrier, started a children's book business after retiring in order to make some extra money and, in his words, 'do something constructive'. Howard takes his business very seriously but doesn't want it to get to 'a point where I can't sleep at night or twisting or turning over as to how I'm going to make an order'. Anne, who creates and markets high end gift products that she makes from hand-painted silk, is careful about growing her business because she suffers from Chronic Fatigue Syndrome. Anne says, 'If I had ready cash, easily accessible to me, there are a lot of things I would do. But it feels like getting the cash is so much work. And I have such limited energy, it's all I can do to just keep the business going .... There just isn't enough of me to go around.' The variety of life situations that lead people to start microbusinesses translate into a variety of goals for the business. Definitions of success are multiple.

Myth 4: Public sector financial support for microcredit should be enough to make microcredit programmes successful

Public support for microenterprise is on the rise. A survey of seven programmes showed that in 1987 they received an average of 16 per cent of their funding from public sources. By 1992, that average had risen to 41 per cent (Servon, 1994). While public sector financial support will certainly aid the viability of these programmes, other policies actually work against microcredit, making it difficult for poor women to view self-employment as a viable option. Federal welfare regulations constitute one of these barriers, placing a $1,000 ceiling on the assets an AFDC recipient can accumulate without risking losing her benefits. According to Gail Christopher (1986), 'a business that is worth less than $1,000 does not represent any potential for financial security, gainful self-employment, or economic self-sufficiency'. Furthermore, most states require self-employed AFDC recipients to use cash accounting, rather than accrual, which penalizes those who have uneven income streams.

Additionally, many programmes see themselves as entrepreneur's first lender, intending that the borrower will begin working with mainstream financial institutions after borrowing successfully from the microcredit programme. Despite the 1977 Community Reinvestment Act (CRA), which requires banks to serve fully the communities in which they operate, discrimination based on gender, race, and class continues to exclude people. CRA is ineffective. Therefore, the policy infrastructure that is needed to make microcredit a stepping-stone rather than a permanent haven is non-existent. Finally, access to training and credit cannot exist in a vacuum. The need for additional universal social policies providing health care and child care is amplified in the case of micro-entrepreneurs.

Myth 5: Microenterprise programmes are the answer to the urban poverty problem

Many of the arguments presented in the literatures that deal with entrepreneurship rest on narrow constructions of the subject. These assumptions derive from talking about 'the poor' as though all low-income people fall into a single, undifferentiated mass. They may also derive from a desire to find a solution to poverty that can 'cure' the majority of the poor population. Recognizing that poverty can be the manifestation of a wide range of circumstances leads to the conclusion that a range of 5 per cent solutions, rather than one or two 50 per cent solutions, is probably necessary. Assumptions about 'the poor' and 'the inner city' need to be revisited. The concentrations of diverse ethnic and racial groups, along with the dramatic rise in female-headed households in these areas, complicate the problem of persistent urban poverty in important ways.

Microenterprise programmes are not sufficient to turn poor urban communities around. In fact, the microenterprise strategy runs the risk of being advocated for the wrong reasons. One of its strong points, from a political economy perspective, is that it can be marketed using bootstrap rhetoric. Credit, on its own, is an attractive solution to the poverty problem because it implies repayment. However, it seems unrealistic to expect that the 'truly disadvantaged' population can exit poverty with credit alone. Programme officials may be tempted to sell their programmes using the bootstrap argument because it translates into bipartisan support. Businesses that can provide significant numbers of jobs and foster substantial investment back into the community are bigger than those microcredit programmes generally serve; it will be important to educate funders and policy-makers about the difference between small and micro-businesses. Social infrastructure needs, such as good public education and the fostering of social networks, and structural forces, such as discrimination by gender and race, must also be addressed. If they are, then perhaps microenterprise can operate as a stepping stone to these larger goals.

In the meantime, self-employment operates more as a survival strategy than a 'get rich quick scheme' for most poor, urban entrepreneurs. Self-employment often constitutes one piece of a larger patchwork quilt that, together, allows a family to get by. While some critics have accused microenterprise programmes of promoting working poverty, many prefer self-employment to remaining on AFDC or working in a dead-end, low-wage job that does not allow the flexibility or potential for creativity that self-employment offers. The point is that microenterprise programmes help low-income people to access another option. Rather than measuring income at a point in time, it would be more valuable to gain a more comprehensive understanding of where these people started out and where they have gone.

Policy recommendations

At first glance, expansion of the microcredit strategy is good news. The danger is that if the proper approach is not taken, the microcredit strategy will continue to be judged through the use of inappropriate assumptions, measures, and definitions of success. While the microcredit strategy alone will not cure the ills of the inner city, it does provide poor people in these communities with one more coping mechanism. The exceptional rags to riches stories that these programmes produce are well known. We know much less about how those stories unfolded and about those whose paths are less linear. Indeed, we are only just beginning to learn what microcredit programmes can and will achieve. Based on what we do know, the following are recommendations both for how to study existing programmes and what to keep in mind when considering expansion of the strategy.

Studies of microcredit programmes must challenge preconceived definitions of success

Broad sociological and economistic approaches to entrepreneurship, as well as more narrow evaluations using traditional economic development indicators, are inadequate for measuring the achievements of microcredit programmes. Economistic approaches tend to focus on the opportunity cost of self-employment as opposed to regular wage labour. In reality, many self-employed people, particularly women who also bear the responsibility for child care, do not perceive themselves as having the option to work in the mainstream economy. Sociological studies generally centre on ethnicity, which must be examined along with class, gender, and race. Traditional evaluations of small business programmes look at easily quantifiable measures of success, such as number of jobs created, number of business starts, and growth rate of businesses started. In general, these measures are arrived at without consulting programme staff and participants about their individual definitions of success.

Evaluation conducted within microcredit programmes has been largely funder driven and has focused on quantitative data including numbers of clients served, business starts, and loans made. The more specific nature of credit relations constructed by these programmes has gone unexplored. Even within the arena of microcredit programmes, little analysis has been done concerning the ways in which credit needs have been both defined and fulfilled by traditional and alternative financial institutions and the extent to which the relationships within these institutions differ along the lines of race, gender, ethnicity, and location. In addition, definitions of success vary greatly from entrepreneur to entrepreneur. Programme staff are not only interested in facilitating a large number of business starts, but also in helping would-be entrepreneurs who do not have the financial and human resources in place to decide to put off their plans to start businesses. Finally, many programmes operate with goals of personal development as well as economic development. Therefore, studies should attempt to document more qualitative outcomes of programmes, such as increases in self-esteem and time management, and the attainment of economic literacy. Funds should be made available for research that incorporates these alternative definitions of success.

If the federal government proceeds with plans to expand funding for microcredit, supervision of funds should occur at the most local level possible

This recommendation is in keeping with recent calls to make government more entrepreneurial and with the recent trends in economic development practice discussed above. Local government institutions and local representatives of federal institutions are in a better position to work with microcredit programmes than Washington-based officials. Relationships with local public funders are more likely to generate desirable flexibility. In addition, local governments are in a better position to motivate the strengthening of programme support networks. These networks not only enhance programme effectiveness but also potentially create positive spillover effects, such as productive public–private partnerships and support systems of community organizations which then operate to build co-operation in arenas often characterized by competition.

Public sector financial support must be accompanied by complementary policy support

As long as policies such as CRA and restrictions on AFDC recipients continue to work at cross purposes to microcredit, it will be impossible to measure the effectiveness of this strategy for poor urbanites. As it stands, fear of losing their safety net operates to keep many, especially women, from viewing self-employment as a viable option. In addition, availability of more universal policies would make self-employment a more realistic option for both the poor and the middle classes.

Conclusion

This chapter offers new ways of framing discussions of the microenterprise strategy instead of perpetuating existing, bipartisan debates.
This work illustrates that microenterprise programmes – in terms of the
ways in which they combine aspects of economic development and
poverty alleviation strategies, and in terms of who they serve and how
they form relationships – are anything but straightforward and deserve a
closer look. Understanding the complexities involved in this strategy will
be essential for government support to function appropriately. Unless
these myths are debunked, the microenterprise strategy may be wrongly
judged and, eventually, defunded. Given the proper context in which to
function, microenterprise programmes may serve as a valuable example
of how we can begin to think creatively about opening up channels of
access to resources, financial and other, to populations that have here-
tofore been excluded.

Notes

1. The terms 'microcredit' and 'microenterprise' are often used interchange-
ably. In reality, microcredit programmes are a subset of microenterprise
programmes, the difference being that microcredit programmes provide
credit as one component of their services, whereas microenterprise programmes may or may not. I have chosen to look only at those programmes
that provide credit, and will therefore use both terms here. I use the term
'microenterprise' when referring to the field in general. Some of the field
experts and programme staff I interviewed resisted using the term 'microcredit', believing that it creates the false impression that credit is the primary
focus of these programmes.
2. The best known of the pioneer programmes in the developing world is
probably the Grameen Bank, started in Bangladesh in 1979 by economics
professor Mohamed Yunus.
3. Michigan and Pennsylvania are two of the leaders in this area. See Osborne
(1988) for further information.
4. David Osborne (1988) explores this assumption in greater detail in his
examination of the array of programmes developed by Pennsylvania state
government. Osborne sees the local emphasis as a way to build the capacity of
local institutions, as well as a way to generate creative ideas that will be
appropriate for a particular context because they are generated within that
context.
5. Ross quoted in Herbers (1990: 47). In a recent article, Roberta Lynch and
Ann Markusen (1994: 132) question whether 'marketizing' government is a
realistic, and even desirable, goal. The authors claim that while Osborne and
Gaebler make some important observations and useful suggestions for
reform, they fail to 'embrace two more fundamental restructuring strategies:
employee empowerment and citizen involvement. Democracy – not markets
– is at the core of both these efforts'.

6. In 1992 the Small Business Administration began making grants to micro-enterprise programmes. The restrictions that the SBA, a federal agency, places on recipients, has made many programmes wary of applying for these grants. See Servon, forthcoming, for a more complete examination of the effects of greater public funding on microenterprise programmes.

7. The Family Assistance Program (FAP), which was proposed in 1969–70, came close to setting in motion a structure of targeting within universalism. FAP would have offered a minimum income for everyone, including the working poor. Interestingly, FAP was defeated by those on the left who thought the income floor was too low. According to Hamilton and Hamilton (1986) this was a critical misstep because passage of FAP would have accomplished the feat of establishing a guaranteed national income for the first time. See 'Social policies, civil rights, and poverty'.

8. Just how small is small? There exists some confusion in the economic development literature around this topic. More precisely, the subject is rarely broached, nor is the term defined. This lack of discussion has resulted in a situation in which very different businesses and, consequently, strategies designed to help them, are erroneously grouped together. Microenterprises generally employ five persons or less, are most often run by one person or one family, and can utilize a loan of $5,000 or less. The US Small Business Administration defines a small business as one that employs less than 100 persons; many SBA loan programmes start at $25,000. We do know enough to claim that very small businesses constitute an important component of the economy. Between 1988 and 1990, small firms created all of the net new jobs in the economy and most of this growth occurred in firms with fewer than 20 employees.

9. U.S. Small Business Administration, *Small business in the American economy*: 90.

10. Tinker, I. 'The human economy of micro-entrepreneurs', unpublished paper.

References

Bates, T. (1993), *Banking on Black Capitalism*. Washington, DC, Joint Center for Political and Economic Studies.

Christopher, G. C. (1986), *Illinois Public Aid Policy Barriers and Disincentives to the Self-employment Initiative of the AFDC Recipient*. Report prepared for The Women's Self-Employment Project, June.

Clark, M., Huston T., Meister B. (ed.) (1994), *1994 Directory of US Microenterprise Programs*. Washington, DC, The Aspen Institute.

Clarke, S. E., Gaile, G. L. (1992), 'The next wave: postfederal local economic development strategies'. *Economic Development Quarterly*, 6: 187–98.

Clavel, P. (1986), *The Progressive City*. Rutgers, Rutgers University Press.

Eisinger, P. (1988), *The Rise of the Entrepreneurial State: State and Local Economic Development Policy in the United States*. Madison, WI, The University of Wisconsin Press.

Friedman, R. E. (1993), 'Paths out: including an antipoverty development strategy in welfare reform', unpublished testimony to the Working Group on

Welfare Reform, Family Support, and Independence. Sacramento, CA, 8 October.

Haberfeld, S. (1981), 'Economic planning in economically distressed communities: the need to take a partisan perspective', *Economic Development and Law Center Report*, October – December: 7–16.

Hamilton, C. V., Hamilton, D.C. (1986), 'Social policies, civil rights, and poverty', in *Fighting poverty: What works and what doesn't*. Cambridge, MA, Harvard University Press.

Herbers, J. (1990), 'A third wave of economic development', *Governing*, June: 43–50.

Herbert, B. (1994), 'Scapegoat time', *The New York Times*, 16 November: A19.

Lynch, R., Markusen, A. (1994), 'Can markets govern?', *The American Prospect*, 16: 125–33.

McLenighan, V., Pogge, J. (1991), *The Business of Self-sufficiency: Microcredit Programs in the United States*. Chicago, The Woodstock Institute.

Mollenkopf, J. H. (1983), *The Contested City*. Princeton, Princeton University Press.

Noponen, H. T. (1977), 'The gender division of labor in the urban informal sector of developing countries: A panel survey of households in Madras India', PhD dissertation, University of California at Berkeley.

Osborne, D. (1988), *Laboratories of Democracy*, Boston, MA, Harvard Business School Press.

Osborne, D. and Gaebler, T. (1992), *Reinventing Government: How the Entrepreneurial Spirit is Transforming the Public Sector*. Reading, MA, Addison-Wesley Publishing Co.

Sclar, E. D., Hook, W. (1993), 'The importance of cities to the national economy', in Cisneros, G. (ed.), *Interwoven Destinies: Cities and the Nation*. New York, W.W. Norton & Company.

Servon, L. J. (1994), 'The institutionalization of microcredit: moving forward by looking back', *Economic Development Commentary*, 18: 23–9.

Sherraden, M. (1991), *Assets and the Poor: A New American Welfare Policy*. New York, M.E. Sharpe.

Skocpol, T. (1991), 'Targeting within universalism: politically viable policies to combat poverty in the United States', in Jencks, C. and Peterson, P. E., *The Urban Underclass*. Washington, DC, The Brookings Institution.

—— (1994), 'The new urban poverty and U.S. social policy, response to W.J. Wilson', *Michigan Quarterly Review*, 33: 274–81.

Stack, C. B. (1974), *All Our Kin: Strategies for Survival in a Black Community*. New York, Harper and Row.

Stiglitz, J. E. (1990), 'Peer monitoring and credit markets', *The World Bank Economic Review*, 4: 351–66.

Tinker, I. (1989), 'Credit for poor women: necessary, but not always sufficient for change'. *Marga*, 10: 31–48.

—— 'The human economy of micro-entrepreneurs', unpublished paper.

Wilson, W. J. (1987), *The Truly Disadvantaged: The Inner City, the Underclass, and Public Policy*. Chicago, The University of Chicago Press.

—— (1991), 'Studying inner city social dislocations: the challenge of public agenda research'. *American Sociological Review*, 56: 1–14.

—— (1994), 'The new urban poverty and the problem of race', *Michigan Quarterly Review*, 33: 247–73.

Wolch, J. (1990), *The Shadow State: Government and Voluntary Sector in Transition*. New York, The Foundation Center.

Part VI

Outlook

15

Future directions in local economic development

PATRICIA A. WILSON

Introduction

Scholarly research in urban and regional economic development has been heading unwittingly towards a post-modern embrace of locality. The literature on urban economic restructuring, influenced by regulation theory, has produced a wealth of case studies that exemplify the importance of the local. The public policy literature, having documented the decreasing influence of the nation state, demonstrates the importance of local initiative in urban economic development. Attention has turned, in particular, to the importance of urban civil society, from business coalitions to grassroots organizations. The collective questioning of grand theory and deterministic constructs leaves the research community open to building a new sense of purpose and process.

Emerging issues

Endogenous development

The broad change in the urban economic development literature over the last two decades points clearly to a shift away from a functionalist perspective of place as the passive location of economic activities according to the grand logic of global capitalism and exogenous business decisions. Instead, the literature is pointing to an endogenous approach, one that emphasizes the unique factors of the spatial milieu in which the activity occurs, while at the same time recognizing the embeddedness in the larger structures.

Ironically, the shift has realized what a number of 'outcasts' had advocated in the late 1970s: a territorial approach (Friedmann and Weaver, 1979; Stöhr and Taylor, 1981; see also Tinbergen, 1976; Nerfin, 1977; Sachs, 1982). Their calls for endogenous regional development

311

were dismissed by many as either utopian or in disregard of class relations. Now with the detailed case studies of innovative milieus and local initiatives, it becomes clear that development is subject to favourable external factors but not the necessary outcome of external factors (Garofoli 1990: 87).

The policy implications of this shift are notable: from regional and national planning of growth poles, emphasis on factor costs and transport costs, recruitment of outside firms and investors, and trust in automatic trickle-down mechanisms, comes a more finely tuned attention to territory as the clustering of social relations (Garofoli, 1990: 89), the place where endogenous and exogenous forces and characteristics meet (see Moulaert *et al.*, 1990, on integrated area development). Thus, what the functionalist literature lumped under external economies, such as propitious urban culture and social psychological factors, become the object of focus under the territorial approach. The new literature, however, does not accept the 'closed economy' prescription of the old territorial literature, instead recognizing the necessary interplay with global forces and the increasingly open nature of the urban economy. On the other hand, the new literature misses one of the subtle contributions that old territorial literature was trying to make – a contribution that is perhaps more timely now: Stöhr (1981) said that endogenous development must include non-economic values. In fact, he stated, it must involve the evolution of human values – a behavioural and socio-psychological change from *homo economicus* to *homo sociales*.

John Friedmann reflects the same idea when he calls for a transcendence of the division between life space and economic space (Friedmann, 1988). See also the French regional scientists and social geographers such as Perrin (1983) on ecosystems, micro regional development and endogenous economic development; Piatier (1979) on *l'espace vécu*; and Guigou (1983) on microregions and intercommunal co-operation, reviewed in Evangelinides-Arachovitou (1990: 65). These authors integrate anthropological and linguistic analysis into their prescriptions for overcoming the duality between life space and economic space. Territorial development should be first a strategy towards the satisfaction of basic needs, using purposeful community action based on decentralized participatory decision-making, small and medium-sized projects, labourintensive modes of production, appropriate technology and self-management, and the development of local small-scale enterprises aimed at providing basic (or social) needs (Evangelinides-Arachovitou, 1990: 64). The third sector – i.e. organized civil society, neither public nor private – is to be the lead actor.

Some observers claim this endogenous approach was tried out in Europe in the late 1970s and 1980s by socialist urban and regional governments in Europe and by OECD and EEC programmes for urban development in a 'burst of new institutions and organizational structures belonging to what in the economic literature is called the "third sector" or the "social sector" ' (Evangelinides-Arachovitou, 1990: 66). This progressive social contract approach to corporatist planning (planning agreements, urban development agencies and enterprises, even municipal enterprises under the umbrella of the local state) diverged, however, in one important aspect from the endogenous approach being advocated by the 'bottom up' territorial literature: instead of civil society playing the lead role, the (local) state was the initiator of the action, the convenor of the participation, and largely the funder of the activities (often with national government assistance).

Other observers put the endogenous paradigm in the context of newer post-modern analysis – a kind of progressive post-modernism. Evangelinides-Arachovitou points out that a post-industrial approach to endogenous development would be based on less government, more (social) entrepreneurialism, and more informal matrix or network organizations (1990: 69). Catalysing the endogenous development would be a loose multi-class network of heterogeneous social groups.

The rainbow coalition and the middle class

One of the emerging post-modern themes that requires investigation and reflection is 'a new type of social movement (that) has its essential social basis in the urban "tertiarized" middle classes, who are themselves subject to strong restructuring processes and have, in part, formed "alternative" milieus' (Esser and Hirsch, 1989). In fact, as Neil Smelser, vice president of the International Sociology Association, points out in his introduction to the programme for the XIII World Congress of Sociology held in Bielefeld, Germany, in July 1994, there is a flourishing of new solidarity groupings with multiple bases – regional, linguistic, religious, ethnic, gender, and lifestyle. Sometimes referred to as the rainbow coalition, this 'bewildering array of novel social movements' pressures the state from above and below (Smelser, 1994), while at the same time evidencing an increasing distance, apathy and alienation towards the established political process.

The informal sector

Another emerging theme brought out at the 1994 World Congress of Sociology is industry's declining capacity to steadily incorporate broad social groups. As formal economic and political structures absorb less and less of the population (even in Europe, especially Mediterranean cities – see Leontidou, 1993: 954), the new research trend in urban economic development will be to look at informal structures. In Europe the clarion call for informal sector or 'ownwork' comes from the research network established around The Other Economic Summit (TOES) (e.g. James Robertson, 1985). Others include Berry (1993); Henderson (1981); and followers of Schumacher (1973) and Gandhi (Diwan and Lutz, 1985).

Much of the research on the informal sector, especially that in the global restructuring literature, does a good job linking the global with the local, the formal with the informal, and the economic with the social (Lawson and Klak, 1990; Sassen, 1991). But it often emphasizes the exploitative aspects of the informal sector (Sassen, 1991), with the implicit policy implication that somehow the state should make the formal sector absorb these people in better conditions .

Two quite different components to the informal sector must be distinguished. First there is the sector of low-paid jobs through contracting out by formal sector firms. These jobs are part of a defensive strategy by Fordist/pre-Fordist firms who cannot modernize. They are informal in advanced countries only because the low wages are illegal. They would be legal and formal in Third World countries. Second, the informal sector includes vital community-based initiatives to produce and reproduce (consume) in non-modern ways – from individual reciprocity, to mutual self-help, to community-based (grassroots) economic development.

Might this latter segment of the informal sector be the germ of a post-modern organization of production and consumption? It transcends Fordist categories and divisions such as the following:

- life space vs. economic space;
- work vs. leisure;
- production vs. consumption;
- employment vs. unemployment
- humans vs. nature.

The community-based segment of the informal sector replaces (at least partially) reliance on the state and the global economy with community self-reliance. It envisions the individual not as a consumer or a worker, etc., but as a whole human being embedded in many networks.

The Latin American experience is particularly useful for indicating the potential role of the informal sector, which is still incipient in North America and Europe. It exemplifies many of the values and approaches that will be required in urban economic development in developed countries, as the formal sector becomes increasingly incapable of fully absorbing the labour force. The informal sector can be characterized as a self-organizing system that cannot be managed or controlled hierarchically. It does not separate economic space from social space and natural space (or economic from social and ecological values).

Friedmann (1992) makes an eloquent plea for the timeliness and instructiveness of observing and supporting the informal sector as a harbinger of new modes of economic and social organization. In the hundreds of low-income *barrios* across Latin America, residents are building a new polity based on convivial social networks, self-reliance, co-operation, and self-governance. Matthew Edel cites the 'great strength and resilience in local communities and networks within the informal sectors' as 'a fundamental source of energy and drive for transformation . . . ' (1992: 77).

The paradigm of socially aware government planning has reached its limits, laments Jorge Hardoy: 'Governments have had little impact on urban problems. Neither politicians nor technocrats have found ways to overcome . . . the growing poverty and squatter settlements. Urban planning has proved fruitless' (Morse and Hardoy, 1992: xvi). Richard Morse, however, captures the essence of the new paradigm:

> From the viewpoint of managerial cadres, cities are 'out of control.' . . . If this be so, the future lies not primarily with the managers but with the people themselves. Their intentions, voices, and traditional or spontaneous forms of association and endeavor must be heeded. The urban design must arise from them and not from ministries, agencies, and universities nor from consecrated urban ideals of the bourgeois, industrial West. (Morse and Hardoy, 1992: x)

Of course the informal sector harbours poverty, hardship, and exploitation. But the 'social energy', innovation, and dynamism present in the disenfranchised informal sector may be the most positive social force for change at the moment. The same social energy that drives the community-based initiatives among low-income populations in Latin America motivates the self-help economic development efforts among the growing ranks of the disenfranchised in North America and Europe – including not just ethnic and racial minorities and the poor, but also the middle class that has lost its place in the formal sector, and even entire localities that have been disenfranchised from the global economy.

Post-modern analysis

The perennial post-modernist since before the term was even coined, Jane Jacobs (1993) makes a case that qualitative methodologies such as ethnography have come back into the limelight in the post-modern era, since cultural factors are now accepted as important for understanding cities and their economic development. Studies of the particular are beginning to be seen as engaging with and extending theory. Good examples are found in recent studies of women workers in the *maquiladoras*, assembly plants along the US-Mexican border (Carrillo,

316   **Patricia A. Wilson**

1992; Heyman, 1991; Kopinak, 1993; Ruiz and Tiano, 1987; Sanchez, 1990; Shaiken, 1990; Staudt, 1986; Young, 1986).

The urban cultural studies tradition has melded ethnography to literary theory and semiotics. Discourse, the built environment, and representations of the environment are seen not only as socially produced, but as a means of communication with encoded messages (of power, usually) that need deconstructing. Feminist theory is helping to deconstruct the 'gendered subject' and to break down the barriers between the researcher and the researched (see, for example, Andrew and Milroy, 1988, cited in Jacobs, 1993, bringing to the fore the role of personal experience in field research).

There is an occasional attempt to go beyond the external appearances of language, discourse, and representation to 'an inner world of meaning and experience' (Jackson, 1989: 177, cited in Jacobs, 1993: 840) where we can actually put our feet in the other's shoes and separate from our own middle class constructions of social reality (see, Thrift, 1991: 144–8). As Gary Bridge (1993: 1–2) expresses in studying gentrification behaviour, 'individual experience cannot be read from social or spatial change (or discourse analysis, I would add) but ... the nature of an individual's perceptions and behavior is necessary for a complete understanding of social change'. But too frequently discourse analysis stops just short of analysing the internal (psychological, spiritual) side of consciousness and transformation and only begins to point a finger back at the researcher.

Semiotics is evident in the US urban economic development literature. Rejecting the proverbial belief that 'sticks and stones (material relations of production) can break my bones, but words can never hurt me', Pratt (1991, cited in Bovaird, 1993) posits that power relations are embedded in language, so that 'social conflict over what and whose discourse becomes accepted has significant material effects' (Bovaird, 1993: 653). In an insightful case study of women's resistance to gendered space in New Orleans, Alma Young and Jyaphia Christos-Rodgers (this volume) describe how the women disempowered themselves by accepting the dominant discourse, and how they were able eventually to change their material conditions through redefining themselves in terms different from those set by the authorities.

Another example is Kevin Archer (this volume), whose case study of Tampa shows the resistance encountered when the growth coalition attempted to redefine ethnic history in a way palatable for marketing to middle-class tourists. As Esser and Hirsch point out, urban cultural policy is becoming an important instrument of economic development policy in the race between locations: 'planned urbanity is becoming an economic strategy' (Esser and Hirsch, 1989: 417).

Latin America is the paragon for semiotics practice in urban economic development, since analysis of discourse has been carried into action

over the last twenty-five years by one of Foucault's students, Paolo
Freire, and now actively used by countless NGOs doing action research
and critical consciousness raising with grassroots groups, both urban and
rural.

Methodology

At an international symposium on urban economic development in Lille,
France, in March, 1994,[1] a consensus seemed to emerge among economic
development scholars that deterministic economistic analysis from global
to local is out. Centralized theory building, grand theory and unidirec-
tional determinist theory must give way to more situational explanations
(Cooke, 1990). Rationalistic approaches to policy in terms of agents,
targets, and instruments (social engineering) are out. A positivist, atom-
istic, quantitative methodology is inadequate to model human agency.
Economic values and motivations are only part of the story. The inter-
dynamics of social agency are a given factor; we must think in terms of
social innovation as well as technical innovation (Moulaert *et al.*, 1990);
we must understand behaviour, discourse and self-oppression. As
Moulaert and Leontidou (1995) conclude, we need a permanent meth-
odological self-questioning, open to untried possibilities and distinct
situational realities, with different interpretations and different ways of
knowing.

Post-modern methodology may open our minds (and hearts) to new
possibilities. But ultimately we need a methodology that values non-
rational knowledge and non-linear thinking. It would allow us, the
'scientific observers', to redefine our roles and transcend the separation
between observer and observed.

New directions

The post-modern transition may provide a quiet space for non-
judgmental appreciation of differences and connectedness and for recognition that the distinction between observer and observed is ambiguous. But it will still take some transformation before we are able to offer
our efforts in service of something larger. By listening to the rainbow
communities – i.e. the panoply of new social movements – we will add
human development and ecological harmony as necessary values in
urban development. It will not be long before we see the interconnected-
ness of biological, psychological, and environmental phenomena along
with the social and economic.

The beginning of the change from the mechanistic and deterministic to
the holistic and interconnected is definitely apparent in the urban economic development literature. With the new acceptance of locality

studies, the literature is embracing the qualitative and the subjective, bringing us closer to setting aside the dominant cultural beliefs in technology, growth, and competition/conflict. Perhaps we shall be able to play a role in the shift of values to the simple, beautiful, and harmonious in the context of community.

Notes

1. 'Cities, Enterprises and Society at the Eve of the XXI Century', Lille, France, March, 1994, sponsored by PIR-Villes, under the academic direction of Frank Moulaert.

References

Andrew, C., Milroy, B.M. (1988), *Life Spaces, Gender, Household, and Employment*. Vancouver, University of British Columbia Press.

Berry, W. (1993), *Sex, Economy, Freedom and Community*. New York, Pantheon.

Bovaird, T. (1993), 'Analysing urban economic development', *Urban Studies*, 30: 631–58.

Bridge, G. (1993), 'People, places and networks', School for Advanced Urban Studies, University of Bristol, Working Paper 113, February.

Carrillo, J. (1992), *Mujeres en la Industria Automotriz en Mexico*. Tijuana, El Colegio de la Frontera Norte.

Cooke, P. (1990), 'Modern urban theory in question', *Transactions of the Institute of British Geographers, NS*, 15: 333–43.

Diwan, R., Lutz, M. (eds) (1985), *Essays in Gandhian Economics*. New Delhi, Gandhi Peace Foundation.

Edel, M. (1992), 'Latin American urban studies, beyond dichotomy', in Morse, R.M., Hardoy, J.E. (eds), *Rethinking the Latin American City*. Washington D.C., Woodrow Wilson Center Press.

Esser, J., Hirsch, J. (1989), 'The crisis of fordism and the dimensions of a "postfordist" regional and urban structure', *International Journal of Urban and Regional Research*, 13: 417–37.

Evangelinides-Arachovitou, M. (1990), 'Some theoretical aspects concerning local development policies in Greece', in Konsolas, N. (ed.), *Local Development*. Athens, Regional Development Institute/Hellenic Agency for Local Development and Local Government.

Fisher, J. (1993), *The Road from Rio: Sustainable Development and the Nongovernmental Movement in the Third World*. Westport, Praeger.

Friedmann, J. (1988), *Life Space and Economic Space*. New Brunswick, Transaction.

—— (1992), *Empowerment: The Politics of Alternative Development*. Cambridge, Blackwell.

Friedmann, J., Salguero, M. (1988), 'The barrio economy and collective self-empowerment in Latin America: a framework and agenda for research', in

Smith, M.P. (ed.), *Power, Community and the City*, Comparative Urban and Community Research, vol. 1. New Brunswick, Transaction.

Friedmann, J., Weaver, C. (1979), *Territory and Function: The Evolution of Regional Planning*. London, Edward Arnold.

Garofoli, G. (1990), 'Local development: patterns and policy implications', in Konsolas, N. (ed.), *Local Development*. Athens, Regional Development Institute and Hellenic Agency for Local Development and Local Government.

Guigou, J.L. (1983), *Coopération intercommunale et développement par la base. Le développement décentralisé*. Paris, LITEC.

Henderson, H. (1981), *The Politics of the Solar Age: Alternatives to Economics*. New York, Anchor/Doubleday.

Heyman, J. (1991), *Life and Labor on the Border*. Tucson, University of Arizona Press.

Jackson, P. (1989), *Maps of Meaning*. London, Unwin Hyman.

Jacobs, J. (1993), 'The city unbound: qualitative approaches to the city', *Urban Studies*, 30: 827–48.

Kopinak, K. (1993), 'Maquiladorization of the Mexican economy', in Cameron, M., Ginspun, R. (eds), *The Political Economy of a North American Free Trade Area*. New York, St. Martin's.

Korten, D. (1987), 'Third generation NGO strategies: a key to people-centered development', *World Development*, 15: 145-59.

Lawson, V., Klak, T. (1990), 'Conceptual linkages in the study of production and reproduction in Latin American cities', *Journal of Economic Geography*, 66: 311–27.

Leontidou, L. (1993), 'Postmodernism and the city: mediterranean versions', *Urban Studies*, 30.

Morse, R. M., Hardoy, J. E. (eds) (1992), *Rethinking the Latin American City*. Washington D.C.: Woodrow Wilson Center Press.

Moulaert, F., Leontidou, L. (1995), 'Localités désintégrées et stratégies de lutte contre la pauvreté: une réflexion méthodologique postmoderne', *Espaces et Sociétés*, forthcoming.

Moulaert, F., Wilson Salinas, P. (eds) (1983), *Regional Analysis and the New International Division of Labor*. Boston, Kluwer-Nijhoff.

Moulaert, F., in collaboration with R. Alaez, Ph. Cooke, C. Courlet, H. Haüßermann and A. da Rosa Pires (1990), *Integrated Area Development and Efficacy of Local Action*. Feasibility study for Animation & Research in the context of Poverty III. Brussels and Lille.

Nerfin, M. (ed.) (1977), *Another Development*. Uppsala, Dag Hammarskjold Foundation.

Peirce, N., Steinbach, C. (1987), *Corrective Capitalism: The Rise of America's Community Development Corporation*. New York, Ford Foundation.

Perrin, J.C. (1983), *Théorie de la planification décentralisée. Le développement décentralisé*. Paris, LITEC.

Piatier, A. (1979), *La structuration du territoire, condition du développement endogène*. Vienna, Club de Genève, INIDO.

Pratt, A. C. (1991), 'Discourses on locality', *Environment and Planning A*, 23: 257–66.

Robertson, J. (1985), *Future Work: Jobs, Self-Employment and Leisure after the Industrial Age*. New York, Universe Books.

Ruiz, V.L., Tiano, S. (1987), *Women on the US-Mexico Border*. Boston: Allen and Unwin.

Sachs, I. (1982), *Ecodesarrollo*. Mexico, El Colegio de Mexico.

Sanchez, R. (1990), 'Condiciones de vida de los trabajadores de la maquiladora en Tijuana y Nogales', *Frontera Norte*, 2: 153–82.

Sassen, S. (1991), *The Global City: New York, London, Tokyo*. Princeton, Princeton University Press.

Schumacher, E.F. (1973), *Small Is Beautiful*. New York, Harper and Row.

Shaiken, H. (1990), *Mexico in the Global Economy: High Technology and Work Organization in Export Industries*. San Diego, Center for US-Mexican Studies, University of California, Monograph Series 33.

Shaiken, H., Herzenberg, S. (1988), *Automation and Global Production: Automobile Engine Production in Mexico, the US and Canada*. San Diego, Center for US-Mexican Studies, University of California at San Diego.

Smelser, N. (1994), 'Contested boundaries and shifting solidarities', Programme notes for the XIII World Congress of Sociology, Bielefeld, Germany, July: 5–6.

Staudt, K. (1986), 'Economic change and ideological lag in households of Maquila workers in Ciudad Juarez', in Young, G. (ed.), *The Social Ecology and Economic Development of Ciudad Juarez*. Boulder, Westview.

Stöhr, W. (1981), 'Development from below: the bottom-up and periphery-inward development paradigm', in Stöhr, W., Taylor, D. (eds), *Development from Above or Below? The Dialectics of Regional Planning in Developing Countries*. Chichester, John Wiley and Sons.

Stöhr, W., Taylor, D. (eds) (1981), *Development from Above or Below? The Dialectics of Regional Planning in Developing Countries*. Chichester, John Wiley and Sons.

Thrift, N. (1991), 'Over-wordy worlds? Thoughts and worries', in Philo, C. (ed.), *New Words, New Worlds: Reconceptualising Social and Cultural Geography*. Proceedings of a Conference organized by the Social and Cultural Geography Study Group of the IBG, Department of Geography, St David's University College, Lampeter.

Tinbergen, J. (1976), *Economics in the Future: Towards a New Paradigm*. Boulder, Westview.

Wilson, P. (1992), *Exports and Local Development: Mexico's New Maquiladoras*. Austin, University of Texas Press.

Young, G. (ed.) (1986), *The Social Ecology and Economic Development of Ciudad Juarez*. Boulder, Westview.

Index